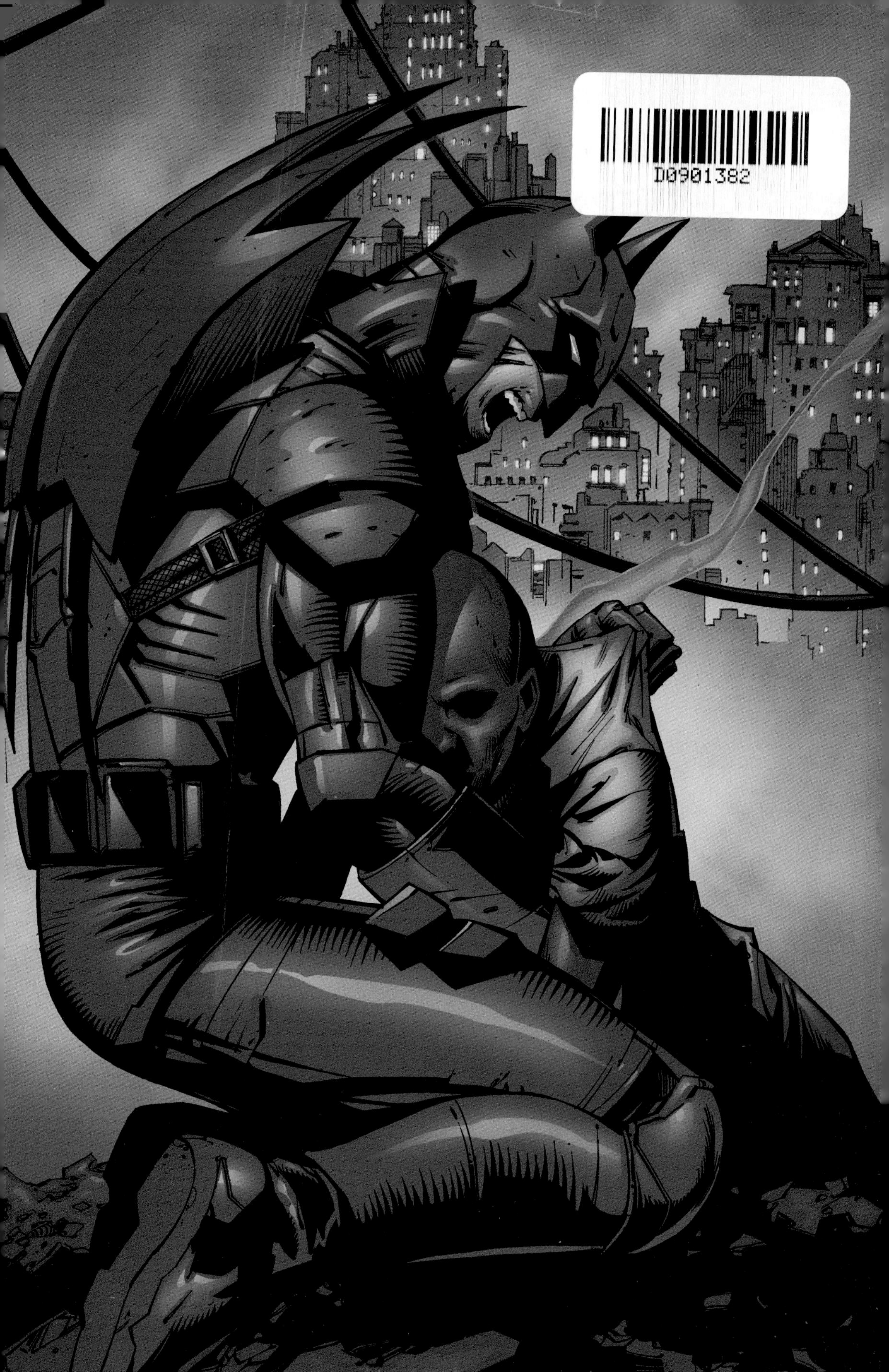

BATMAN: LIFE AFTER DEATH

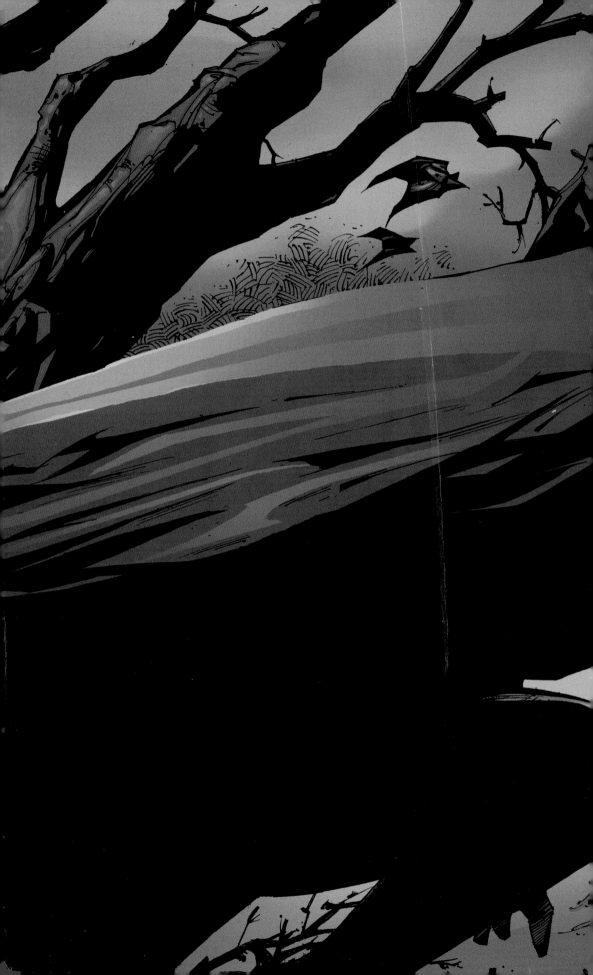

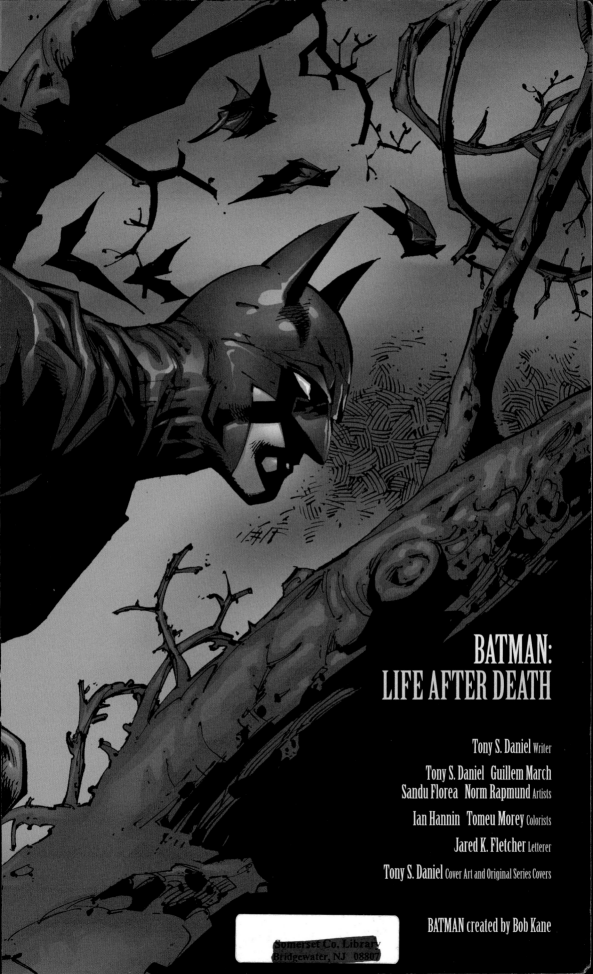

BATMAN: LIFE AFTER DEATH

Tony S. Daniel Writer

Tony S. Daniel Guillem March
Sandu Florea Norm Rapmund Artists

Ian Hannin Tomeu Morey Colorists

Jared K. Fletcher Letterer

Tony S. Daniel Cover Art and Original Series Covers

BATMAN created by Bob Kane

Somerset Co. Library
Bridgewater, NJ 08807

Mike Marts Editor – Original Series
Janelle Siegel Assistant Editor – Original Series
Bob Harras Group Editor – Collected Editions
Scott Nybakken Editor
Robbin Brosterman Design Director – Books

DC COMICS
Diane Nelson President
Dan DiDio and Jim Lee Co-Publishers
Geoff Johns Chief Creative Officer
Patrick Caldon EVP – Finance and Administration
John Rood EVP – Sales, Marketing and Business Development
Amy Genkins SVP – Business and Legal Affairs
Steve Rotterdam SVP – Sales and Marketing
John Cunningham VP – Marketing
Terri Cunningham VP – Managing Editor
Alison Gill VP – Manufacturing
David Hyde VP – Publicity
Sue Pohja VP – Book Trade Sales
Alysse Soll VP – Advertising and Custom Publishing
Bob Wayne VP – Sales
Mark Chiarello Art Director

BATMAN: LIFE AFTER DEATH

Published by DC Comics. Cover and compilation Copyright
© 2010 DC Comics. All Rights Reserved. Originally published
in single magazine form in BATMAN 692-699. Copyright ©
2009, 2010 DC Comics. All Rights Reserved. All characters,
their distinctive likenesses and related elements featured in
this publication are trademarks of DC Comics. The stories,
characters and incidents featured in this publication are
entirely fictional. DC Comics does not read or accept
unsolicited submissions of ideas, stories or artwork.

DC Comics, 1700 Broadway, New York, NY 10019
A Warner Bros. Entertainment Company
Printed by RR Donnelley, Salem, VA, USA
9/9/11. First Printing.
ISBN: 978-1-4012-2975-7

SUSTAINABLE
FORESTRY
INITIATIVE

Certified Chain of Custody
Promoting Sustainable
Forest Management
www.sfiprogram.org

Fiber used in this product line meets the
sourcing requirements of the SFI program.
www.sfiprogram.org SGS-SFI/COC-US10/81072

Table of Contents

LIFE AFTER DEATH

Pencils by **Tony S. Daniel** Colors by **Ian Hannin**

Riddle Me This

Pencils and inks by **Guillem March** Colors by **Tomeu Morey**

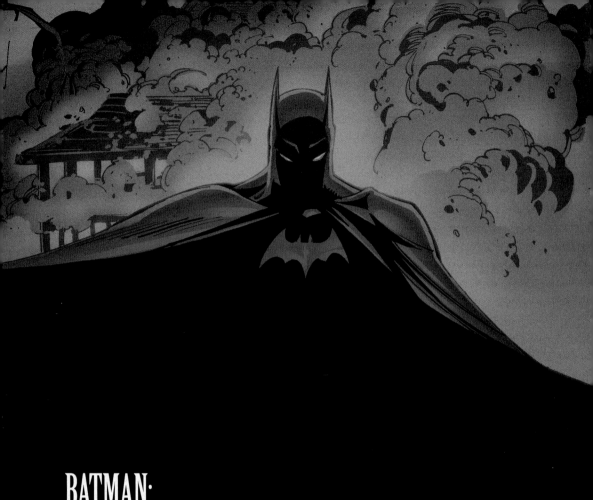

BATMAN:
LIFE AFTER DEATH

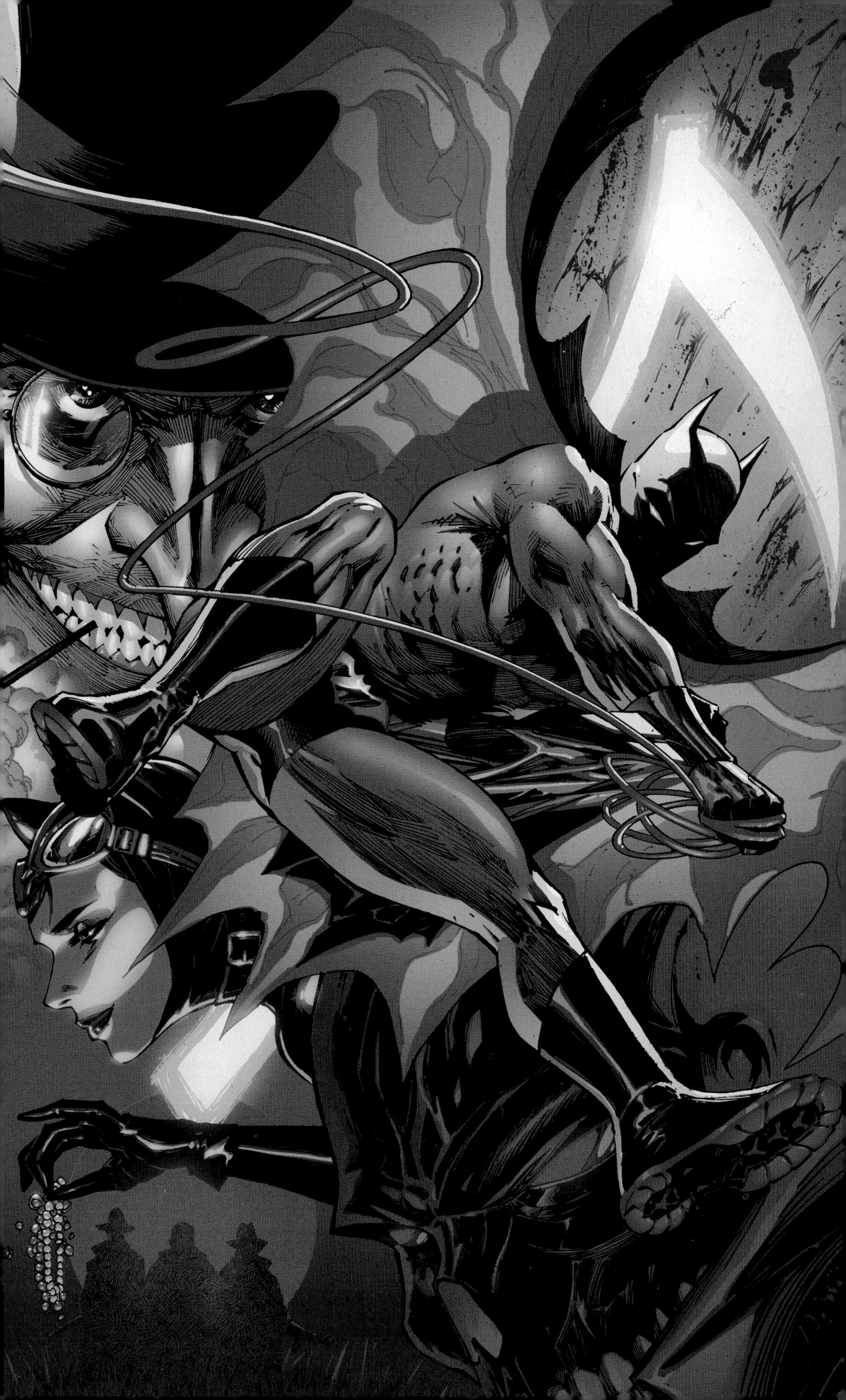

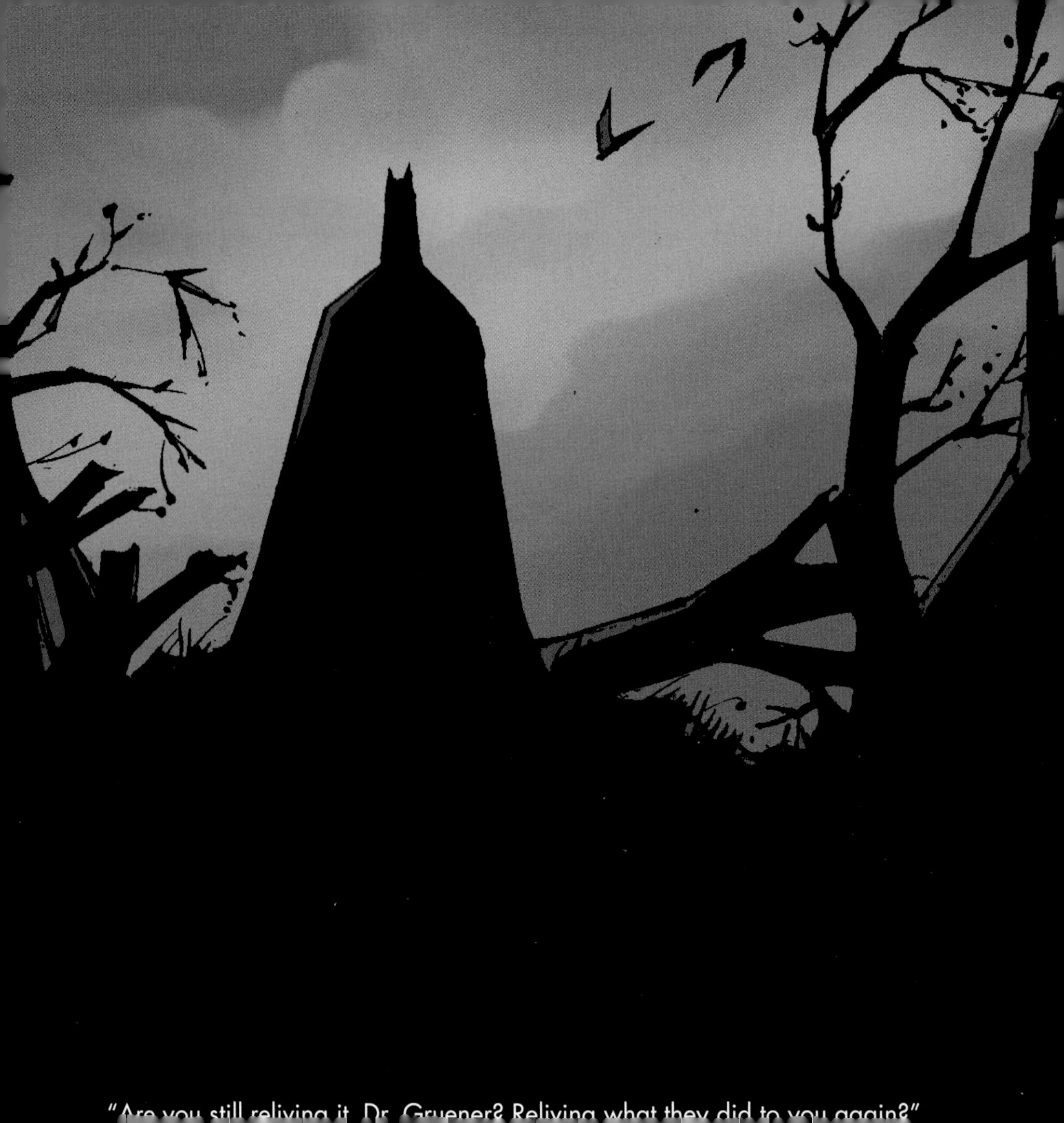
"Are you still reliving it, Dr. Gruener? Reliving what they did to you again?"

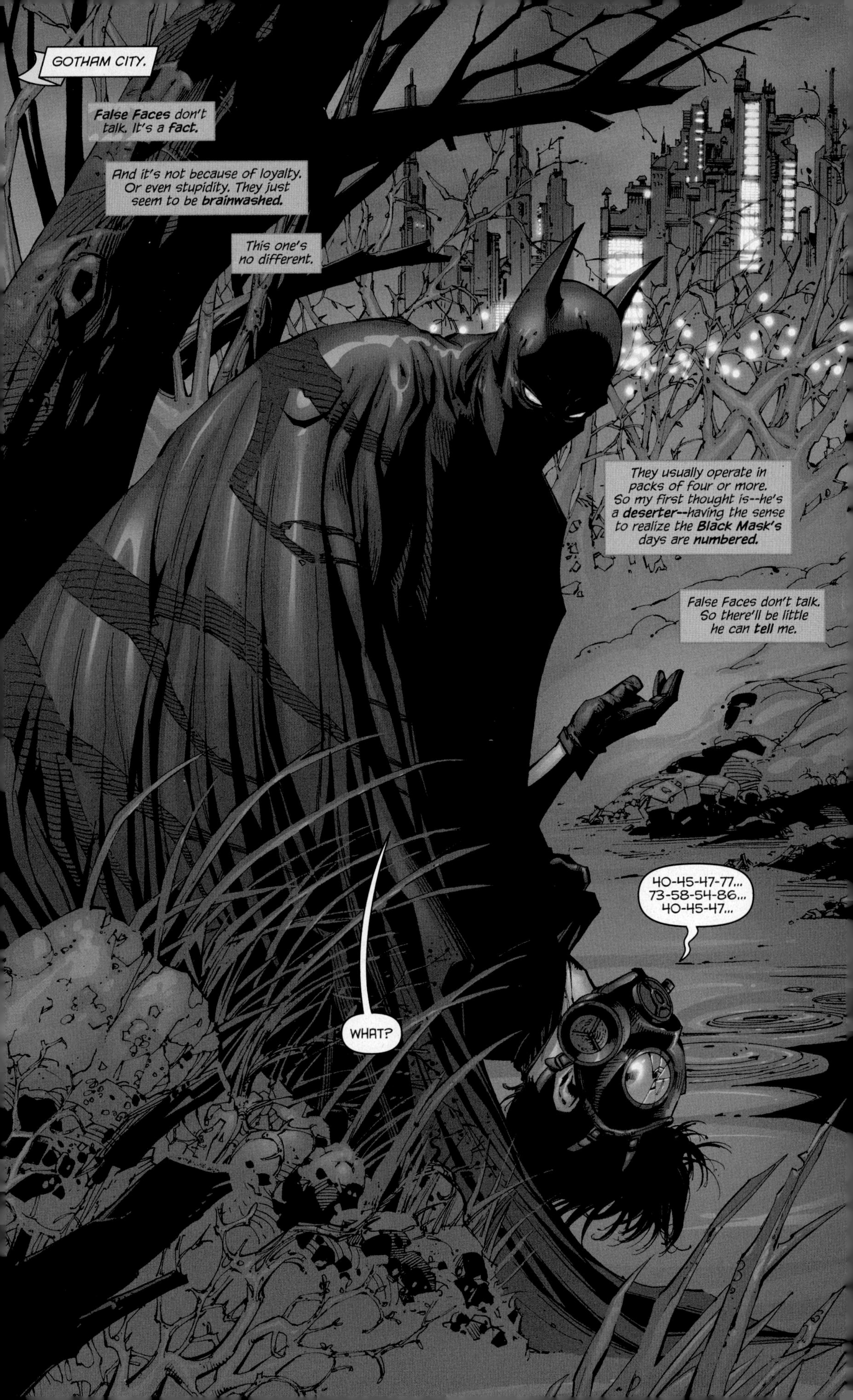
GOTHAM CITY.
False Faces don't talk. It's a fact.
And it's not because of loyalty. Or even stupidity. They just seem to be brainwashed.
This one's no different.
They usually operate in packs of four or more. So my first thought is--he's a deserter--having the sense to realize the Black Mask's days are numbered.
False Faces don't talk. So there'll be little he can tell me.
40-45-47-77... 73-58-54-86... 40-45-47...
WHAT?

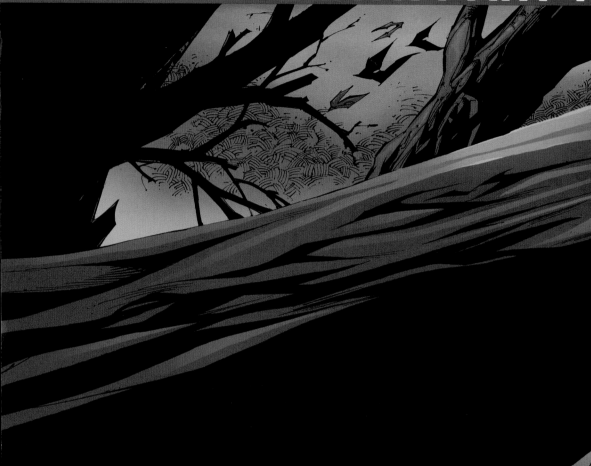

A coppery, metallic rust-scent fills my nostrils--the smell of *blood.* And then a whiff of *gunpowder.*

Death.

More *False Faces...* the first one's buddies.

Judging by the bullet wounds and points of entry, I'd wager these men were caught in an *ambush.*

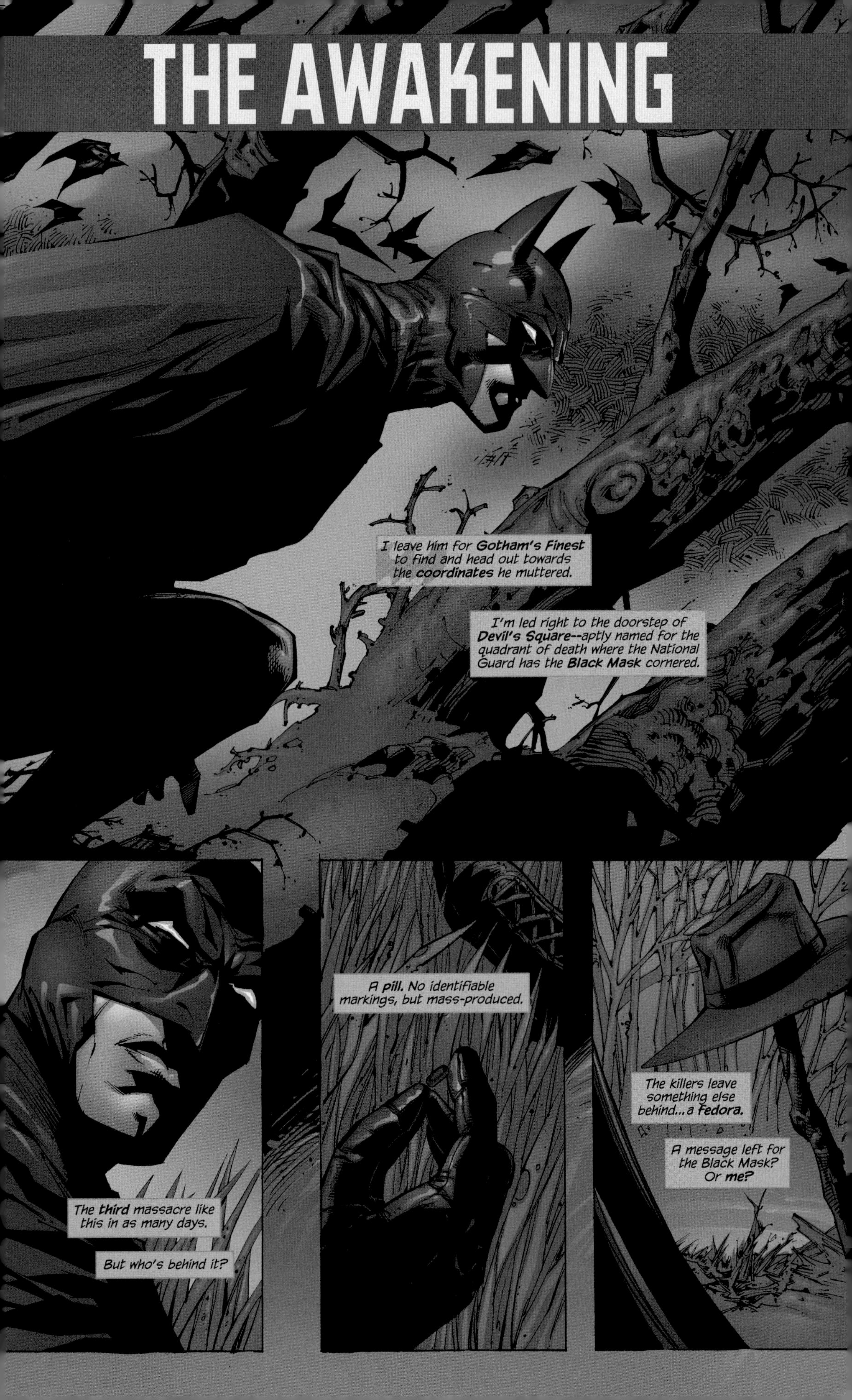
THE AWAKENING
I leave him for Gotham's Finest to find and head out towards the coordinates he muttered.
I'm led right to the doorstep of Devil's Square--aptly named for the quadrant of death where the National Guard has the Black Mask cornered.
The third massacre like this in as many days.
But who's behind it?
A pill. No identifiable markings, but mass-produced.
The killers leave something else behind...a Fedora.
A message left for the Black Mask? Or me?

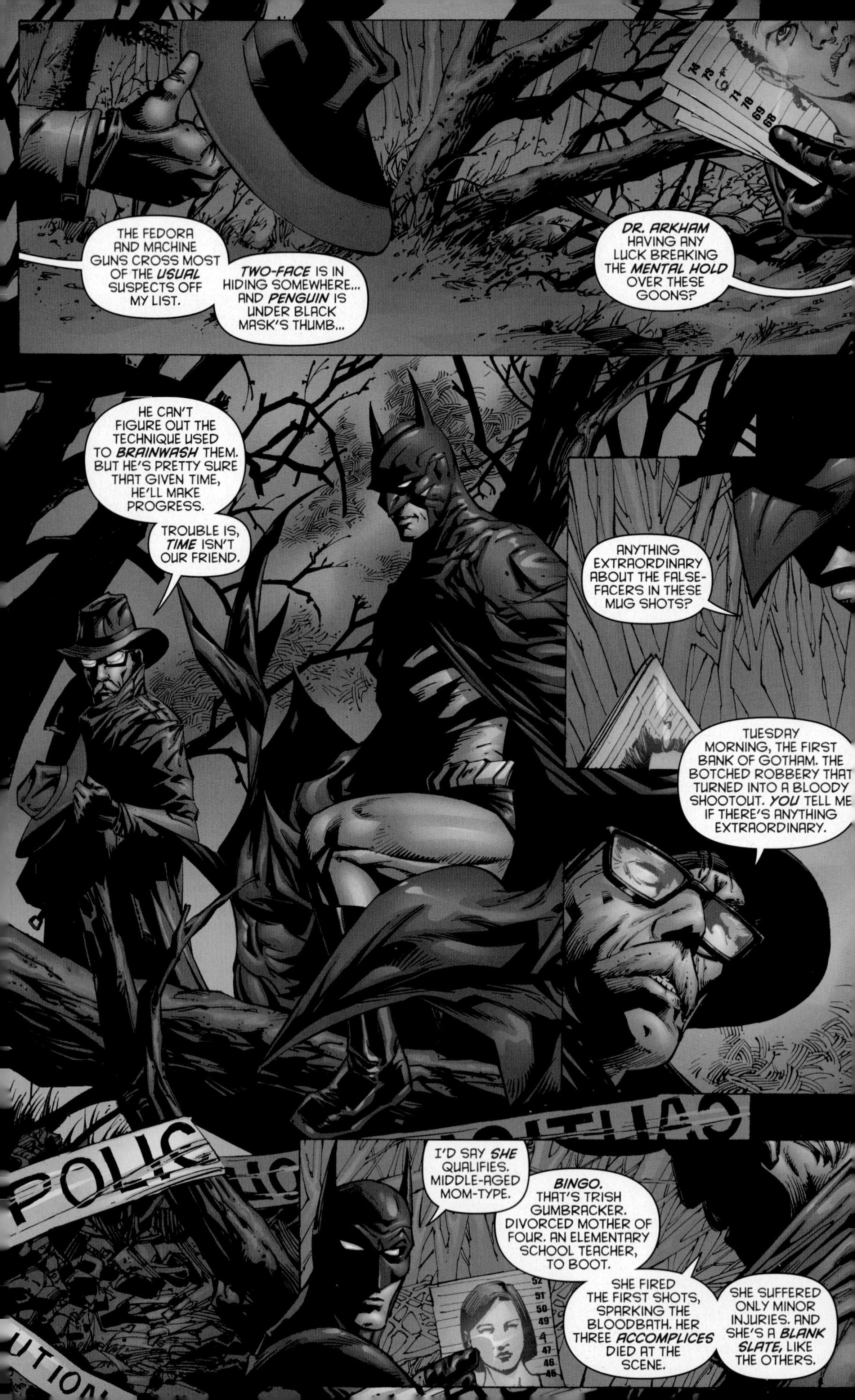
THE FEDORA AND MACHINE GUNS CROSS MOST OF THE USUAL SUSPECTS OFF MY LIST.
TWO-FACE IS IN HIDING SOMEWHERE... AND PENGUIN IS UNDER BLACK MASK'S THUMB...
DR. ARKHAM HAVING ANY LUCK BREAKING THE MENTAL HOLD OVER THESE GOONS?
HE CAN'T FIGURE OUT THE TECHNIQUE USED TO BRAINWASH THEM. BUT HE'S PRETTY SURE THAT GIVEN TIME, HE'LL MAKE PROGRESS.
TROUBLE IS, TIME ISN'T OUR FRIEND.
ANYTHING EXTRAORDINARY ABOUT THE FALSE-FACERS IN THESE MUG SHOTS?
TUESDAY MORNING, THE FIRST BANK OF GOTHAM. THE BOTCHED ROBBERY THAT TURNED INTO A BLOODY SHOOTOUT. YOU TELL ME IF THERE'S ANYTHING EXTRAORDINARY.
POLIC
I'D SAY SHE QUALIFIES. MIDDLE-AGED MOM-TYPE.
BINGO. THAT'S TRISH GUMBRACKER. DIVORCED MOTHER OF FOUR. AN ELEMENTARY SCHOOL TEACHER, TO BOOT.
SHE FIRED THE FIRST SHOTS, SPARKING THE BLOODBATH. HER THREE ACCOMPLICES DIED AT THE SCENE.
SHE SUFFERED ONLY MINOR INJURIES. AND SHE'S A BLANK SLATE, LIKE THE OTHERS.
UTION

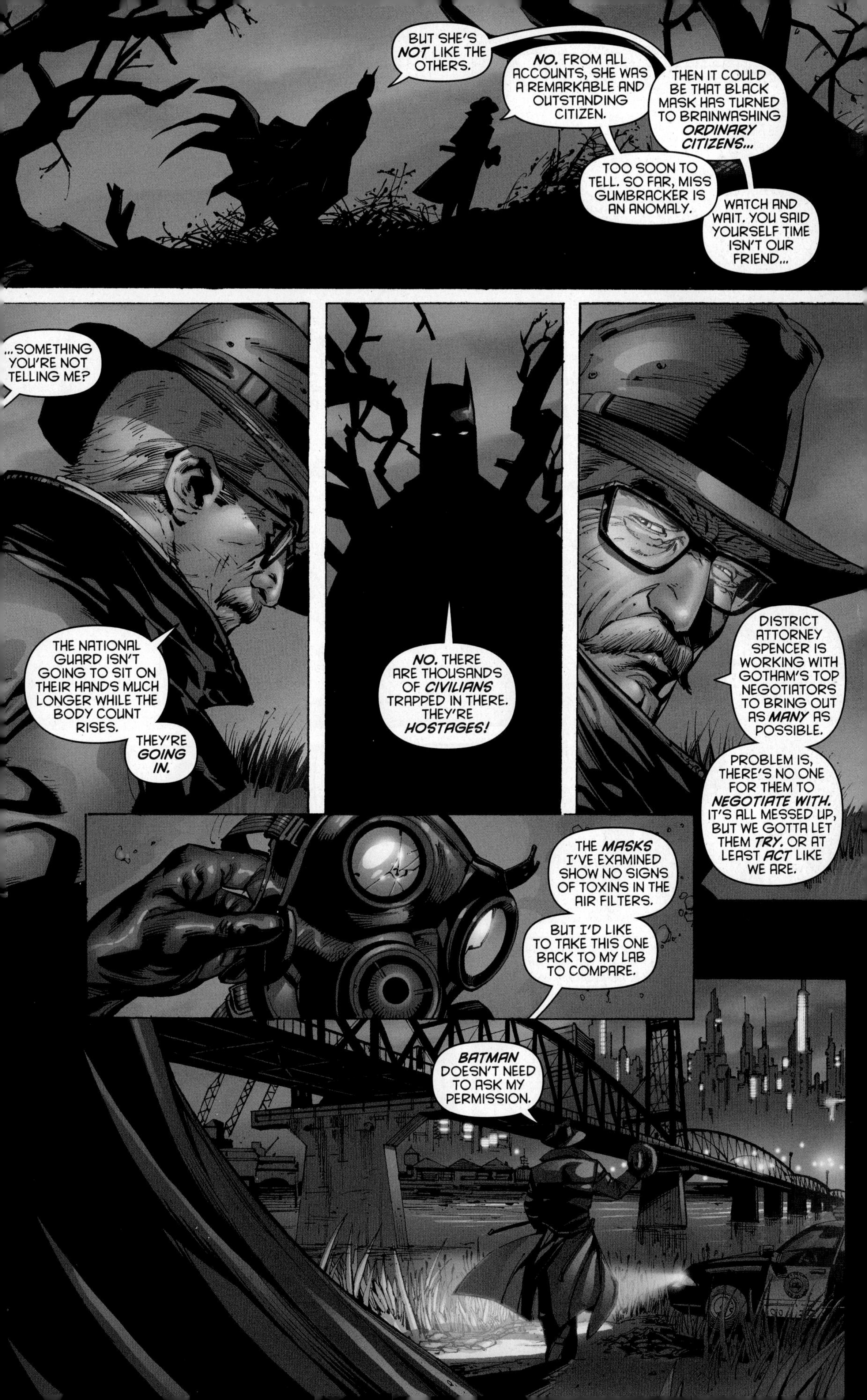

BUT SHE'S NOT LIKE THE OTHERS.
NO. FROM ALL ACCOUNTS, SHE WAS A REMARKABLE AND OUTSTANDING CITIZEN.
THEN IT COULD BE THAT BLACK MASK HAS TURNED TO BRAINWASHING ORDINARY CITIZENS...
TOO SOON TO TELL. SO FAR, MISS GUMBRACKER IS AN ANOMALY.
WATCH AND WAIT. YOU SAID YOURSELF TIME ISN'T OUR FRIEND...
...SOMETHING YOU'RE NOT TELLING ME?
THE NATIONAL GUARD ISN'T GOING TO SIT ON THEIR HANDS MUCH LONGER WHILE THE BODY COUNT RISES.
THEY'RE GOING IN.
NO. THERE ARE THOUSANDS OF CIVILIANS TRAPPED IN THERE. THEY'RE HOSTAGES!
DISTRICT ATTORNEY SPENCER IS WORKING WITH GOTHAM'S TOP NEGOTIATORS TO BRING OUT AS MANY AS POSSIBLE.
PROBLEM IS, THERE'S NO ONE FOR THEM TO NEGOTIATE WITH. IT'S ALL MESSED UP, BUT WE GOTTA LET THEM TRY. OR AT LEAST ACT LIKE WE ARE.
THE MASKS I'VE EXAMINED SHOW NO SIGNS OF TOXINS IN THE AIR FILTERS.
BUT I'D LIKE TO TAKE THIS ONE BACK TO MY LAB TO COMPARE.
BATMAN DOESN'T NEED TO ASK MY PERMISSION.

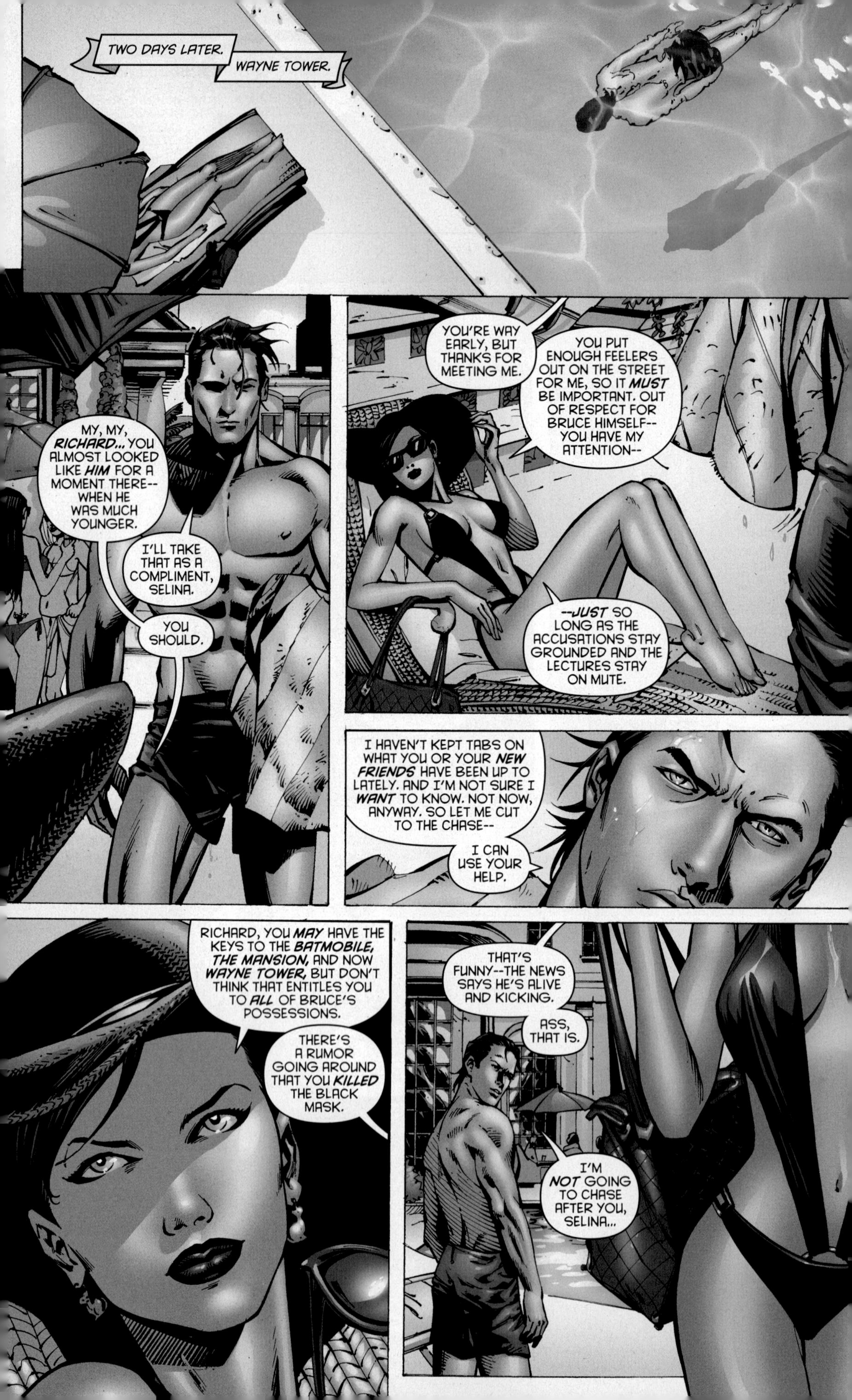

TWO DAYS LATER.
WAYNE TOWER.
MY, MY, RICHARD... YOU ALMOST LOOKED LIKE HIM FOR A MOMENT THERE-- WHEN HE WAS MUCH YOUNGER.
I'LL TAKE THAT AS A COMPLIMENT, SELINA.
YOU SHOULD.
YOU'RE WAY EARLY, BUT THANKS FOR MEETING ME.
YOU PUT ENOUGH FEELERS OUT ON THE STREET FOR ME, SO IT MUST BE IMPORTANT. OUT OF RESPECT FOR BRUCE HIMSELF-- YOU HAVE MY ATTENTION--
--JUST SO LONG AS THE ACCUSATIONS STAY GROUNDED AND THE LECTURES STAY ON MUTE.
I HAVEN'T KEPT TABS ON WHAT YOU OR YOUR NEW FRIENDS HAVE BEEN UP TO LATELY. AND I'M NOT SURE I WANT TO KNOW. NOT NOW, ANYWAY. SO LET ME CUT TO THE CHASE--
I CAN USE YOUR HELP.
RICHARD, YOU MAY HAVE THE KEYS TO THE BATMOBILE, THE MANSION, AND NOW WAYNE TOWER, BUT DON'T THINK THAT ENTITLES YOU TO ALL OF BRUCE'S POSSESSIONS.
THERE'S A RUMOR GOING AROUND THAT YOU KILLED THE BLACK MASK.
THAT'S FUNNY--THE NEWS SAYS HE'S ALIVE AND KICKING.
ASS, THAT IS.
I'M NOT GOING TO CHASE AFTER YOU, SELINA...

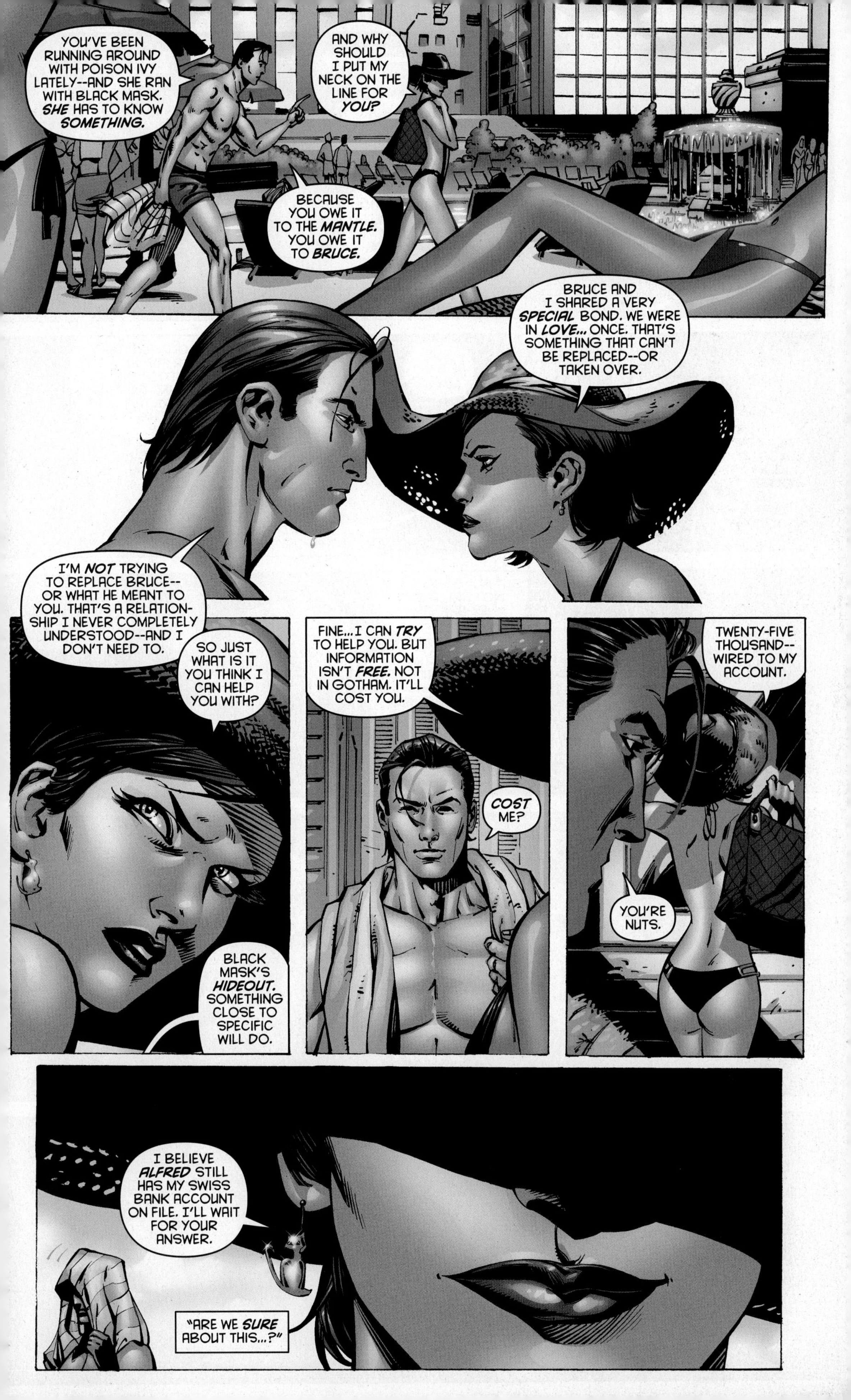

YOU'VE BEEN RUNNING AROUND WITH POISON IVY LATELY--AND SHE RAN WITH BLACK MASK. SHE HAS TO KNOW SOMETHING.
AND WHY SHOULD I PUT MY NECK ON THE LINE FOR YOU?
BECAUSE YOU OWE IT TO THE MANTLE. YOU OWE IT TO BRUCE.
BRUCE AND I SHARED A VERY SPECIAL BOND. WE WERE IN LOVE... ONCE. THAT'S SOMETHING THAT CAN'T BE REPLACED--OR TAKEN OVER.
I'M NOT TRYING TO REPLACE BRUCE--OR WHAT HE MEANT TO YOU. THAT'S A RELATIONSHIP I NEVER COMPLETELY UNDERSTOOD--AND I DON'T NEED TO.
SO JUST WHAT IS IT YOU THINK I CAN HELP YOU WITH?
BLACK MASK'S HIDEOUT. SOMETHING CLOSE TO SPECIFIC WILL DO.
FINE... I CAN TRY TO HELP YOU. BUT INFORMATION ISN'T FREE. NOT IN GOTHAM. IT'LL COST YOU.
COST ME?
TWENTY-FIVE THOUSAND--WIRED TO MY ACCOUNT.
YOU'RE NUTS.
I BELIEVE ALFRED STILL HAS MY SWISS BANK ACCOUNT ON FILE. I'LL WAIT FOR YOUR ANSWER.
"ARE WE SURE ABOUT THIS...?"

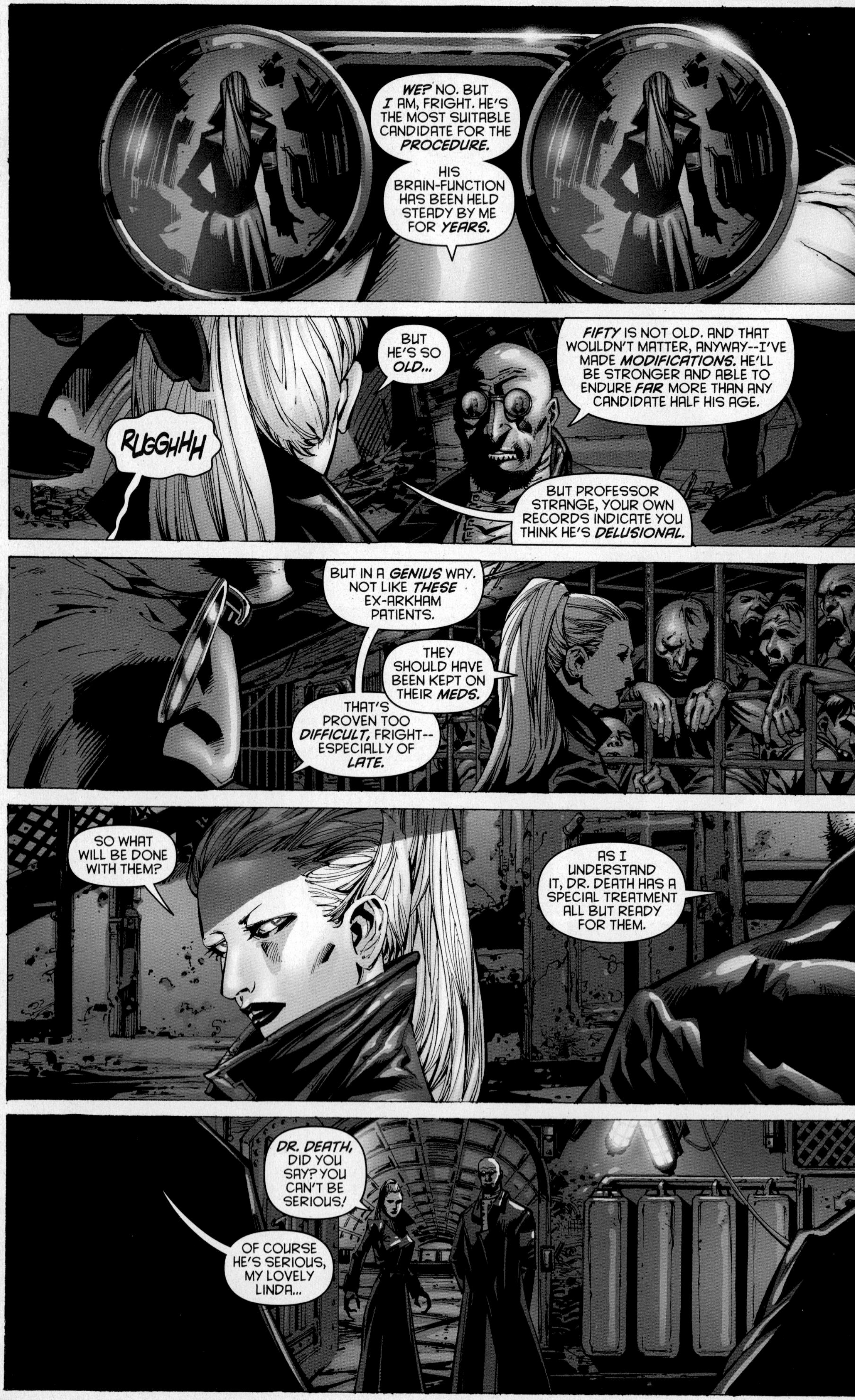

WE? NO. BUT *I* AM, FRIGHT. HE'S THE MOST SUITABLE CANDIDATE FOR THE *PROCEDURE.*
HIS BRAIN-FUNCTION HAS BEEN HELD STEADY BY ME FOR *YEARS.*
BUT HE'S SO *OLD...*
FIFTY IS NOT OLD. AND THAT WOULDN'T MATTER, ANYWAY--I'VE MADE *MODIFICATIONS.* HE'LL BE STRONGER AND ABLE TO ENDURE *FAR* MORE THAN ANY CANDIDATE HALF HIS AGE.
RUGGHHH
BUT PROFESSOR STRANGE, YOUR OWN RECORDS INDICATE YOU THINK HE'S *DELUSIONAL.*
BUT IN A *GENIUS* WAY. NOT LIKE *THESE* EX-ARKHAM PATIENTS.
THEY SHOULD HAVE BEEN KEPT ON THEIR *MEDS.*
THAT'S PROVEN TOO *DIFFICULT,* FRIGHT--ESPECIALLY OF *LATE.*
SO WHAT WILL BE DONE WITH THEM?
AS I UNDERSTAND IT, DR. DEATH HAS A SPECIAL TREATMENT ALL BUT READY FOR THEM.
DR. DEATH, DID YOU SAY? YOU CAN'T BE SERIOUS!
OF COURSE HE'S SERIOUS, MY LOVELY LINDA...

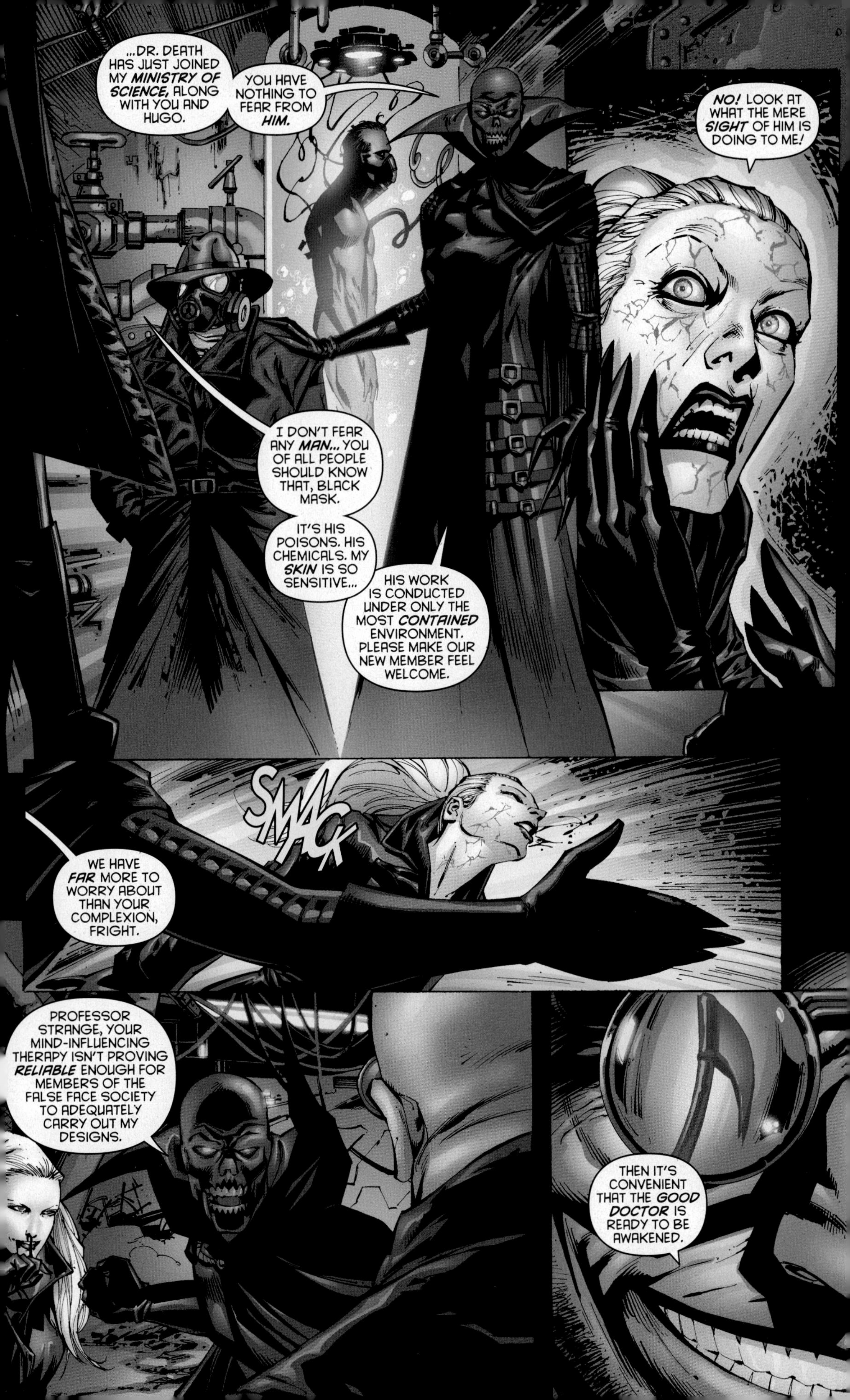
...DR. DEATH HAS JUST JOINED MY MINISTRY OF SCIENCE, ALONG WITH YOU AND HUGO.
YOU HAVE NOTHING TO FEAR FROM HIM.
NO! LOOK AT WHAT THE MERE SIGHT OF HIM IS DOING TO ME!
I DON'T FEAR ANY MAN... YOU OF ALL PEOPLE SHOULD KNOW THAT, BLACK MASK.
IT'S HIS POISONS. HIS CHEMICALS. MY SKIN IS SO SENSITIVE...
HIS WORK IS CONDUCTED UNDER ONLY THE MOST CONTAINED ENVIRONMENT. PLEASE MAKE OUR NEW MEMBER FEEL WELCOME.
SMACK
WE HAVE FAR MORE TO WORRY ABOUT THAN YOUR COMPLEXION, FRIGHT.
PROFESSOR STRANGE, YOUR MIND-INFLUENCING THERAPY ISN'T PROVING RELIABLE ENOUGH FOR MEMBERS OF THE FALSE FACE SOCIETY TO ADEQUATELY CARRY OUT MY DESIGNS.
THEN IT'S CONVENIENT THAT THE GOOD DOCTOR IS READY TO BE AWAKENED.

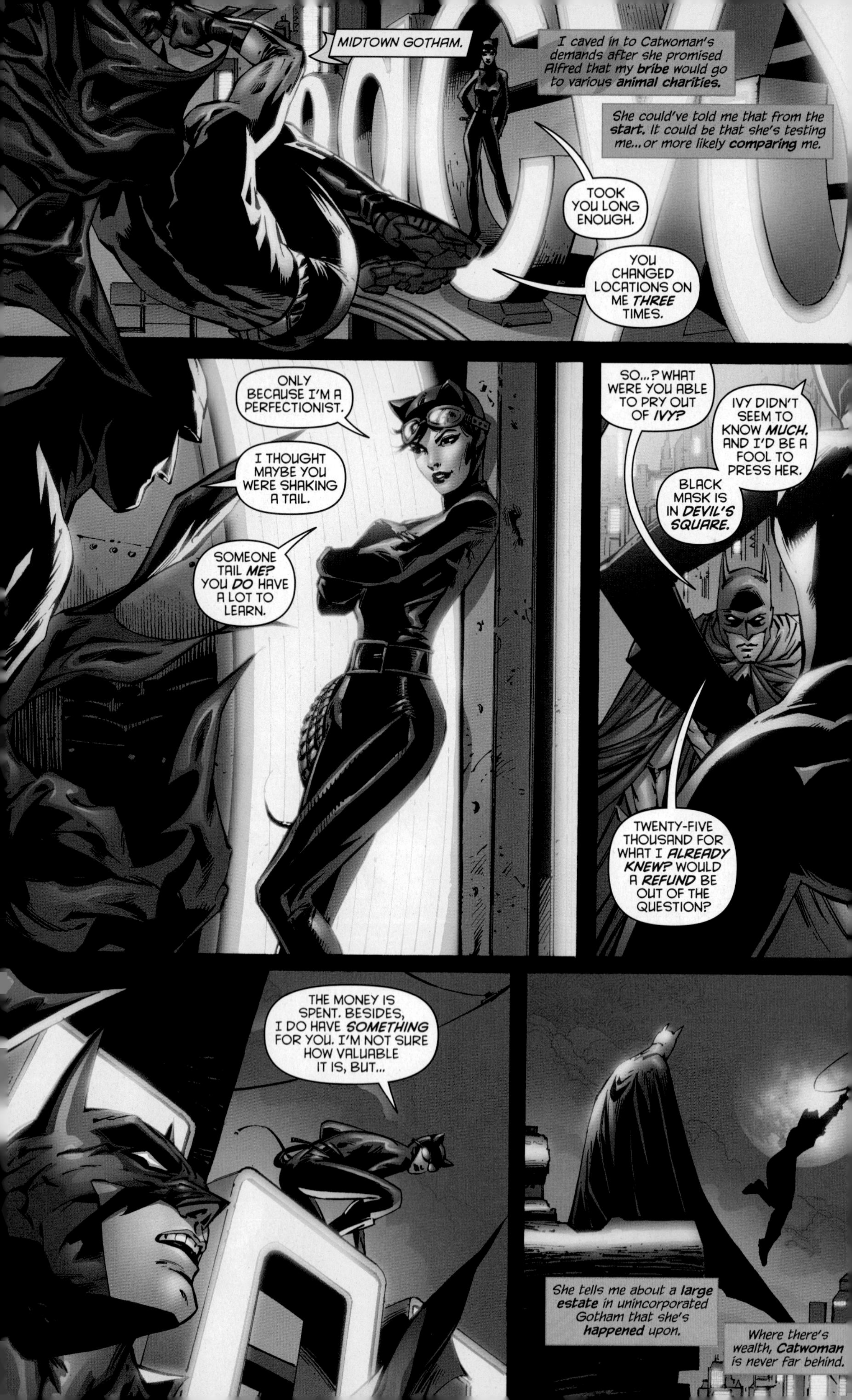
MIDTOWN GOTHAM.
I caved in to Catwoman's demands after she promised Alfred that my bribe would go to various animal charities.
She could've told me that from the start. It could be that she's testing me...or more likely comparing me.
TOOK YOU LONG ENOUGH.
YOU CHANGED LOCATIONS ON ME THREE TIMES.
ONLY BECAUSE I'M A PERFECTIONIST.
I THOUGHT MAYBE YOU WERE SHAKING A TAIL.
SOMEONE TAIL ME? YOU DO HAVE A LOT TO LEARN.
SO...? WHAT WERE YOU ABLE TO PRY OUT OF IVY?
IVY DIDN'T SEEM TO KNOW MUCH. AND I'D BE A FOOL TO PRESS HER.
BLACK MASK IS IN DEVIL'S SQUARE.
TWENTY-FIVE THOUSAND FOR WHAT I ALREADY KNEW? WOULD A REFUND BE OUT OF THE QUESTION?
THE MONEY IS SPENT. BESIDES, I DO HAVE SOMETHING FOR YOU. I'M NOT SURE HOW VALUABLE IT IS, BUT...
She tells me about a large estate in unincorporated Gotham that she's happened upon.
Where there's wealth, Catwoman is never far behind.

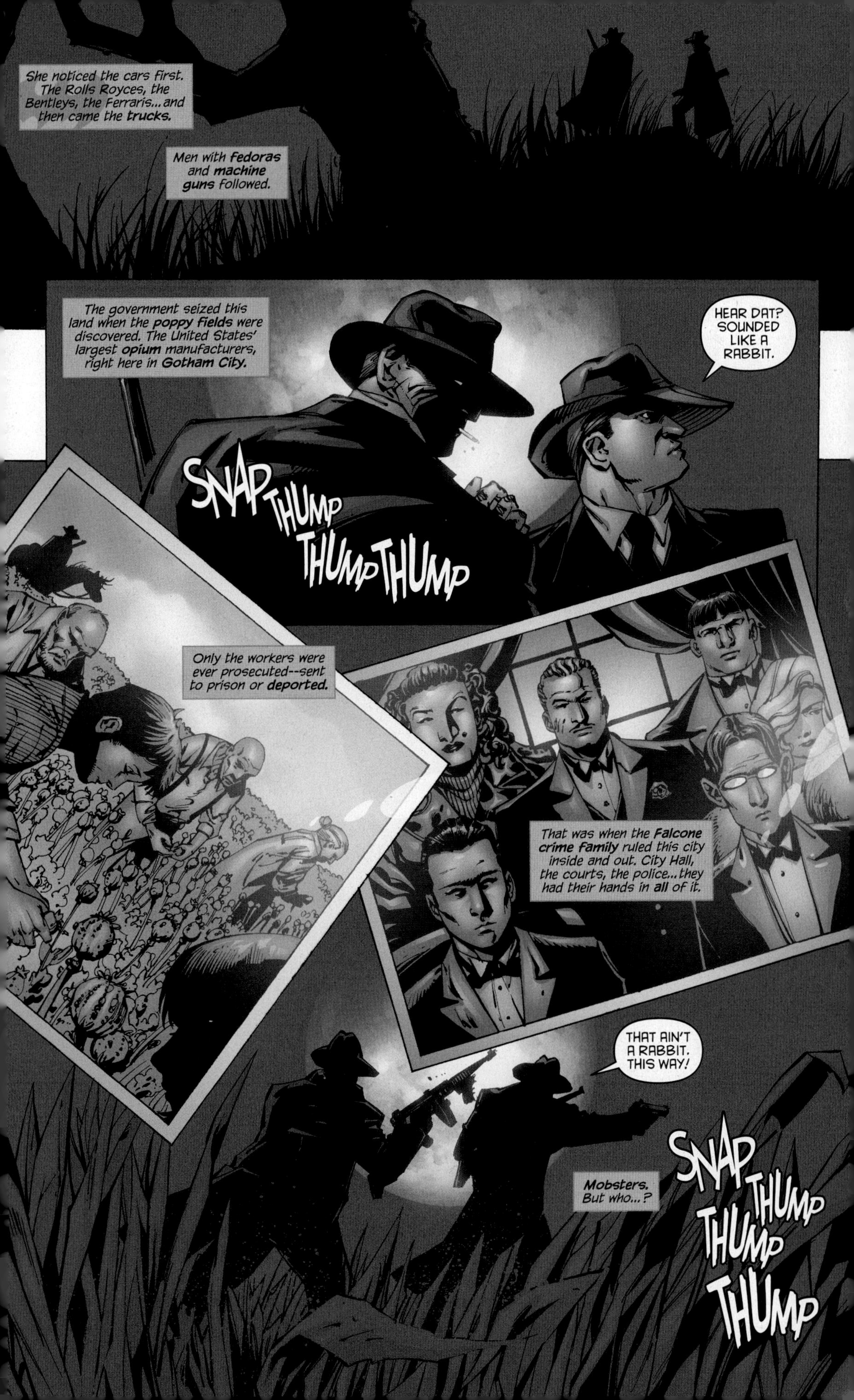
She noticed the cars first. The Rolls Royces, the Bentleys, the Ferraris...and then came the trucks.
Men with fedoras and machine guns followed.
The government seized this land when the poppy fields were discovered. The United States' largest opium manufacturers, right here in Gotham City.
HEAR DAT? SOUNDED LIKE A RABBIT.
SNAP THUMP THUMP THUMP
Only the workers were ever prosecuted--sent to prison or deported.
That was when the Falcone crime family ruled this city inside and out. City Hall, the courts, the police...they had their hands in all of it.
THAT AIN'T A RABBIT. THIS WAY!
Mobsters. But who...?
SNAP THUMP THUMP THUMP

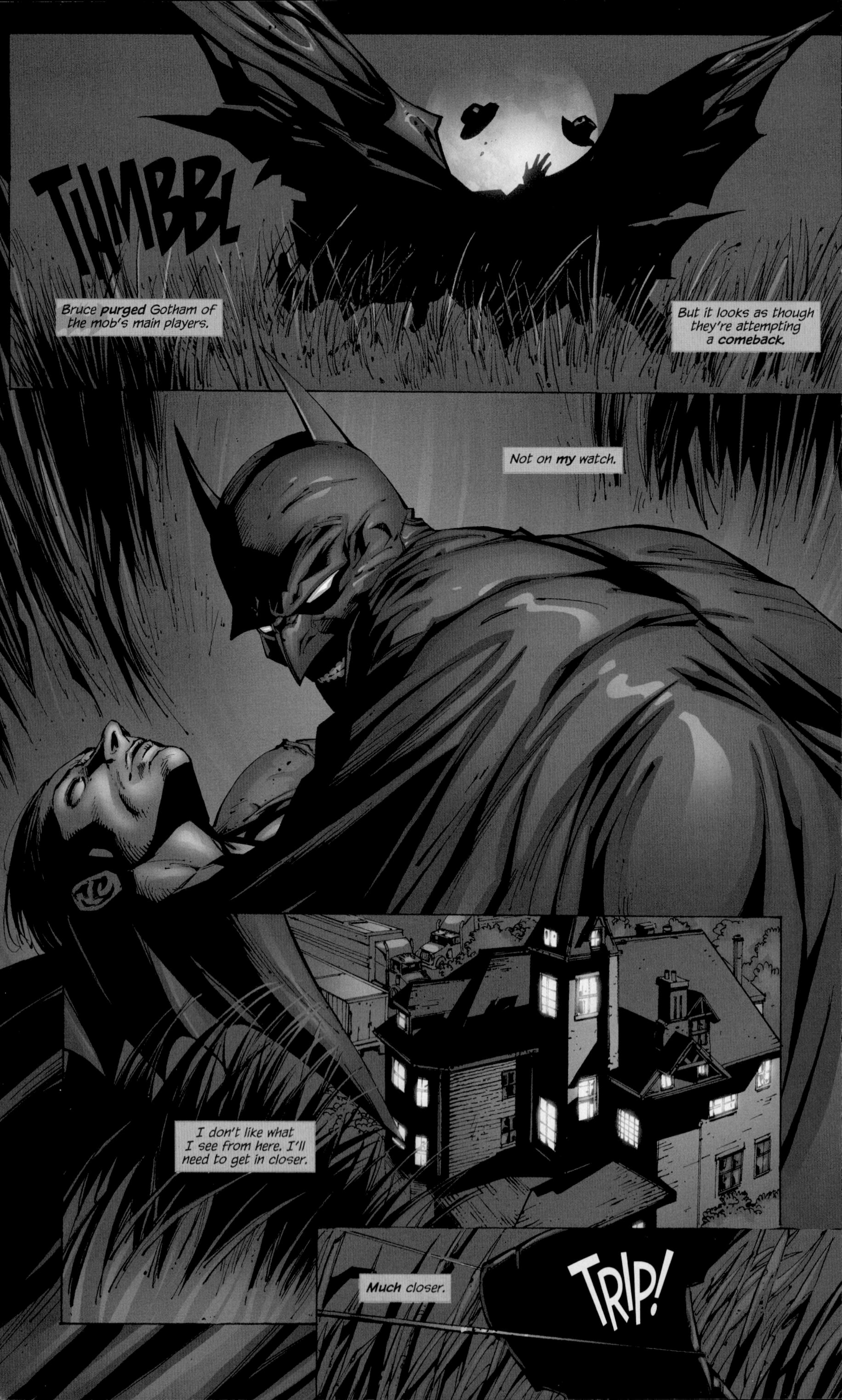
THMBBL
Bruce purged Gotham of the mob's main players.
But it looks as though they're attempting a comeback.
Not on my watch.
I don't like what I see from here. I'll need to get in closer.
Much closer.
TRIP!

There goes the element of surprise.
BOOOM
SEE WHO THE HELL IS OUT THERE!
WE'LL FIND OUT, MR. FALCONE.
Mario Falcone. If I wasn't seeing it with my own magnified lenses, I wouldn't believe it.

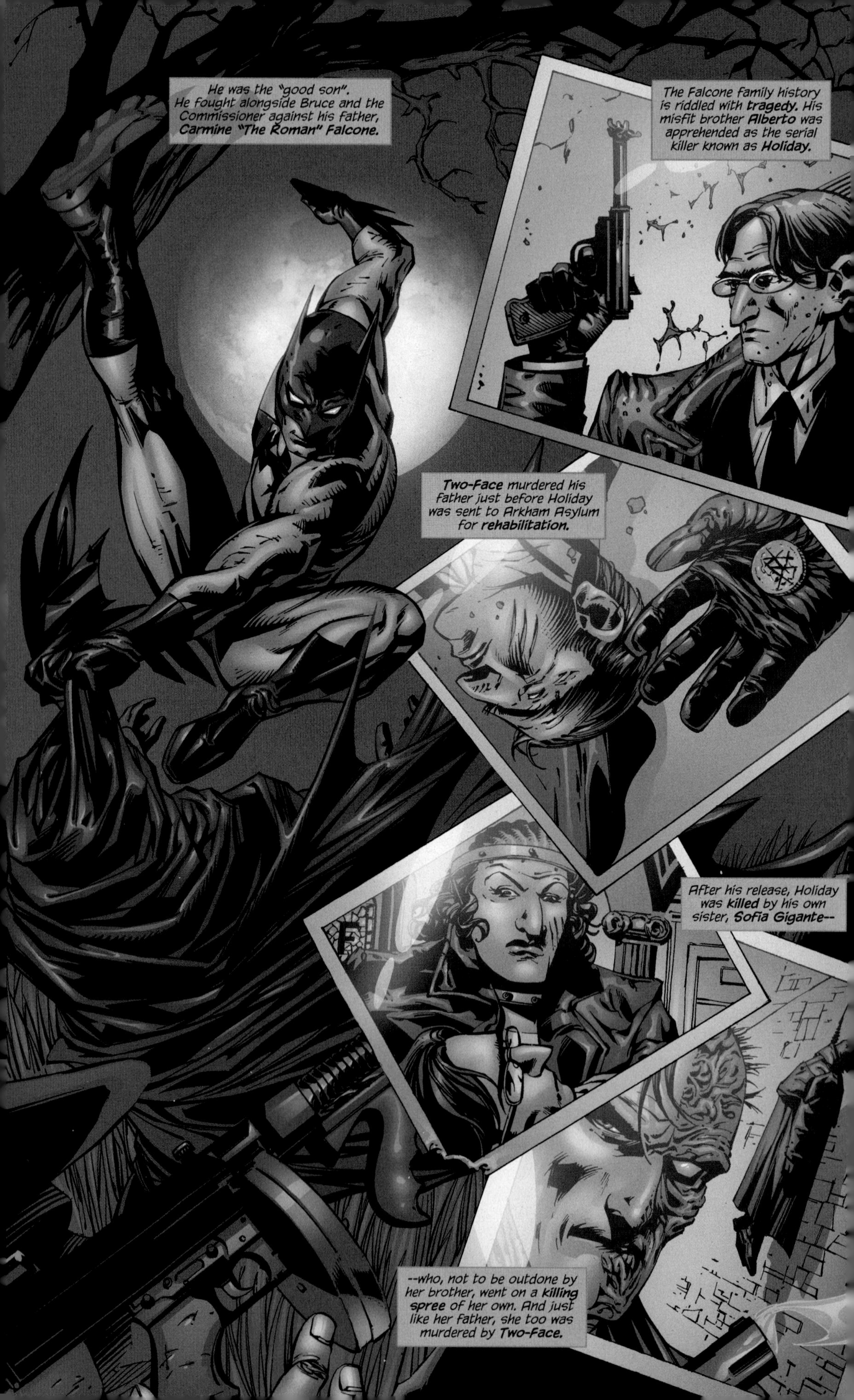
He was the "good son". He fought alongside Bruce and the Commissioner against his father, **Carmine "The Roman" Falcone.**
The Falcone family history is riddled with **tragedy.** His misfit brother **Alberto** was apprehended as the serial killer known as **Holiday.**
Two-Face murdered his father just before Holiday was sent to Arkham Asylum for **rehabilitation.**
After his release, Holiday was **killed** by his own sister, **Sofia Gigante--**
--who, not to be outdone by her brother, went on a **killing spree** of her own. And just like her father, she too was murdered by **Two-Face.**

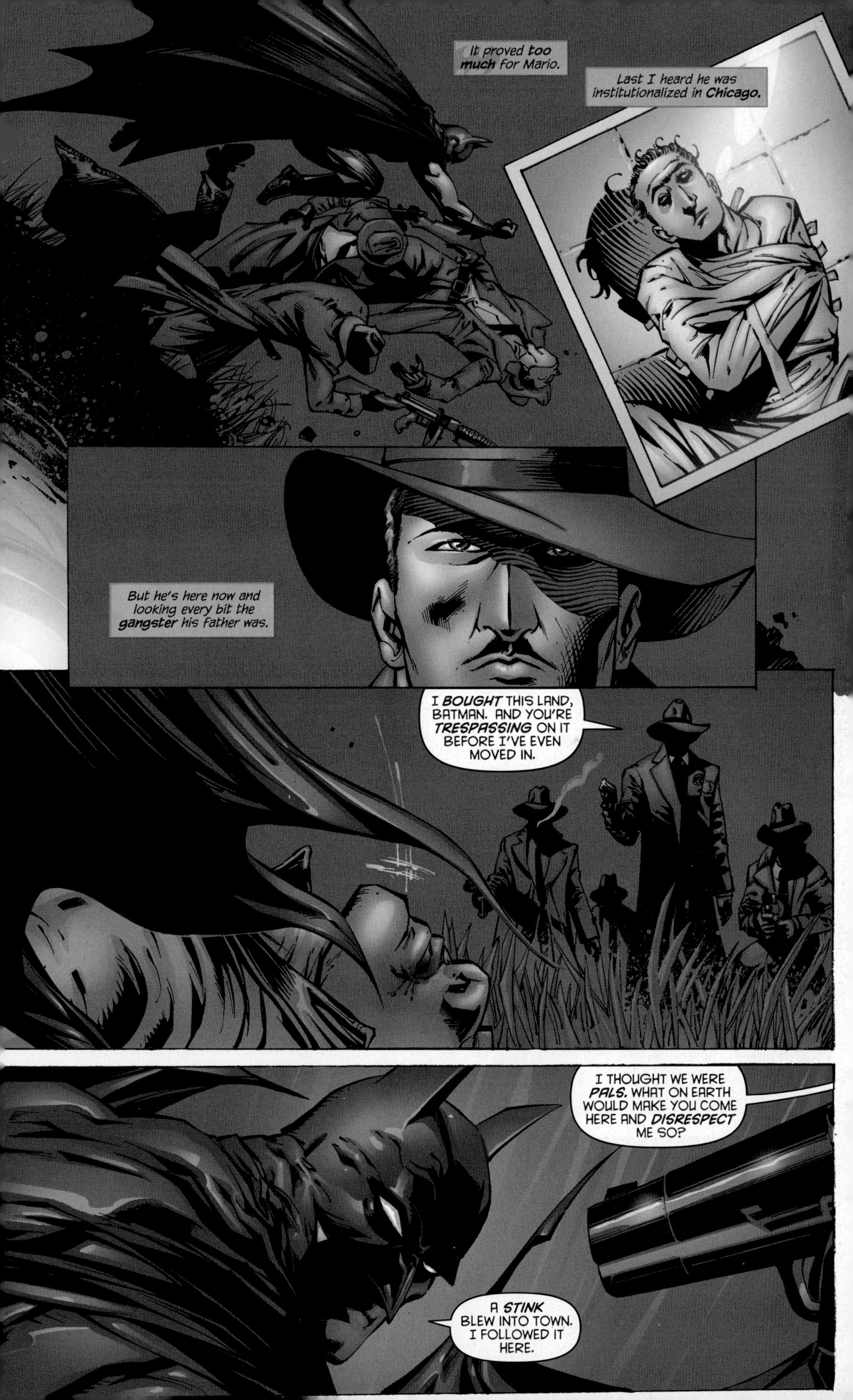
It proved too much for Mario.
Last I heard he was institutionalized in Chicago.
But he's here now and looking every bit the gangster his father was.
I BOUGHT THIS LAND, BATMAN. AND YOU'RE TRESPASSING ON IT BEFORE I'VE EVEN MOVED IN.
I THOUGHT WE WERE PALS. WHAT ON EARTH WOULD MAKE YOU COME HERE AND DISRESPECT ME SO?
A STINK BLEW INTO TOWN. I FOLLOWED IT HERE.

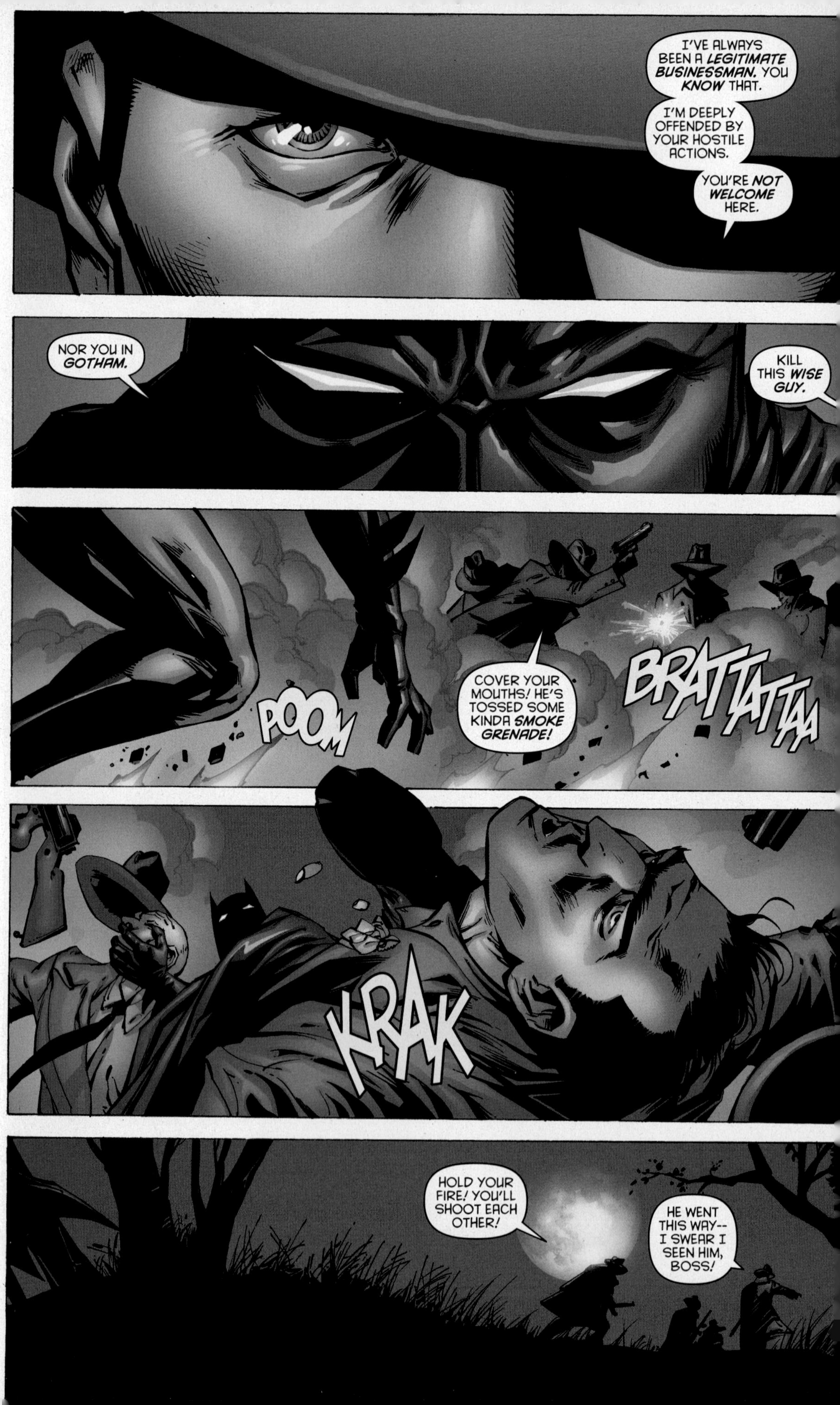

I'VE ALWAYS BEEN A LEGITIMATE BUSINESSMAN. YOU KNOW THAT.
I'M DEEPLY OFFENDED BY YOUR HOSTILE ACTIONS.
YOU'RE NOT WELCOME HERE.
NOR YOU IN GOTHAM.
KILL THIS WISE GUY.
POOM
COVER YOUR MOUTHS! HE'S TOSSED SOME KINDA SMOKE GRENADE!
BRATTATTAA
KRAK
HOLD YOUR FIRE! YOU'LL SHOOT EACH OTHER!
HE WENT THIS WAY-- I SWEAR I SEEN HIM, BOSS!

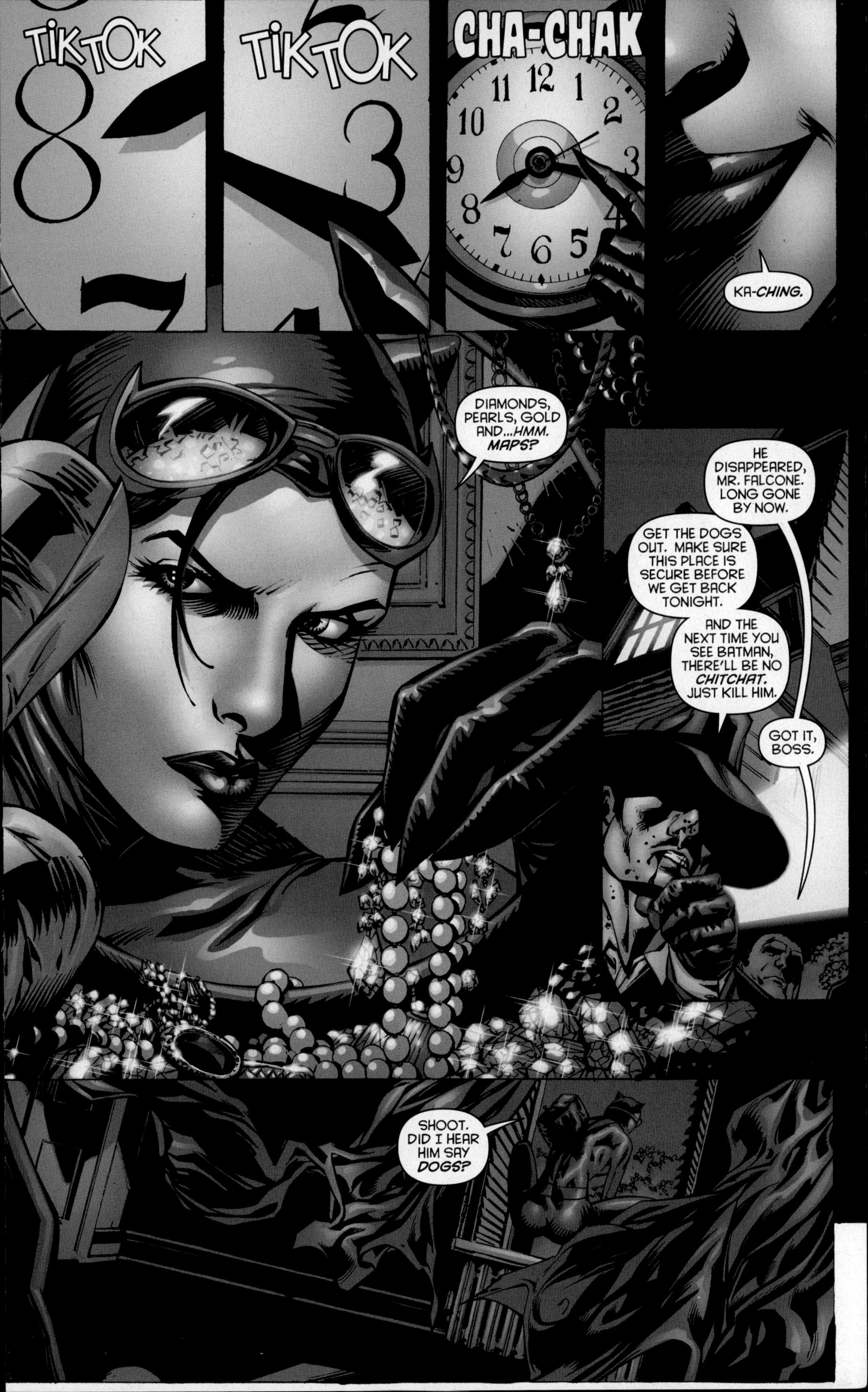
TIKTOK
TIKTOK
CHA-CHAK
KA-CHING.
DIAMONDS, PEARLS, GOLD AND...HMM. MAPS?
HE DISAPPEARED, MR. FALCONE. LONG GONE BY NOW.
GET THE DOGS OUT. MAKE SURE THIS PLACE IS SECURE BEFORE WE GET BACK TONIGHT.
AND THE NEXT TIME YOU SEE BATMAN, THERE'LL BE NO CHITCHAT. JUST KILL HIM.
GOT IT, BOSS.
SHOOT. DID I HEAR HIM SAY DOGS?

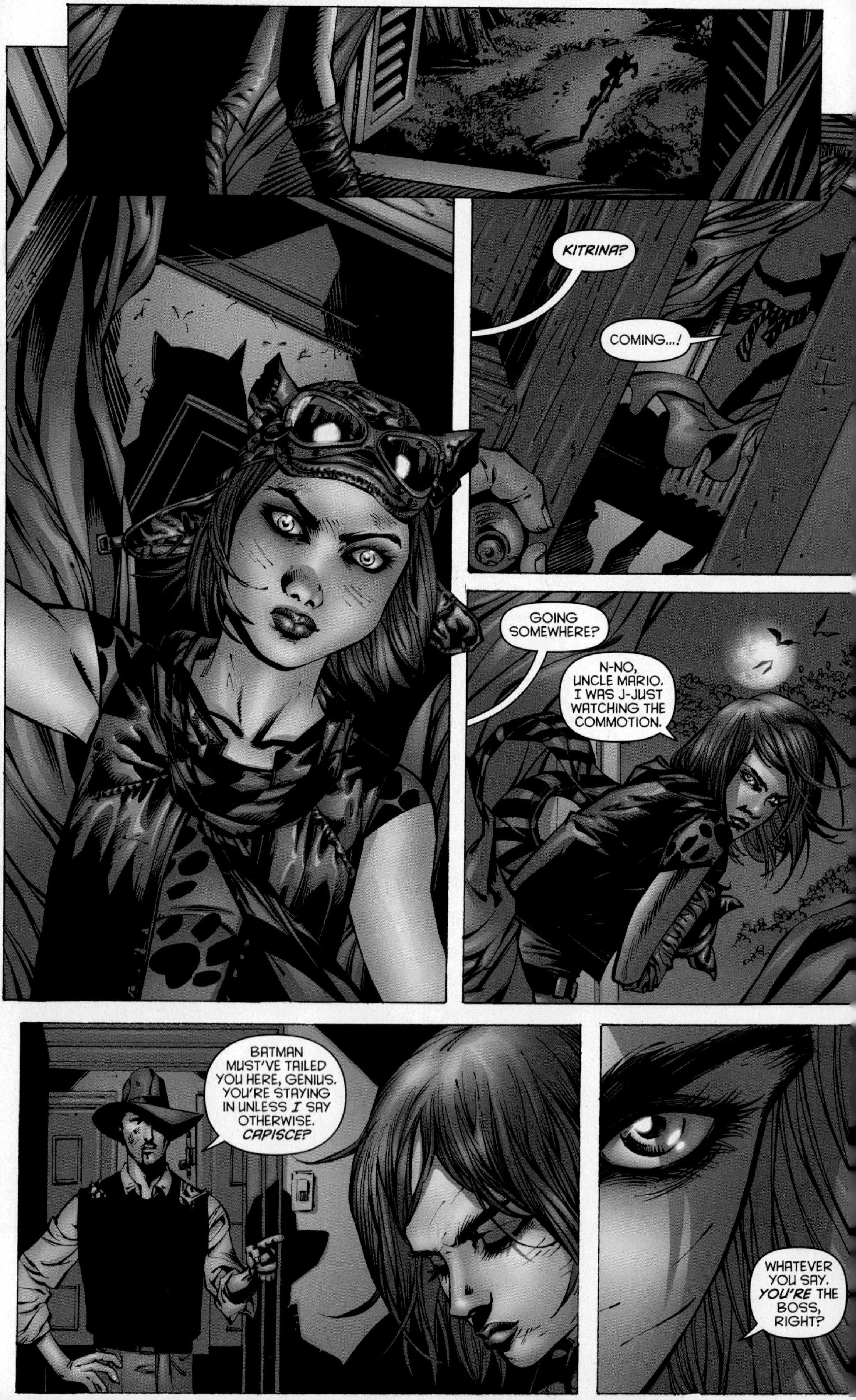
KITRINA?
COMING...!
GOING SOMEWHERE?
N-NO, UNCLE MARIO. I WAS J-JUST WATCHING THE COMMOTION.
BATMAN MUST'VE TAILED YOU HERE, GENIUS. YOU'RE STAYING IN UNLESS *I* SAY OTHERWISE. *CAPISCE?*
WHATEVER YOU SAY. *YOU'RE* THE BOSS, RIGHT?

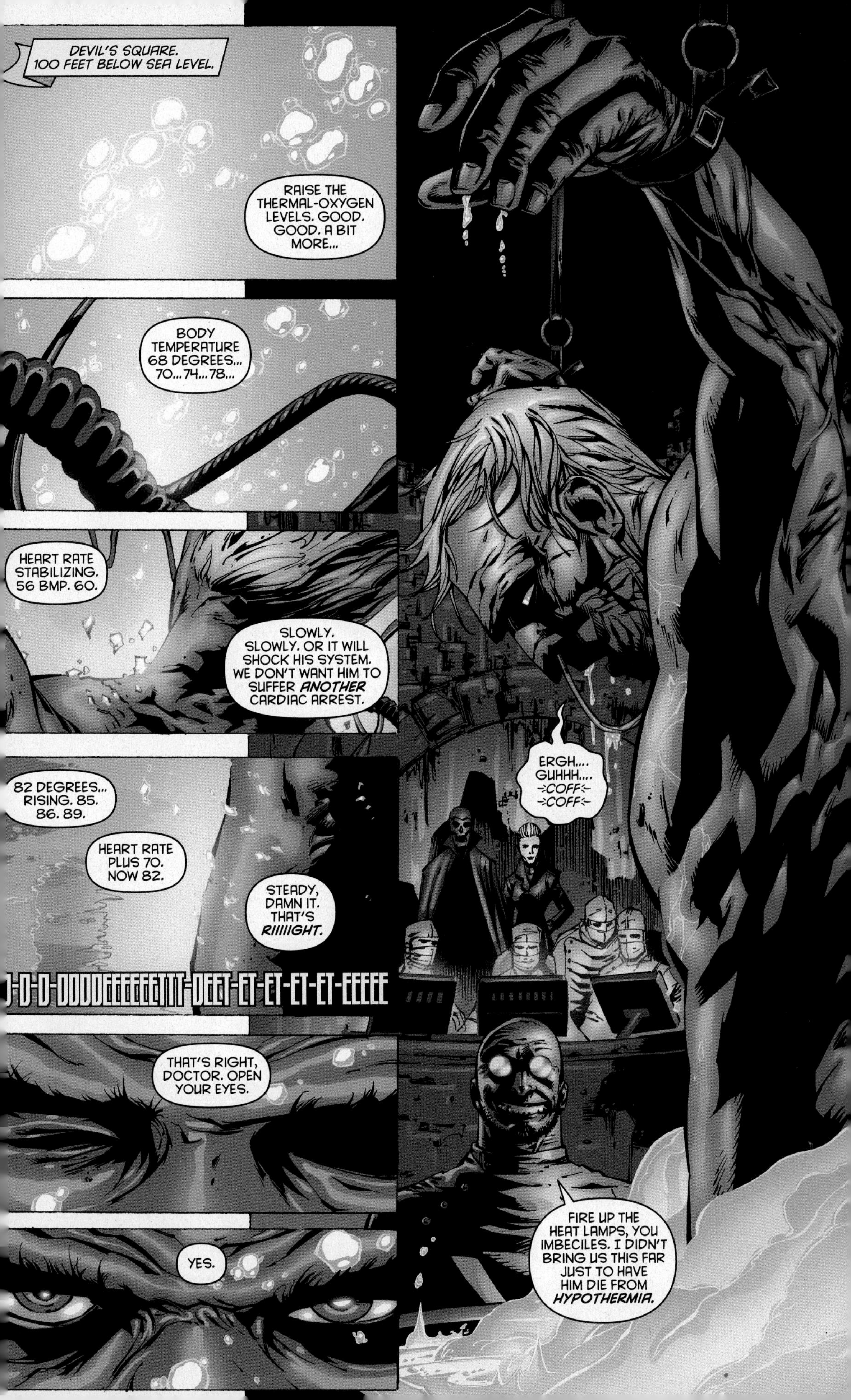

DEVIL'S SQUARE. 100 FEET BELOW SEA LEVEL.
RAISE THE THERMAL-OXYGEN LEVELS. GOOD. GOOD. A BIT MORE...
BODY TEMPERATURE 68 DEGREES... 70...74...78...
HEART RATE STABILIZING. 56 BMP. 60.
SLOWLY. SLOWLY. OR IT WILL SHOCK HIS SYSTEM. WE DON'T WANT HIM TO SUFFER ANOTHER CARDIAC ARREST.
82 DEGREES... RISING. 85. 86. 89.
HEART RATE PLUS 70. NOW 82.
STEADY, DAMN IT. THAT'S RIIIIGHT.
ERGH.... GUHHH.... COFF COFF
D-D-D-DDDDEEEEEEETTT-DEET-ET-ET-ET-ET-EEEEE
THAT'S RIGHT, DOCTOR. OPEN YOUR EYES.
YES.
FIRE UP THE HEAT LAMPS, YOU IMBECILES. I DIDN'T BRING US THIS FAR JUST TO HAVE HIM DIE FROM HYPOTHERMIA.

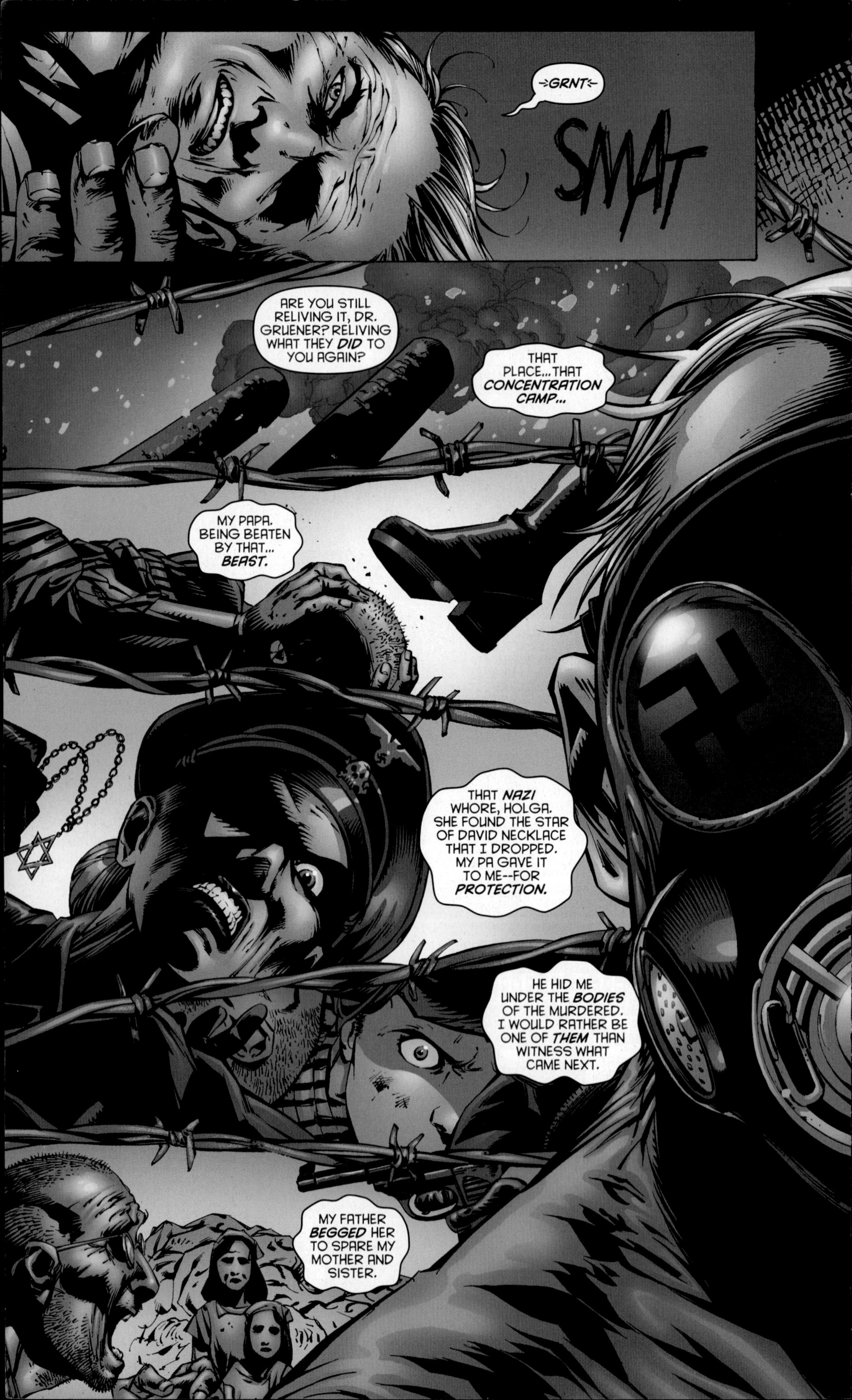

GRNT
SMAT
ARE YOU STILL RELIVING IT, DR. GRUENER? RELIVING WHAT THEY DID TO YOU AGAIN?
THAT PLACE...THAT CONCENTRATION CAMP...
MY PAPA. BEING BEATEN BY THAT... BEAST.
THAT NAZI WHORE, HOLGA. SHE FOUND THE STAR OF DAVID NECKLACE THAT I DROPPED. MY PA GAVE IT TO ME--FOR PROTECTION.
HE HID ME UNDER THE BODIES OF THE MURDERED. I WOULD RATHER BE ONE OF THEM THAN WITNESS WHAT CAME NEXT.
MY FATHER BEGGED HER TO SPARE MY MOTHER AND SISTER.

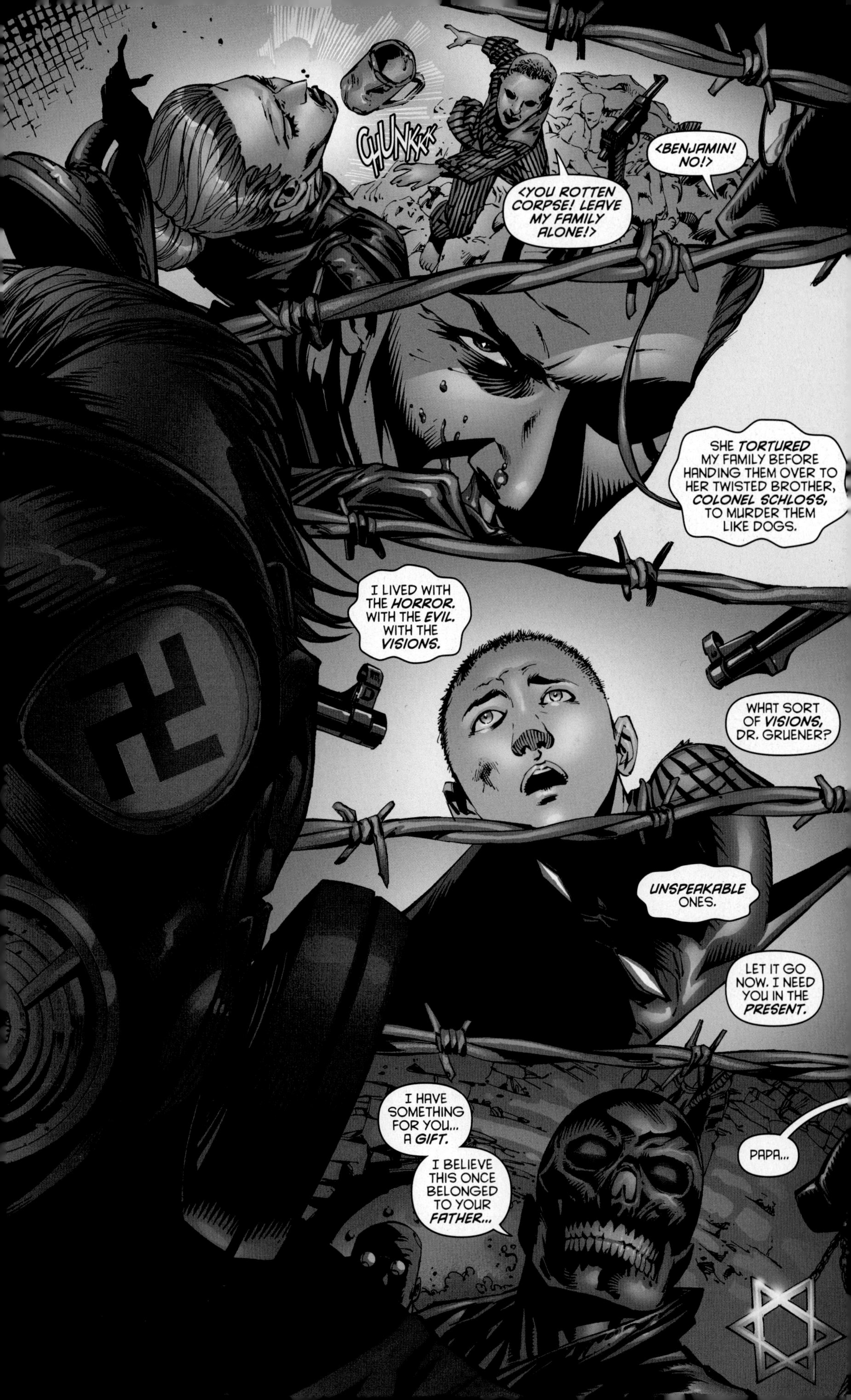
CHUNKK
<YOU ROTTEN CORPSE! LEAVE MY FAMILY ALONE!>
<BENJAMIN! NO!>
SHE TORTURED MY FAMILY BEFORE HANDING THEM OVER TO HER TWISTED BROTHER, COLONEL SCHLOSS, TO MURDER THEM LIKE DOGS.
I LIVED WITH THE HORROR. WITH THE EVIL. WITH THE VISIONS.
WHAT SORT OF VISIONS, DR. GRUENER?
UNSPEAKABLE ONES.
LET IT GO NOW. I NEED YOU IN THE PRESENT.
I HAVE SOMETHING FOR YOU... A GIFT.
I BELIEVE THIS ONCE BELONGED TO YOUR FATHER...
PAPA...

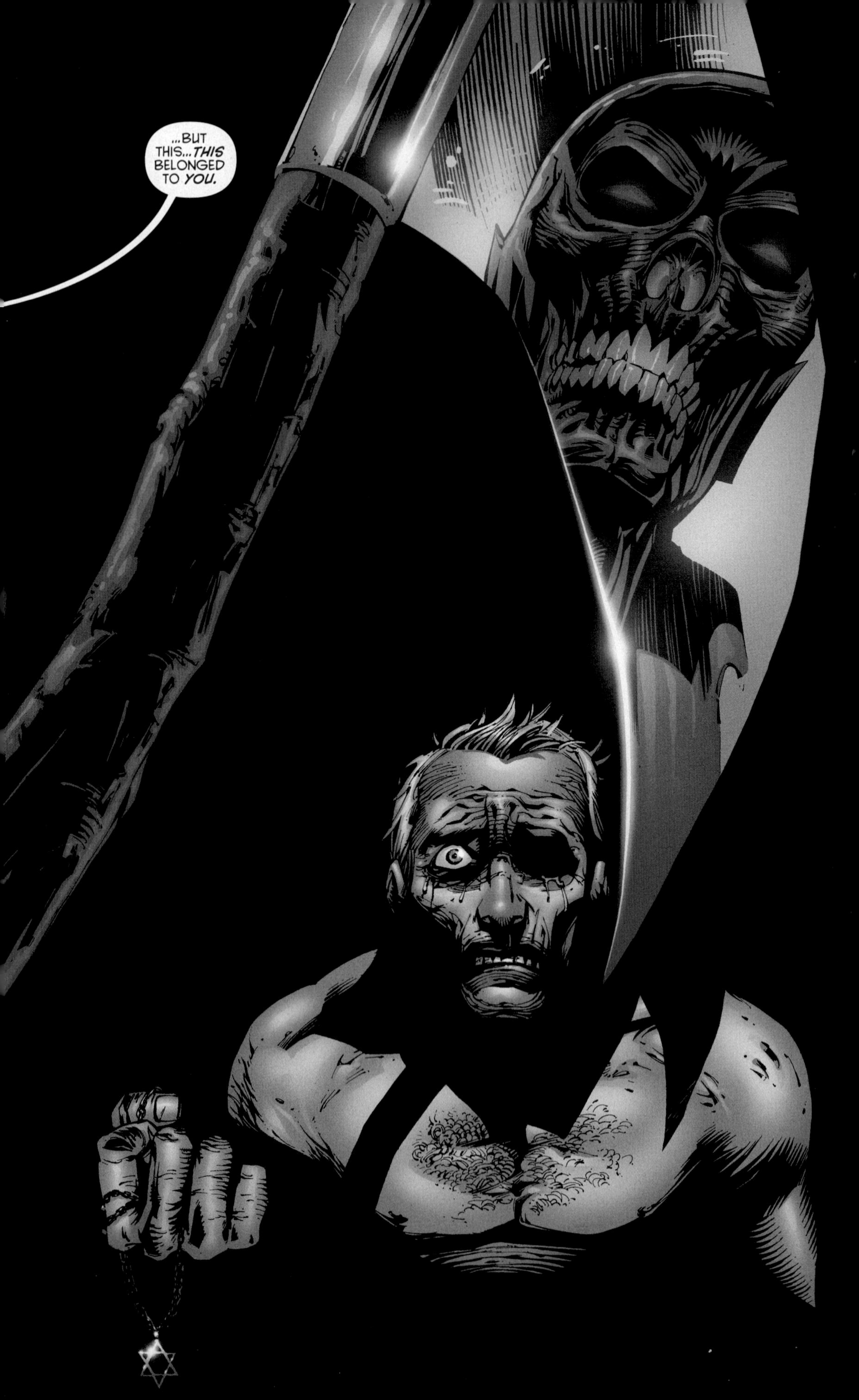
...BUT THIS...THIS BELONGED TO YOU.

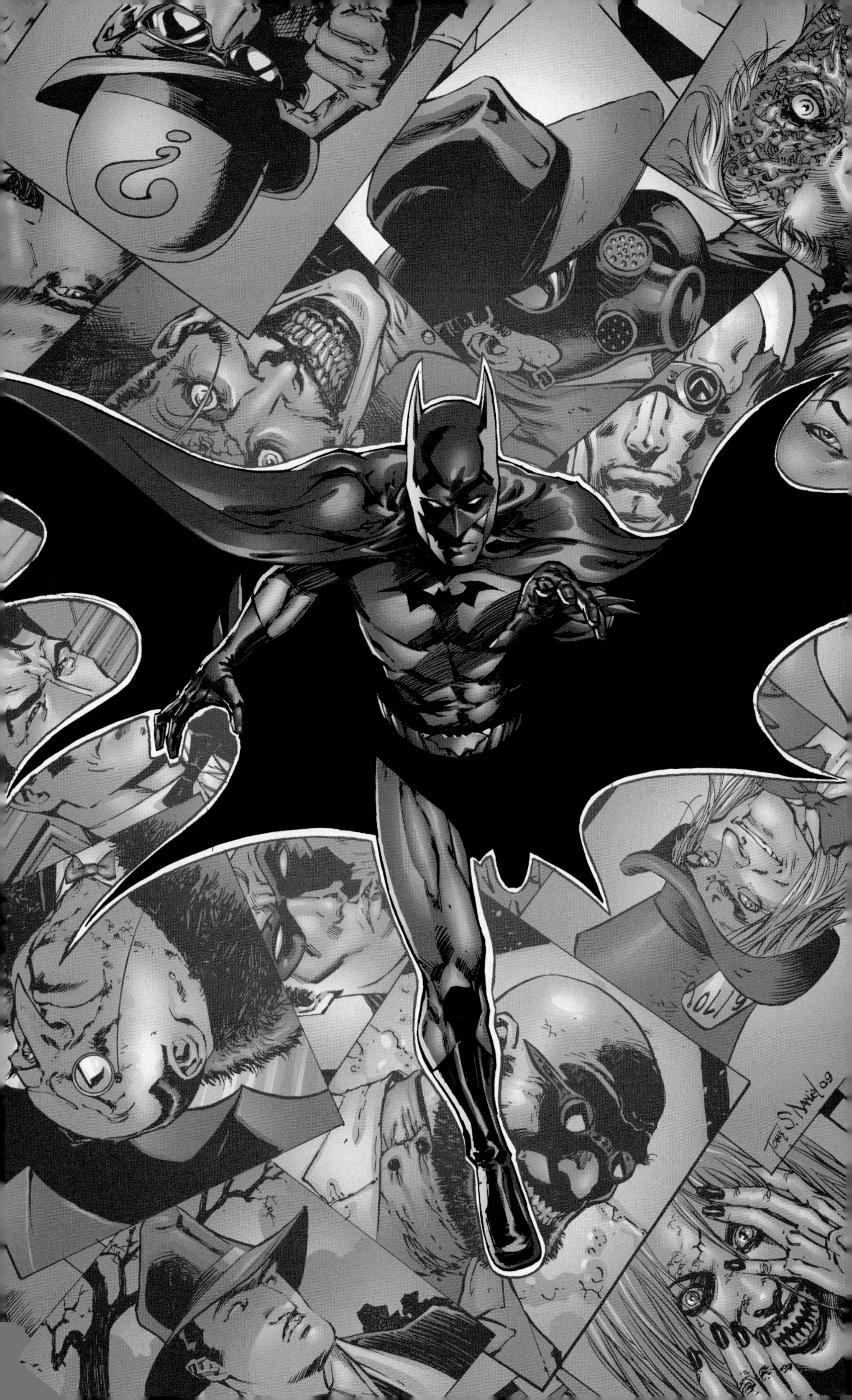

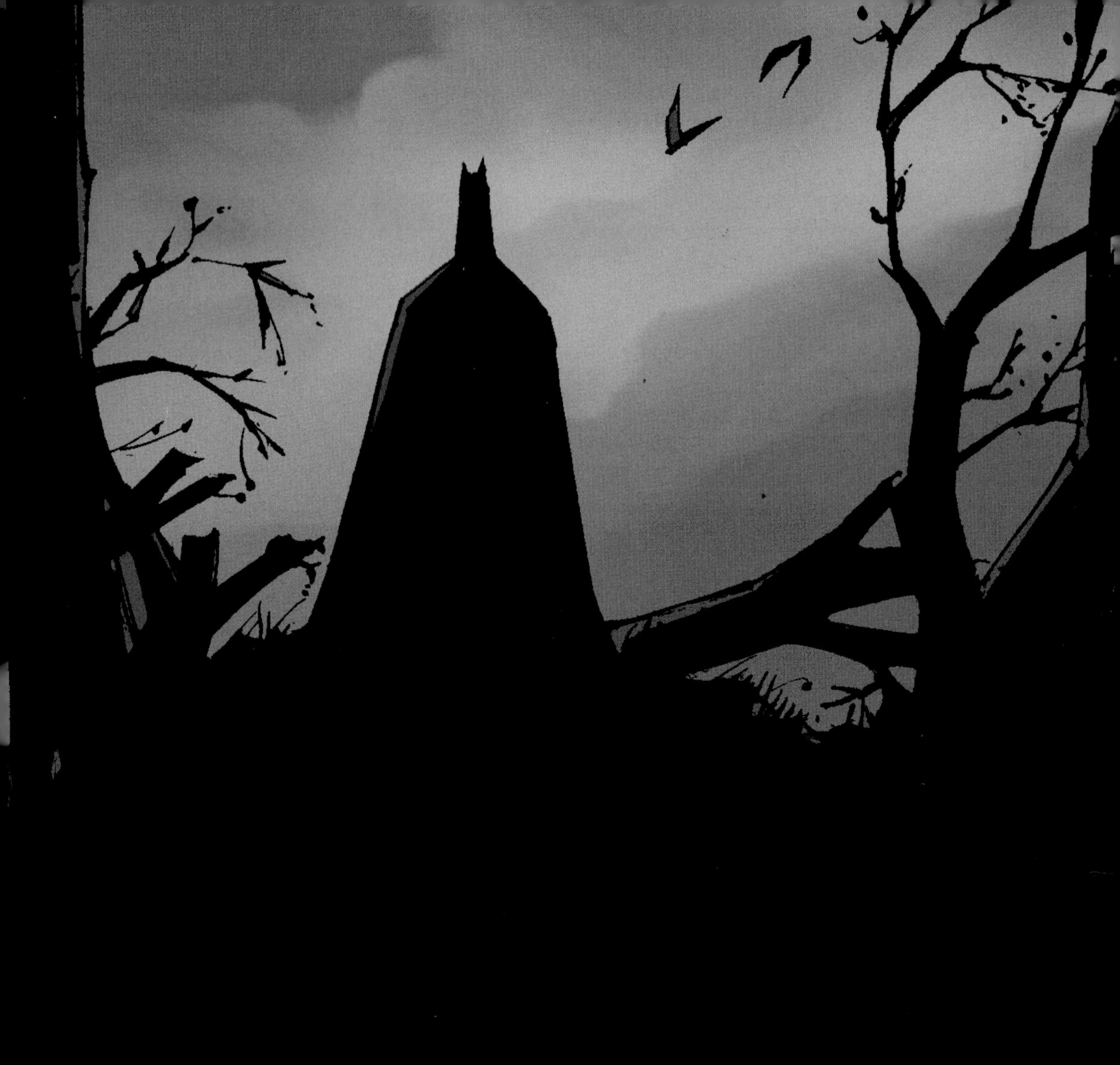

"I have an hour and a half of darkness left. That's all I need to get started."

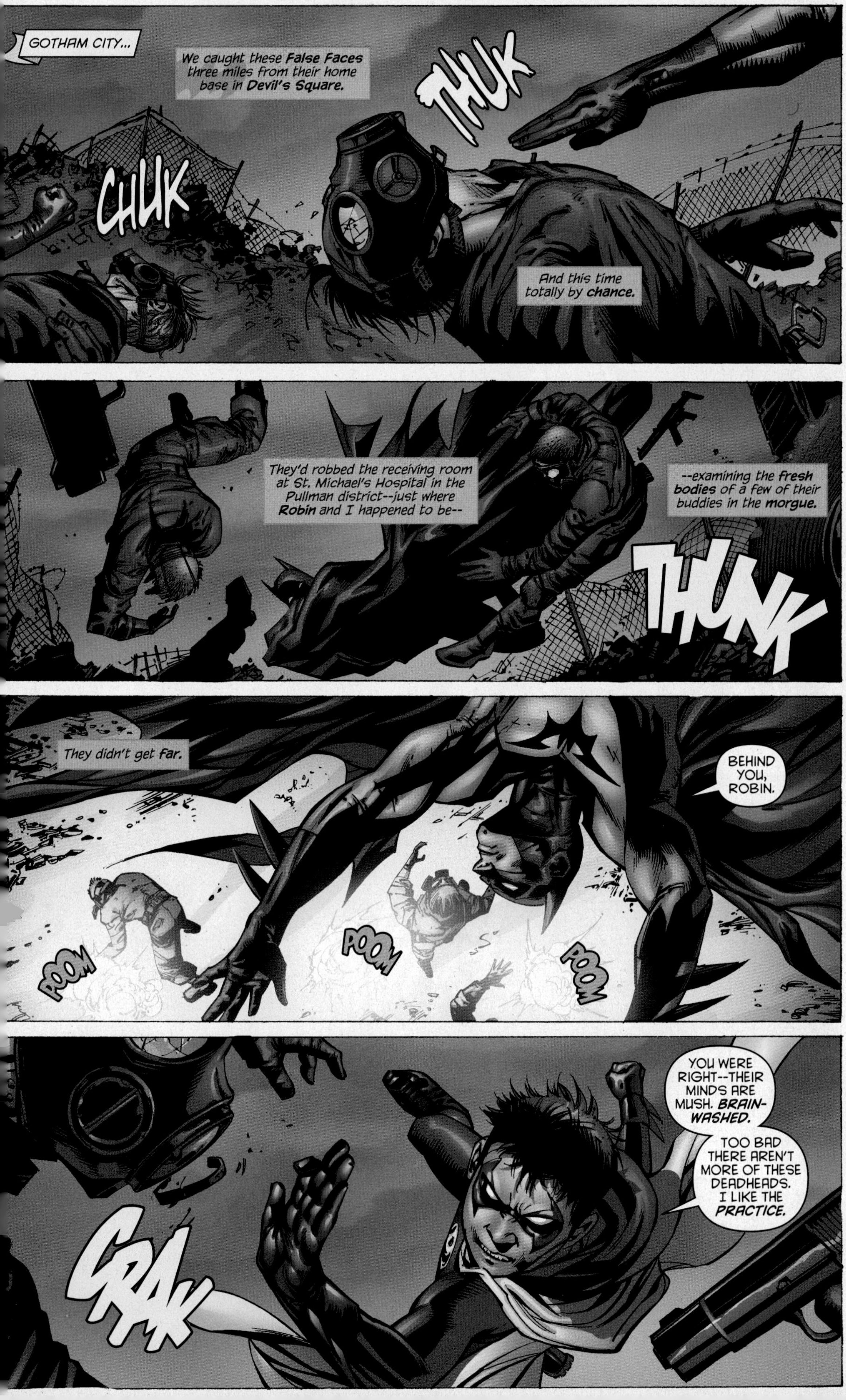
GOTHAM CITY...
We caught these False Faces three miles from their home base in Devil's Square.
THUK
CHUK
And this time totally by chance.
They'd robbed the receiving room at St. Michael's Hospital in the Pullman district--just where Robin and I happened to be--
--examining the fresh bodies of a few of their buddies in the morgue.
THUNK
They didn't get far.
BEHIND YOU, ROBIN.
POOM
POOM
POOM
YOU WERE RIGHT--THEIR MINDS ARE MUSH. BRAIN-WASHED.
TOO BAD THERE AREN'T MORE OF THESE DEADHEADS. I LIKE THE PRACTICE.
CRAK

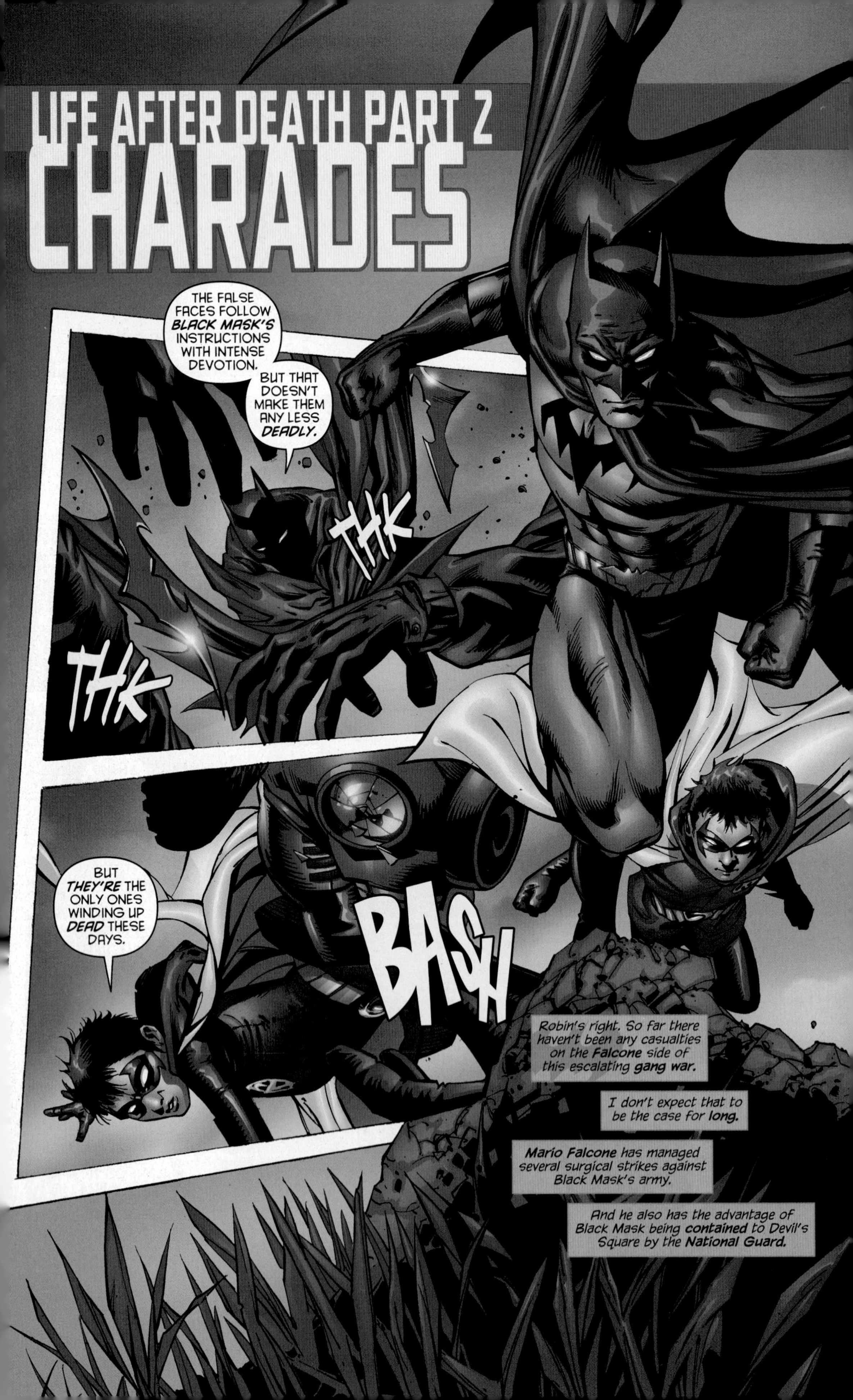
LIFE AFTER DEATH PART 2
CHARADES
THE FALSE FACES FOLLOW BLACK MASK'S INSTRUCTIONS WITH INTENSE DEVOTION.
BUT THAT DOESN'T MAKE THEM ANY LESS DEADLY.
THK
THK
BUT THEY'RE THE ONLY ONES WINDING UP DEAD THESE DAYS.
BASH
Robin's right. So far there haven't been any casualties on the Falcone side of this escalating gang war.
I don't expect that to be the case for long.
Mario Falcone has managed several surgical strikes against Black Mask's army.
And he also has the advantage of Black Mask being contained to Devil's Square by the National Guard.

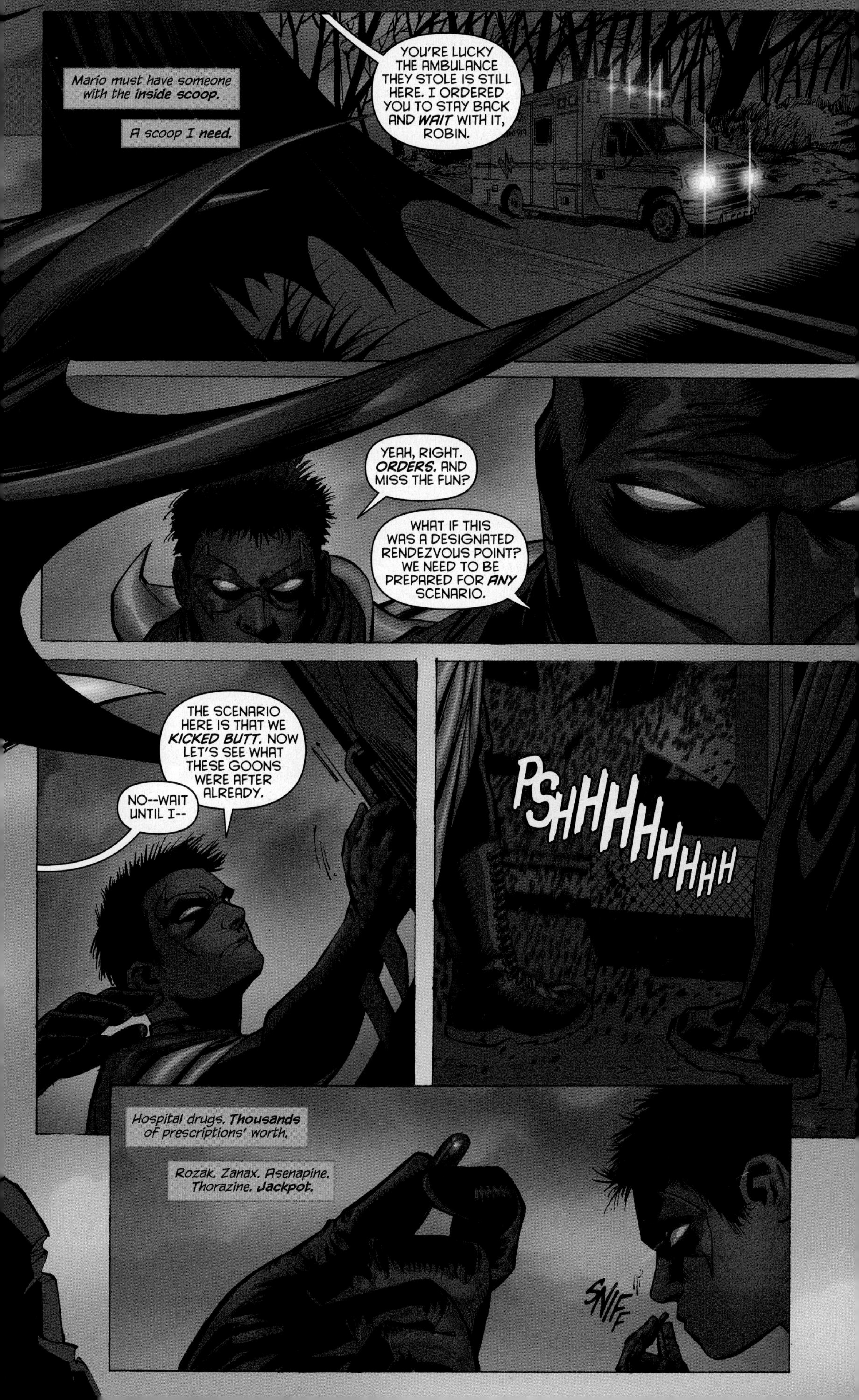

Mario must have someone with the inside scoop.
A scoop I need.
YOU'RE LUCKY THE AMBULANCE THEY STOLE IS STILL HERE. I ORDERED YOU TO STAY BACK AND WAIT WITH IT, ROBIN.
YEAH, RIGHT. ORDERS. AND MISS THE FUN?
WHAT IF THIS WAS A DESIGNATED RENDEZVOUS POINT? WE NEED TO BE PREPARED FOR ANY SCENARIO.
THE SCENARIO HERE IS THAT WE KICKED BUTT. NOW LET'S SEE WHAT THESE GOONS WERE AFTER ALREADY.
NO--WAIT UNTIL I--
PSHHHHHHHHH
Hospital drugs. Thousands of prescriptions' worth.
Rozak. Zanax. Asenapine. Thorazine. Jackpot.
SNIFF

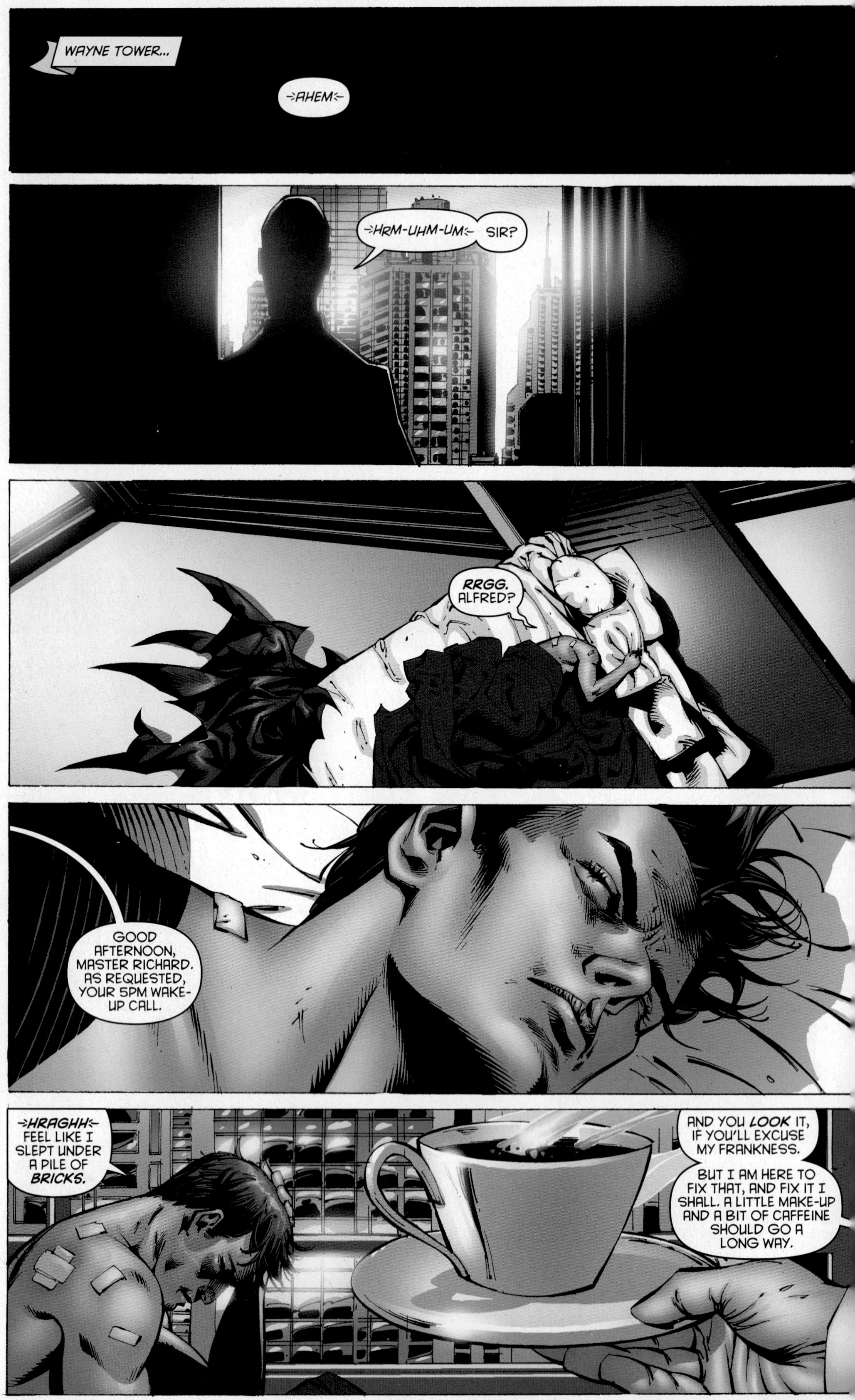
WAYNE TOWER...
AHEM
HRM-UHM-UM SIR?
RRGG. ALFRED?
GOOD AFTERNOON, MASTER RICHARD. AS REQUESTED, YOUR 5PM WAKE-UP CALL.
HRAGHH FEEL LIKE I SLEPT UNDER A PILE OF BRICKS.
AND YOU LOOK IT, IF YOU'LL EXCUSE MY FRANKNESS.
BUT I AM HERE TO FIX THAT, AND FIX IT I SHALL. A LITTLE MAKE-UP AND A BIT OF CAFFEINE SHOULD GO A LONG WAY.

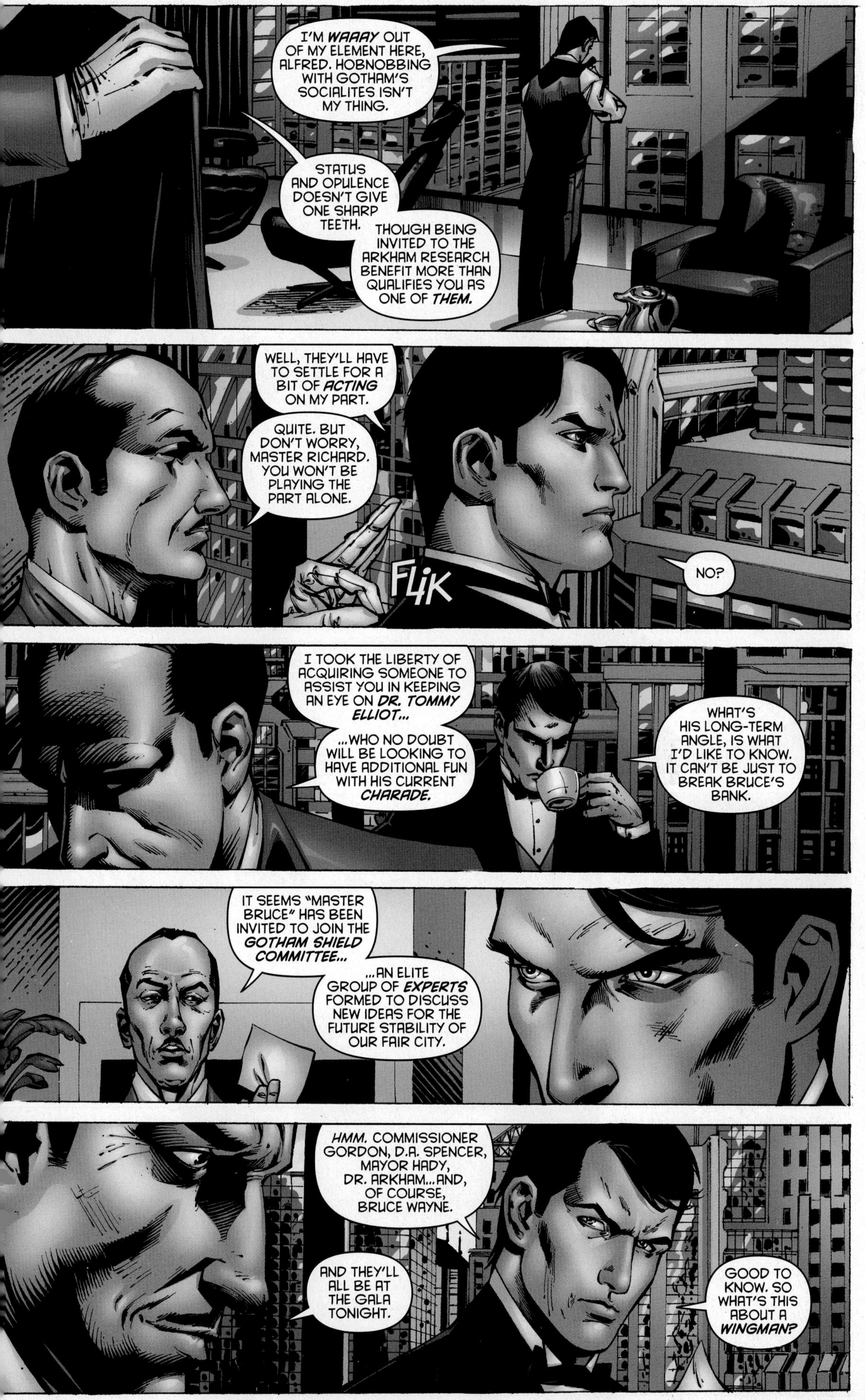
I'M WAAAY OUT OF MY ELEMENT HERE, ALFRED. HOBNOBBING WITH GOTHAM'S SOCIALITES ISN'T MY THING.
STATUS AND OPULENCE DOESN'T GIVE ONE SHARP TEETH.
THOUGH BEING INVITED TO THE ARKHAM RESEARCH BENEFIT MORE THAN QUALIFIES YOU AS ONE OF THEM.
WELL, THEY'LL HAVE TO SETTLE FOR A BIT OF ACTING ON MY PART.
QUITE. BUT DON'T WORRY, MASTER RICHARD. YOU WON'T BE PLAYING THE PART ALONE.
FLIK
NO?
I TOOK THE LIBERTY OF ACQUIRING SOMEONE TO ASSIST YOU IN KEEPING AN EYE ON DR. TOMMY ELLIOT...
...WHO NO DOUBT WILL BE LOOKING TO HAVE ADDITIONAL FUN WITH HIS CURRENT CHARADE.
WHAT'S HIS LONG-TERM ANGLE, IS WHAT I'D LIKE TO KNOW. IT CAN'T BE JUST TO BREAK BRUCE'S BANK.
IT SEEMS "MASTER BRUCE" HAS BEEN INVITED TO JOIN THE GOTHAM SHIELD COMMITTEE...
...AN ELITE GROUP OF EXPERTS FORMED TO DISCUSS NEW IDEAS FOR THE FUTURE STABILITY OF OUR FAIR CITY.
HMM. COMMISSIONER GORDON, D.A. SPENCER, MAYOR HADY, DR. ARKHAM...AND, OF COURSE, BRUCE WAYNE.
AND THEY'LL ALL BE AT THE GALA TONIGHT.
GOOD TO KNOW. SO WHAT'S THIS ABOUT A WINGMAN?

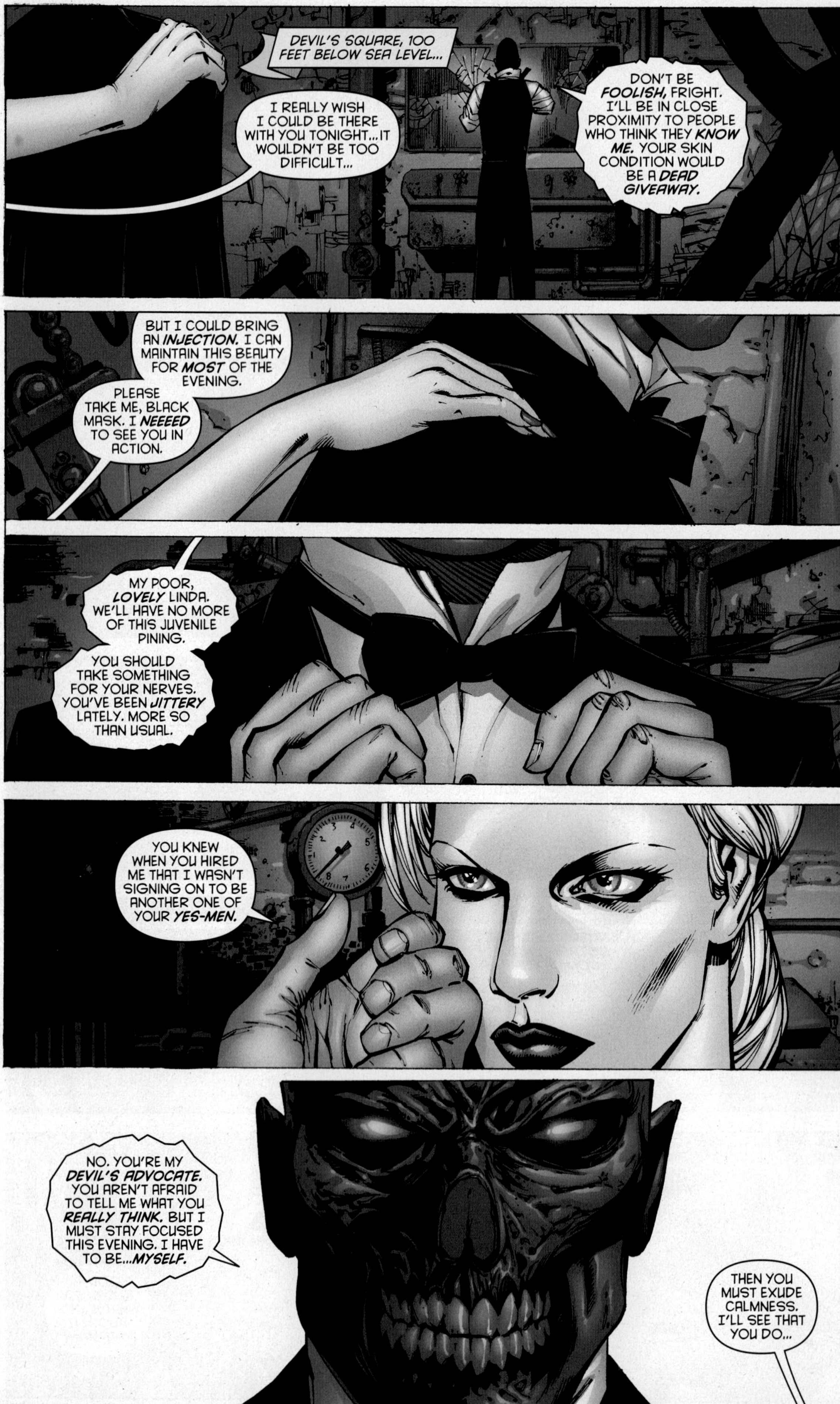
DEVIL'S SQUARE, 100 FEET BELOW SEA LEVEL...
I REALLY WISH I COULD BE THERE WITH YOU TONIGHT...IT WOULDN'T BE TOO DIFFICULT...
DON'T BE FOOLISH, FRIGHT. I'LL BE IN CLOSE PROXIMITY TO PEOPLE WHO THINK THEY KNOW ME. YOUR SKIN CONDITION WOULD BE A DEAD GIVEAWAY.
BUT I COULD BRING AN INJECTION. I CAN MAINTAIN THIS BEAUTY FOR MOST OF THE EVENING.
PLEASE TAKE ME, BLACK MASK. I NEEEED TO SEE YOU IN ACTION.
MY POOR, LOVELY LINDA. WE'LL HAVE NO MORE OF THIS JUVENILE PINING.
YOU SHOULD TAKE SOMETHING FOR YOUR NERVES. YOU'VE BEEN JITTERY LATELY. MORE SO THAN USUAL.
YOU KNEW WHEN YOU HIRED ME THAT I WASN'T SIGNING ON TO BE ANOTHER ONE OF YOUR YES-MEN.
NO. YOU'RE MY DEVIL'S ADVOCATE. YOU AREN'T AFRAID TO TELL ME WHAT YOU REALLY THINK. BUT I MUST STAY FOCUSED THIS EVENING. I HAVE TO BE...MYSELF.
THEN YOU MUST EXUDE CALMNESS. I'LL SEE THAT YOU DO...

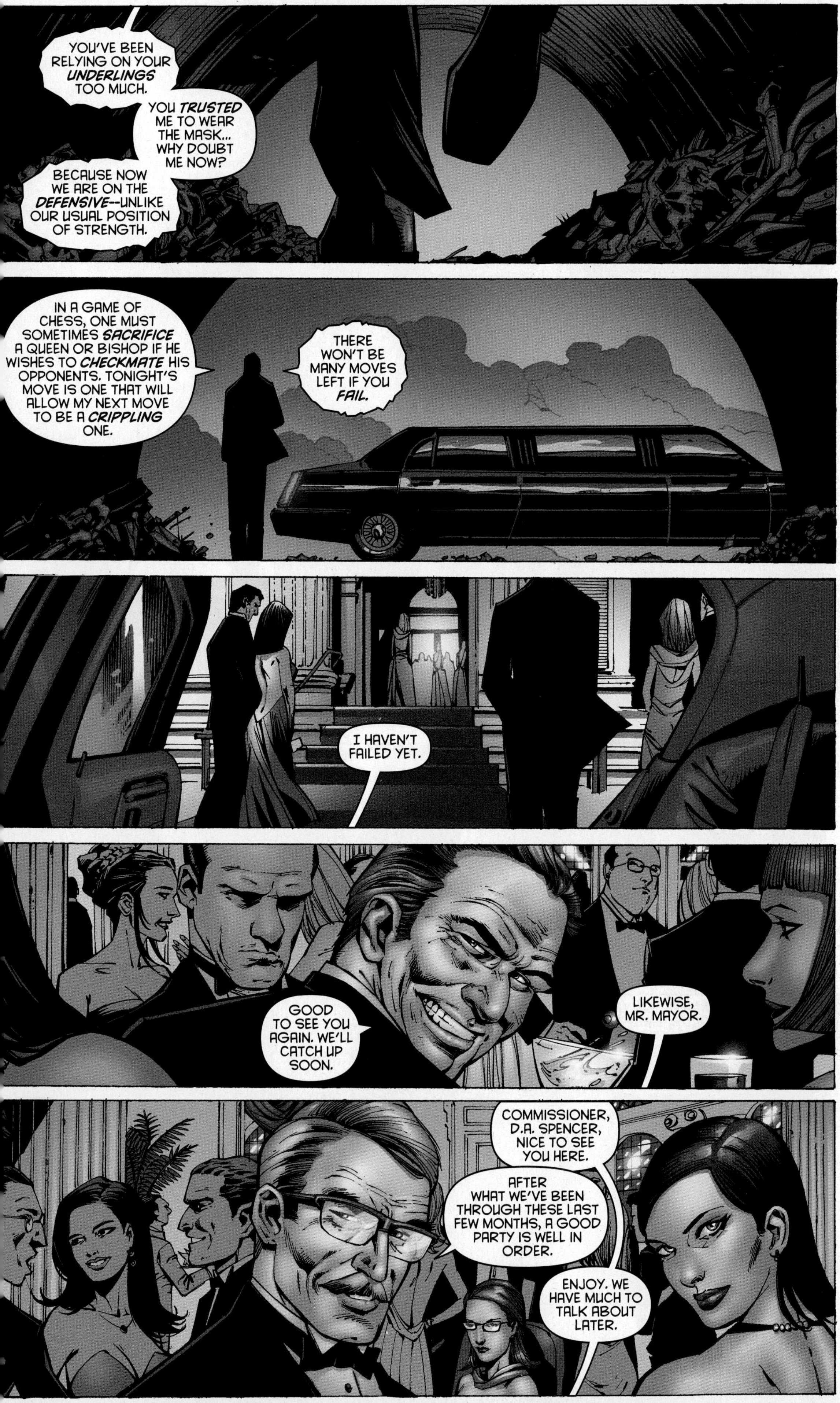
YOU'VE BEEN RELYING ON YOUR UNDERLINGS TOO MUCH.
YOU TRUSTED ME TO WEAR THE MASK... WHY DOUBT ME NOW?
BECAUSE NOW WE ARE ON THE DEFENSIVE--UNLIKE OUR USUAL POSITION OF STRENGTH.
IN A GAME OF CHESS, ONE MUST SOMETIMES SACRIFICE A QUEEN OR BISHOP IF HE WISHES TO CHECKMATE HIS OPPONENTS. TONIGHT'S MOVE IS ONE THAT WILL ALLOW MY NEXT MOVE TO BE A CRIPPLING ONE.
THERE WON'T BE MANY MOVES LEFT IF YOU FAIL.
I HAVEN'T FAILED YET.
GOOD TO SEE YOU AGAIN. WE'LL CATCH UP SOON.
LIKEWISE, MR. MAYOR.
COMMISSIONER, D.A. SPENCER, NICE TO SEE YOU HERE.
AFTER WHAT WE'VE BEEN THROUGH THESE LAST FEW MONTHS, A GOOD PARTY IS WELL IN ORDER.
ENJOY. WE HAVE MUCH TO TALK ABOUT LATER.

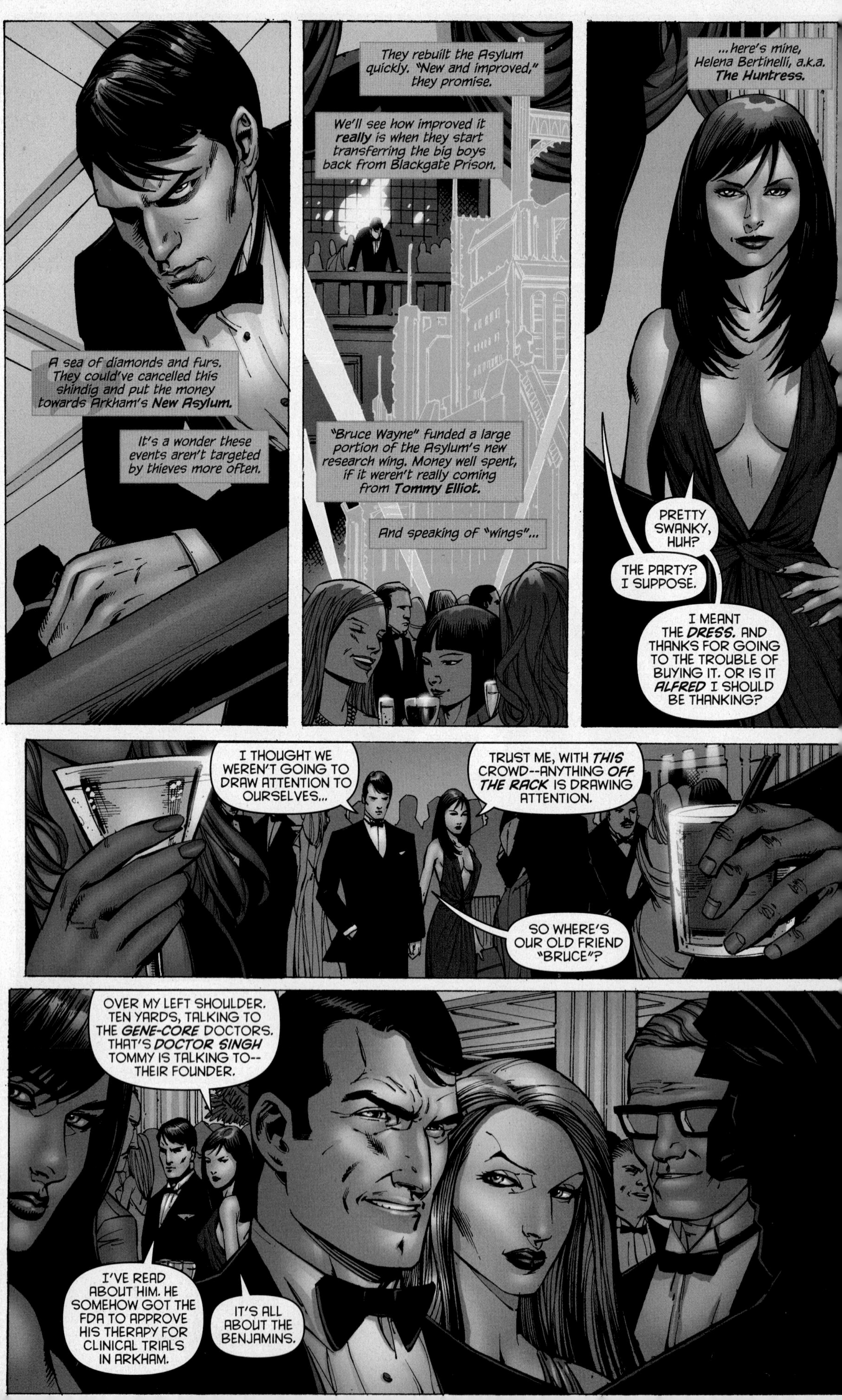

A sea of diamonds and furs. They could've cancelled this shindig and put the money towards Arkham's New Asylum.
It's a wonder these events aren't targeted by thieves more often.
They rebuilt the Asylum quickly. "New and improved," they promise.
We'll see how improved it really is when they start transferring the big boys back from Blackgate Prison.
"Bruce Wayne" funded a large portion of the Asylum's new research wing. Money well spent, if it weren't really coming from Tommy Elliot.
And speaking of "wings"...
...here's mine, Helena Bertinelli, a.k.a. The Huntress.
PRETTY SWANKY, HUH?
THE PARTY? I SUPPOSE.
I MEANT THE DRESS. AND THANKS FOR GOING TO THE TROUBLE OF BUYING IT. OR IS IT ALFRED I SHOULD BE THANKING?
I THOUGHT WE WEREN'T GOING TO DRAW ATTENTION TO OURSELVES...
TRUST ME, WITH THIS CROWD--ANYTHING OFF THE RACK IS DRAWING ATTENTION.
SO WHERE'S OUR OLD FRIEND "BRUCE"?
OVER MY LEFT SHOULDER. TEN YARDS, TALKING TO THE GENE-CORE DOCTORS. THAT'S DOCTOR SINGH TOMMY IS TALKING TO--THEIR FOUNDER.
I'VE READ ABOUT HIM. HE SOMEHOW GOT THE FDA TO APPROVE HIS THERAPY FOR CLINICAL TRIALS IN ARKHAM.
IT'S ALL ABOUT THE BENJAMINS.

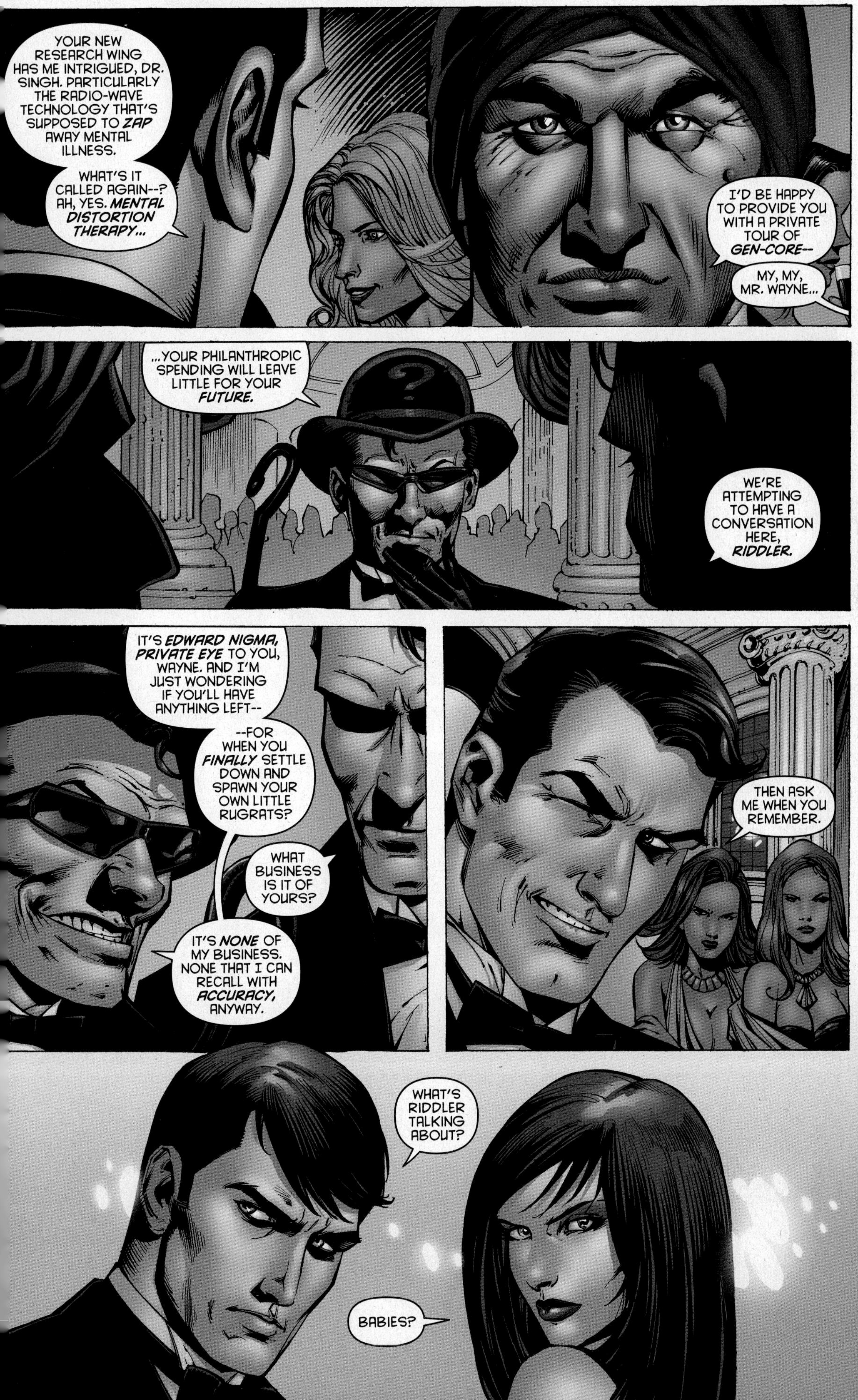

YOUR NEW RESEARCH WING HAS ME INTRIGUED, DR. SINGH. PARTICULARLY THE RADIO-WAVE TECHNOLOGY THAT'S SUPPOSED TO ZAP AWAY MENTAL ILLNESS.
WHAT'S IT CALLED AGAIN--? AH, YES. MENTAL DISTORTION THERAPY...
I'D BE HAPPY TO PROVIDE YOU WITH A PRIVATE TOUR OF GEN-CORE--
MY, MY, MR. WAYNE...
...YOUR PHILANTHROPIC SPENDING WILL LEAVE LITTLE FOR YOUR FUTURE.
WE'RE ATTEMPTING TO HAVE A CONVERSATION HERE, RIDDLER.
IT'S EDWARD NIGMA, PRIVATE EYE TO YOU, WAYNE. AND I'M JUST WONDERING IF YOU'LL HAVE ANYTHING LEFT--
--FOR WHEN YOU FINALLY SETTLE DOWN AND SPAWN YOUR OWN LITTLE RUGRATS?
WHAT BUSINESS IS IT OF YOURS?
IT'S NONE OF MY BUSINESS. NONE THAT I CAN RECALL WITH ACCURACY, ANYWAY.
THEN ASK ME WHEN YOU REMEMBER.
WHAT'S RIDDLER TALKING ABOUT?
BABIES?

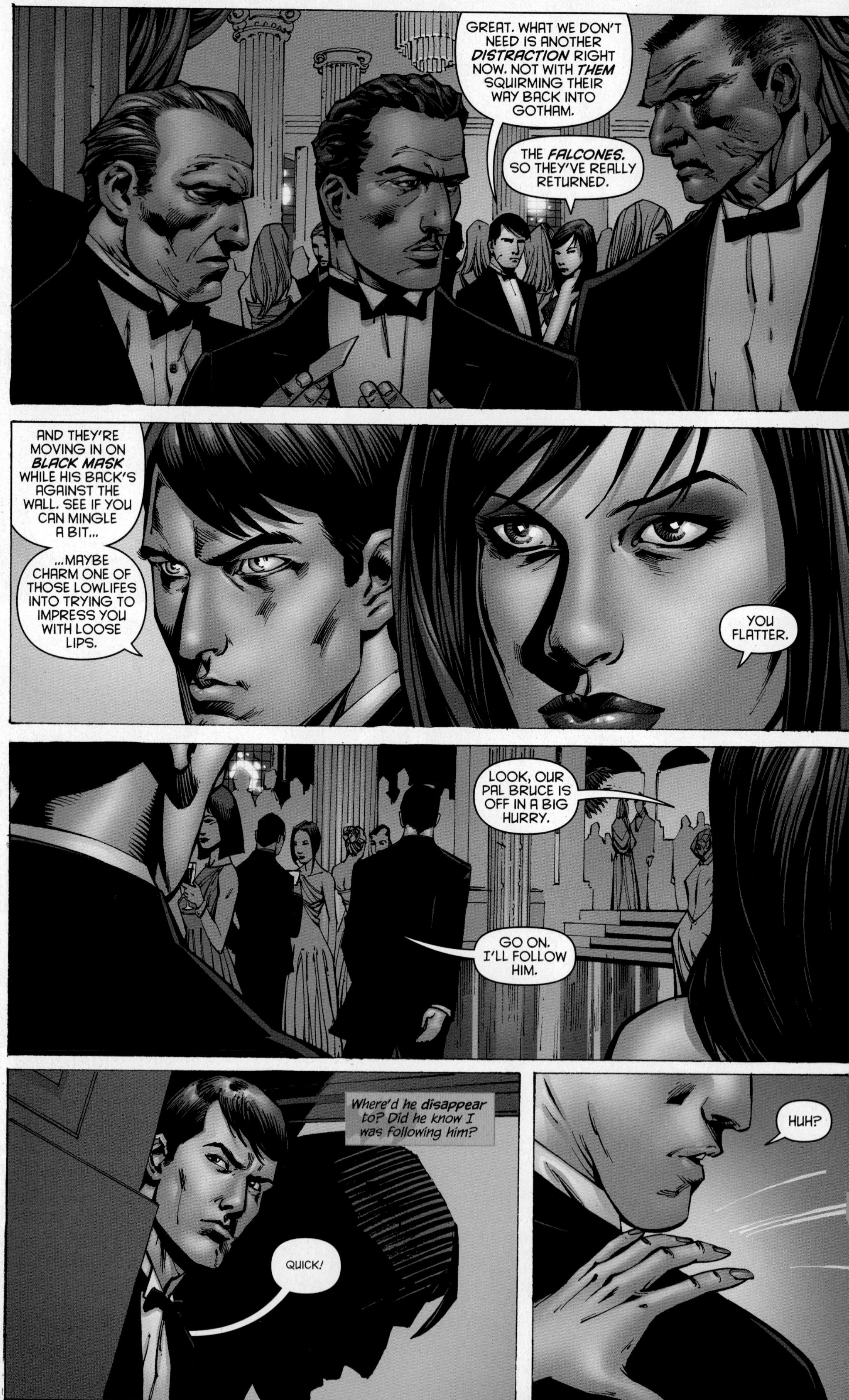

GREAT. WHAT WE DON'T NEED IS ANOTHER DISTRACTION RIGHT NOW. NOT WITH THEM SQUIRMING THEIR WAY BACK INTO GOTHAM.
THE FALCONES. SO THEY'VE REALLY RETURNED.
AND THEY'RE MOVING IN ON BLACK MASK WHILE HIS BACK'S AGAINST THE WALL. SEE IF YOU CAN MINGLE A BIT...
...MAYBE CHARM ONE OF THOSE LOWLIFES INTO TRYING TO IMPRESS YOU WITH LOOSE LIPS.
YOU FLATTER.
LOOK, OUR PAL BRUCE IS OFF IN A BIG HURRY.
GO ON. I'LL FOLLOW HIM.
Where'd he disappear to? Did he know I was following him?
QUICK!
HUH?

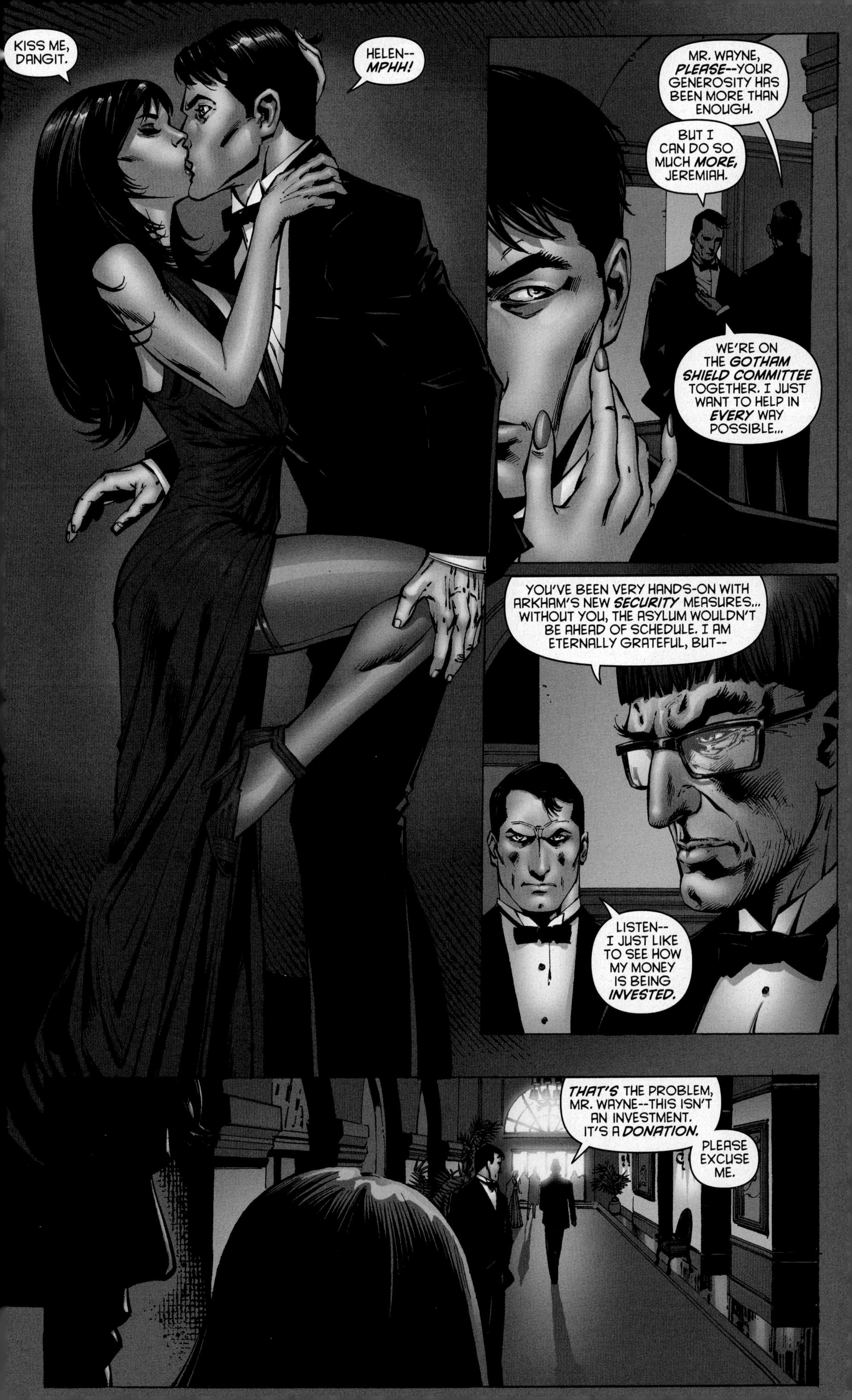
KISS ME, DANGIT.
HELEN-- MPHH!
MR. WAYNE, PLEASE--YOUR GENEROSITY HAS BEEN MORE THAN ENOUGH.
BUT I CAN DO SO MUCH MORE, JEREMIAH.
WE'RE ON THE GOTHAM SHIELD COMMITTEE TOGETHER. I JUST WANT TO HELP IN EVERY WAY POSSIBLE...
YOU'VE BEEN VERY HANDS-ON WITH ARKHAM'S NEW SECURITY MEASURES... WITHOUT YOU, THE ASYLUM WOULDN'T BE AHEAD OF SCHEDULE. I AM ETERNALLY GRATEFUL, BUT--
LISTEN-- I JUST LIKE TO SEE HOW MY MONEY IS BEING INVESTED.
THAT'S THE PROBLEM, MR. WAYNE--THIS ISN'T AN INVESTMENT. IT'S A DONATION.
PLEASE EXCUSE ME.

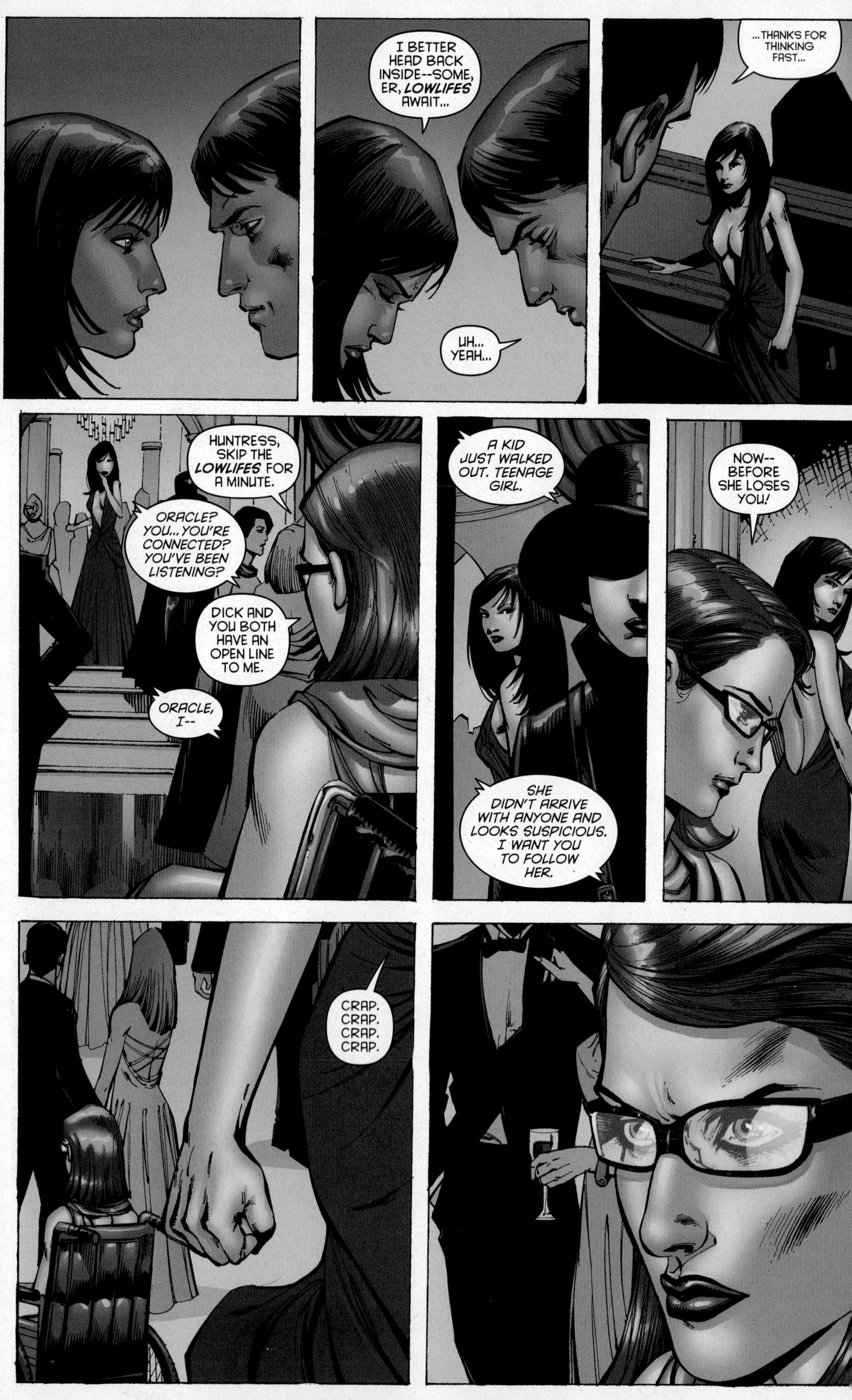
I BETTER HEAD BACK INSIDE--SOME, ER, *LOWLIFES* AWAIT...
UH... YEAH...
...THANKS FOR THINKING FAST...
HUNTRESS, SKIP THE *LOWLIFES* FOR A MINUTE.
ORACLE? YOU... YOU'RE CONNECTED? YOU'VE BEEN LISTENING?
DICK AND YOU BOTH HAVE AN OPEN LINE TO ME.
ORACLE, I--
A KID JUST WALKED OUT. TEENAGE GIRL.
SHE DIDN'T ARRIVE WITH ANYONE AND LOOKS SUSPICIOUS. I WANT YOU TO FOLLOW HER.
NOW-- BEFORE SHE LOSES YOU!
CRAP. CRAP. CRAP. CRAP.

DAG!

YOU'RE BEING FOLLOWED, KITRINA.

LIKE I DON'T KNOW. AND *DON'T* TALK TO ME. YOU'RE RUINING MY INNER CHI.

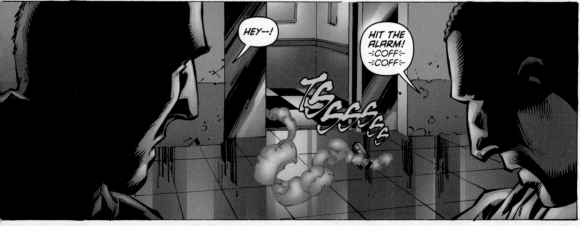

HEY--!

HIT THE ALARM! →COFF← →COFF←

TSSSSS

TWO GUARDS EQUALS CHILD'S PLAY.

PLAYTIME IS LATER. GET WHAT YOU CAME FOR. YOU DON'T HAVE MUCH TIME.

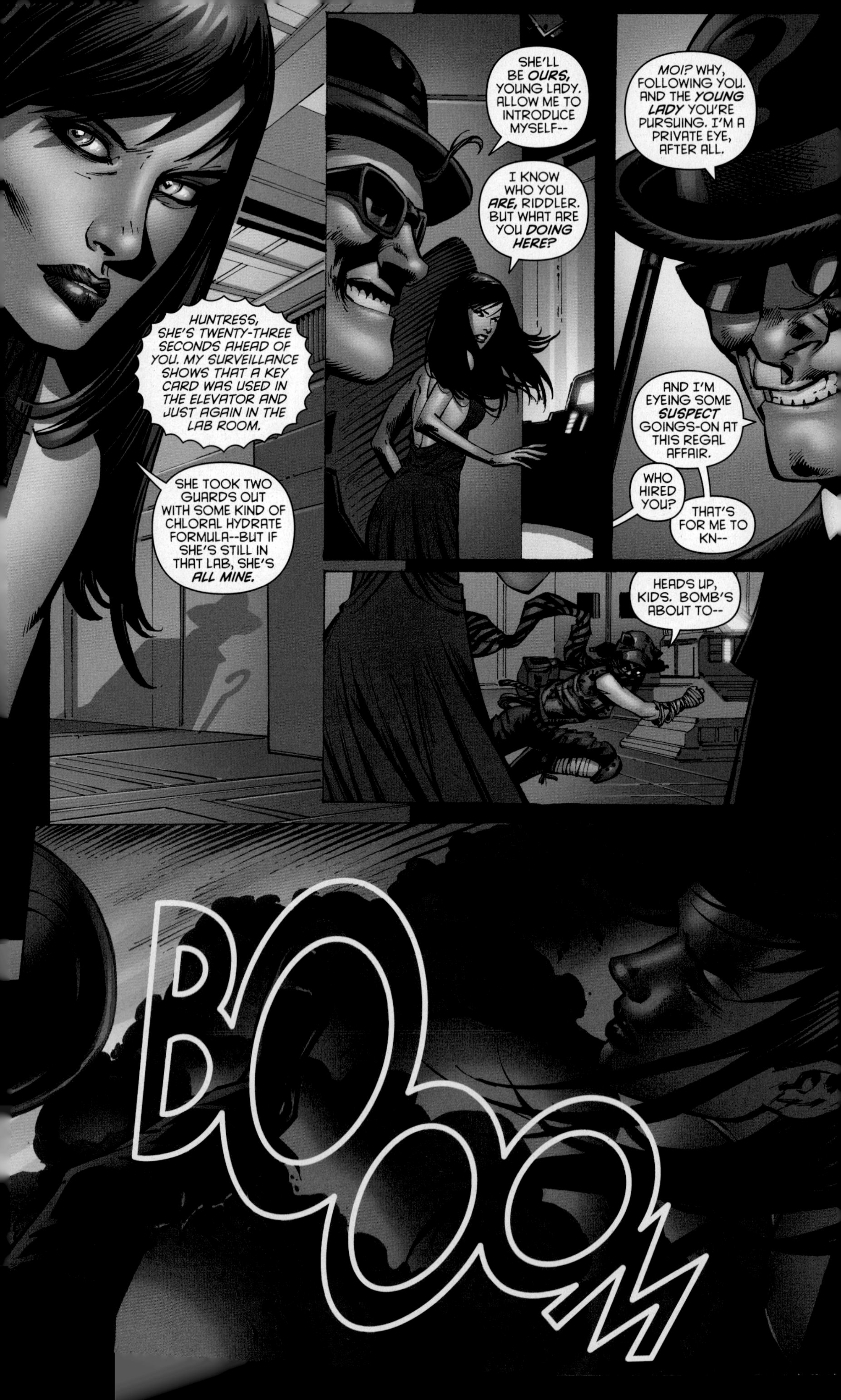

HUNTRESS, SHE'S TWENTY-THREE SECONDS AHEAD OF YOU. MY SURVEILLANCE SHOWS THAT A KEY CARD WAS USED IN THE ELEVATOR AND JUST AGAIN IN THE LAB ROOM.
SHE TOOK TWO GUARDS OUT WITH SOME KIND OF CHLORAL HYDRATE FORMULA--BUT IF SHE'S STILL IN THAT LAB, SHE'S ALL MINE.
SHE'LL BE OURS, YOUNG LADY. ALLOW ME TO INTRODUCE MYSELF--
I KNOW WHO YOU ARE, RIDDLER. BUT WHAT ARE YOU DOING HERE?
MOI? WHY, FOLLOWING YOU. AND THE YOUNG LADY YOU'RE PURSUING. I'M A PRIVATE EYE, AFTER ALL.
AND I'M EYEING SOME SUSPECT GOINGS-ON AT THIS REGAL AFFAIR.
WHO HIRED YOU?
THAT'S FOR ME TO KN--
HEADS UP, KIDS. BOMB'S ABOUT TO--
BOOOM

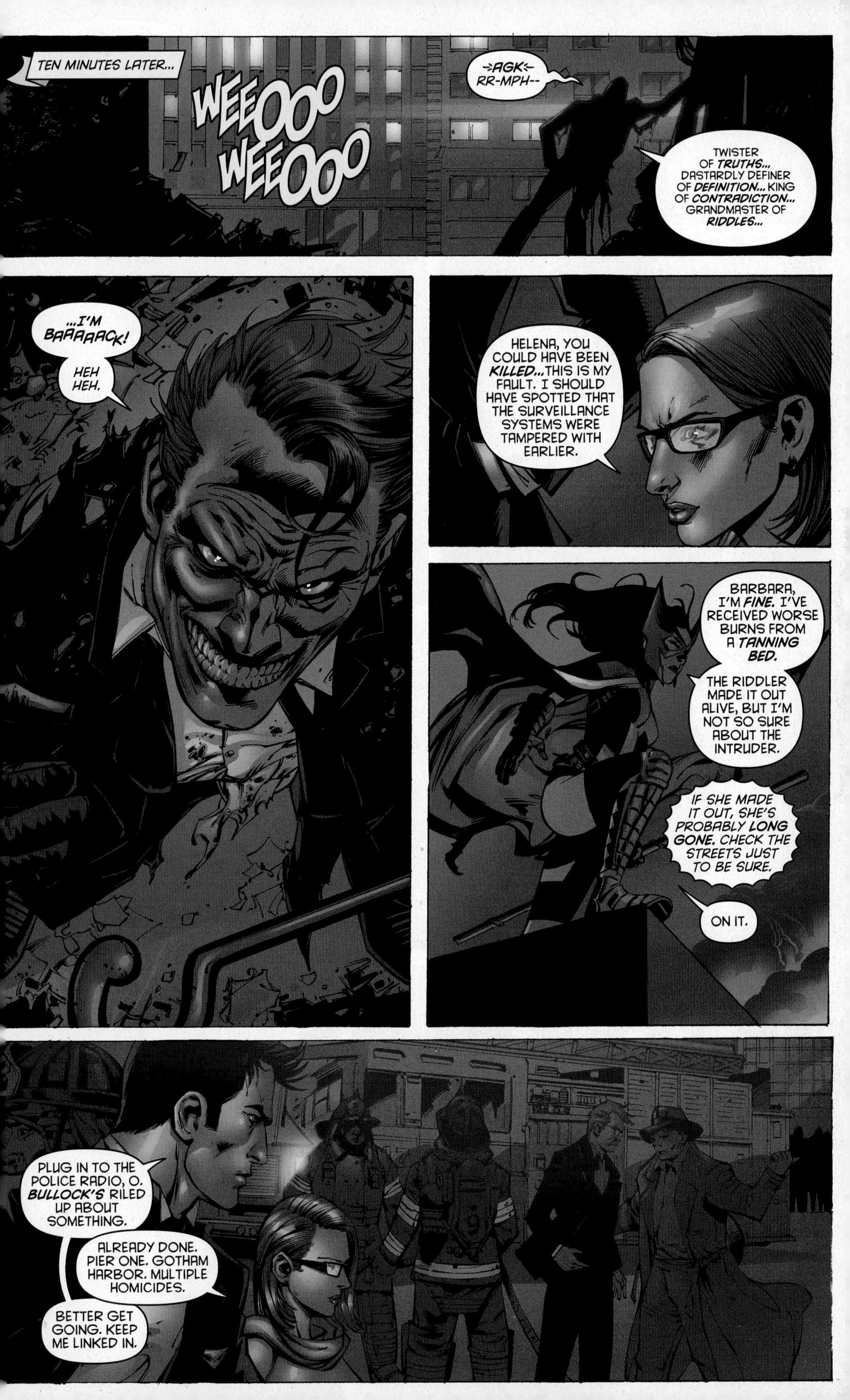

TEN MINUTES LATER...
WEEOOO WEEOOO
AGK RR-MPH--
TWISTER OF TRUTHS... DASTARDLY DEFINER OF DEFINITION... KING OF CONTRADICTION... GRANDMASTER OF RIDDLES...
...I'M BAAAAACK!
HEH HEH.
HELENA, YOU COULD HAVE BEEN KILLED... THIS IS MY FAULT. I SHOULD HAVE SPOTTED THAT THE SURVEILLANCE SYSTEMS WERE TAMPERED WITH EARLIER.
BARBARA, I'M FINE. I'VE RECEIVED WORSE BURNS FROM A TANNING BED.
THE RIDDLER MADE IT OUT ALIVE, BUT I'M NOT SO SURE ABOUT THE INTRUDER.
IF SHE MADE IT OUT, SHE'S PROBABLY LONG GONE. CHECK THE STREETS JUST TO BE SURE.
ON IT.
PLUG IN TO THE POLICE RADIO, O. BULLOCK'S RILED UP ABOUT SOMETHING.
ALREADY DONE. PIER ONE. GOTHAM HARBOR. MULTIPLE HOMICIDES.
BETTER GET GOING. KEEP ME LINKED IN.

WELL, THE OTHER SHOE HAS DROPPED.

AND EVERY *OTHER* BODY PART. MUST'VE BEEN SOME *BONFIRE*, HUH? THERE'S LIKE, FIFTEEN--SIXTEEN BODIES IN THAT *HEAP*.

I COUNT *EIGHT*, SERGEANT. SO FAR. THE MEDICAL EXAMINER WILL HAVE TO PRY THEM APART. THE HEAT FROM THE FIRE FUSED SOME BONES TOGETHER.

WHAT DO YOU THINK WENT DOWN HERE WITH FALCONE'S MEN, BATMAN?

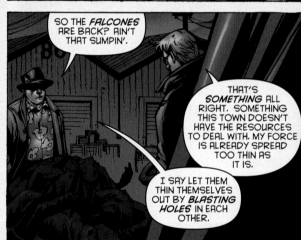

SO THE *FALCONES* ARE BACK? AIN'T THAT SUMPIN'.

THAT'S *SOMETHING* ALL RIGHT. SOMETHING THIS TOWN DOESN'T HAVE THE RESOURCES TO DEAL WITH. MY FORCE IS ALREADY SPREAD TOO THIN AS IT IS.

I SAY LET THEM THIN THEMSELVES OUT BY *BLASTING HOLES* IN EACH OTHER.

FALCONE'S MEN DIDN'T STAND A CHANCE AGAINST WHOEVER *CUT* THEM UP.

WHAT ARE YOU SAYING? THESE GUYS WERE CHOPPED UP, BUT *SURELY* THAT WAS DONE *AFTER*--

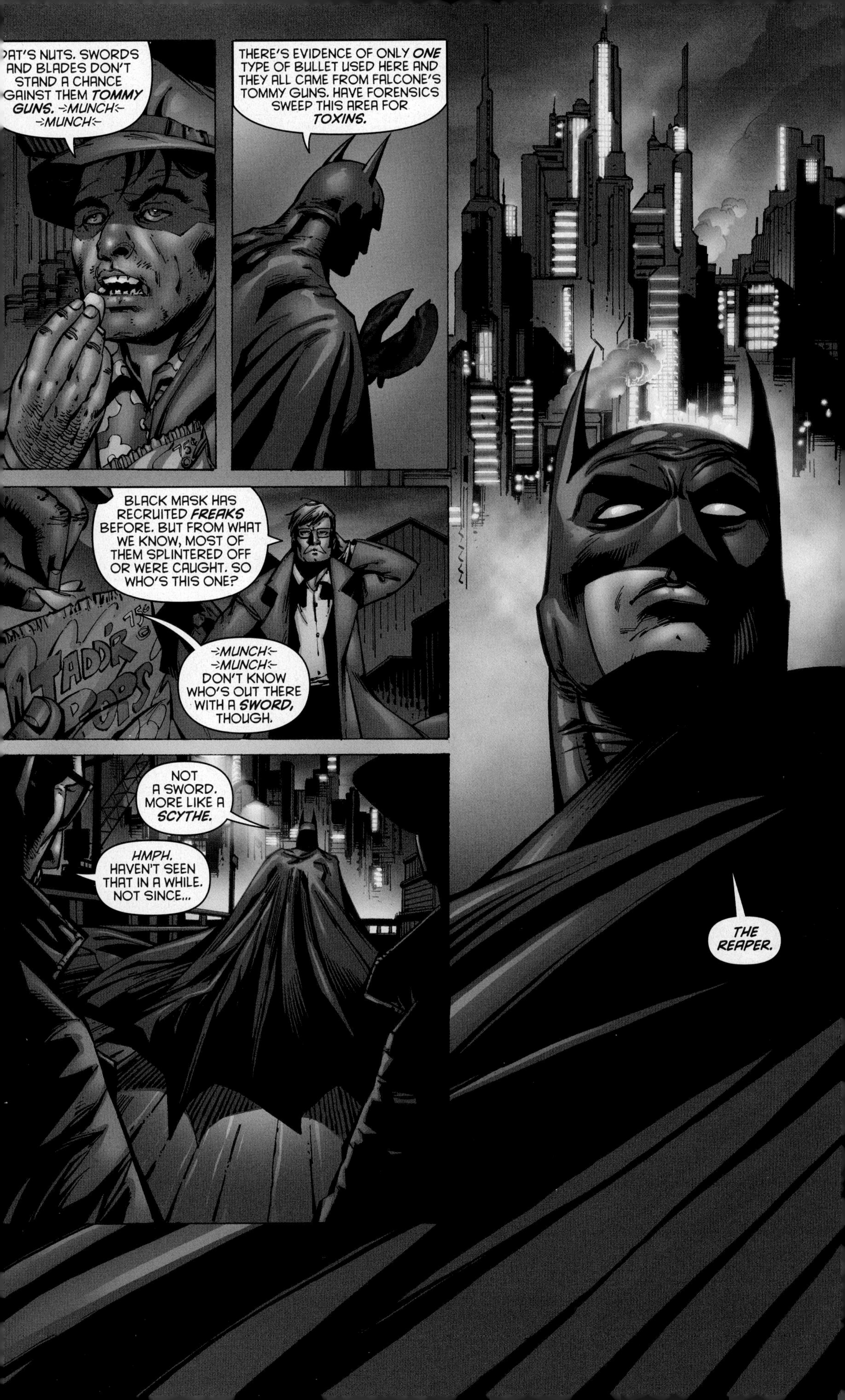

DAT'S NUTS. SWORDS AND BLADES DON'T STAND A CHANCE GAINST THEM TOMMY GUNS. ≈MUNCH≈ ≈MUNCH≈
THERE'S EVIDENCE OF ONLY ONE TYPE OF BULLET USED HERE AND THEY ALL CAME FROM FALCONE'S TOMMY GUNS. HAVE FORENSICS SWEEP THIS AREA FOR TOXINS.
BLACK MASK HAS RECRUITED FREAKS BEFORE. BUT FROM WHAT WE KNOW, MOST OF THEM SPLINTERED OFF OR WERE CAUGHT. SO WHO'S THIS ONE?
≈MUNCH≈ ≈MUNCH≈ DON'T KNOW WHO'S OUT THERE WITH A SWORD, THOUGH.
NOT A SWORD. MORE LIKE A SCYTHE.
HMPH. HAVEN'T SEEN THAT IN A WHILE. NOT SINCE...
THE REAPER.

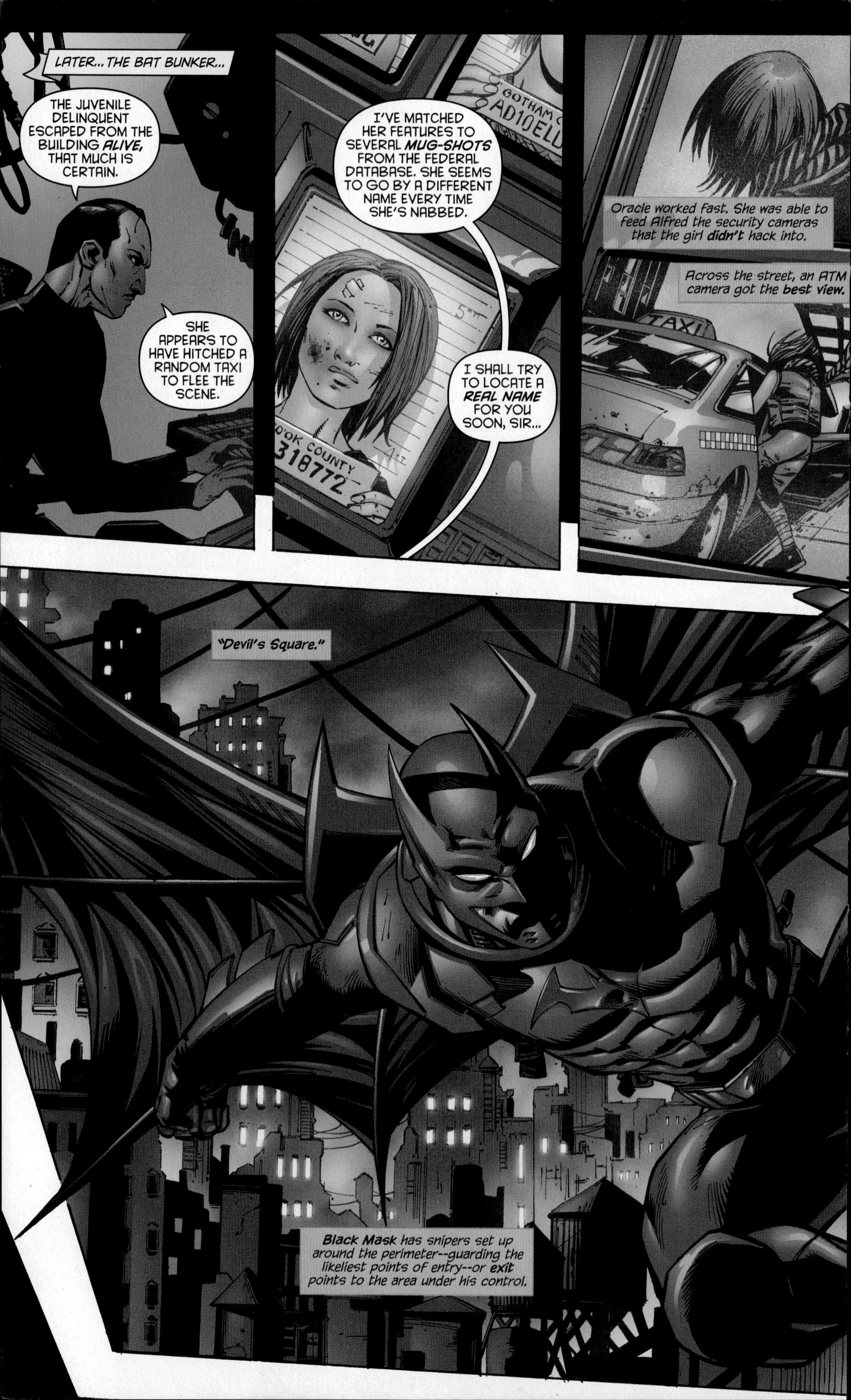
LATER... THE BAT BUNKER...
THE JUVENILE DELINQUENT ESCAPED FROM THE BUILDING ALIVE, THAT MUCH IS CERTAIN.
SHE APPEARS TO HAVE HITCHED A RANDOM TAXI TO FLEE THE SCENE.
GOTHAM
AD10ELL
I'VE MATCHED HER FEATURES TO SEVERAL MUG-SHOTS FROM THE FEDERAL DATABASE. SHE SEEMS TO GO BY A DIFFERENT NAME EVERY TIME SHE'S NABBED.
I SHALL TRY TO LOCATE A REAL NAME FOR YOU SOON, SIR...
COOK COUNTY
318772
Oracle worked fast. She was able to feed Alfred the security cameras that the girl didn't hack into.
Across the street, an ATM camera got the best view.
TAXI
"Devil's Square."
Black Mask has snipers set up around the perimeter--guarding the likeliest points of entry--or exit points to the area under his control.

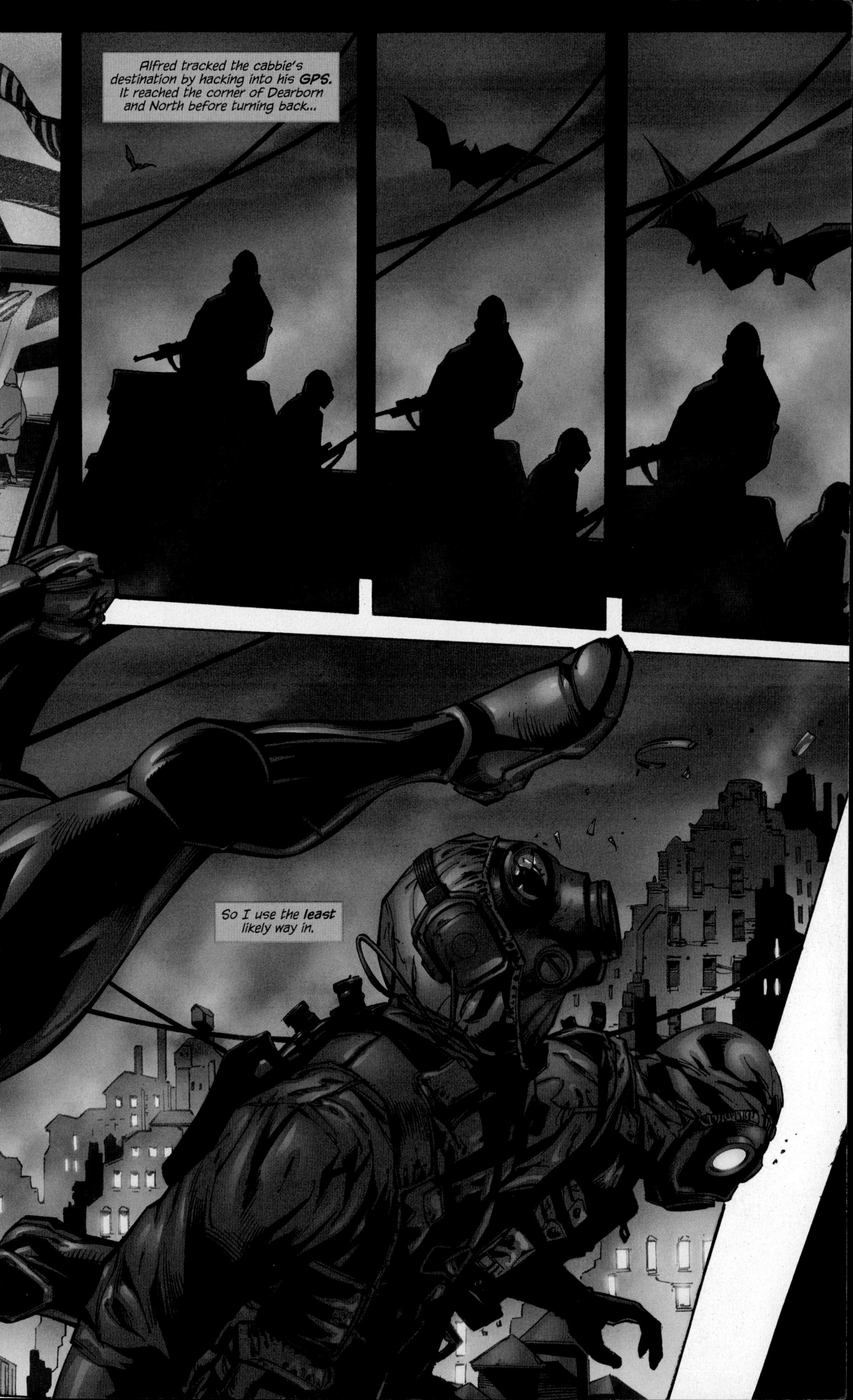

Alfred tracked the cabbie's destination by hacking into his GPS. It reached the corner of Dearborn and North before turning back...
So I use the least likely way in.

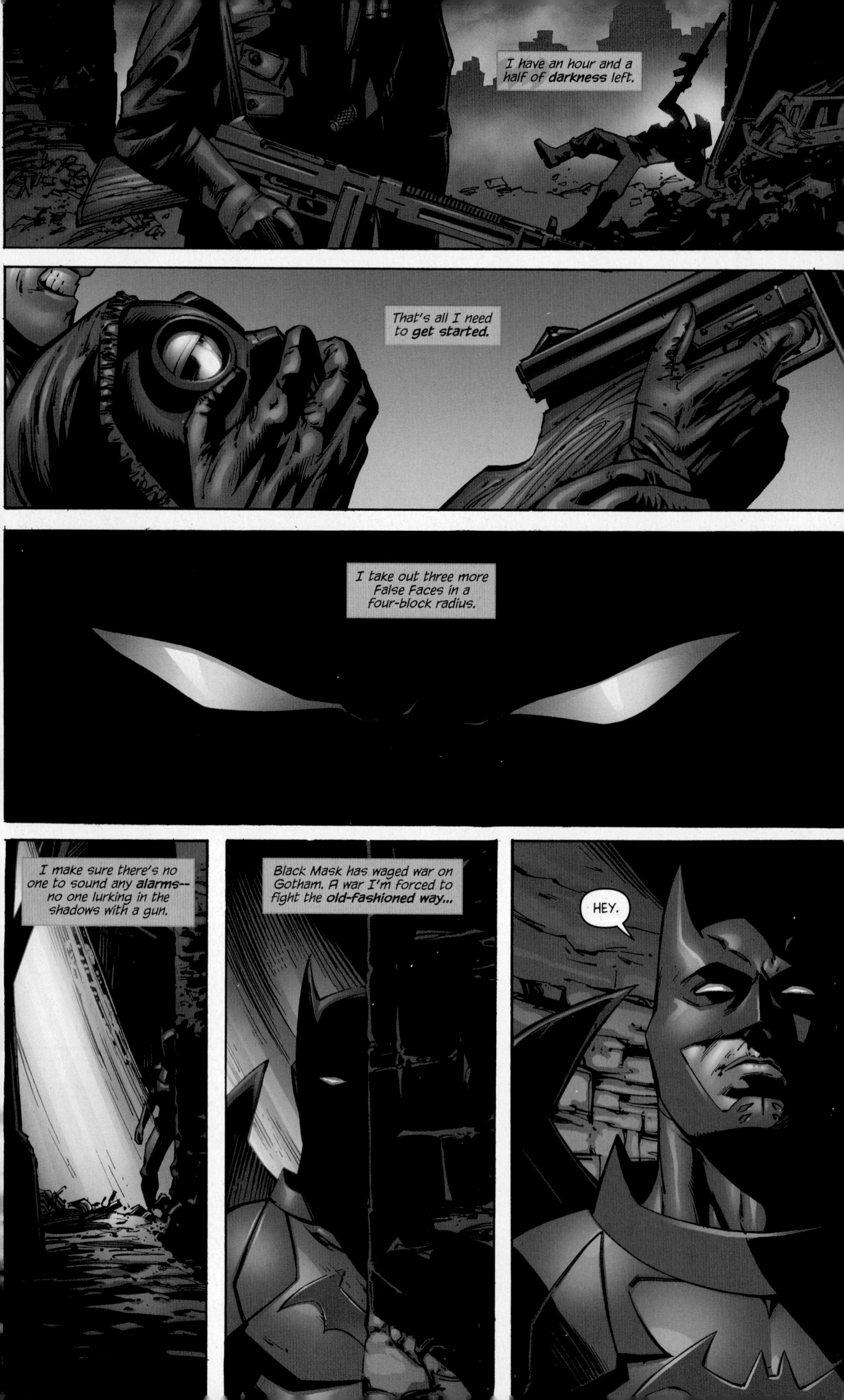
I have an hour and a half of darkness left.
That's all I need to get started.
I take out three more False Faces in a four-block radius.
I make sure there's no one to sound any alarms-- no one lurking in the shadows with a gun.
Black Mask has waged war on Gotham. A war I'm forced to fight the old-fashioned way...
HEY.

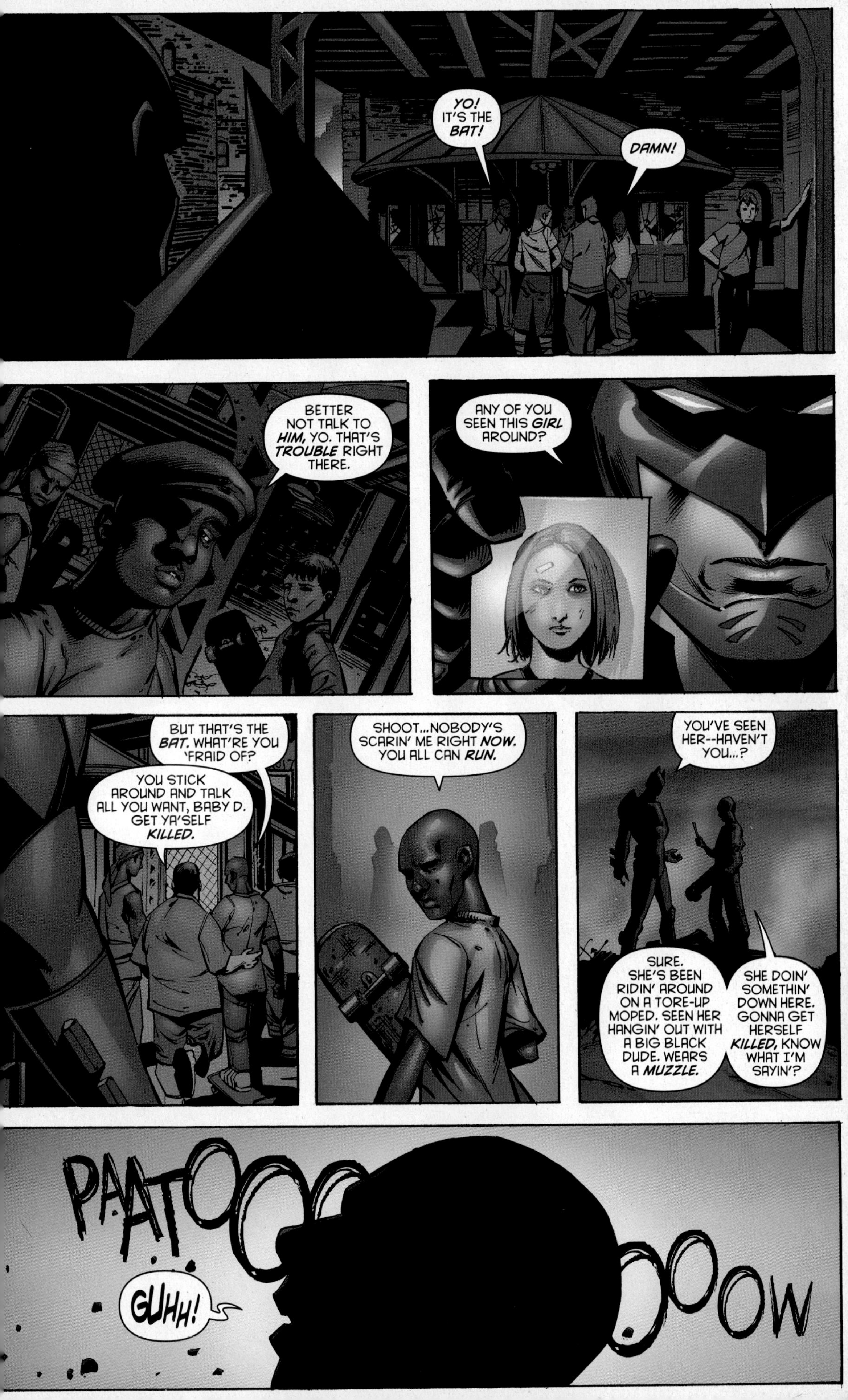
YO! IT'S THE BAT!
DAMN!
BETTER NOT TALK TO HIM, YO. THAT'S TROUBLE RIGHT THERE.
ANY OF YOU SEEN THIS GIRL AROUND?
BUT THAT'S THE BAT. WHAT'RE YOU 'FRAID OF?
YOU STICK AROUND AND TALK ALL YOU WANT, BABY D. GET YA'SELF KILLED.
SHOOT...NOBODY'S SCARIN' ME RIGHT NOW. YOU ALL CAN RUN.
YOU'VE SEEN HER--HAVEN'T YOU...?
SURE. SHE'S BEEN RIDIN' AROUND ON A TORE-UP MOPED. SEEN HER HANGIN' OUT WITH A BIG BLACK DUDE. WEARS A MUZZLE.
SHE DOIN' SOMETHIN' DOWN HERE. GONNA GET HERSELF KILLED, KNOW WHAT I'M SAYIN'?
PAATOOOOOOOOOW
GUHH!

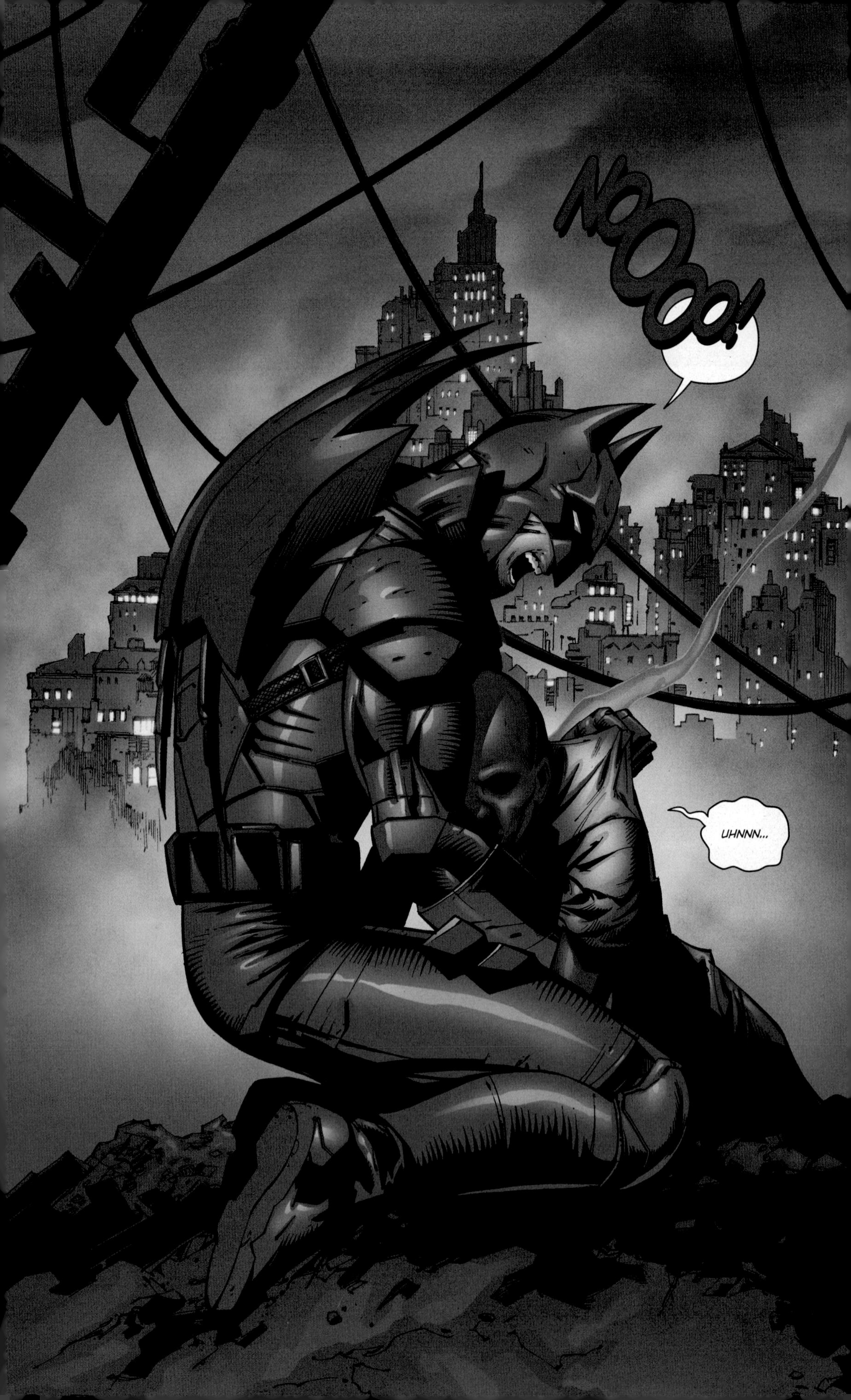
NOOOOO!
UHNNN...

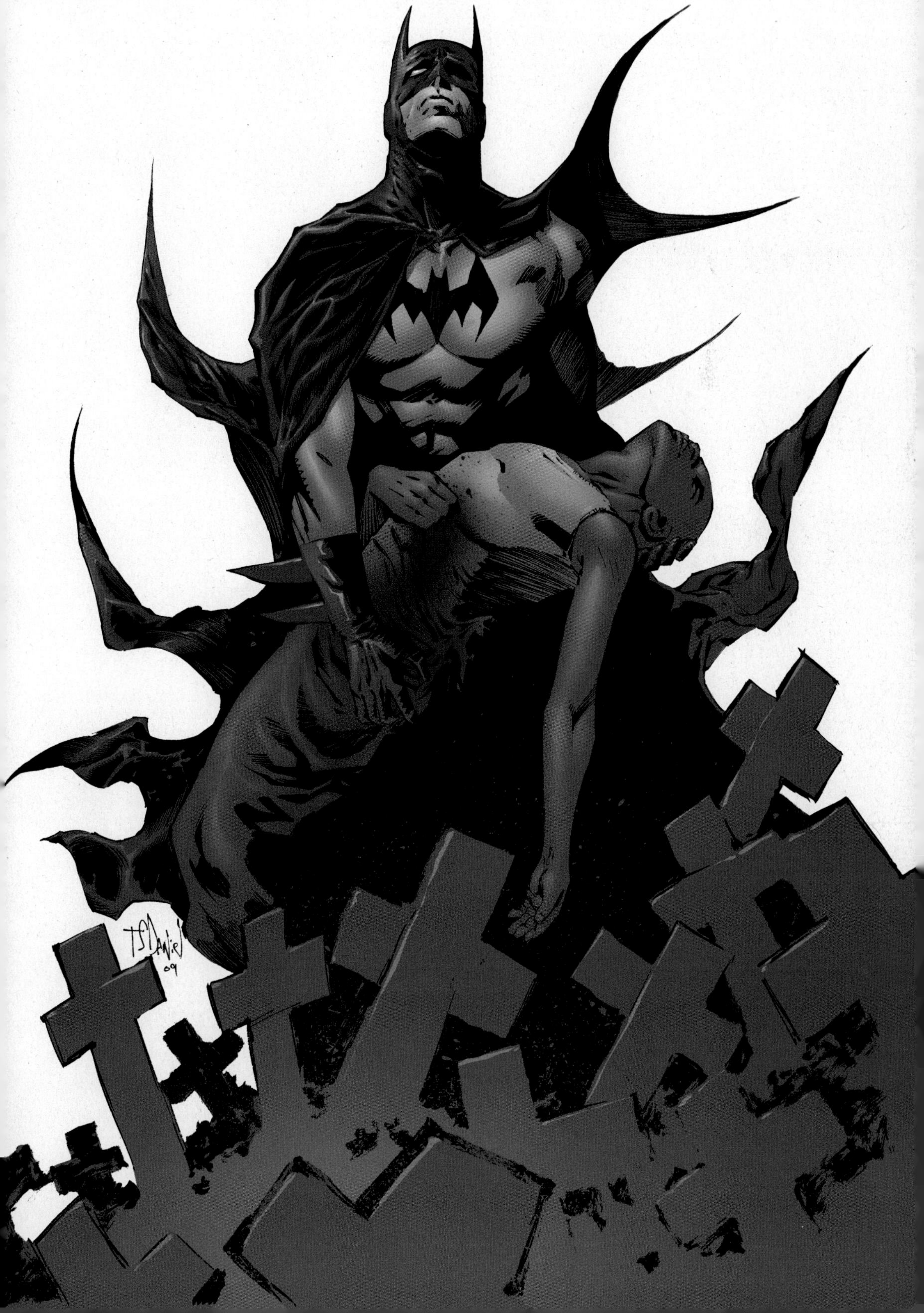

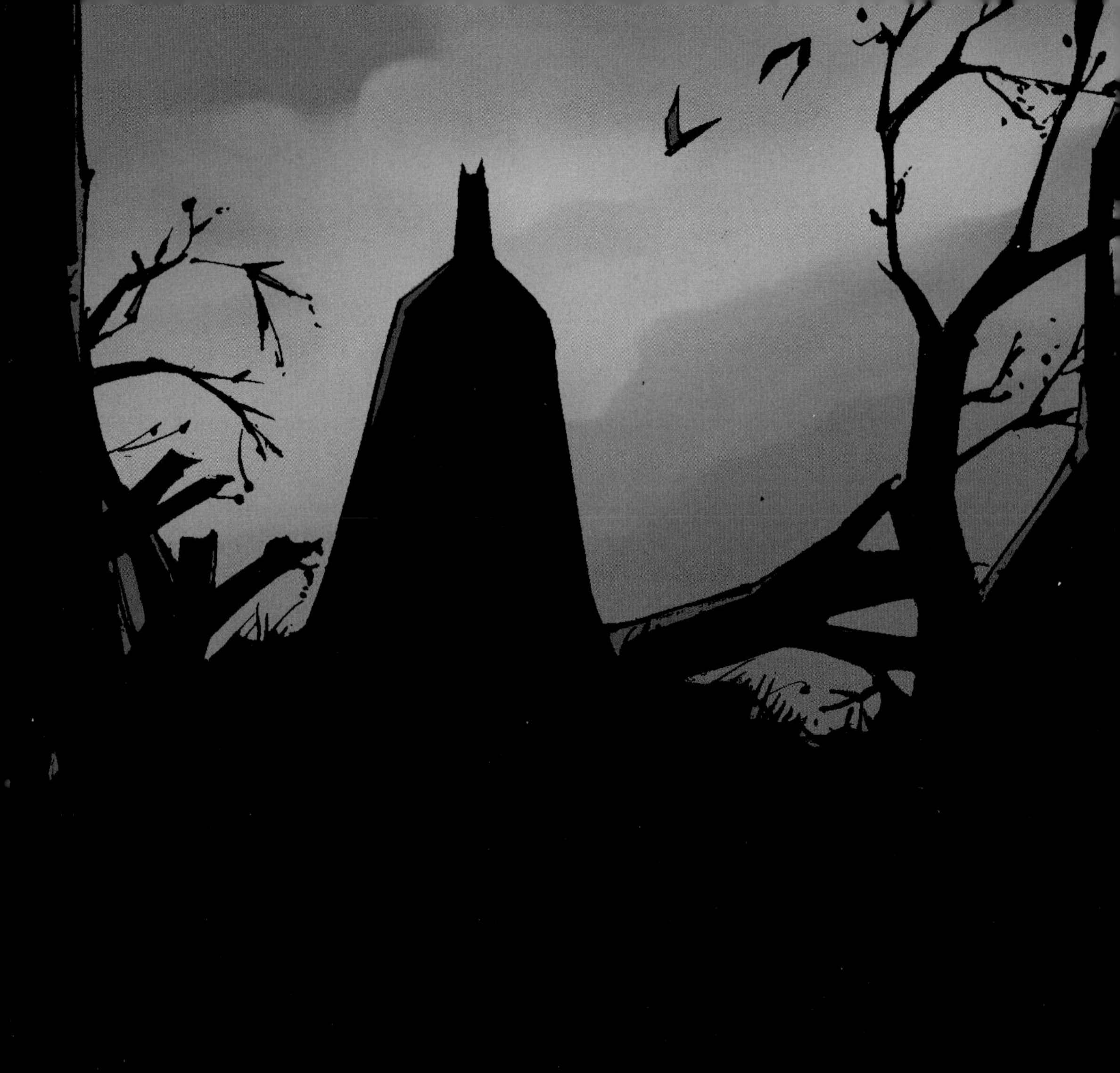

"Children of Gotham, fear no more —
for I will purge your city of the animals that seek to destroy you."

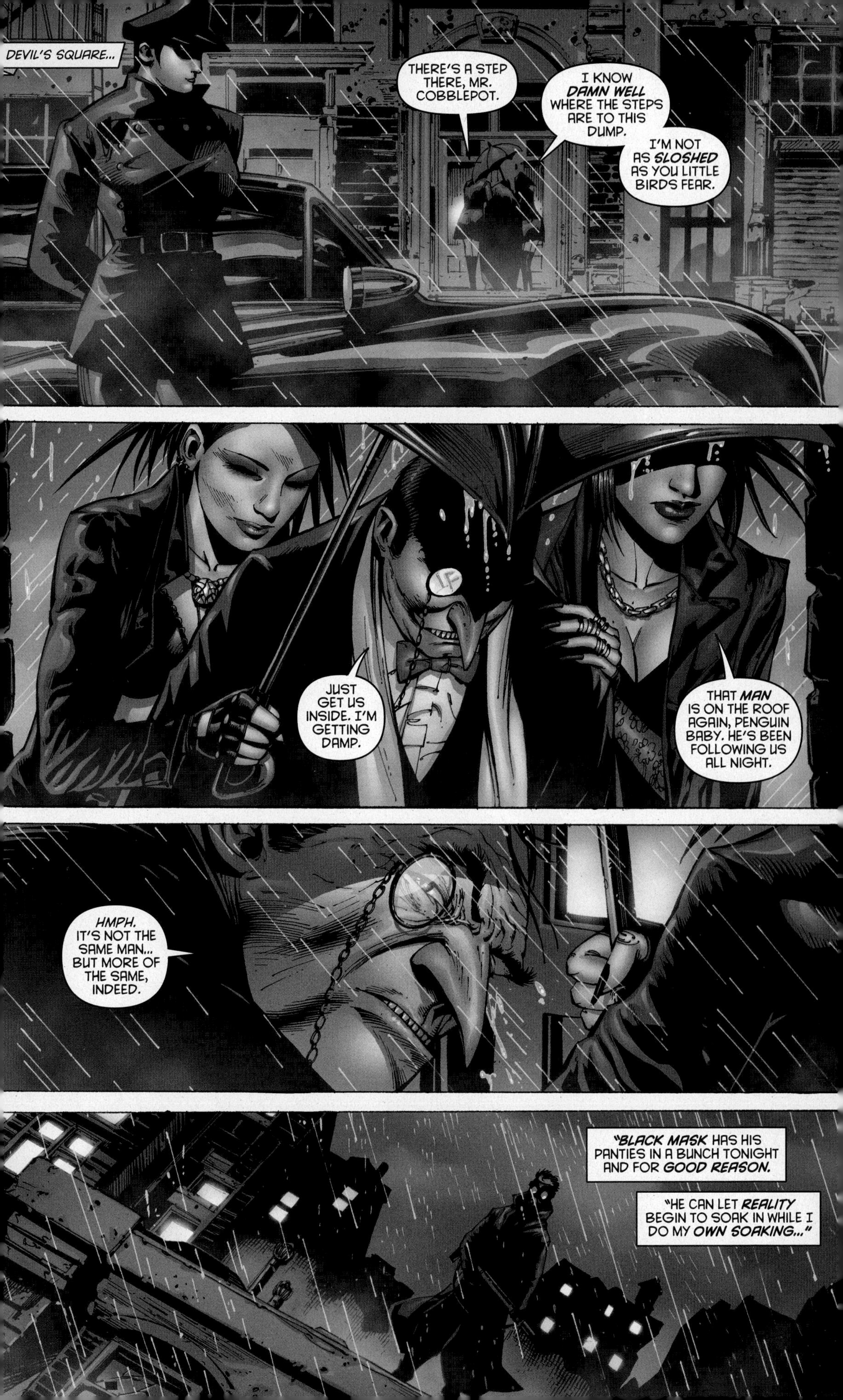
DEVIL'S SQUARE...
THERE'S A STEP THERE, MR. COBBLEPOT.
I KNOW DAMN WELL WHERE THE STEPS ARE TO THIS DUMP.
I'M NOT AS SLOSHED AS YOU LITTLE BIRDS FEAR.
JUST GET US INSIDE. I'M GETTING DAMP.
THAT MAN IS ON THE ROOF AGAIN, PENGUIN BABY. HE'S BEEN FOLLOWING US ALL NIGHT.
HMPH. IT'S NOT THE SAME MAN... BUT MORE OF THE SAME, INDEED.
"BLACK MASK HAS HIS PANTIES IN A BUNCH TONIGHT AND FOR GOOD REASON.
"HE CAN LET REALITY BEGIN TO SOAK IN WHILE I DO MY OWN SOAKING..."

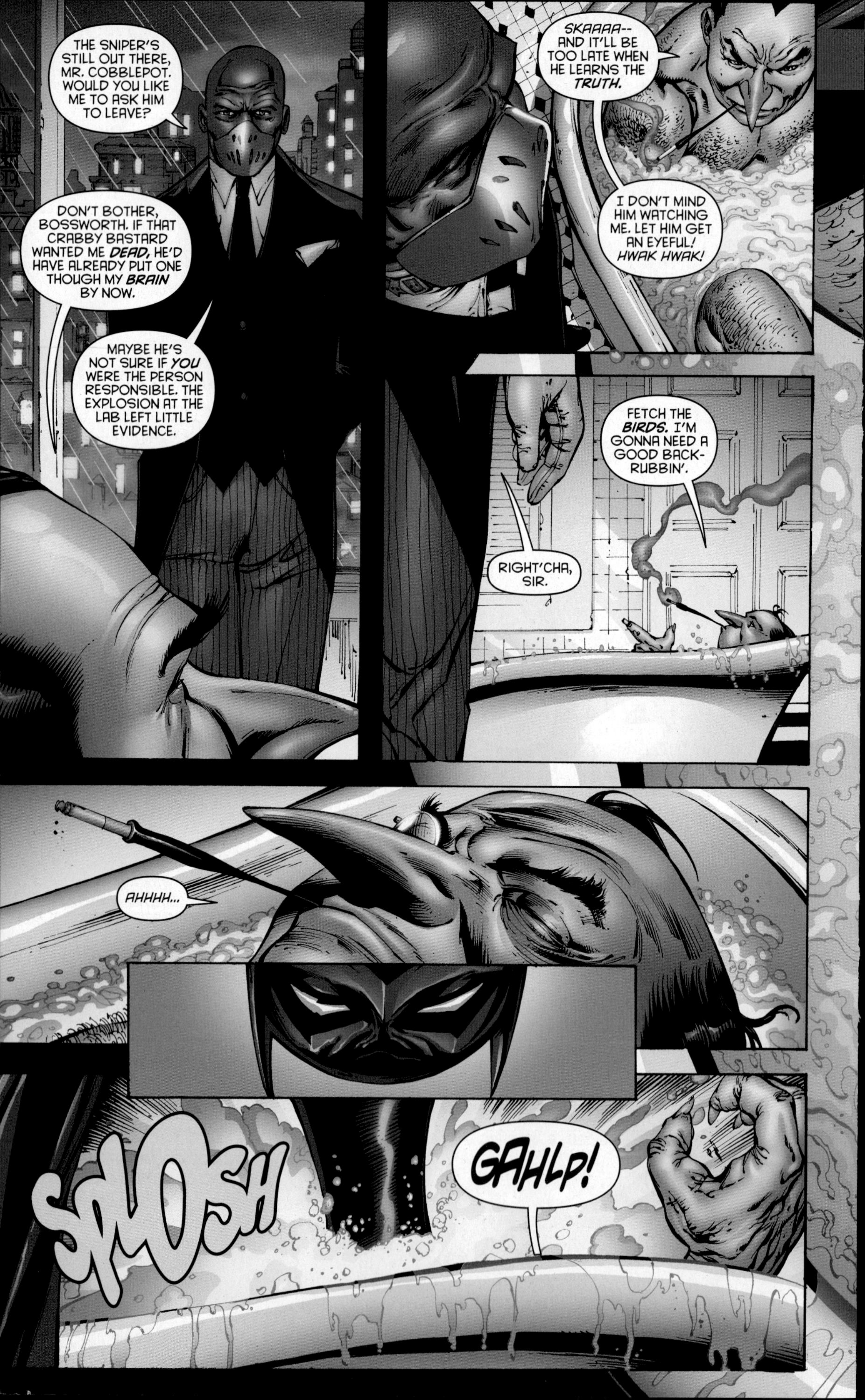
THE SNIPER'S STILL OUT THERE, MR. COBBLEPOT. WOULD YOU LIKE ME TO ASK HIM TO LEAVE?
DON'T BOTHER, BOSSWORTH. IF THAT CRABBY BASTARD WANTED ME DEAD, HE'D HAVE ALREADY PUT ONE THOUGH MY BRAIN BY NOW.
MAYBE HE'S NOT SURE IF YOU WERE THE PERSON RESPONSIBLE. THE EXPLOSION AT THE LAB LEFT LITTLE EVIDENCE.
SKAAAA-- AND IT'LL BE TOO LATE WHEN HE LEARNS THE TRUTH.
I DON'T MIND HIM WATCHING ME. LET HIM GET AN EYEFUL! HWAK HWAK!
FETCH THE BIRDS. I'M GONNA NEED A GOOD BACK-RUBBIN'.
RIGHT'CHA, SIR.
AHHHH...
SPLOSH
GAHLP!

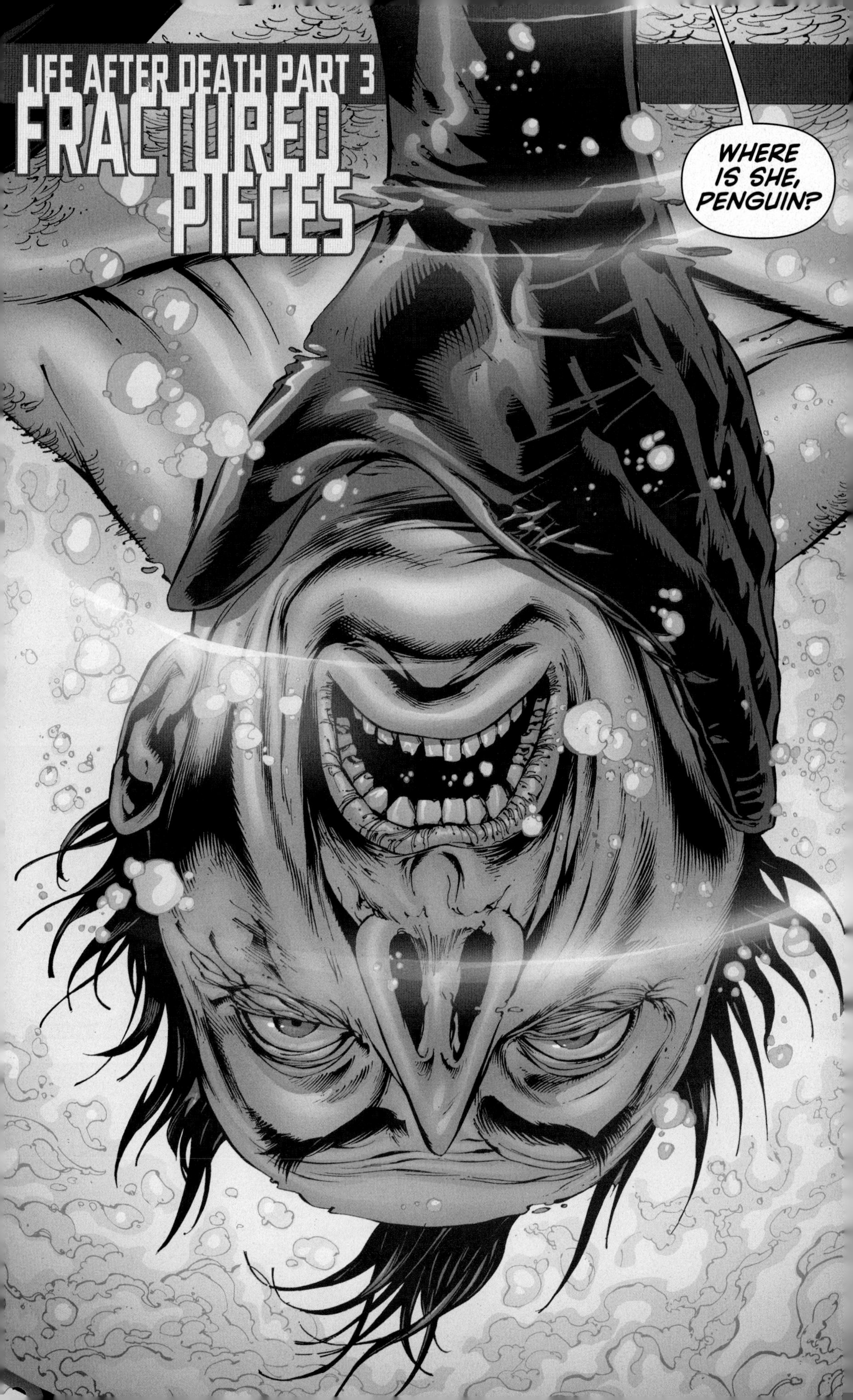
LIFE AFTER DEATH PART 3
FRACTURED PIECES
WHERE IS SHE, PENGUIN?

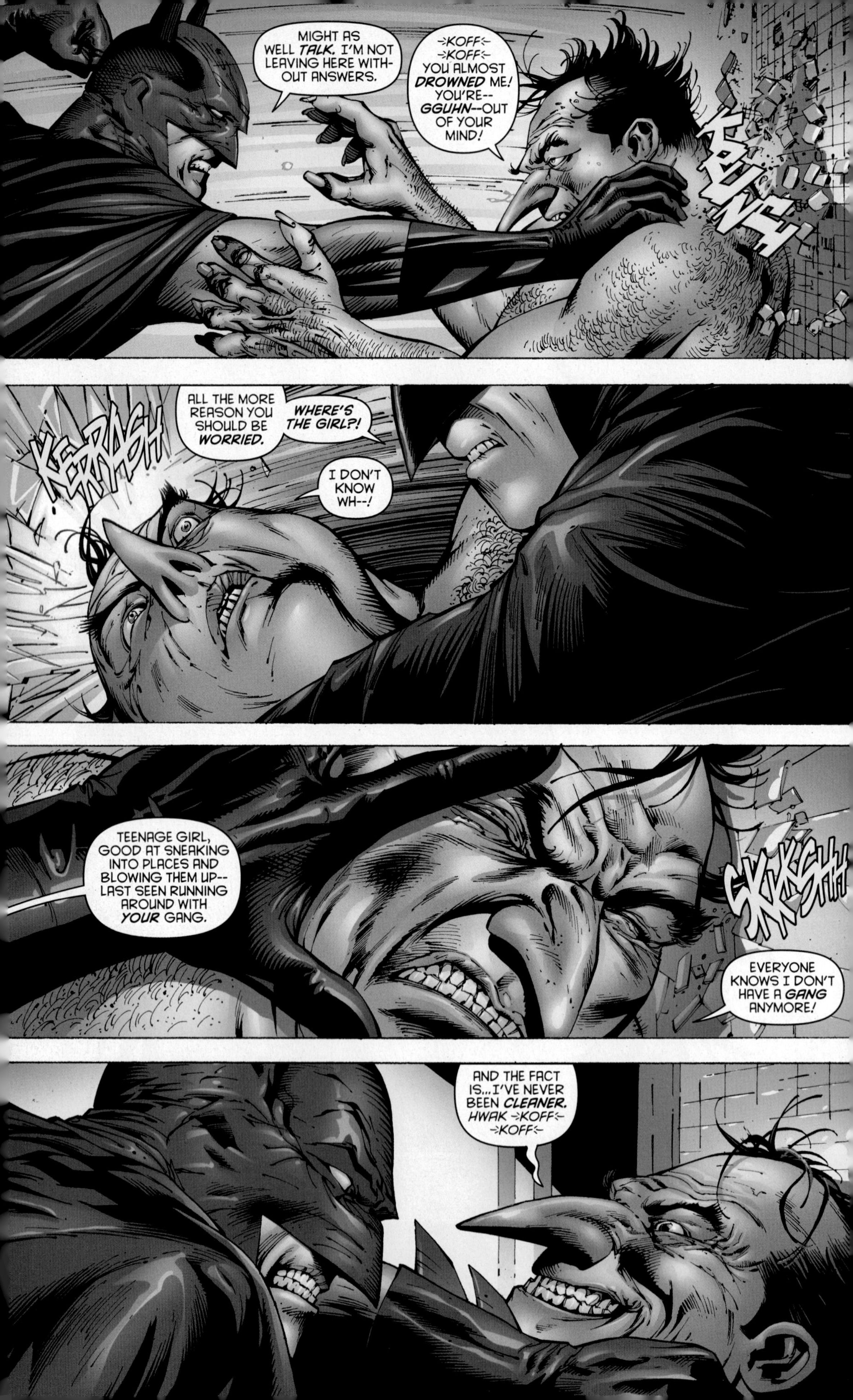

MIGHT AS WELL TALK. I'M NOT LEAVING HERE WITH-OUT ANSWERS.
-KOFF- -KOFF- YOU ALMOST DROWNED ME! YOU'RE--GGUHN--OUT OF YOUR MIND!
KRUNSH
KERRASH
ALL THE MORE REASON YOU SHOULD BE WORRIED.
WHERE'S THE GIRL?!
I DON'T KNOW WH--!
TEENAGE GIRL, GOOD AT SNEAKING INTO PLACES AND BLOWING THEM UP--LAST SEEN RUNNING AROUND WITH YOUR GANG.
SKKKSHH
EVERYONE KNOWS I DON'T HAVE A GANG ANYMORE!
AND THE FACT IS...I'VE NEVER BEEN CLEANER. HWAK -KOFF- -KOFF-

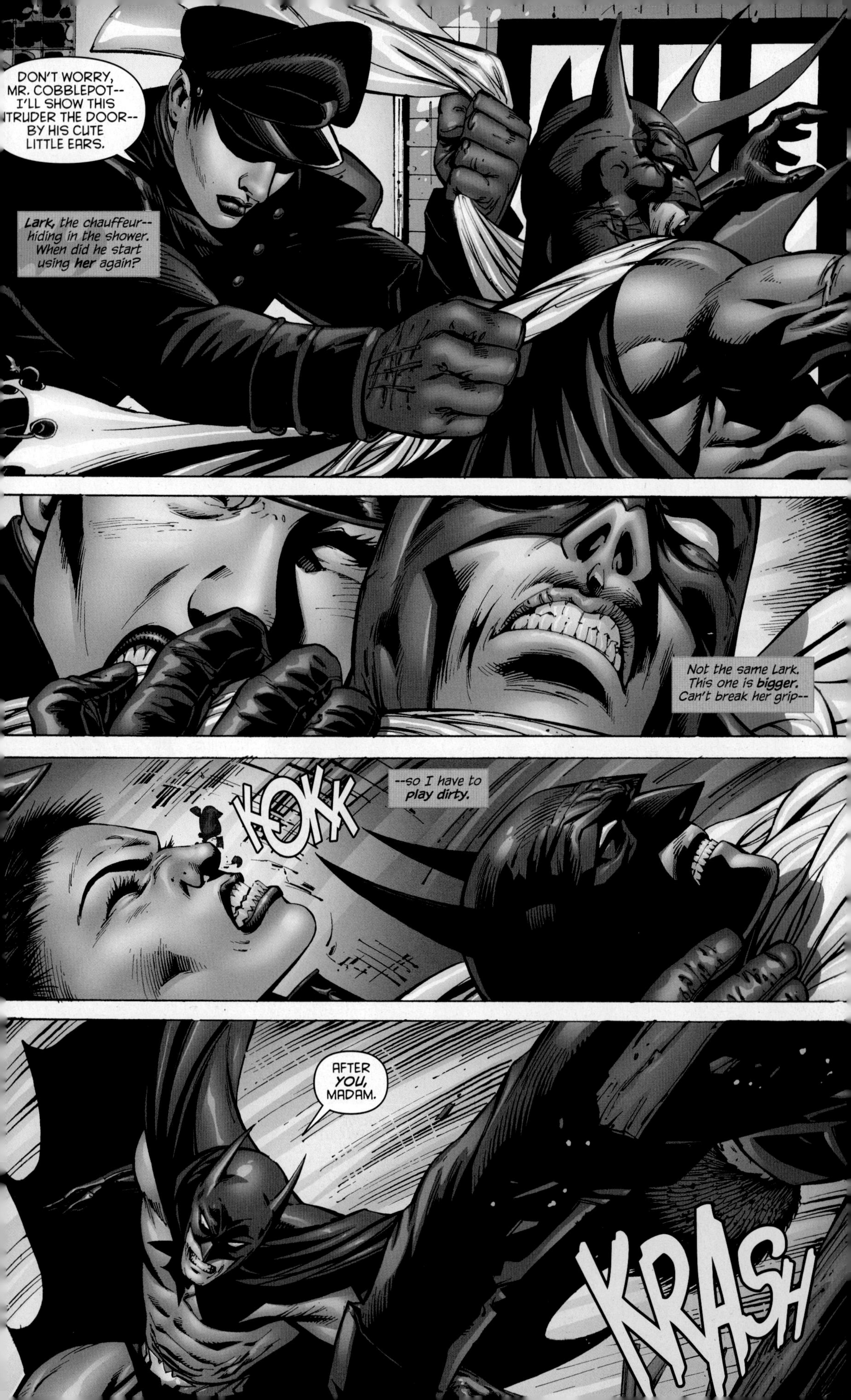

DON'T WORRY, MR. COBBLEPOT-- I'LL SHOW THIS TRUDER THE DOOR-- BY HIS CUTE LITTLE EARS.
Lark, the chauffeur-- hiding in the shower. When did he start using her again?
Not the same Lark. This one is bigger. Can't break her grip--
KOKK
--so I have to play dirty.
AFTER YOU, MADAM.
KRASH

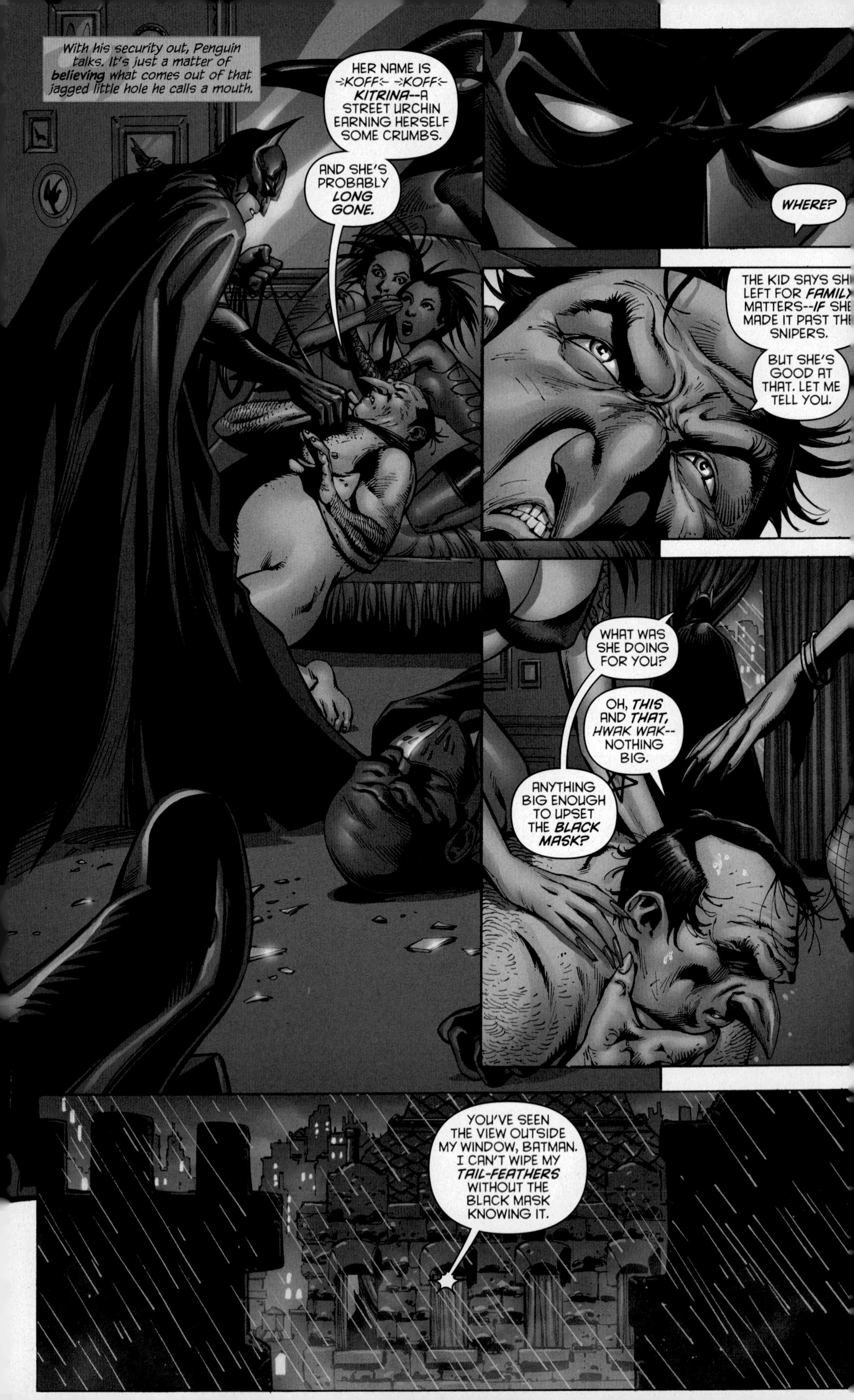

With his security out, Penguin talks. It's just a matter of believing what comes out of that jagged little hole he calls a mouth.
HER NAME IS -KOFF- -KOFF- KITRINA--A STREET URCHIN EARNING HERSELF SOME CRUMBS.
AND SHE'S PROBABLY LONG GONE.
WHERE?
THE KID SAYS SHE LEFT FOR FAMILY MATTERS--IF SHE MADE IT PAST THE SNIPERS.
BUT SHE'S GOOD AT THAT. LET ME TELL YOU.
WHAT WAS SHE DOING FOR YOU?
OH, THIS AND THAT, HWAK WAK--NOTHING BIG.
ANYTHING BIG ENOUGH TO UPSET THE BLACK MASK?
YOU'VE SEEN THE VIEW OUTSIDE MY WINDOW, BATMAN. I CAN'T WIPE MY TAIL-FEATHERS WITHOUT THE BLACK MASK KNOWING IT.

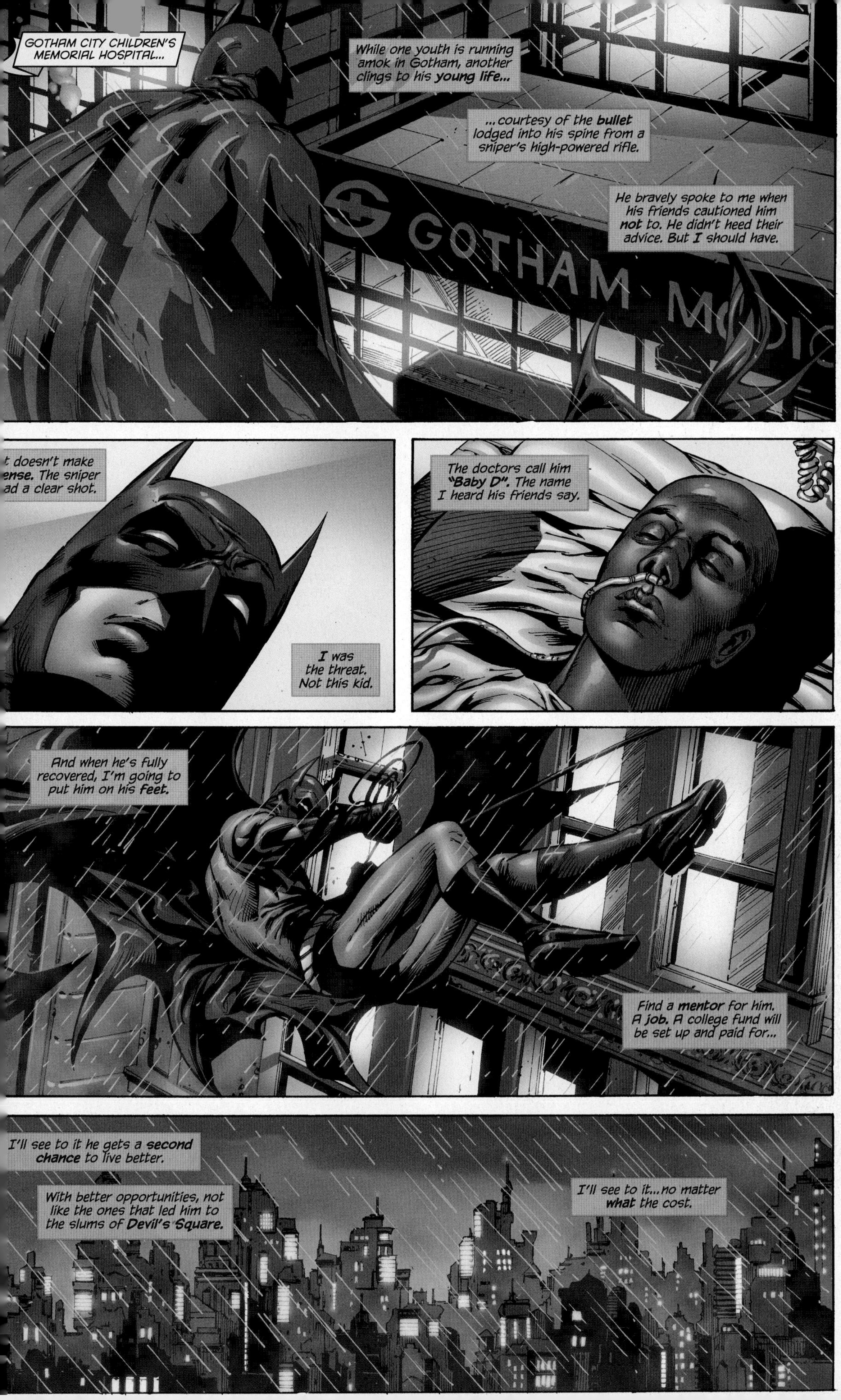
GOTHAM CITY CHILDREN'S MEMORIAL HOSPITAL...
While one youth is running amok in Gotham, another clings to his young life...
...courtesy of the bullet lodged into his spine from a sniper's high-powered rifle.
He bravely spoke to me when his friends cautioned him not to. He didn't heed their advice. But I should have.
GOTHAM M
t doesn't make ense. The sniper ad a clear shot.
I was the threat. Not this kid.
The doctors call him "Baby D". The name I heard his friends say.
And when he's fully recovered, I'm going to put him on his feet.
Find a mentor for him. A job. A college fund will be set up and paid for...
I'll see to it he gets a second chance to live better.
With better opportunities, not like the ones that led him to the slums of Devil's Square.
I'll see to it...no matter what the cost.

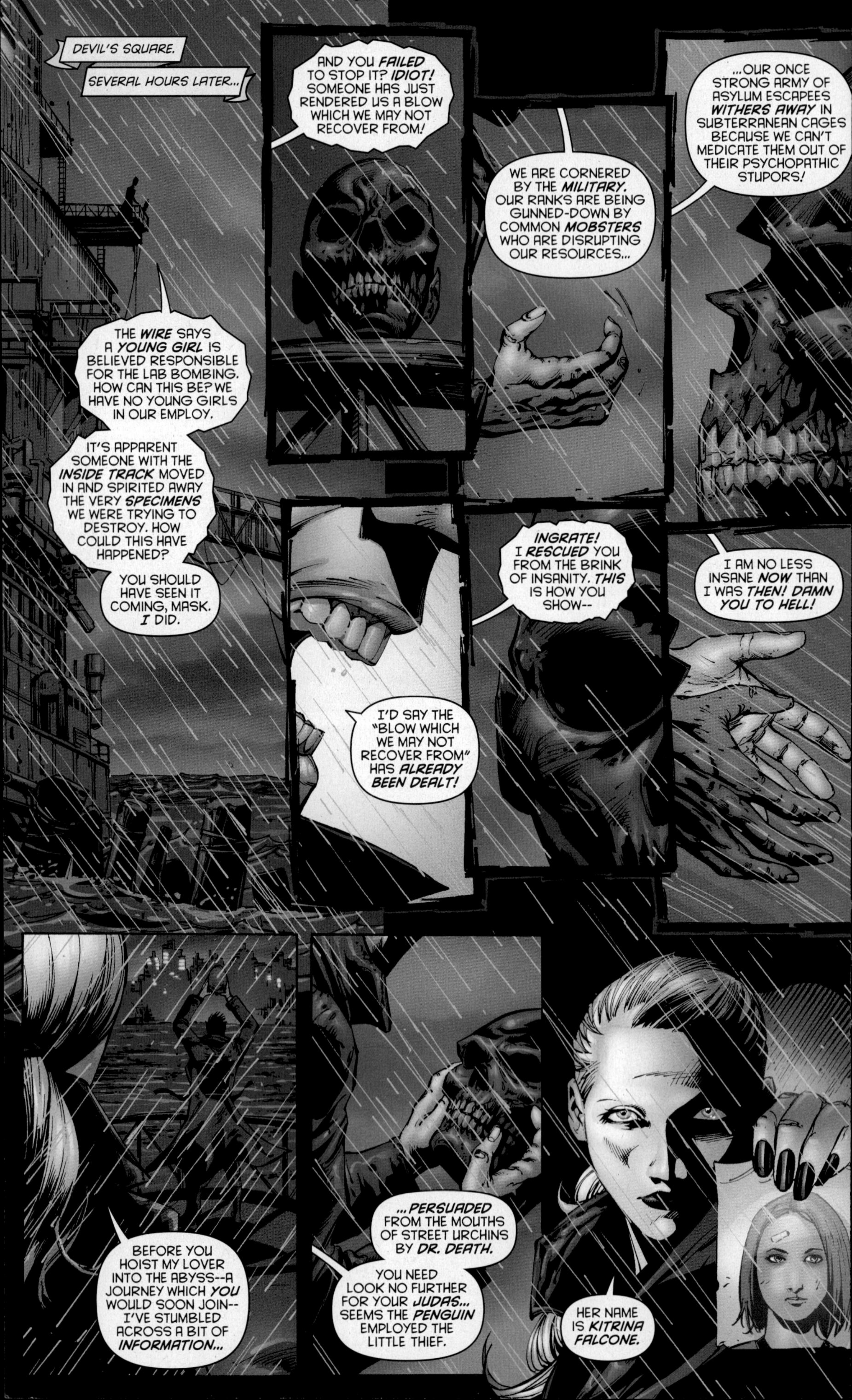
DEVIL'S SQUARE.
SEVERAL HOURS LATER...
THE WIRE SAYS A YOUNG GIRL IS BELIEVED RESPONSIBLE FOR THE LAB BOMBING. HOW CAN THIS BE? WE HAVE NO YOUNG GIRLS IN OUR EMPLOY.
IT'S APPARENT SOMEONE WITH THE INSIDE TRACK MOVED IN AND SPIRITED AWAY THE VERY SPECIMENS WE WERE TRYING TO DESTROY. HOW COULD THIS HAVE HAPPENED?
YOU SHOULD HAVE SEEN IT COMING, MASK. I DID.
AND YOU FAILED TO STOP IT? IDIOT! SOMEONE HAS JUST RENDERED US A BLOW WHICH WE MAY NOT RECOVER FROM!
WE ARE CORNERED BY THE MILITARY. OUR RANKS ARE BEING GUNNED-DOWN BY COMMON MOBSTERS WHO ARE DISRUPTING OUR RESOURCES...
...OUR ONCE STRONG ARMY OF ASYLUM ESCAPEES WITHERS AWAY IN SUBTERRANEAN CAGES BECAUSE WE CAN'T MEDICATE THEM OUT OF THEIR PSYCHOPATHIC STUPORS!
I'D SAY THE "BLOW WHICH WE MAY NOT RECOVER FROM" HAS ALREADY BEEN DEALT!
INGRATE! I RESCUED YOU FROM THE BRINK OF INSANITY. THIS IS HOW YOU SHOW--
I AM NO LESS INSANE NOW THAN I WAS THEN! DAMN YOU TO HELL!
BEFORE YOU HOIST MY LOVER INTO THE ABYSS--A JOURNEY WHICH YOU WOULD SOON JOIN--I'VE STUMBLED ACROSS A BIT OF INFORMATION...
...PERSUADED FROM THE MOUTHS OF STREET URCHINS BY DR. DEATH.
YOU NEED LOOK NO FURTHER FOR YOUR JUDAS... SEEMS THE PENGUIN EMPLOYED THE LITTLE THIEF.
HER NAME IS KITRINA FALCONE.

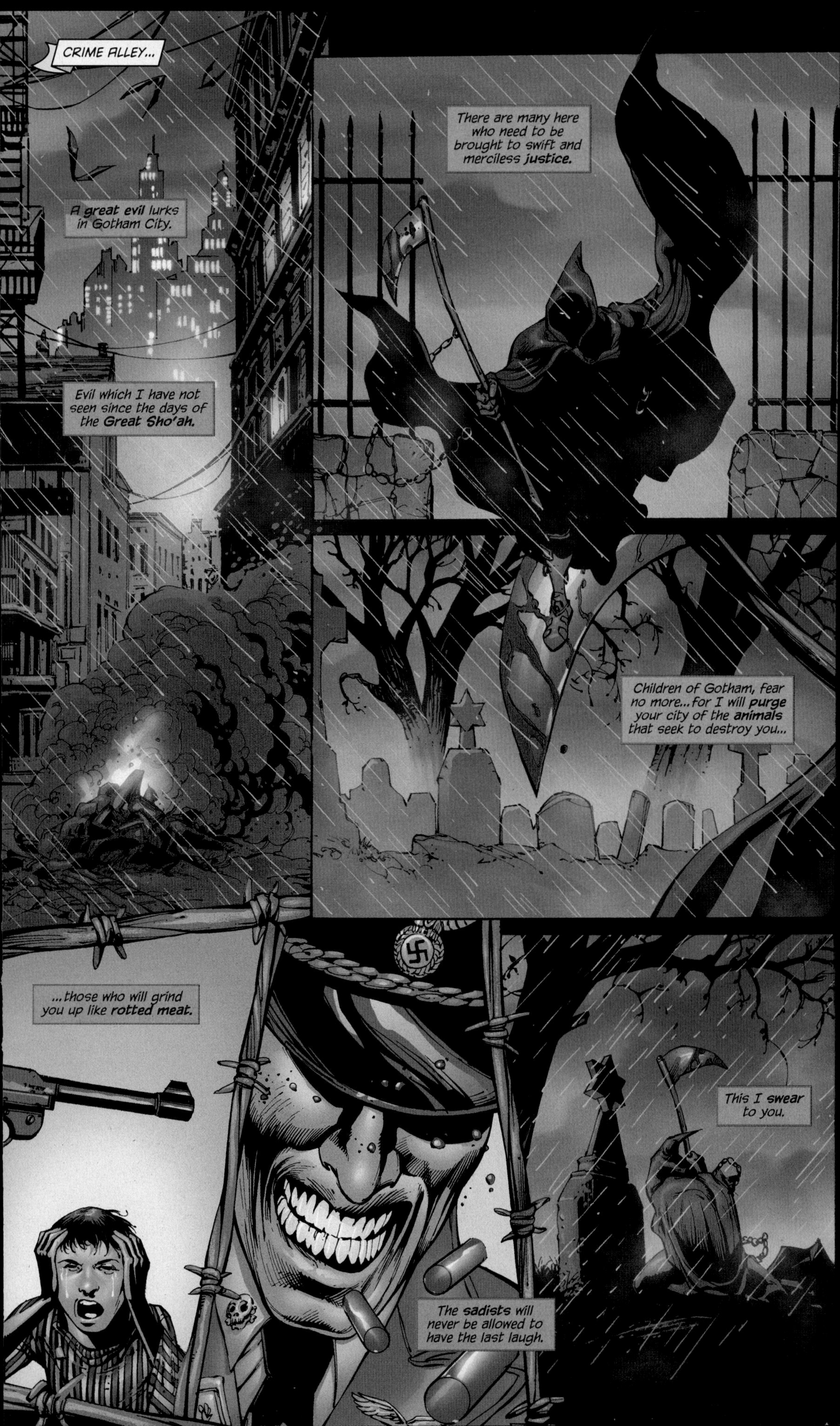
CRIME ALLEY...
A great evil lurks in Gotham City.
Evil which I have not seen since the days of the Great Sho'ah.
There are many here who need to be brought to swift and merciless justice.
Children of Gotham, fear no more... for I will purge your city of the animals that seek to destroy you...
...those who will grind you up like rotted meat.
The sadists will never be allowed to have the last laugh.
This I swear to you.

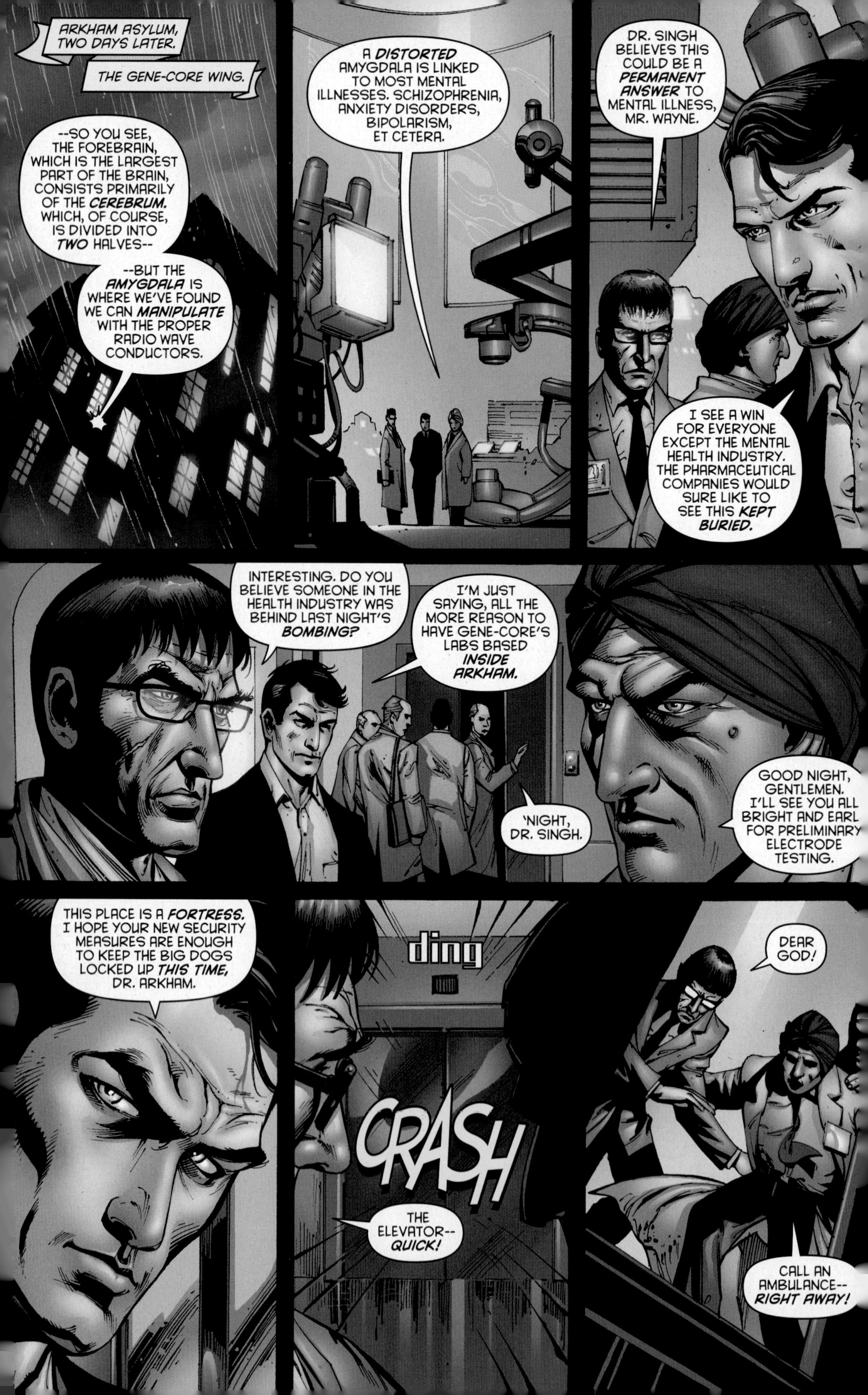

ARKHAM ASYLUM, TWO DAYS LATER.
THE GENE-CORE WING.
--SO YOU SEE, THE FOREBRAIN, WHICH IS THE LARGEST PART OF THE BRAIN, CONSISTS PRIMARILY OF THE CEREBRUM. WHICH, OF COURSE, IS DIVIDED INTO TWO HALVES--
--BUT THE AMYGDALA IS WHERE WE'VE FOUND WE CAN MANIPULATE WITH THE PROPER RADIO WAVE CONDUCTORS.
A DISTORTED AMYGDALA IS LINKED TO MOST MENTAL ILLNESSES. SCHIZOPHRENIA, ANXIETY DISORDERS, BIPOLARISM, ET CETERA.
DR. SINGH BELIEVES THIS COULD BE A PERMANENT ANSWER TO MENTAL ILLNESS, MR. WAYNE.
I SEE A WIN FOR EVERYONE EXCEPT THE MENTAL HEALTH INDUSTRY. THE PHARMACEUTICAL COMPANIES WOULD SURE LIKE TO SEE THIS KEPT BURIED.
INTERESTING. DO YOU BELIEVE SOMEONE IN THE HEALTH INDUSTRY WAS BEHIND LAST NIGHT'S BOMBING?
I'M JUST SAYING, ALL THE MORE REASON TO HAVE GENE-CORE'S LABS BASED INSIDE ARKHAM.
'NIGHT, DR. SINGH.
GOOD NIGHT, GENTLEMEN. I'LL SEE YOU ALL BRIGHT AND EARL FOR PRELIMINARY ELECTRODE TESTING.
THIS PLACE IS A FORTRESS. I HOPE YOUR NEW SECURITY MEASURES ARE ENOUGH TO KEEP THE BIG DOGS LOCKED UP THIS TIME, DR. ARKHAM.
ding
CRASH
THE ELEVATOR-- QUICK!
DEAR GOD!
CALL AN AMBULANCE-- RIGHT AWAY!

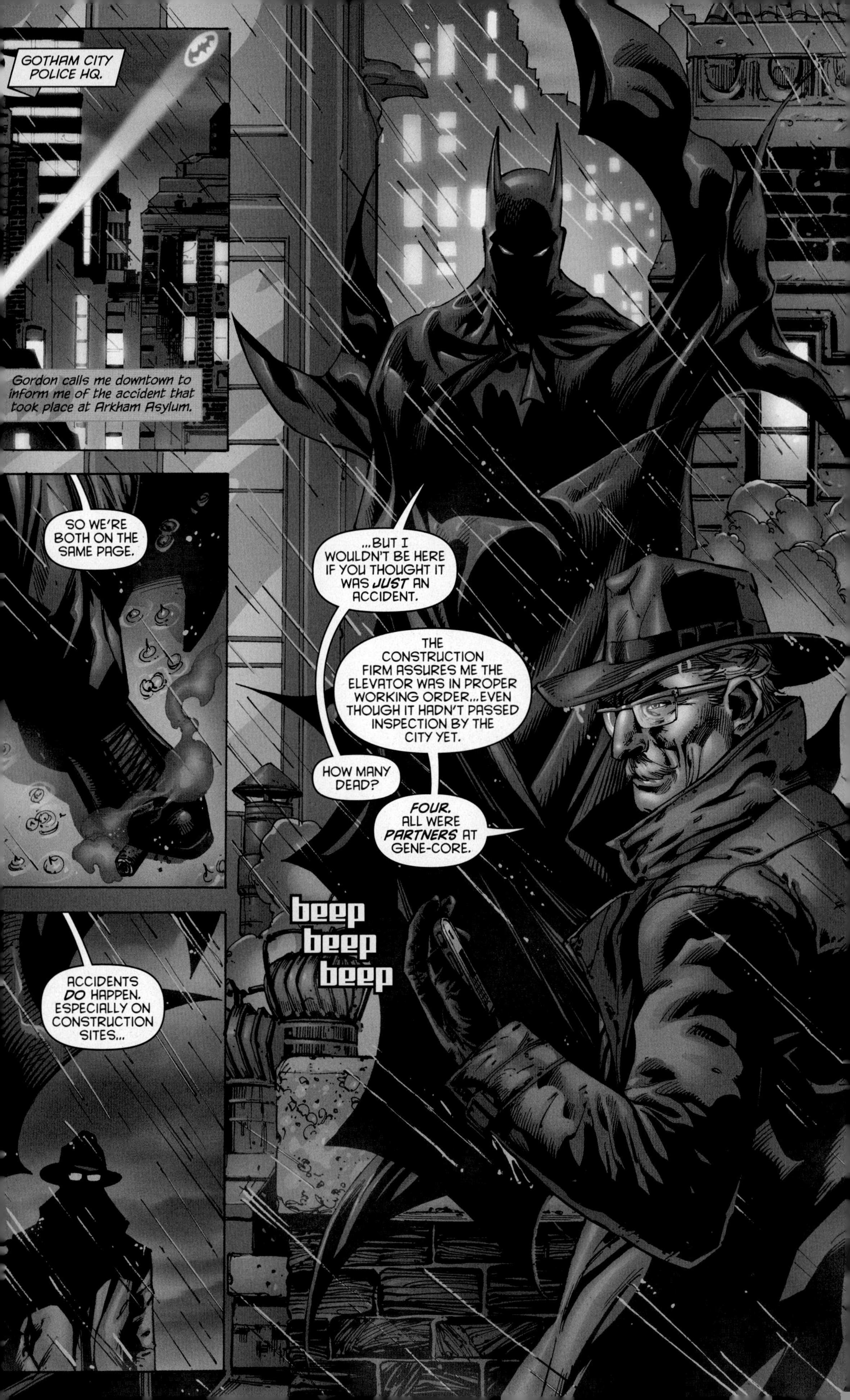
GOTHAM CITY POLICE HQ.
Gordon calls me downtown to inform me of the accident that took place at Arkham Asylum.
SO WE'RE BOTH ON THE SAME PAGE.
ACCIDENTS *DO* HAPPEN. ESPECIALLY ON CONSTRUCTION SITES...
...BUT I WOULDN'T BE HERE IF YOU THOUGHT IT WAS *JUST* AN ACCIDENT.
THE CONSTRUCTION FIRM ASSURES ME THE ELEVATOR WAS IN PROPER WORKING ORDER...EVEN THOUGH IT HADN'T PASSED INSPECTION BY THE CITY YET.
HOW MANY DEAD?
FOUR. ALL WERE *PARTNERS* AT GENE-CORE.
beep beep beep

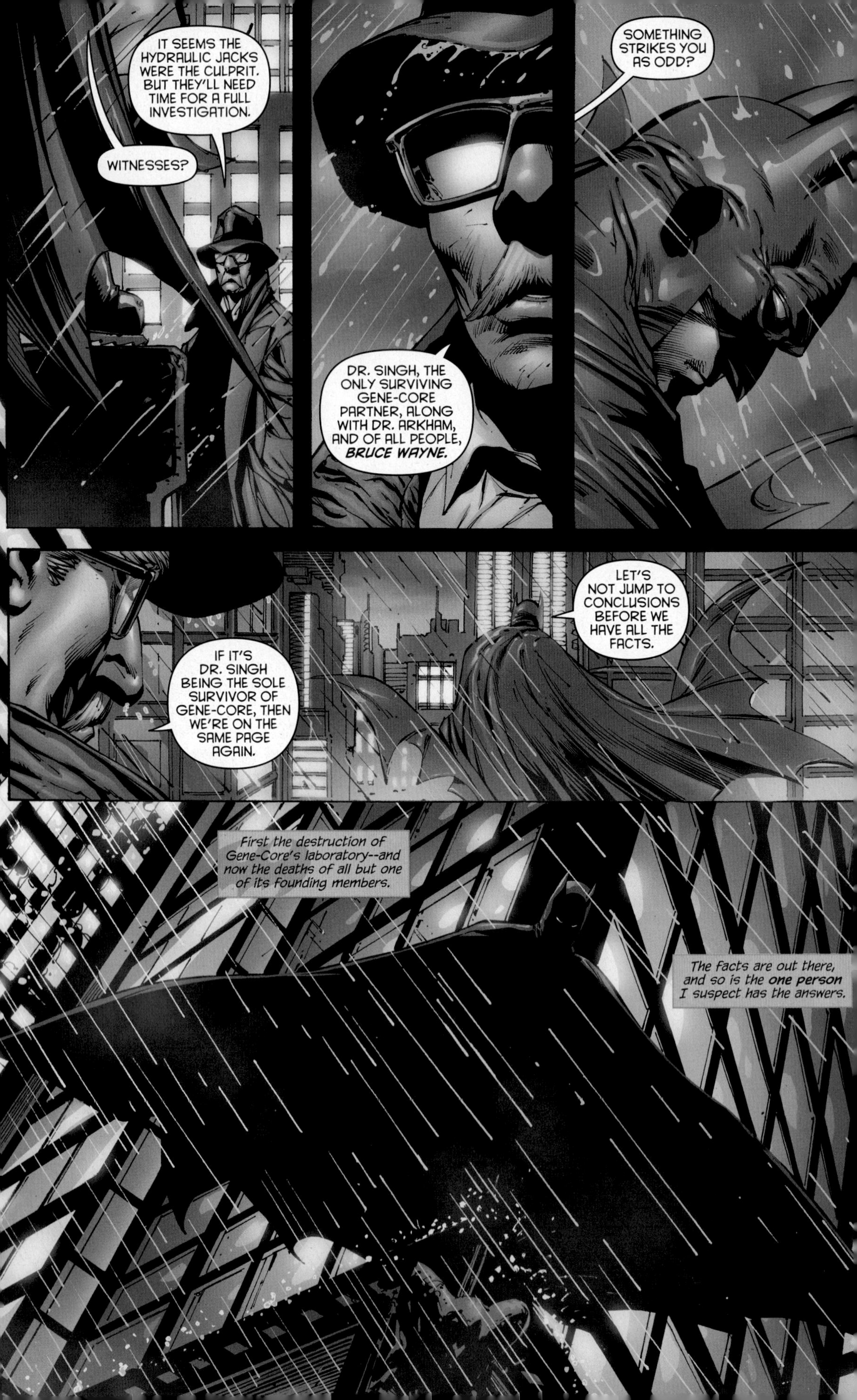
IT SEEMS THE HYDRAULIC JACKS WERE THE CULPRIT. BUT THEY'LL NEED TIME FOR A FULL INVESTIGATION.
WITNESSES?
DR. SINGH, THE ONLY SURVIVING GENE-CORE PARTNER, ALONG WITH DR. ARKHAM, AND OF ALL PEOPLE, BRUCE WAYNE.
SOMETHING STRIKES YOU AS ODD?
IF IT'S DR. SINGH BEING THE SOLE SURVIVOR OF GENE-CORE, THEN WE'RE ON THE SAME PAGE AGAIN.
LET'S NOT JUMP TO CONCLUSIONS BEFORE WE HAVE ALL THE FACTS.
First the destruction of Gene-Core's laboratory--and now the deaths of all but one of its founding members.
The facts are out there, and so is the one person I suspect has the answers.

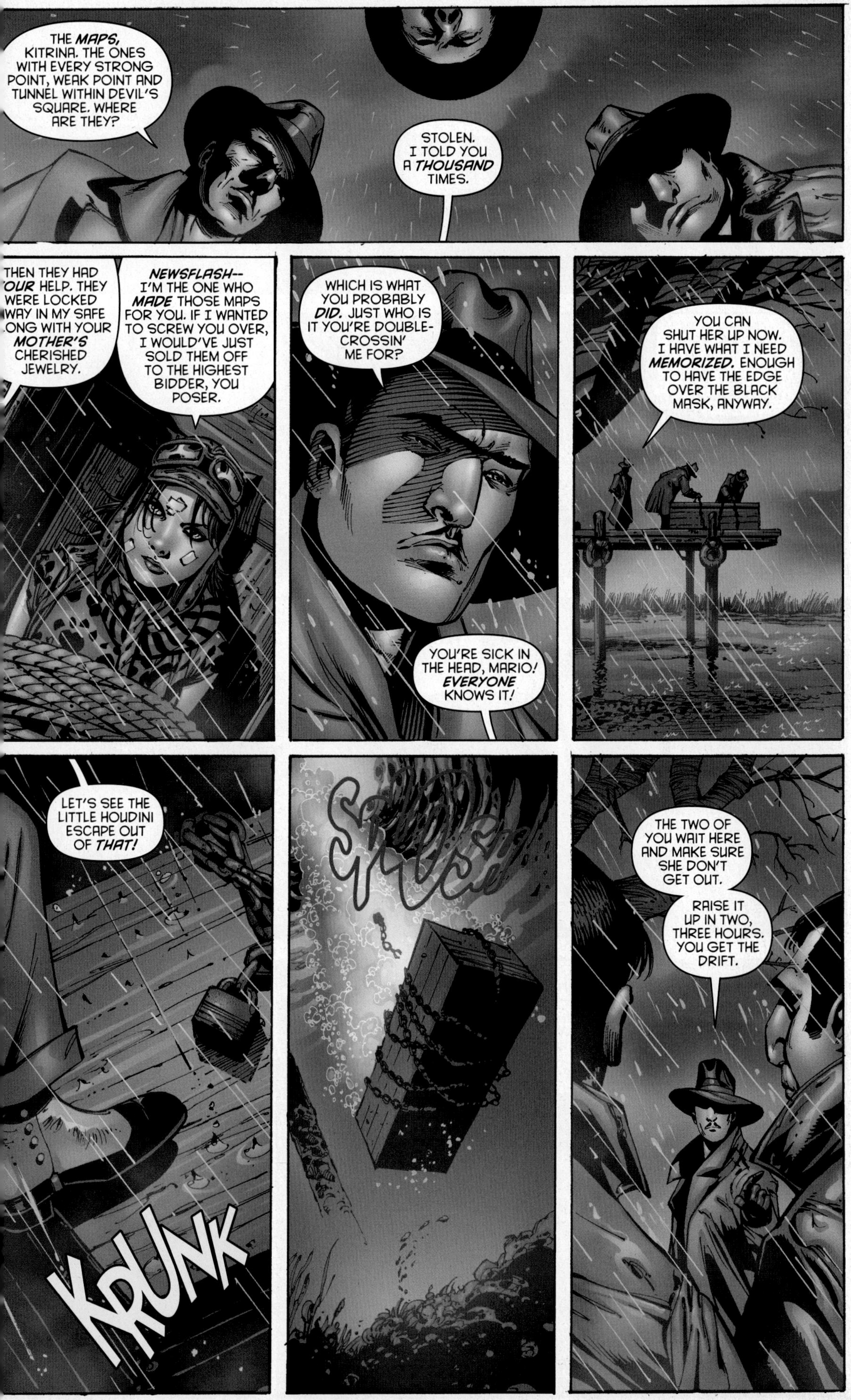
THE MAPS, KITRINA. THE ONES WITH EVERY STRONG POINT, WEAK POINT AND TUNNEL WITHIN DEVIL'S SQUARE. WHERE ARE THEY?
STOLEN. I TOLD YOU A THOUSAND TIMES.
THEN THEY HAD YOUR HELP. THEY WERE LOCKED AWAY IN MY SAFE ALONG WITH YOUR MOTHER'S CHERISHED JEWELRY.
NEWSFLASH-- I'M THE ONE WHO MADE THOSE MAPS FOR YOU. IF I WANTED TO SCREW YOU OVER, I WOULD'VE JUST SOLD THEM OFF TO THE HIGHEST BIDDER, YOU POSER.
WHICH IS WHAT YOU PROBABLY DID. JUST WHO IS IT YOU'RE DOUBLE-CROSSIN' ME FOR?
YOU'RE SICK IN THE HEAD, MARIO! EVERYONE KNOWS IT!
YOU CAN SHUT HER UP NOW. I HAVE WHAT I NEED MEMORIZED. ENOUGH TO HAVE THE EDGE OVER THE BLACK MASK, ANYWAY.
LET'S SEE THE LITTLE HOUDINI ESCAPE OUT OF THAT!
KRUNK
THE TWO OF YOU WAIT HERE AND MAKE SURE SHE DON'T GET OUT.
RAISE IT UP IN TWO, THREE HOURS. YOU GET THE DRIFT.

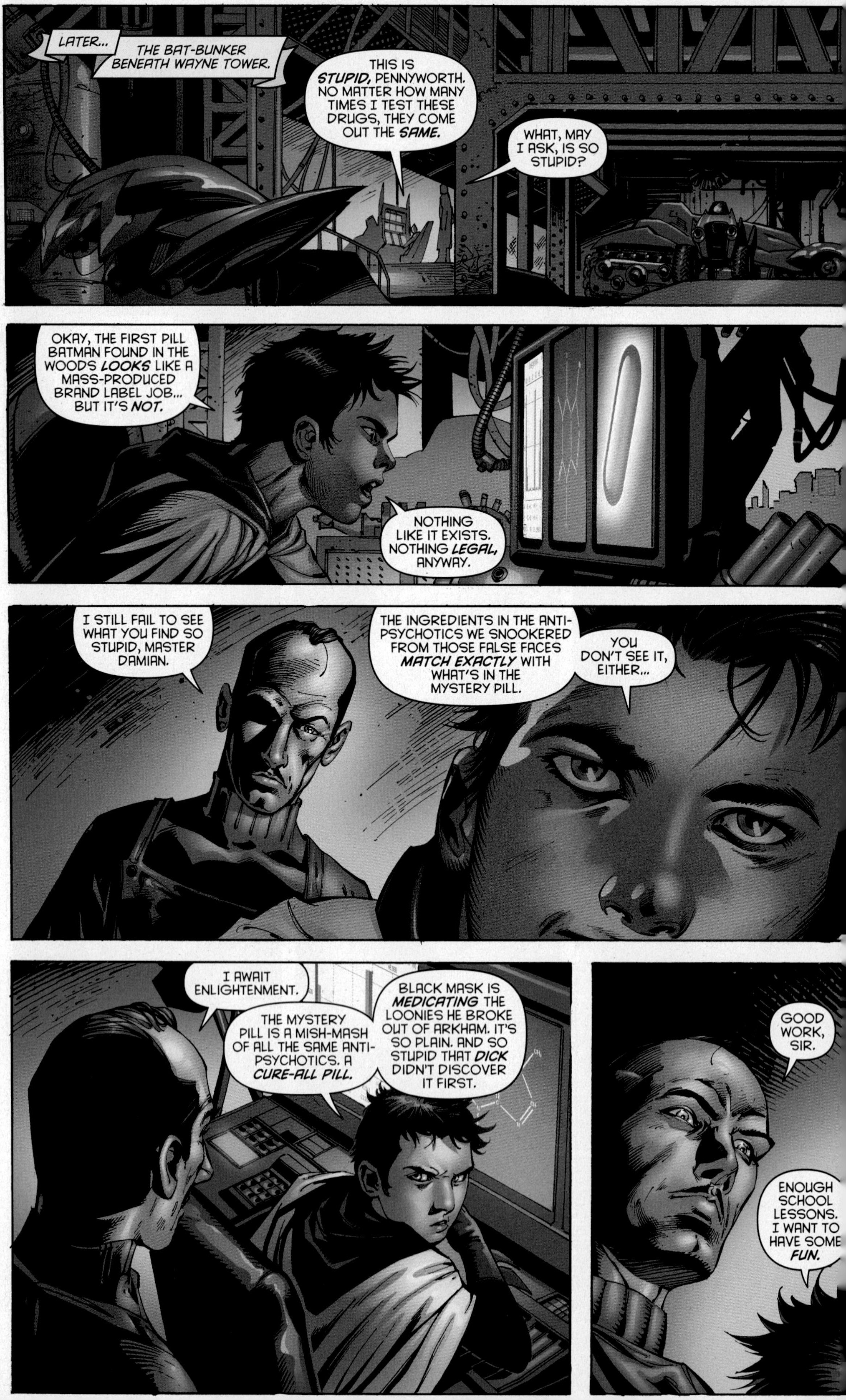
LATER...
THE BAT-BUNKER BENEATH WAYNE TOWER.
THIS IS STUPID, PENNYWORTH. NO MATTER HOW MANY TIMES I TEST THESE DRUGS, THEY COME OUT THE SAME.
WHAT, MAY I ASK, IS SO STUPID?
OKAY, THE FIRST PILL BATMAN FOUND IN THE WOODS LOOKS LIKE A MASS-PRODUCED BRAND LABEL JOB... BUT IT'S NOT.
NOTHING LIKE IT EXISTS. NOTHING LEGAL, ANYWAY.
I STILL FAIL TO SEE WHAT YOU FIND SO STUPID, MASTER DAMIAN.
THE INGREDIENTS IN THE ANTI-PSYCHOTICS WE SNOOKERED FROM THOSE FALSE FACES MATCH EXACTLY WITH WHAT'S IN THE MYSTERY PILL.
YOU DON'T SEE IT, EITHER...
I AWAIT ENLIGHTENMENT.
THE MYSTERY PILL IS A MISH-MASH OF ALL THE SAME ANTI-PSYCHOTICS. A CURE-ALL PILL.
BLACK MASK IS MEDICATING THE LOONIES HE BROKE OUT OF ARKHAM. IT'S SO PLAIN. AND SO STUPID THAT DICK DIDN'T DISCOVER IT FIRST.
GOOD WORK, SIR.
ENOUGH SCHOOL LESSONS. I WANT TO HAVE SOME FUN.

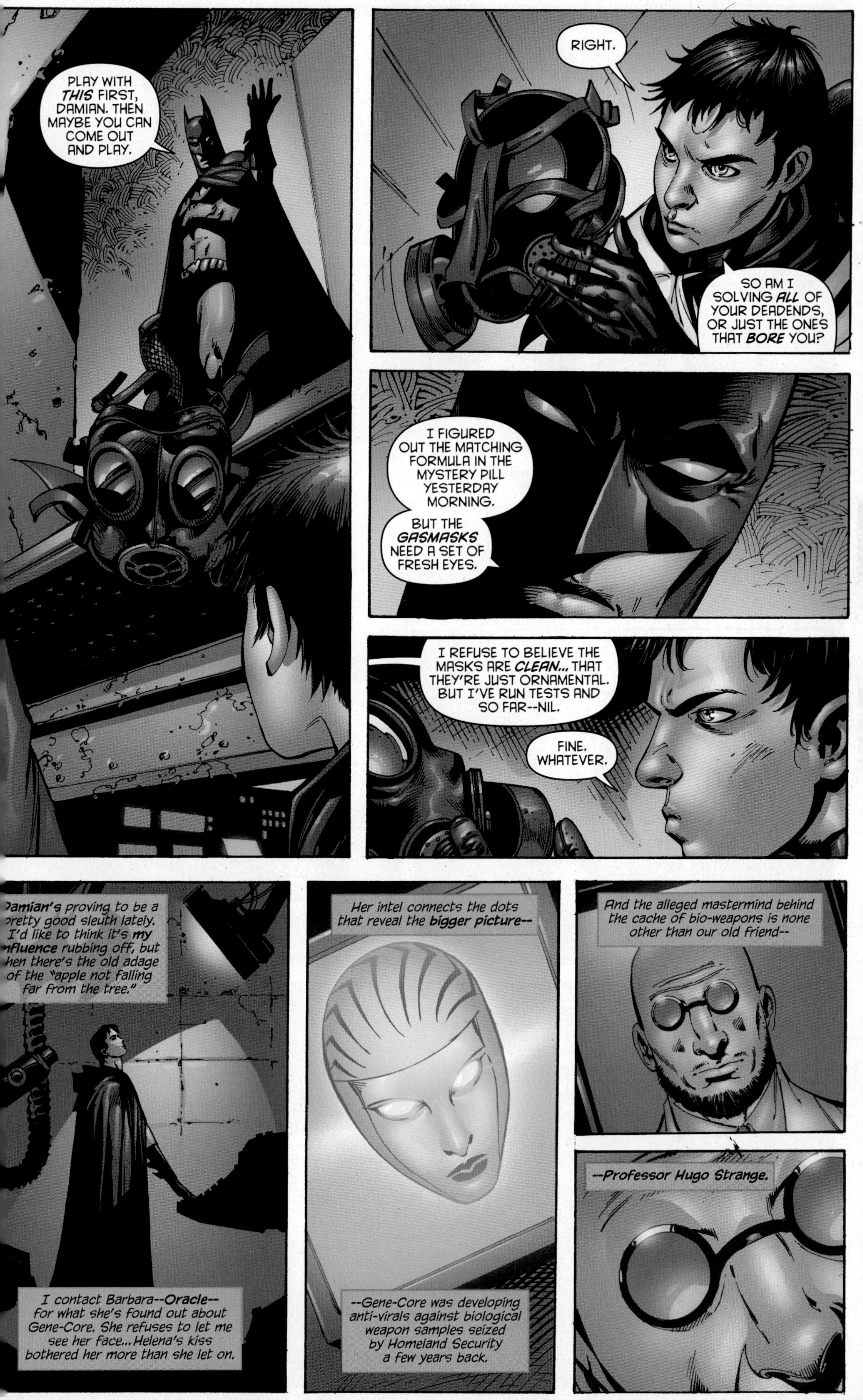
PLAY WITH THIS FIRST, DAMIAN. THEN MAYBE YOU CAN COME OUT AND PLAY.
RIGHT.
SO AM I SOLVING ALL OF YOUR DEADENDS, OR JUST THE ONES THAT BORE YOU?
I FIGURED OUT THE MATCHING FORMULA IN THE MYSTERY PILL YESTERDAY MORNING.
BUT THE GASMASKS NEED A SET OF FRESH EYES.
I REFUSE TO BELIEVE THE MASKS ARE CLEAN... THAT THEY'RE JUST ORNAMENTAL. BUT I'VE RUN TESTS AND SO FAR--NIL.
FINE. WHATEVER.
Damian's proving to be a pretty good sleuth lately. I'd like to think it's my influence rubbing off, but then there's the old adage of the "apple not falling far from the tree."
I contact Barbara--Oracle--for what she's found out about Gene-Core. She refuses to let me see her face...Helena's kiss bothered her more than she let on.
Her intel connects the dots that reveal the bigger picture--
--Gene-Core was developing anti-virals against biological weapon samples seized by Homeland Security a few years back.
And the alleged mastermind behind the cache of bio-weapons is none other than our old friend--
--Professor Hugo Strange.

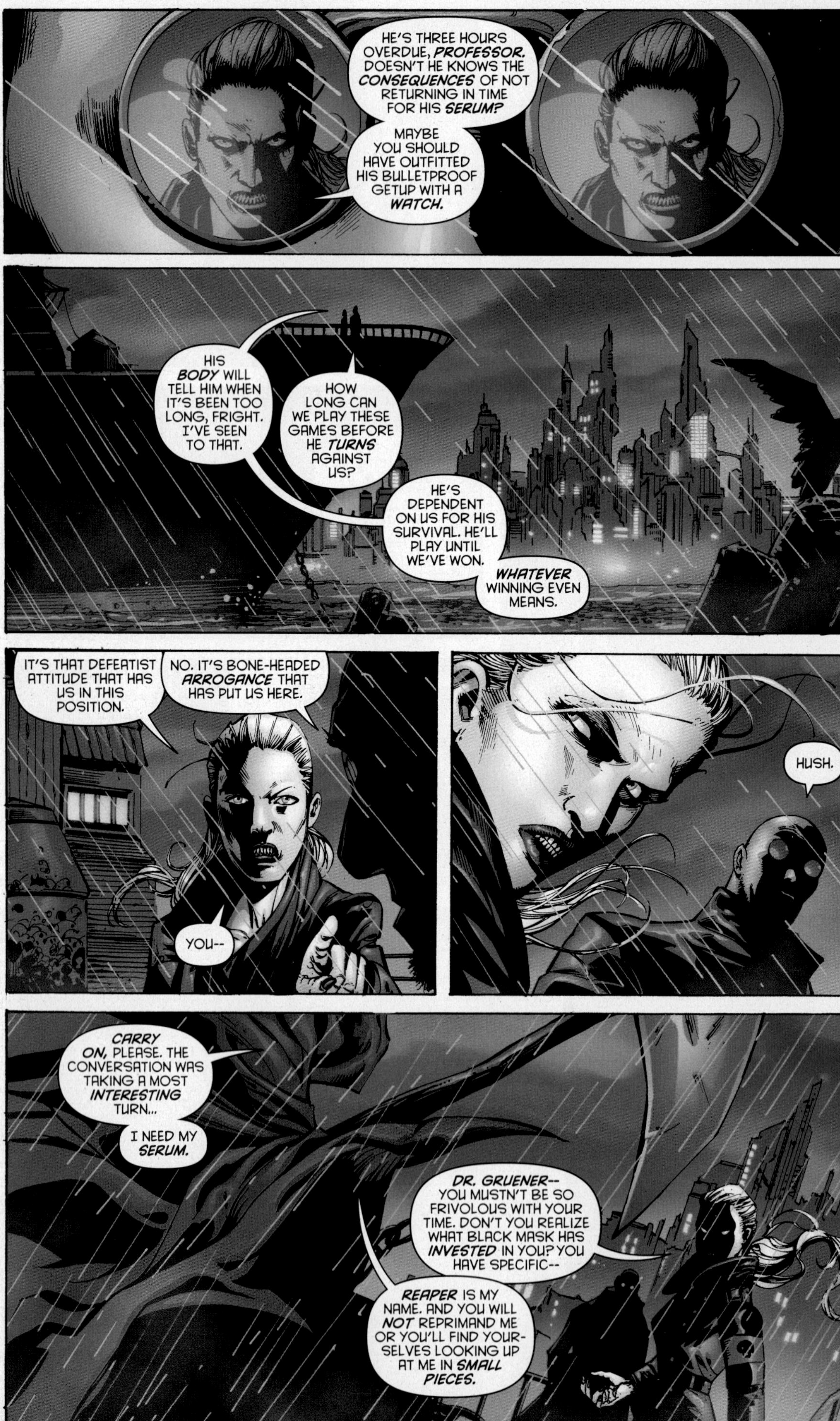
HE'S THREE HOURS OVERDUE, PROFESSOR. DOESN'T HE KNOWS THE CONSEQUENCES OF NOT RETURNING IN TIME FOR HIS SERUM?
MAYBE YOU SHOULD HAVE OUTFITTED HIS BULLETPROOF GETUP WITH A WATCH.
HIS BODY WILL TELL HIM WHEN IT'S BEEN TOO LONG, FRIGHT. I'VE SEEN TO THAT.
HOW LONG CAN WE PLAY THESE GAMES BEFORE HE TURNS AGAINST US?
HE'S DEPENDENT ON US FOR HIS SURVIVAL. HE'LL PLAY UNTIL WE'VE WON.
WHATEVER WINNING EVEN MEANS.
IT'S THAT DEFEATIST ATTITUDE THAT HAS US IN THIS POSITION.
NO. IT'S BONE-HEADED ARROGANCE THAT HAS PUT US HERE.
YOU--
HUSH.
CARRY ON, PLEASE. THE CONVERSATION WAS TAKING A MOST INTERESTING TURN...
I NEED MY SERUM.
DR. GRUENER-- YOU MUSTN'T BE SO FRIVOLOUS WITH YOUR TIME. DON'T YOU REALIZE WHAT BLACK MASK HAS INVESTED IN YOU? YOU HAVE SPECIFIC--
REAPER IS MY NAME. AND YOU WILL NOT REPRIMAND ME OR YOU'LL FIND YOUR-SELVES LOOKING UP AT ME IN SMALL PIECES.

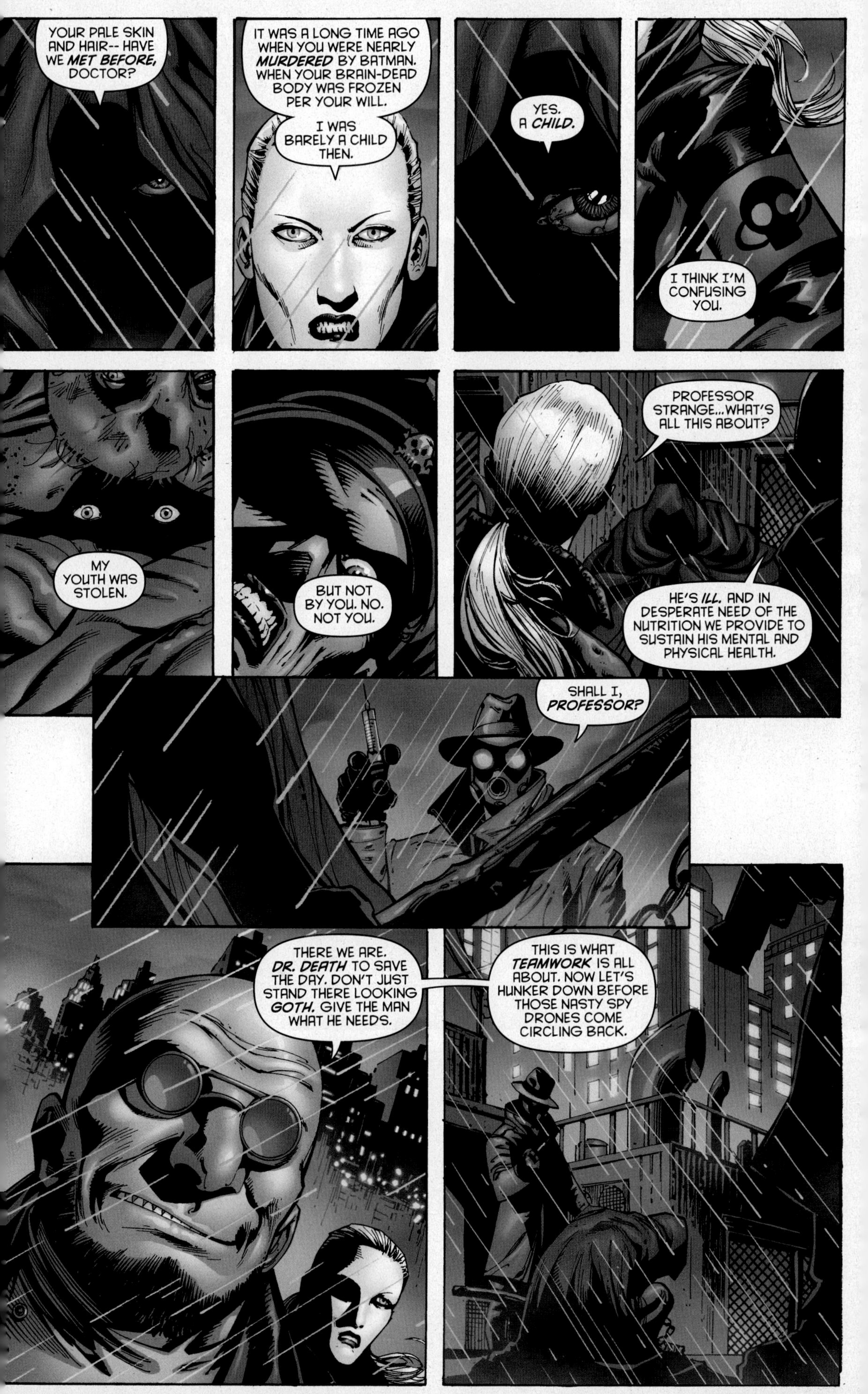
YOUR PALE SKIN AND HAIR-- HAVE WE *MET BEFORE,* DOCTOR?
IT WAS A LONG TIME AGO WHEN YOU WERE NEARLY *MURDERED* BY BATMAN. WHEN YOUR BRAIN-DEAD BODY WAS FROZEN PER YOUR WILL.
I WAS BARELY A CHILD THEN.
YES. A *CHILD.*
I THINK I'M CONFUSING YOU.
MY YOUTH WAS STOLEN.
BUT NOT BY YOU. NO. NOT YOU.
PROFESSOR STRANGE...WHAT'S ALL THIS ABOUT?
HE'S *ILL.* AND IN DESPERATE NEED OF THE NUTRITION WE PROVIDE TO SUSTAIN HIS MENTAL AND PHYSICAL HEALTH.
SHALL I, *PROFESSOR?*
THERE WE ARE. *DR. DEATH* TO SAVE THE DAY. DON'T JUST STAND THERE LOOKING *GOTH.* GIVE THE MAN WHAT HE NEEDS.
THIS IS WHAT *TEAMWORK* IS ALL ABOUT. NOW LET'S HUNKER DOWN BEFORE THOSE NASTY SPY DRONES COME CIRCLING BACK.

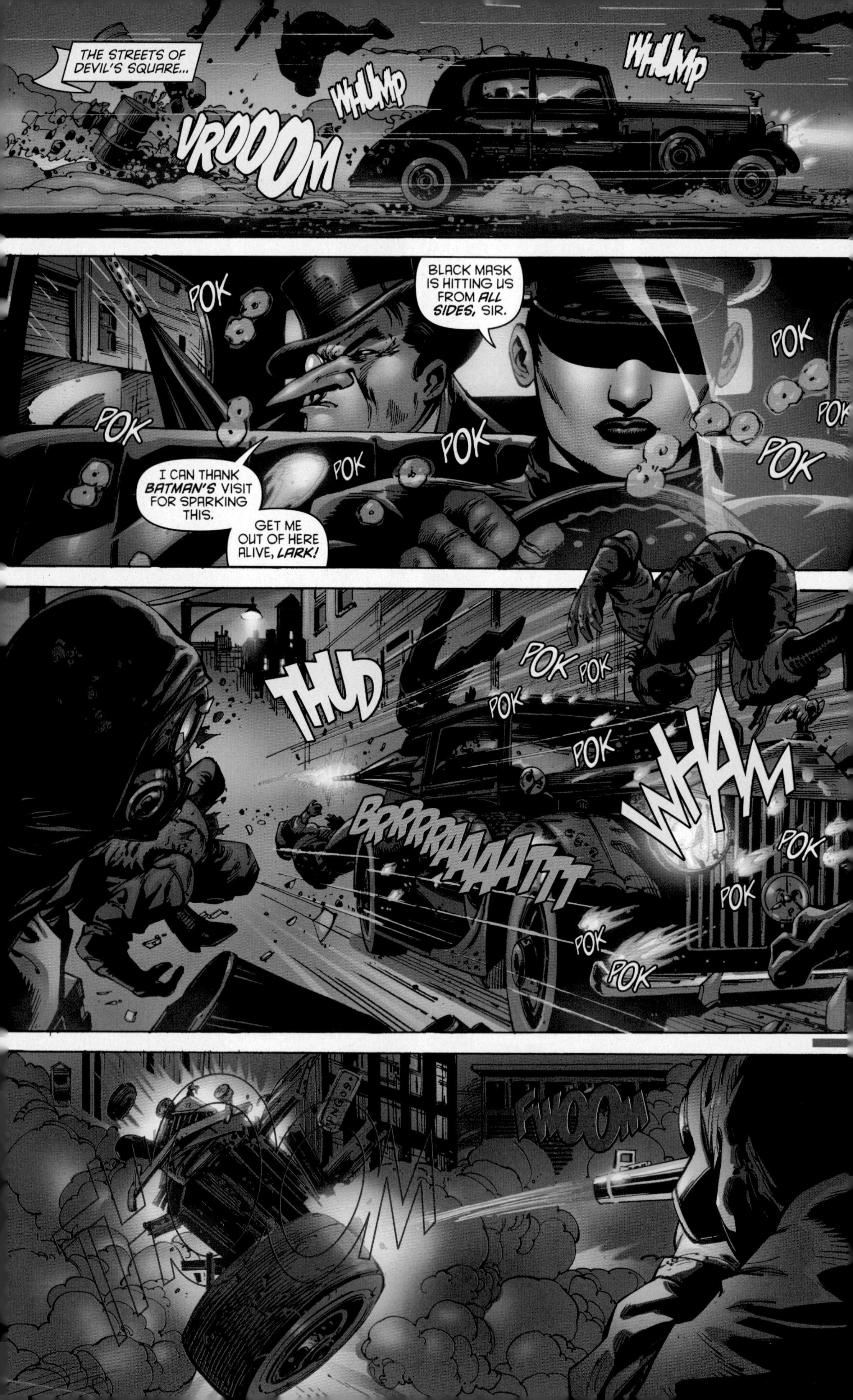
THE STREETS OF DEVIL'S SQUARE...
WHUMP
VROOOOM
WHUMP
POK
BLACK MASK IS HITTING US FROM ALL SIDES, SIR.
POK
POK
POK
POK
POK
POK
I CAN THANK BATMAN'S VISIT FOR SPARKING THIS.
GET ME OUT OF HERE ALIVE, LARK!
THUD
POK
POK
POK
POK
WHAM
BRRRRAAAAATTTT
POK
POK
POK
POK
FWOOM

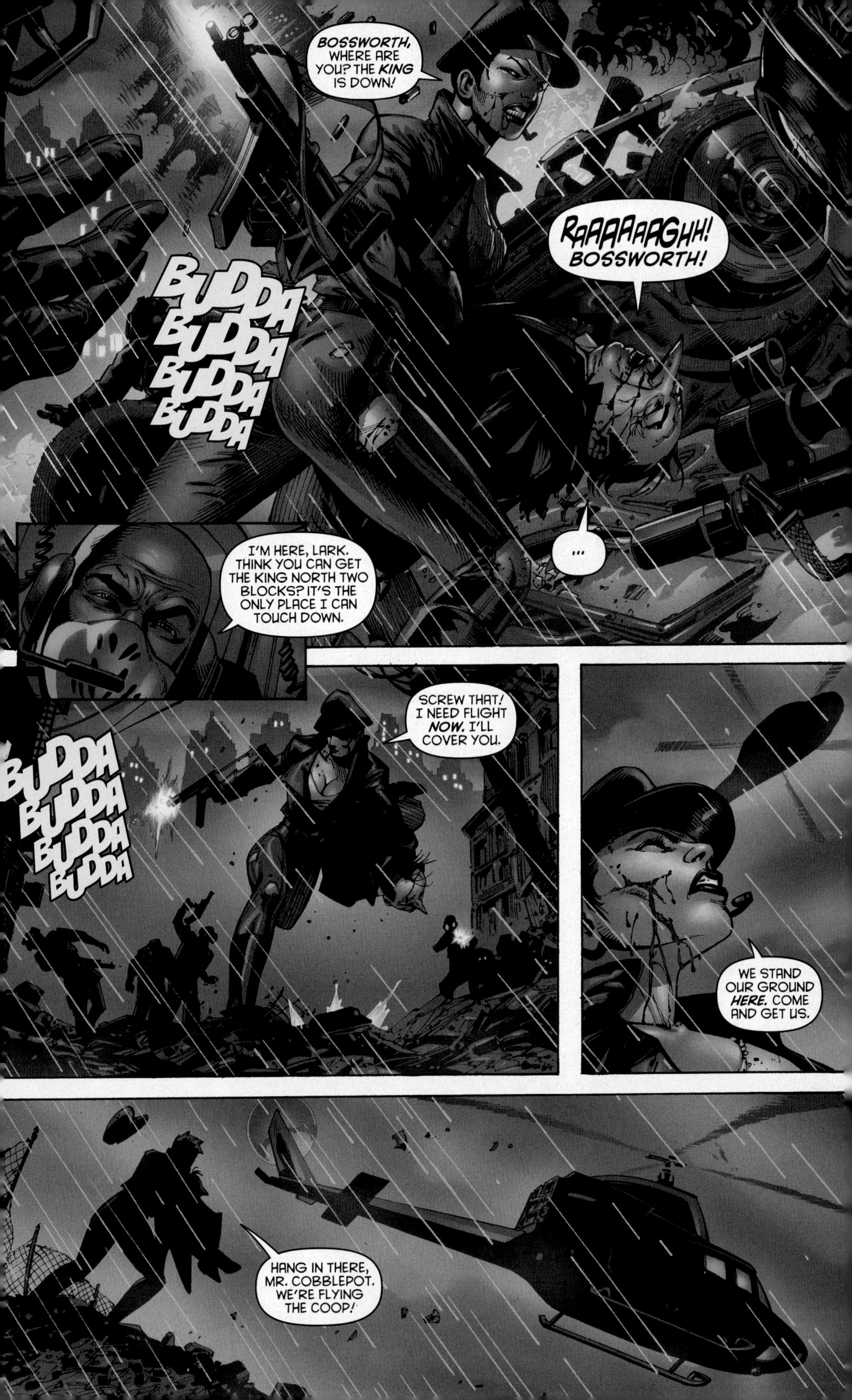
BOSSWORTH, WHERE ARE YOU? THE KING IS DOWN!
RAAAAAAGHH! BOSSWORTH!
BUDDA BUDDA BUDDA BUDDA
...
I'M HERE, LARK. THINK YOU CAN GET THE KING NORTH TWO BLOCKS? IT'S THE ONLY PLACE I CAN TOUCH DOWN.
BUDDA BUDDA BUDDA BUDDA
SCREW THAT! I NEED FLIGHT NOW. I'LL COVER YOU.
WE STAND OUR GROUND HERE. COME AND GET US.
HANG IN THERE, MR. COBBLEPOT. WE'RE FLYING THE COOP!

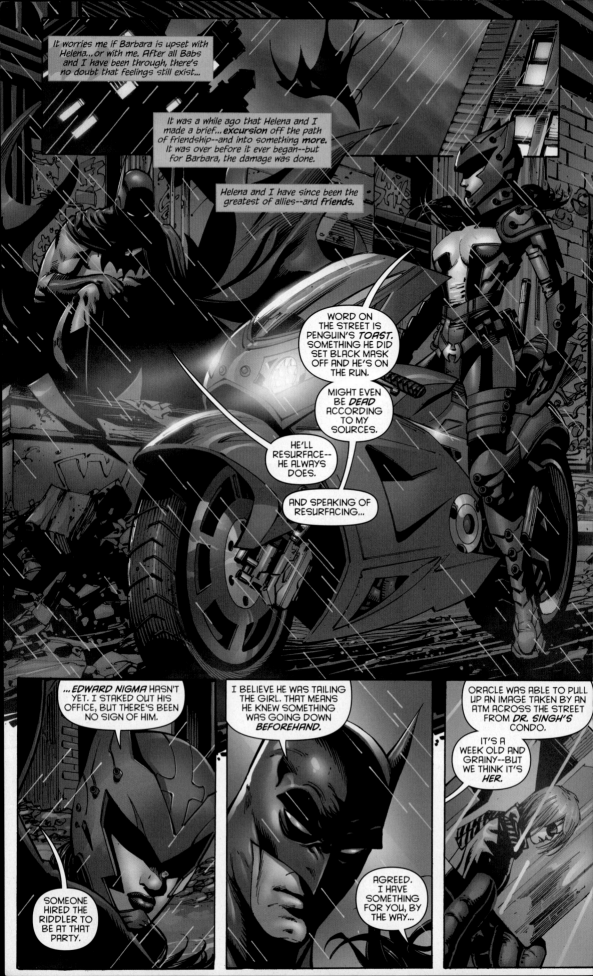

It worries me if Barbara is upset with Helena...or with me. After all Babs and I have been through, there's no doubt that feelings still exist...

It was a while ago that Helena and I made a brief...excursion off the path of friendship--and into something *more*. It was over before it ever began--but for Barbara, the damage was done.

Helena and I have since been the greatest of allies--and *friends*.

WORD ON THE STREET IS PENGUIN'S *TOAST.* SOMETHING HE DID SET BLACK MASK OFF AND HE'S ON THE RUN.

MIGHT EVEN BE *DEAD* ACCORDING TO MY SOURCES.

HE'LL RESURFACE-- HE ALWAYS DOES.

AND SPEAKING OF RESURFACING...

...*EDWARD NIGMA* HASN'T YET. I STAKED OUT HIS OFFICE, BUT THERE'S BEEN NO SIGN OF HIM.

SOMEONE HIRED THE RIDDLER TO BE AT THAT PARTY.

I BELIEVE HE WAS TAILING THE GIRL. THAT MEANS HE KNEW SOMETHING WAS GOING DOWN *BEFOREHAND.*

AGREED. I HAVE SOMETHING FOR YOU, BY THE WAY...

ORACLE WAS ABLE TO PULL UP AN IMAGE TAKEN BY AN ATM ACROSS THE STREET FROM *DR. SINGH'S* CONDO.

IT'S A WEEK OLD AND GRAINY--BUT WE THINK IT'S *HER.*

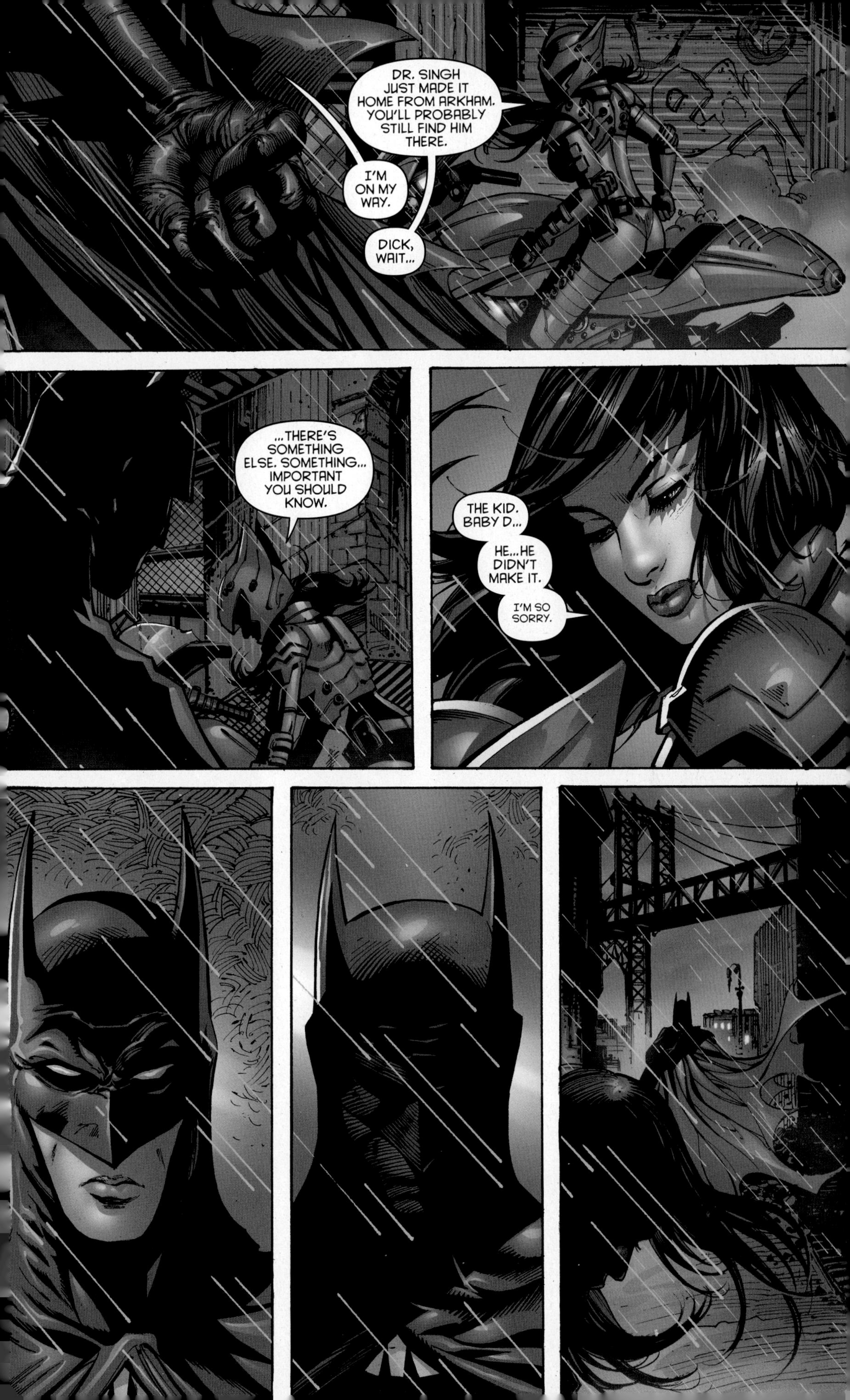
DR. SINGH JUST MADE IT HOME FROM ARKHAM. YOU'LL PROBABLY STILL FIND HIM THERE.
I'M ON MY WAY.
DICK, WAIT...
...THERE'S SOMETHING ELSE. SOMETHING... IMPORTANT YOU SHOULD KNOW.
THE KID. BABY D...
HE...HE DIDN'T MAKE IT.
I'M SO SORRY.

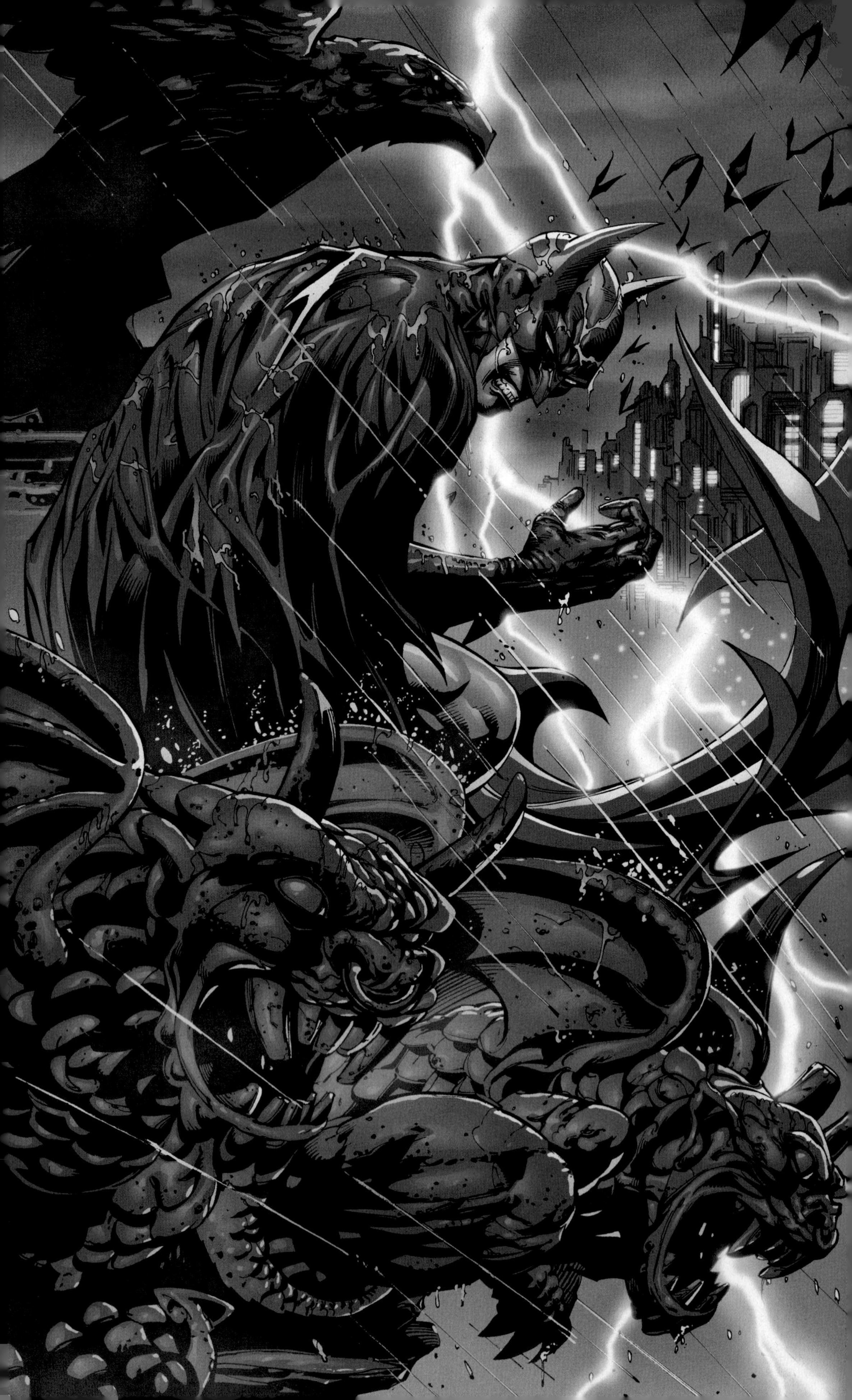

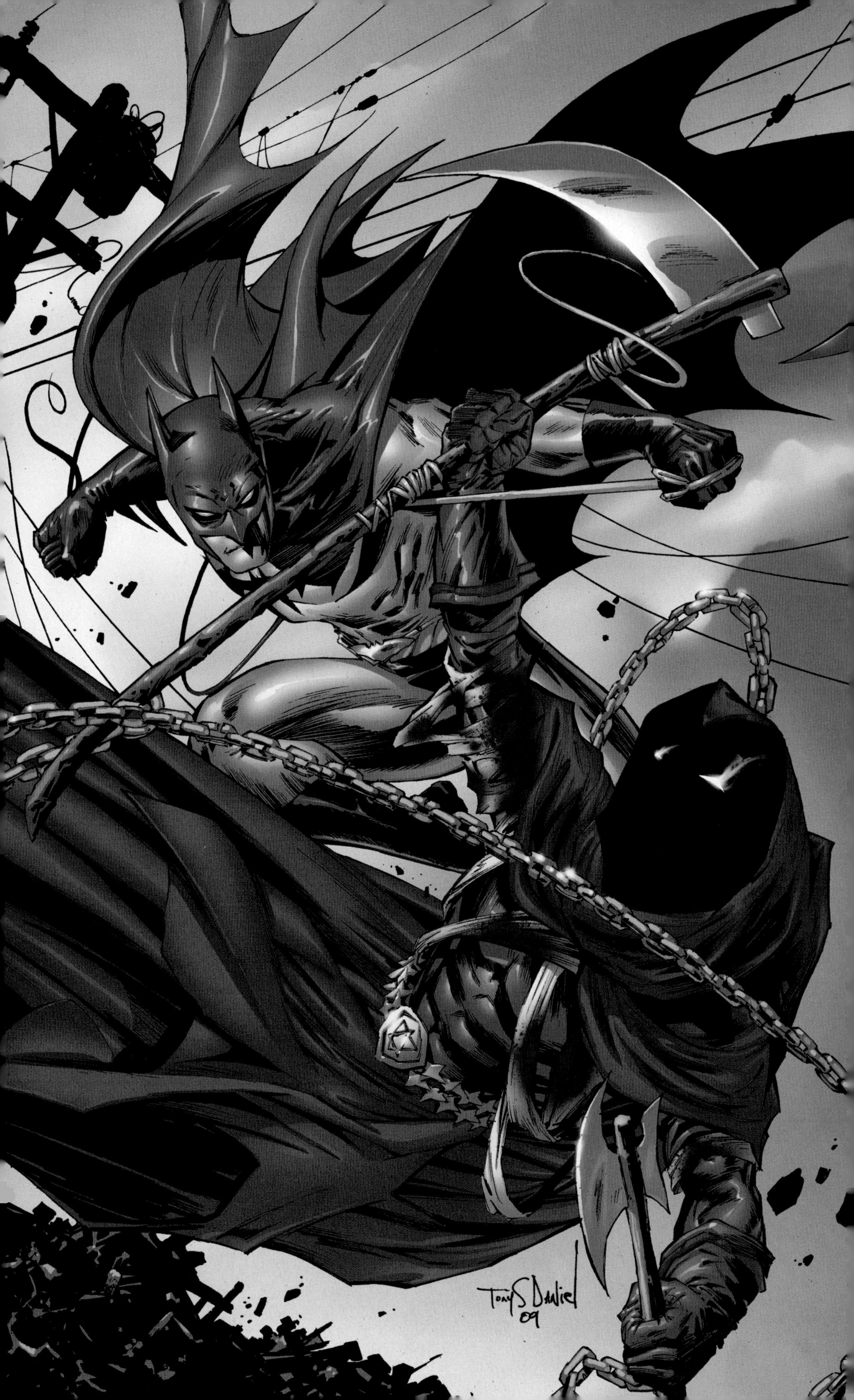
Tony S Daniel
09

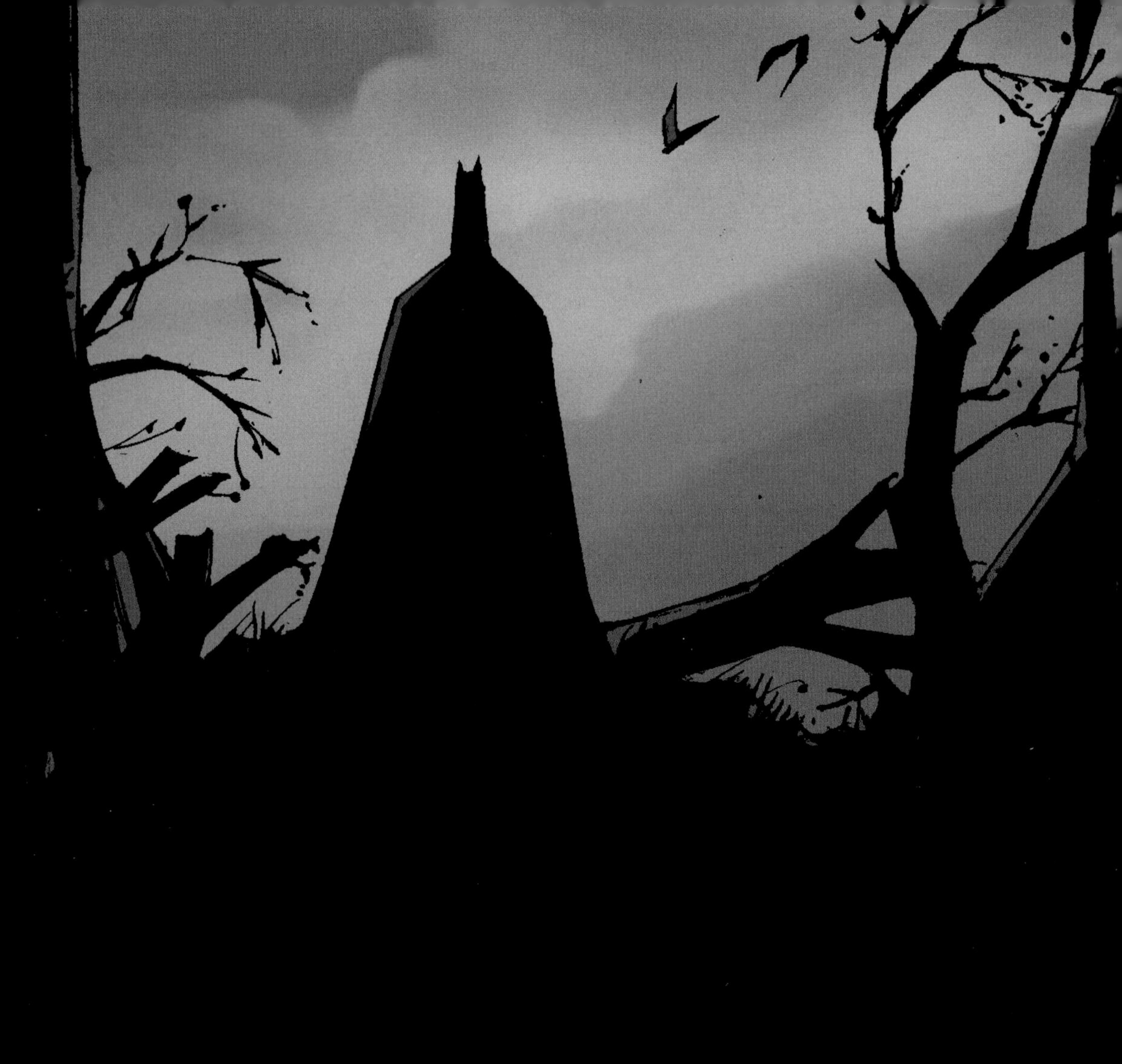

"Your time is up, Falcone. Let's not keep hell waiting."

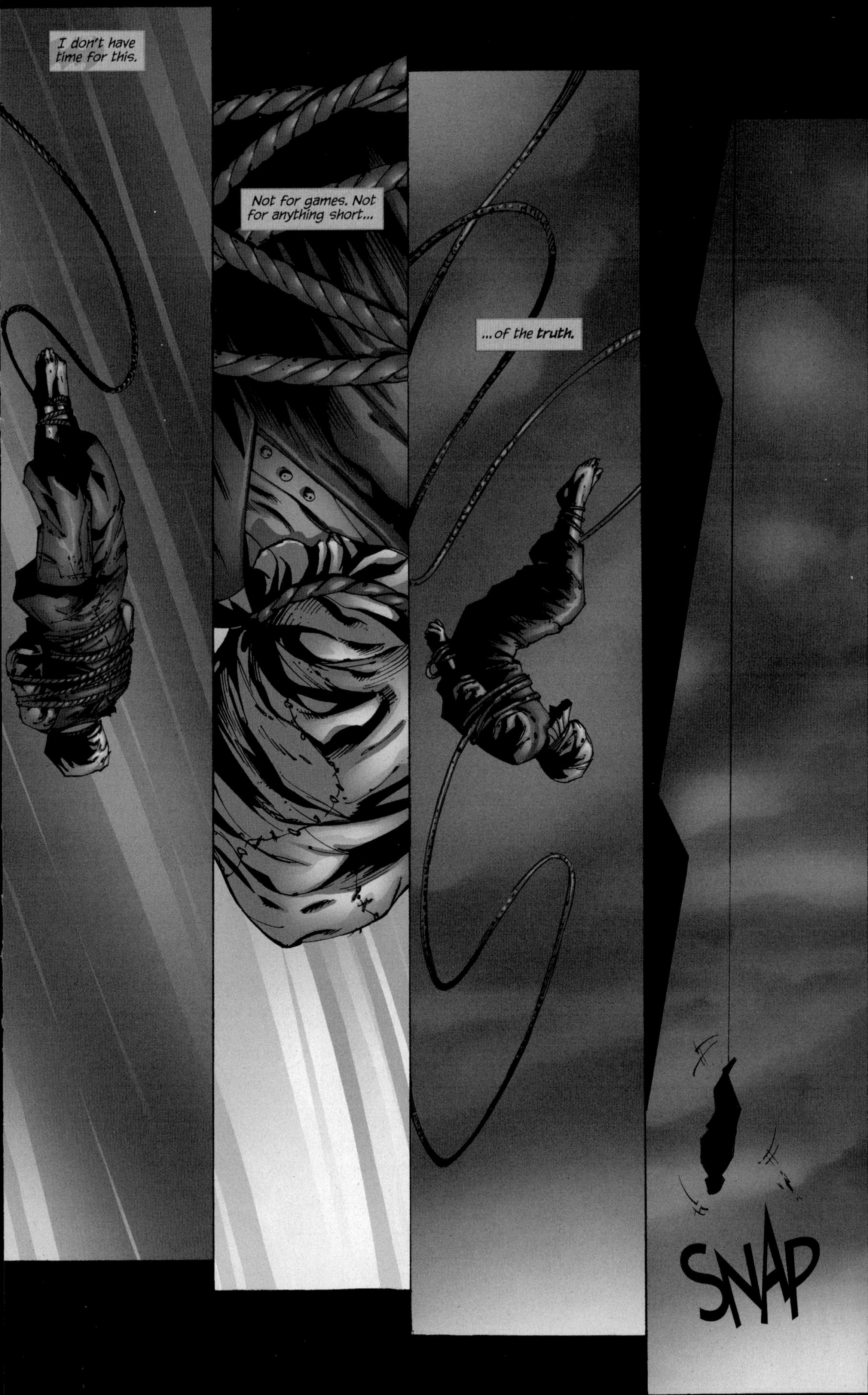
I don't have time for this.
Not for games. Not for anything short...
...of the **truth.**
SNAP

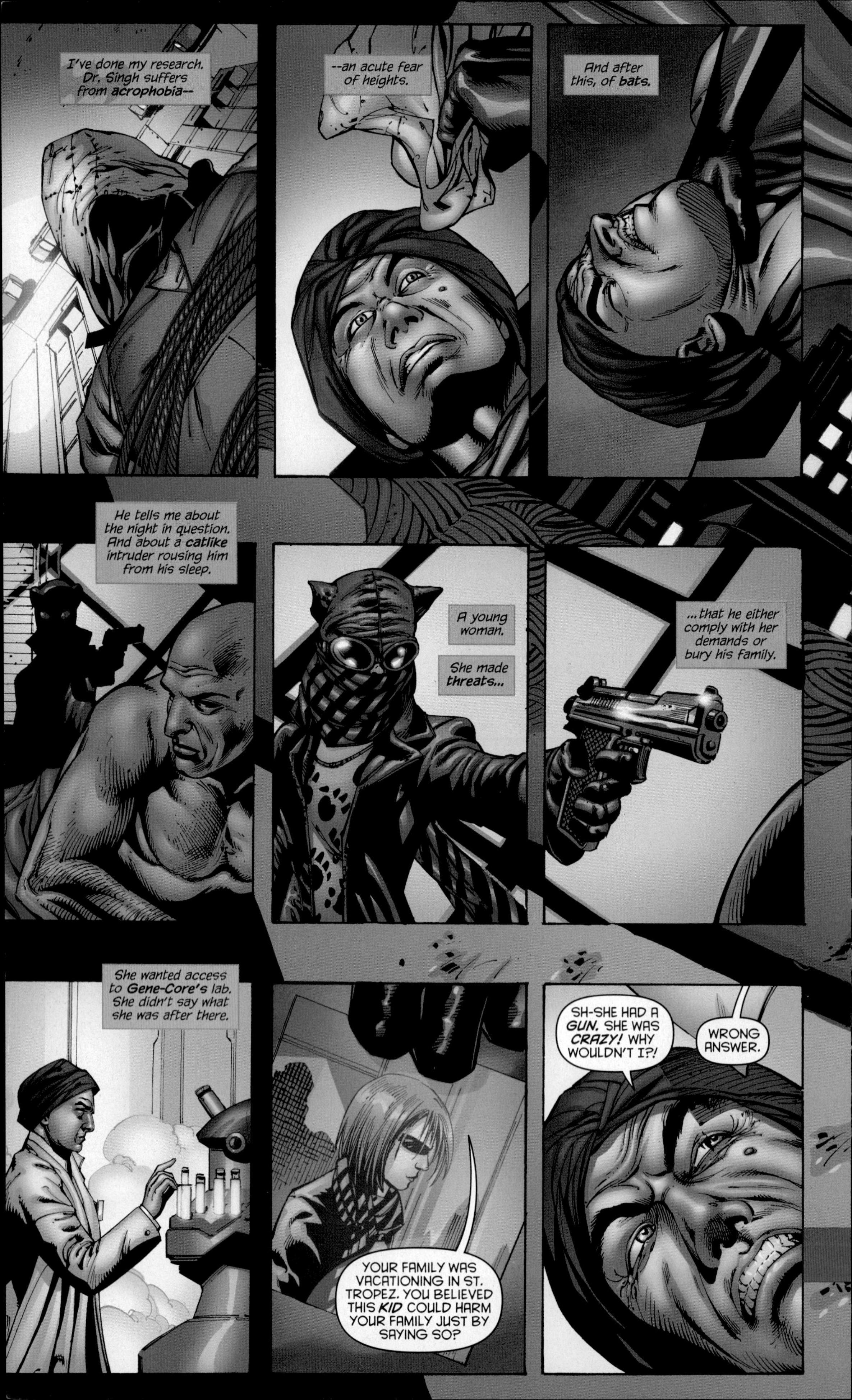
I've done my research. Dr. Singh suffers from acrophobia--
--an acute fear of heights.
And after this, of bats.
He tells me about the night in question. And about a catlike intruder rousing him from his sleep.
A young woman.
She made threats...
...that he either comply with her demands or bury his family.
She wanted access to Gene-Core's lab. She didn't say what she was after there.
YOUR FAMILY WAS VACATIONING IN ST. TROPEZ. YOU BELIEVED THIS KID COULD HARM YOUR FAMILY JUST BY SAYING SO?
SH-SHE HAD A GUN. SHE WAS CRAZY! WHY WOULDN'T I?!
WRONG ANSWER.

He knows more, and he's afraid of spilling it to me.
But he's even more afraid of heights.
Between the gagging and vomiting he spits out something useful.
A **name** which leaves me no doubt where to go next.
LIFE AFTER DEATH PART 4
SMOKE AND MIRRORS

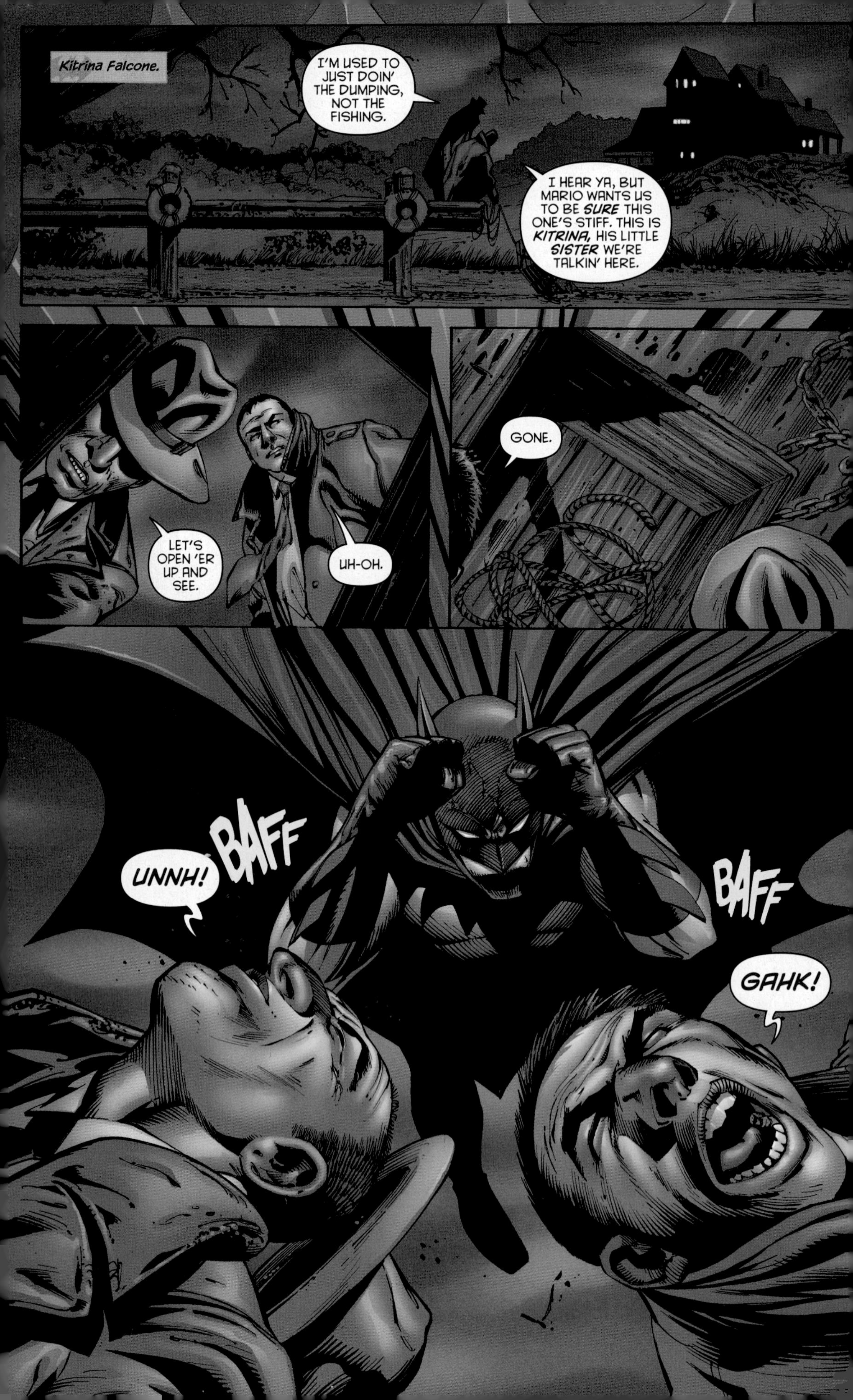
Kitrina Falcone.
I'M USED TO JUST DOIN' THE DUMPING, NOT THE FISHING.
I HEAR YA, BUT MARIO WANTS US TO BE SURE THIS ONE'S STIFF. THIS IS KITRINA, HIS LITTLE SISTER WE'RE TALKIN' HERE.
LET'S OPEN 'ER UP AND SEE.
UH-OH.
GONE.
BAFF
UNNH!
BAFF
GAHK!

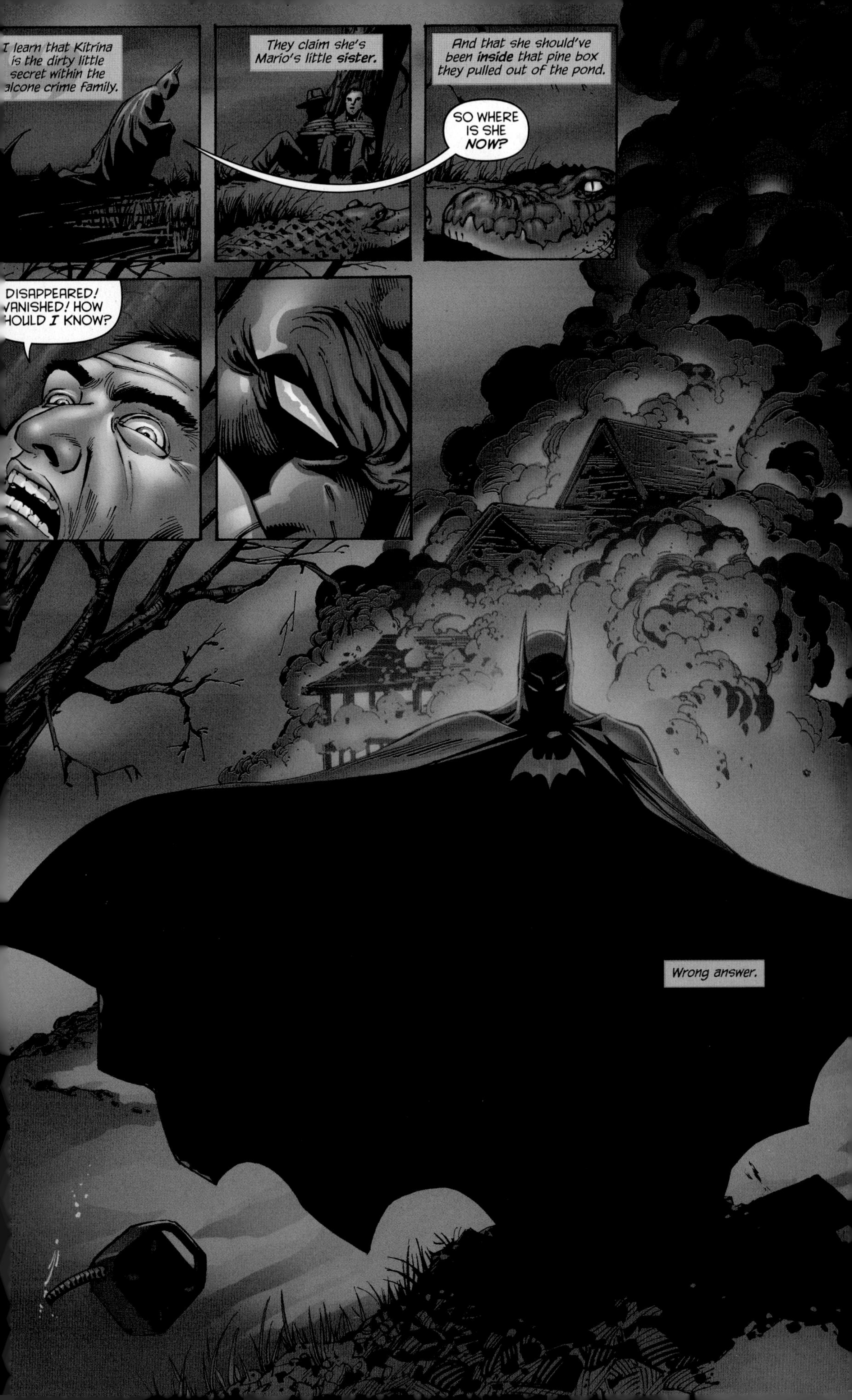

I learn that Kitrina is the dirty little secret within the alcone crime family.
They claim she's Mario's little sister.
And that she should've been inside that pine box they pulled out of the pond.
SO WHERE IS SHE NOW?
DISAPPEARED! VANISHED! HOW HOULD I KNOW?
Wrong answer.

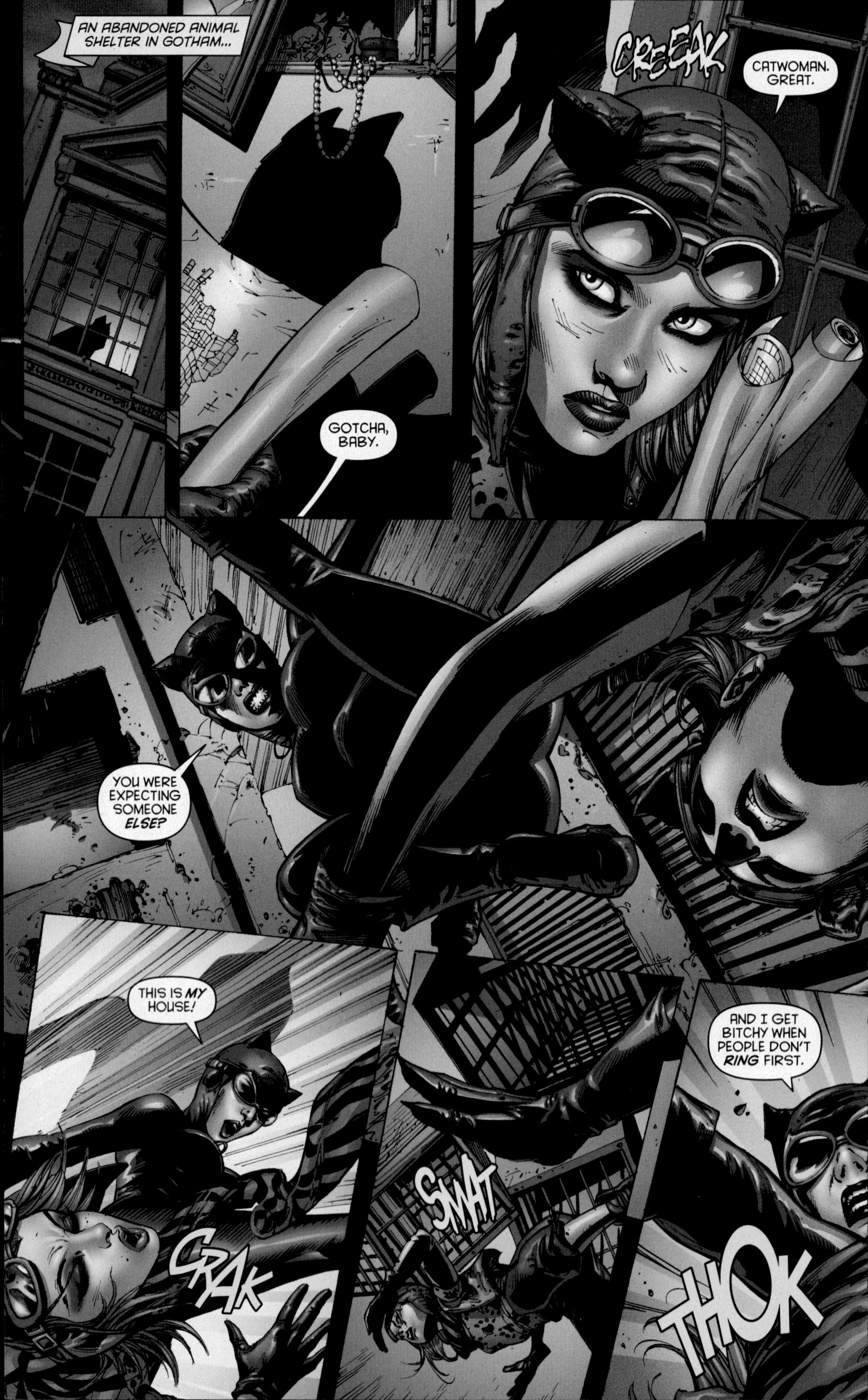
AN ABANDONED ANIMAL SHELTER IN GOTHAM...
GOTCHA, BABY.
CREEAK
CATWOMAN. GREAT.
YOU WERE EXPECTING SOMEONE ELSE?
THIS IS MY HOUSE!
CRAK
SMAT
AND I GET BITCHY WHEN PEOPLE DON'T RING FIRST.
THOK

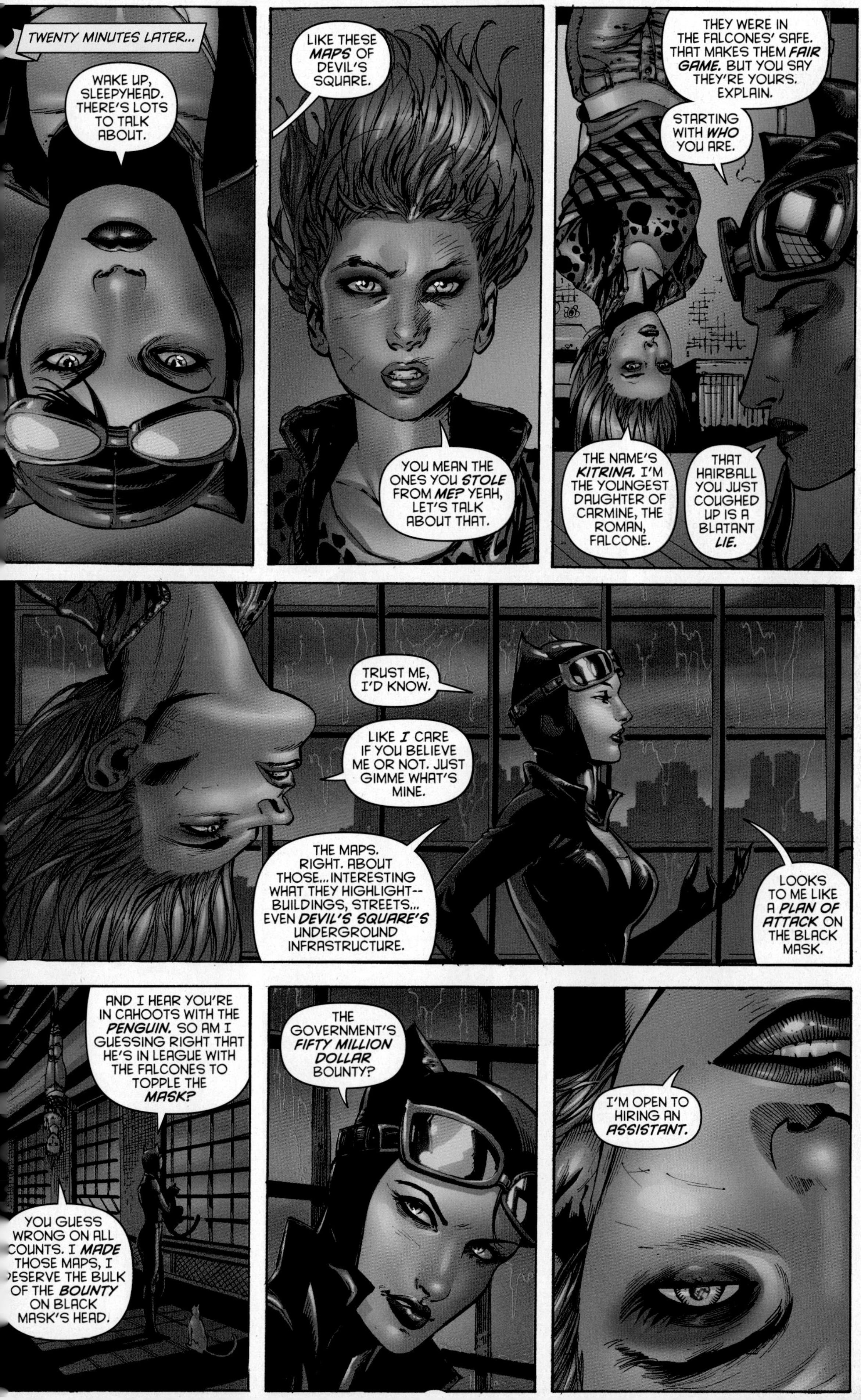
TWENTY MINUTES LATER...
WAKE UP, SLEEPYHEAD. THERE'S LOTS TO TALK ABOUT.
LIKE THESE MAPS OF DEVIL'S SQUARE.
YOU MEAN THE ONES YOU STOLE FROM ME? YEAH, LET'S TALK ABOUT THAT.
THEY WERE IN THE FALCONES' SAFE. THAT MAKES THEM FAIR GAME. BUT YOU SAY THEY'RE YOURS. EXPLAIN.
STARTING WITH WHO YOU ARE.
THE NAME'S KITRINA. I'M THE YOUNGEST DAUGHTER OF CARMINE, THE ROMAN, FALCONE.
THAT HAIRBALL YOU JUST COUGHED UP IS A BLATANT LIE.
TRUST ME, I'D KNOW.
LIKE I CARE IF YOU BELIEVE ME OR NOT. JUST GIMME WHAT'S MINE.
THE MAPS. RIGHT. ABOUT THOSE... INTERESTING WHAT THEY HIGHLIGHT-- BUILDINGS, STREETS... EVEN DEVIL'S SQUARE'S UNDERGROUND INFRASTRUCTURE.
LOOKS TO ME LIKE A PLAN OF ATTACK ON THE BLACK MASK.
AND I HEAR YOU'RE IN CAHOOTS WITH THE PENGUIN. SO AM I GUESSING RIGHT THAT HE'S IN LEAGUE WITH THE FALCONES TO TOPPLE THE MASK?
YOU GUESS WRONG ON ALL COUNTS. I MADE THOSE MAPS, I DESERVE THE BULK OF THE BOUNTY ON BLACK MASK'S HEAD.
THE GOVERNMENT'S FIFTY MILLION DOLLAR BOUNTY?
I'M OPEN TO HIRING AN ASSISTANT.

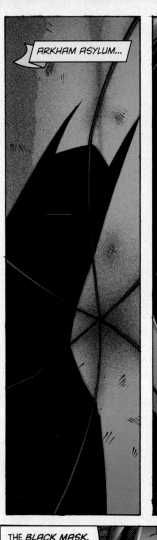

SORRY TO KEEP YOU WAITING, **BATMAN.** BUT YOU COULD'VE WAITED IN MY OFFICE.

I SEIZED THE OPPORTUNITY TO HAVE A LOOK AROUND THE ASYLUM'S NEW ADDITIONS. PARTICULARLY THE **PANIC ROOM,** DR. ARKHAM.

IT'S THE SAFEST PLACE IN ALL OF GOTHAM CITY. STRONG AS ANY NUCLEAR SHELTER. A BIT **COLD** AT THE MOMENT, BUT THAT WILL SOON BE FIXED.

SMART MOVE. ESPECIALLY CONSIDERING THE ASYLUM'S RECENT SECURITY BREACHES.

BUT I'M HERE TO TALK ABOUT SOMETHING ELSE. **SOMEONE** ELSE...

THE **BLACK MASK.** I'VE ASSEMBLED A **PROFILE** ON HIM AND WOULD LIKE TO SEE IF HE MATCHES ANYONE YOU'VE SEEN HERE BEFORE.

I'VE ALREADY PUT MY OWN CHARACTER STUDY TOGETHER BASED ON WHAT I KNOW. BUT I DON'T BELIEVE HE'S EVER BEEN A PATIENT HERE...

GOOD. THEN WE CAN COMPARE NOTES. YOU START.

AS A **PERSON,** I'D GUESS HE'S HIGHLY INTELLIGENT, NEAR GENIUS-LEVEL. AND HE OOZES CHARISMA.

PEOPLE **TRUST** HIM--TO THE POINT OF FOLLOWING HIM NO MATTER WHERE HE LEADS.

HE'S WEALTHY. PERHAPS NEWFOUND WEALTH...WHICH WOULD EXPLAIN HIS STARTLINGLY ABRUPT RISE TO POWER.

HE'S NOT YOUR EVERY-DAY CRIMINAL MASTERMIND, BATMAN.

I'VE ALREADY COME TO MOST OF THOSE CONCLUSIONS MYSELF, DOCTOR. BUT I'M MORE INTERESTED IN HIS *WEAKNESSES*.

HE'S DERANGED, OBSESSED WITH POWER, UNSYMPATHETIC...

THOUGH HE ATTEMPTED TO KEEP HIS ARMY-- THE PATIENTS TAKEN FROM ME-- MEDICATED. SO THERE MUST BE SYMPATHY...

HE'S MEDICATING THEM AND *BRAIN-WASHING* THEM TO SERVE ONLY *HIS* NEEDS.

I'M LOOKING AT A DELUSIONAL, BLACK-HEARTED, CHARISMATIC, LEADER-TYPE. A MODERN DAY HITLER WOULDN'T BE TOO FAR OFF BASE, DOCTOR.

LIKE I SAID, WHOEVER HE IS, HE'S NEVER BEEN UNDER MY CARE.

I'VE SEEN *EVIL* BEFORE.

I'M SURE YOU *HAVE*. AND YOU'RE AFRAID OF IT. THAT EXPLAINS THE BULGE IN YOUR COAT.

ONLY A *TEMPORARY* MEASURE, BATMAN. UNTIL THE ASYLUM IS COMPLETE, I MUST TAKE EVERY PRECAUTION.

RUBBER BULLETS. I REFUSE TO USE LETHAL FORCE EVEN AT MY OWN PERIL.

IF IT BUYS ME ENOUGH TIME TO MAKE IT DOWN HERE WHERE IT'S SAFE, IT'S SERVED ITS PURPOSE.

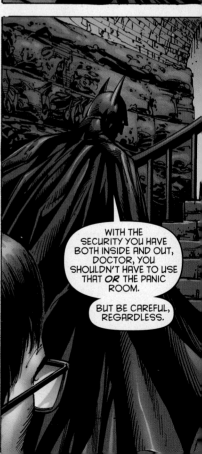

WITH THE SECURITY YOU HAVE BOTH INSIDE AND OUT, DOCTOR, YOU SHOULDN'T HAVE TO USE THAT *OR* THE PANIC ROOM.

BUT BE CAREFUL, REGARDLESS.

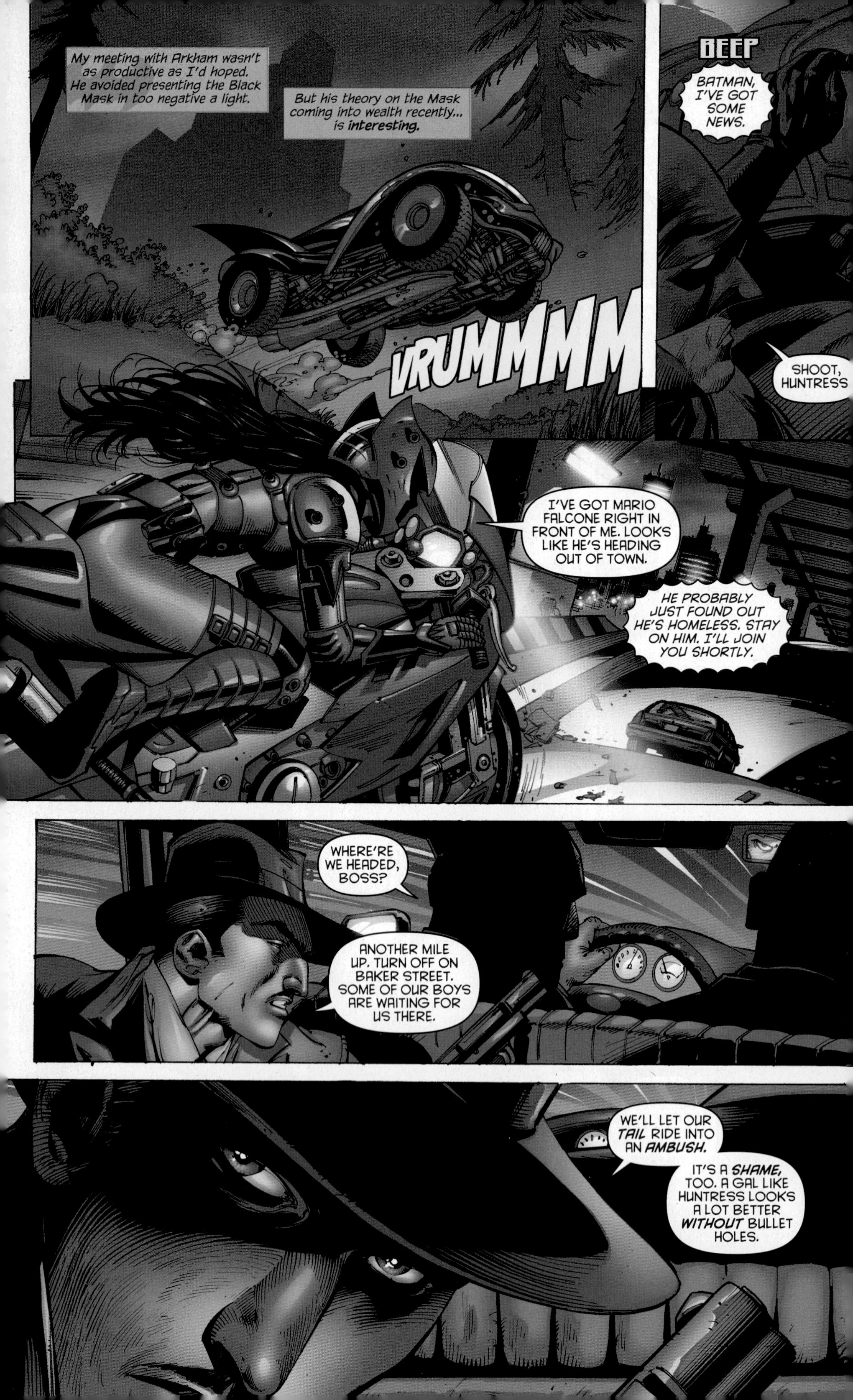
My meeting with Arkham wasn't as productive as I'd hoped. He avoided presenting the Black Mask in too negative a light.
But his theory on the Mask coming into wealth recently... is interesting.
VRUMMMM
BEEP
BATMAN, I'VE GOT SOME NEWS.
SHOOT, HUNTRESS
I'VE GOT MARIO FALCONE RIGHT IN FRONT OF ME. LOOKS LIKE HE'S HEADING OUT OF TOWN.
HE PROBABLY JUST FOUND OUT HE'S HOMELESS. STAY ON HIM. I'LL JOIN YOU SHORTLY.
WHERE'RE WE HEADED, BOSS?
ANOTHER MILE UP. TURN OFF ON BAKER STREET. SOME OF OUR BOYS ARE WAITING FOR US THERE.
WE'LL LET OUR TAIL RIDE INTO AN AMBUSH.
IT'S A SHAME, TOO. A GAL LIKE HUNTRESS LOOKS A LOT BETTER WITHOUT BULLET HOLES.

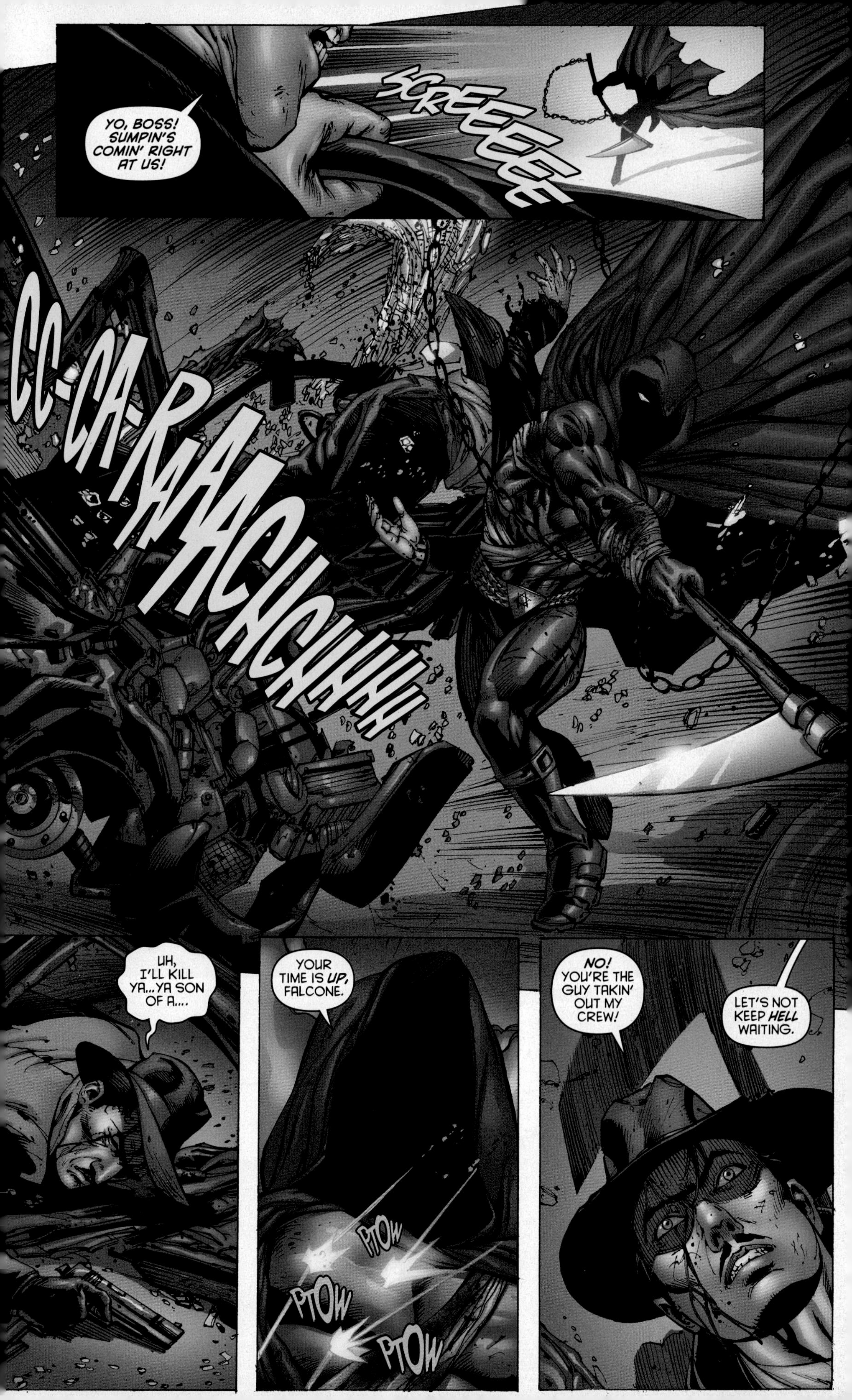
YO, BOSS! SUMPIN'S COMIN' RIGHT AT US!
SCREEEEE
CC-CA-RAAACHCHHHH
UH, I'LL KILL YA...YA SON OF A....
YOUR TIME IS UP, FALCONE.
PTOW
PTOW
PTOW
NO! YOU'RE THE GUY TAKIN' OUT MY CREW!
LET'S NOT KEEP HELL WAITING.

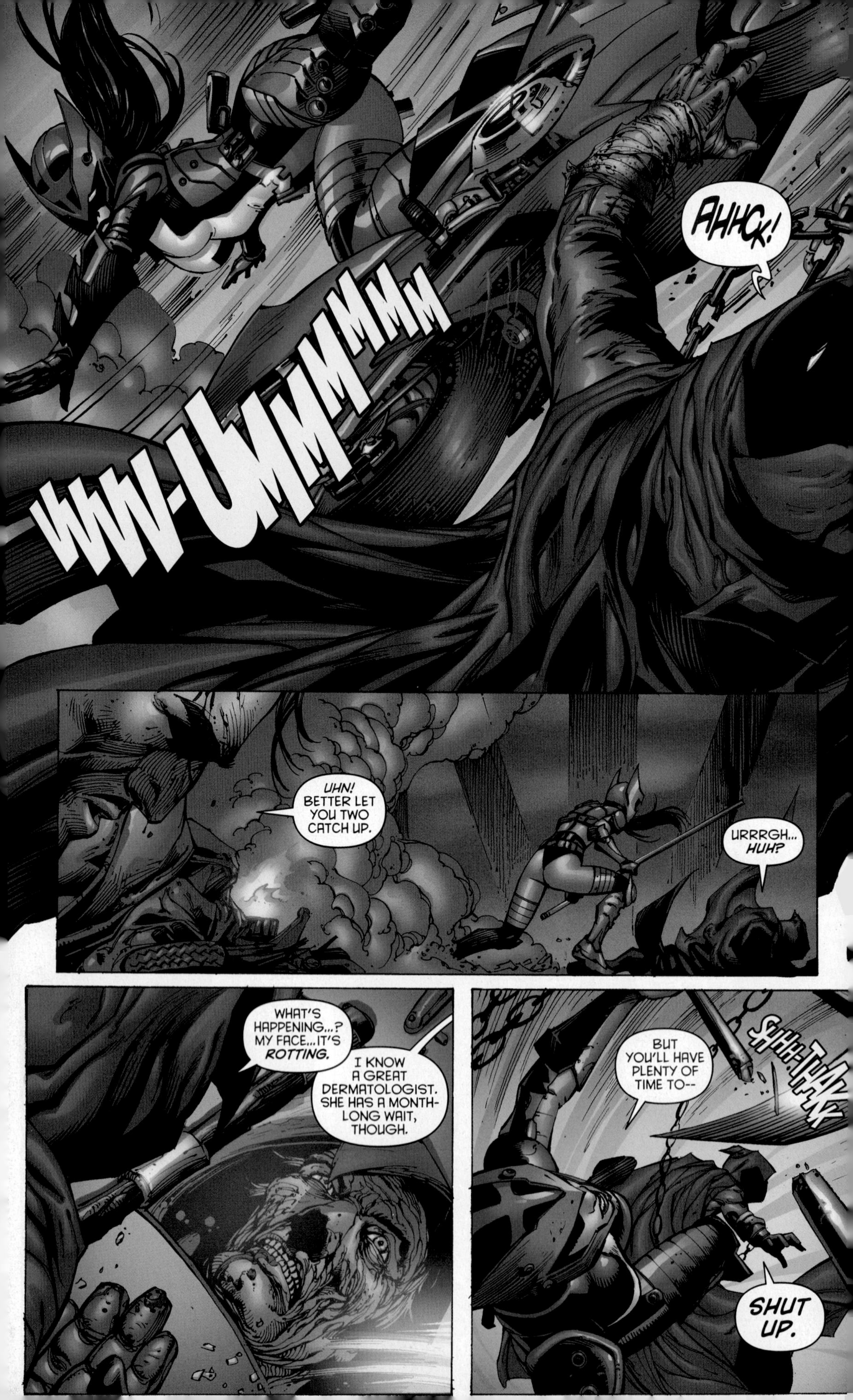
AHHCK!
VVVV-UMMMMMMM
UHN! BETTER LET YOU TWO CATCH UP.
URRRGH... HUH?
WHAT'S HAPPENING...? MY FACE...IT'S ROTTING.
I KNOW A GREAT DERMATOLOGIST. SHE HAS A MONTH-LONG WAIT, THOUGH.
BUT YOU'LL HAVE PLENTY OF TIME TO--
SHHH-THAKK
SHUT UP.

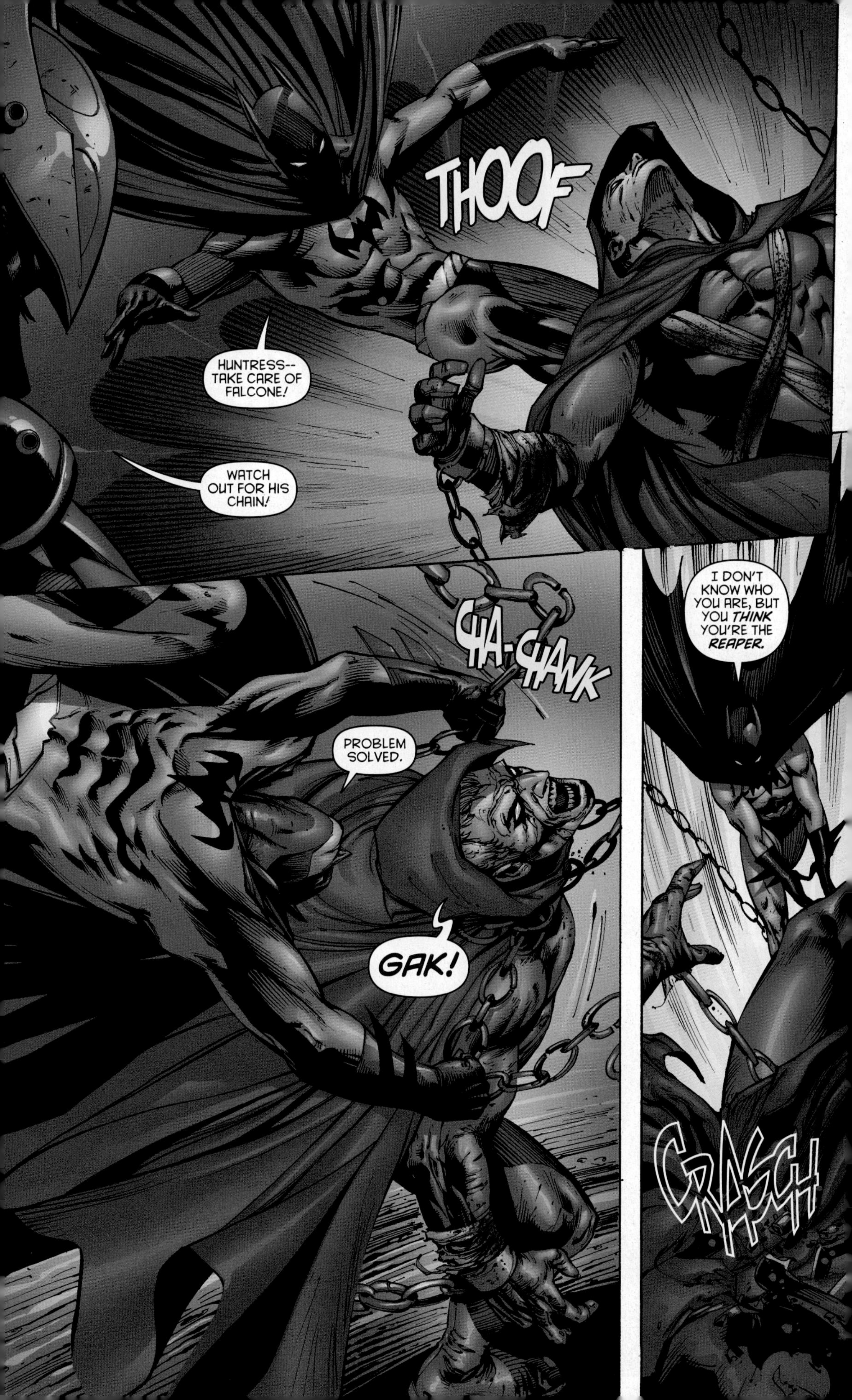
THOOF
HUNTRESS--TAKE CARE OF FALCONE!
WATCH OUT FOR HIS CHAIN!
CHA-CHANK
PROBLEM SOLVED.
GAK!
I DON'T KNOW WHO YOU ARE, BUT YOU *THINK* YOU'RE THE *REAPER.*
CRASCH

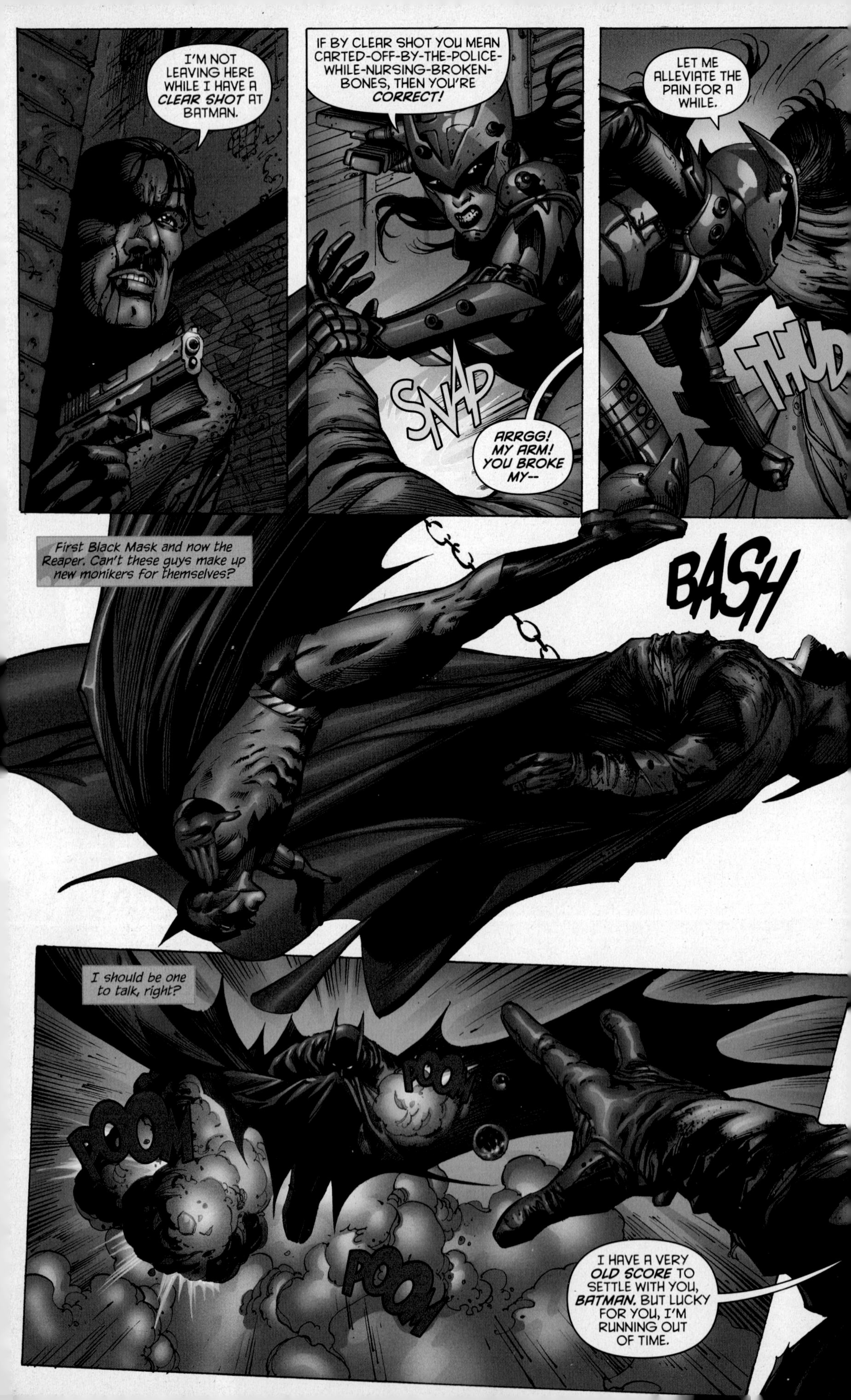
I'M NOT LEAVING HERE WHILE I HAVE A CLEAR SHOT AT BATMAN.
IF BY CLEAR SHOT YOU MEAN CARTED-OFF-BY-THE-POLICE-WHILE-NURSING-BROKEN-BONES, THEN YOU'RE CORRECT!
SNAP
ARRGG! MY ARM! YOU BROKE MY--
LET ME ALLEVIATE THE PAIN FOR A WHILE.
THUD
First Black Mask and now the Reaper. Can't these guys make up new monikers for themselves?
BASH
I should be one to talk, right?
POOM
POOM
POOM
I HAVE A VERY OLD SCORE TO SETTLE WITH YOU, BATMAN. BUT LUCKY FOR YOU, I'M RUNNING OUT OF TIME.

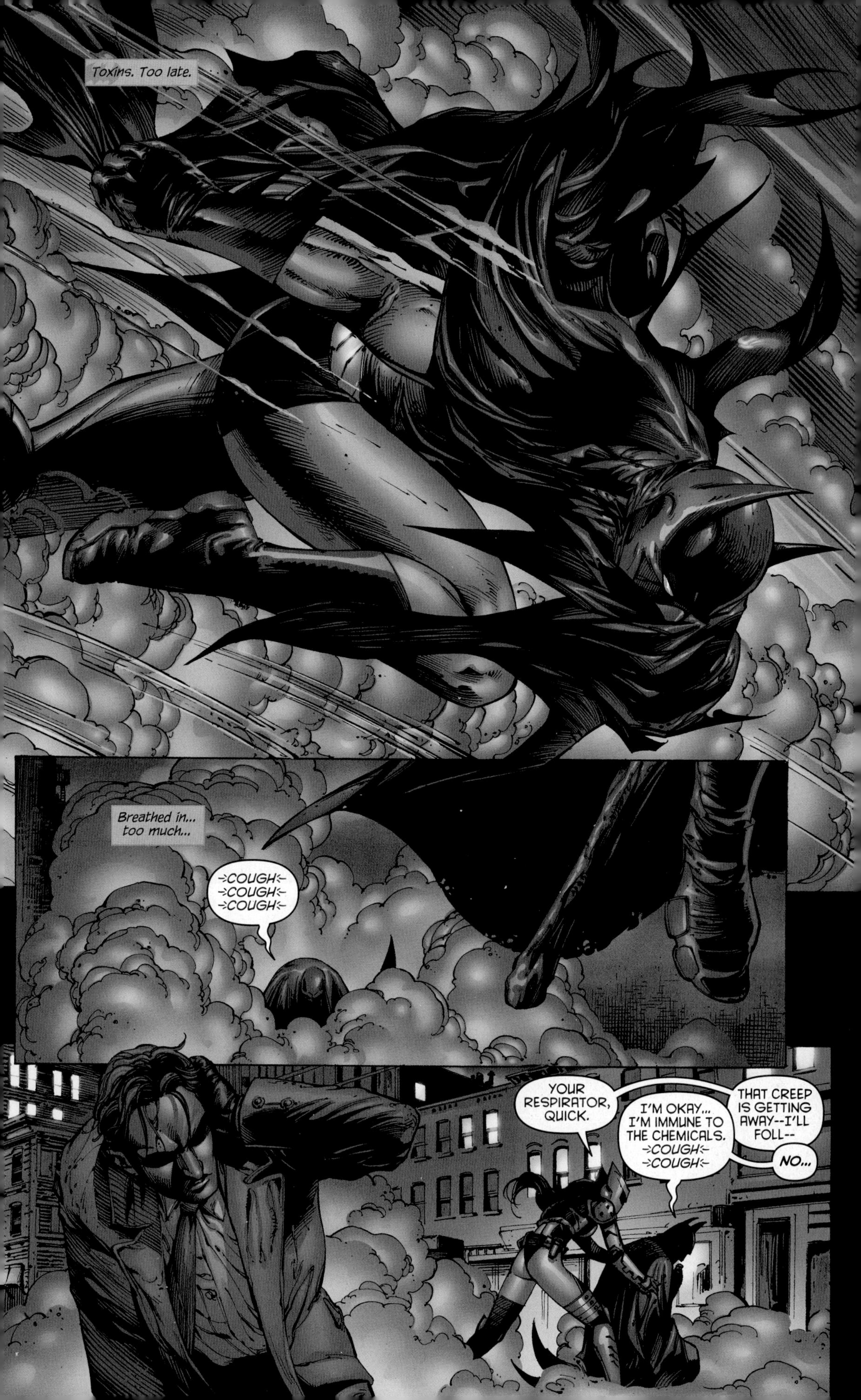
Toxins. Too late.
Breathed in... too much...
COUGH COUGH COUGH
YOUR RESPIRATOR, QUICK.
I'M OKAY... I'M IMMUNE TO THE CHEMICALS. COUGH COUGH
THAT CREEP IS GETTING AWAY--I'LL FOLL--
NO...

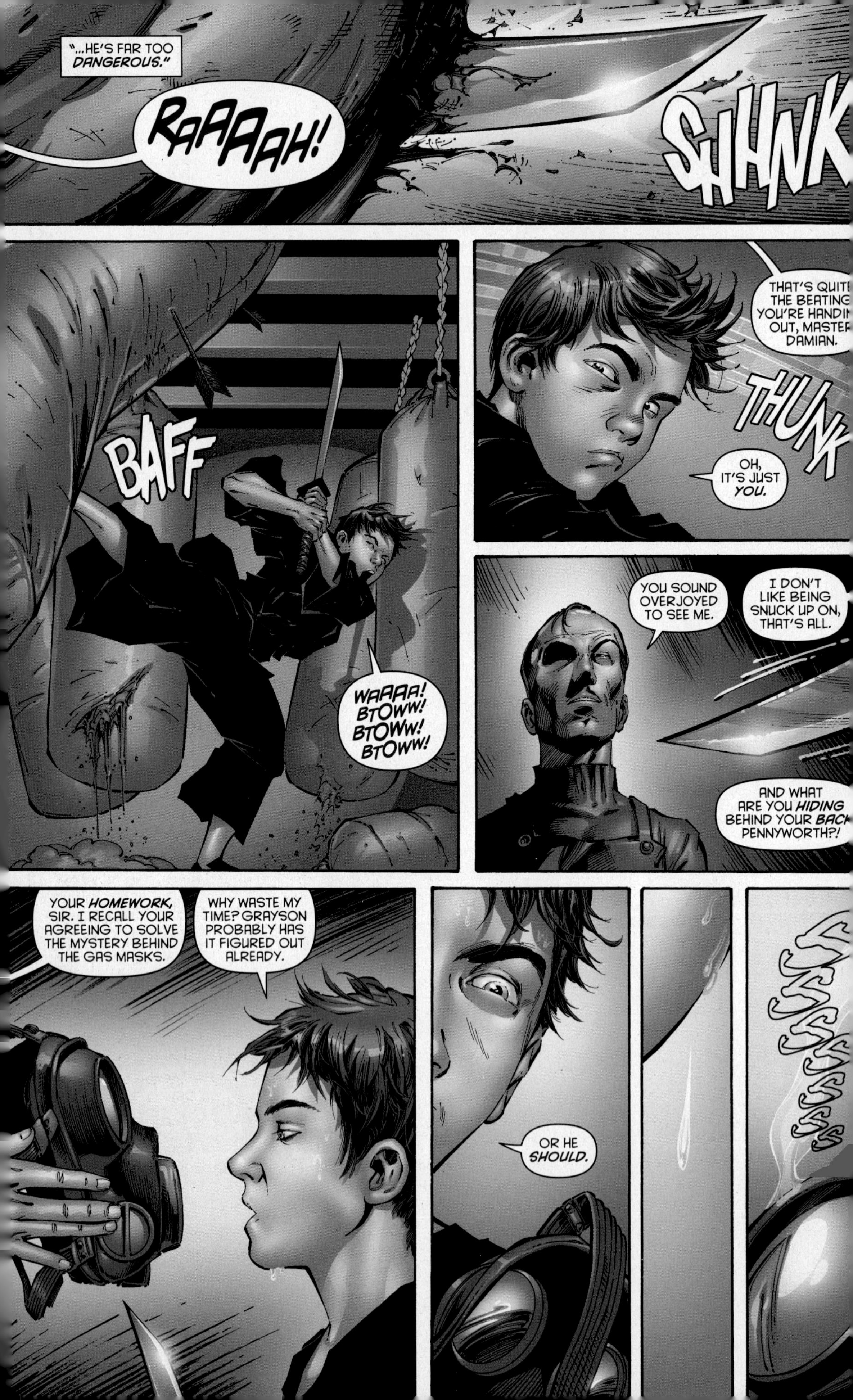
"...HE'S FAR TOO DANGEROUS."
RAAAAAH!
SHHNK
BAFF
WAAAA! BTOWW! BTOWW! BTOWW!
THAT'S QUITE THE BEATING YOU'RE HANDIN OUT, MASTER DAMIAN.
THUNK
OH, IT'S JUST YOU.
YOU SOUND OVERJOYED TO SEE ME.
I DON'T LIKE BEING SNUCK UP ON, THAT'S ALL.
AND WHAT ARE YOU HIDING BEHIND YOUR BACK PENNYWORTH?!
YOUR HOMEWORK, SIR. I RECALL YOUR AGREEING TO SOLVE THE MYSTERY BEHIND THE GAS MASKS.
WHY WASTE MY TIME? GRAYSON PROBABLY HAS IT FIGURED OUT ALREADY.
OR HE SHOULD.
SSSSSSSS

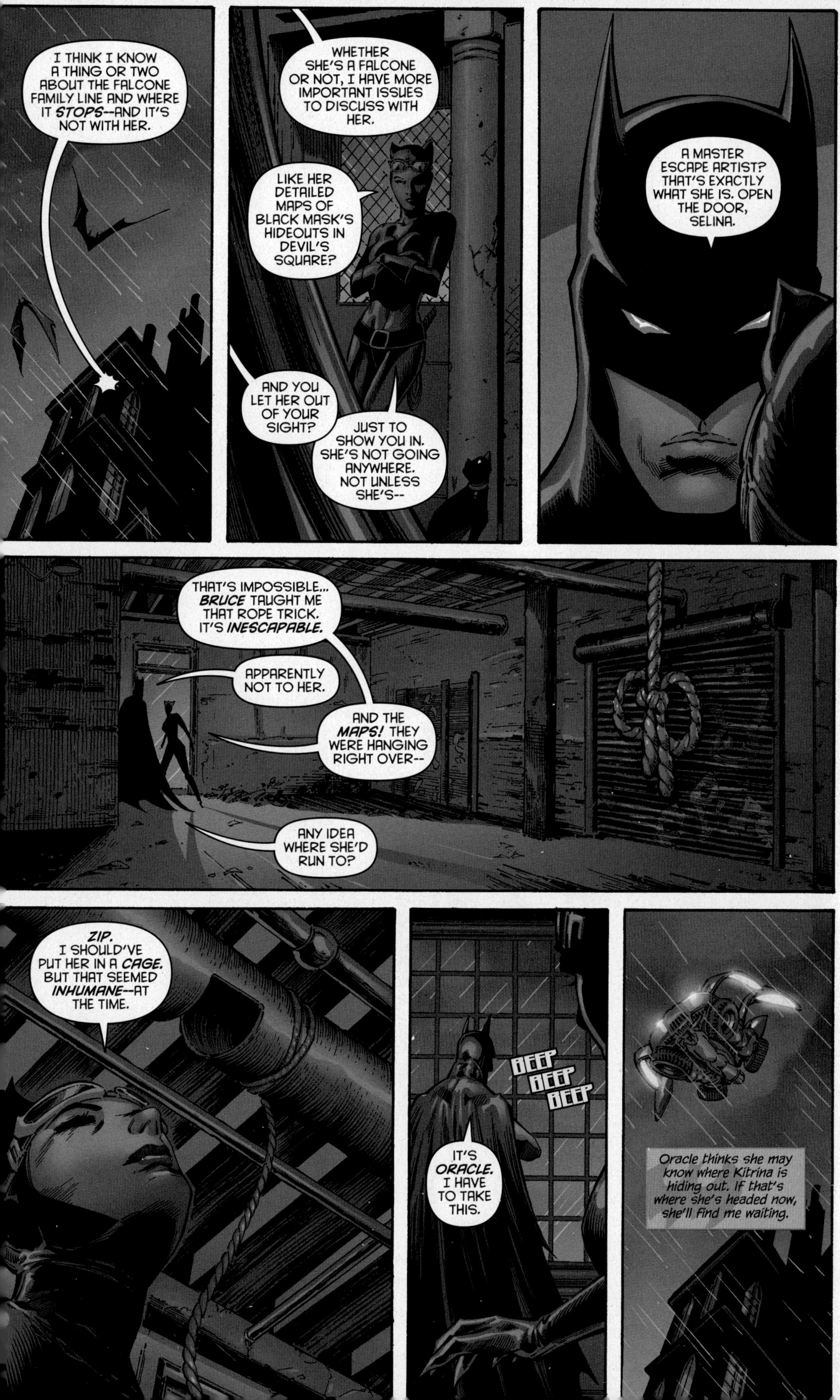

I THINK I KNOW A THING OR TWO ABOUT THE FALCONE FAMILY LINE AND WHERE IT *STOPS*--AND IT'S NOT WITH HER.
WHETHER SHE'S A FALCONE OR NOT, I HAVE MORE IMPORTANT ISSUES TO DISCUSS WITH HER.
LIKE HER DETAILED MAPS OF BLACK MASK'S HIDEOUTS IN DEVIL'S SQUARE?
AND YOU LET HER OUT OF YOUR SIGHT?
JUST TO SHOW YOU IN. SHE'S NOT GOING ANYWHERE. NOT UNLESS SHE'S--
A MASTER ESCAPE ARTIST? THAT'S EXACTLY WHAT SHE IS. OPEN THE DOOR, SELINA.
THAT'S IMPOSSIBLE... *BRUCE* TAUGHT ME THAT ROPE TRICK. IT'S *INESCAPABLE.*
APPARENTLY NOT TO HER.
AND THE *MAPS!* THEY WERE HANGING RIGHT OVER--
ANY IDEA WHERE SHE'D RUN TO?
ZIP. I SHOULD'VE PUT HER IN A *CAGE.* BUT THAT SEEMED *INHUMANE*--AT THE TIME.
BEEP BEEP BEEP
IT'S *ORACLE.* I HAVE TO TAKE THIS.
Oracle thinks she may know where Kitrina is hiding out. If that's where she's headed now, she'll find me waiting.

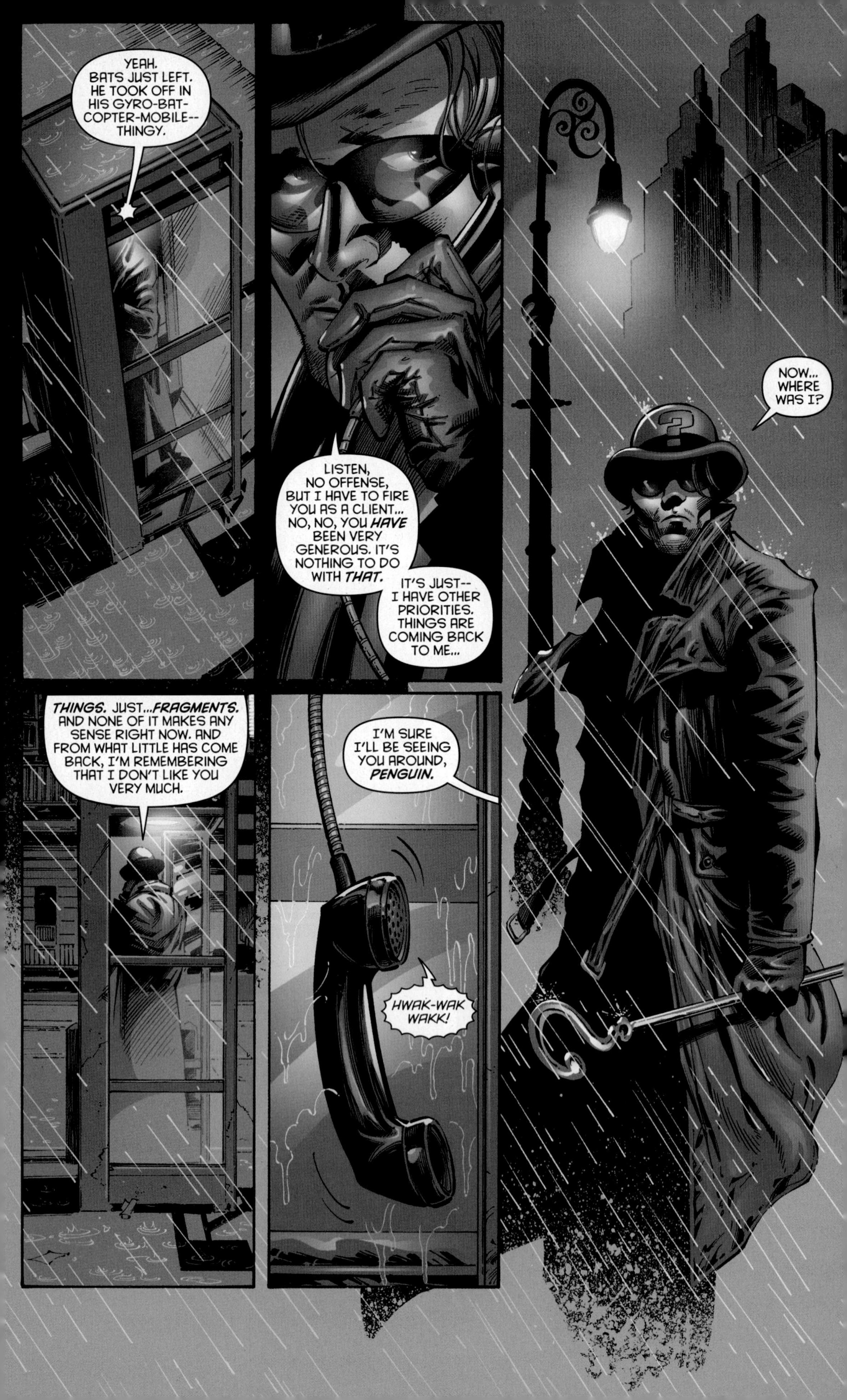
YEAH. BATS JUST LEFT. HE TOOK OFF IN HIS GYRO-BAT-COPTER-MOBILE--THINGY.
LISTEN, NO OFFENSE, BUT I HAVE TO FIRE YOU AS A CLIENT... NO, NO, YOU *HAVE* BEEN VERY GENEROUS. IT'S NOTHING TO DO WITH *THAT.*
IT'S JUST-- I HAVE OTHER PRIORITIES. THINGS ARE COMING BACK TO ME...
THINGS. JUST...*FRAGMENTS.* AND NONE OF IT MAKES ANY SENSE RIGHT NOW. AND FROM WHAT LITTLE HAS COME BACK, I'M REMEMBERING THAT I DON'T LIKE YOU VERY MUCH.
I'M SURE I'LL BE SEEING YOU AROUND, *PENGUIN.*
HWAK-WAK WAKK!
NOW... WHERE WAS I?

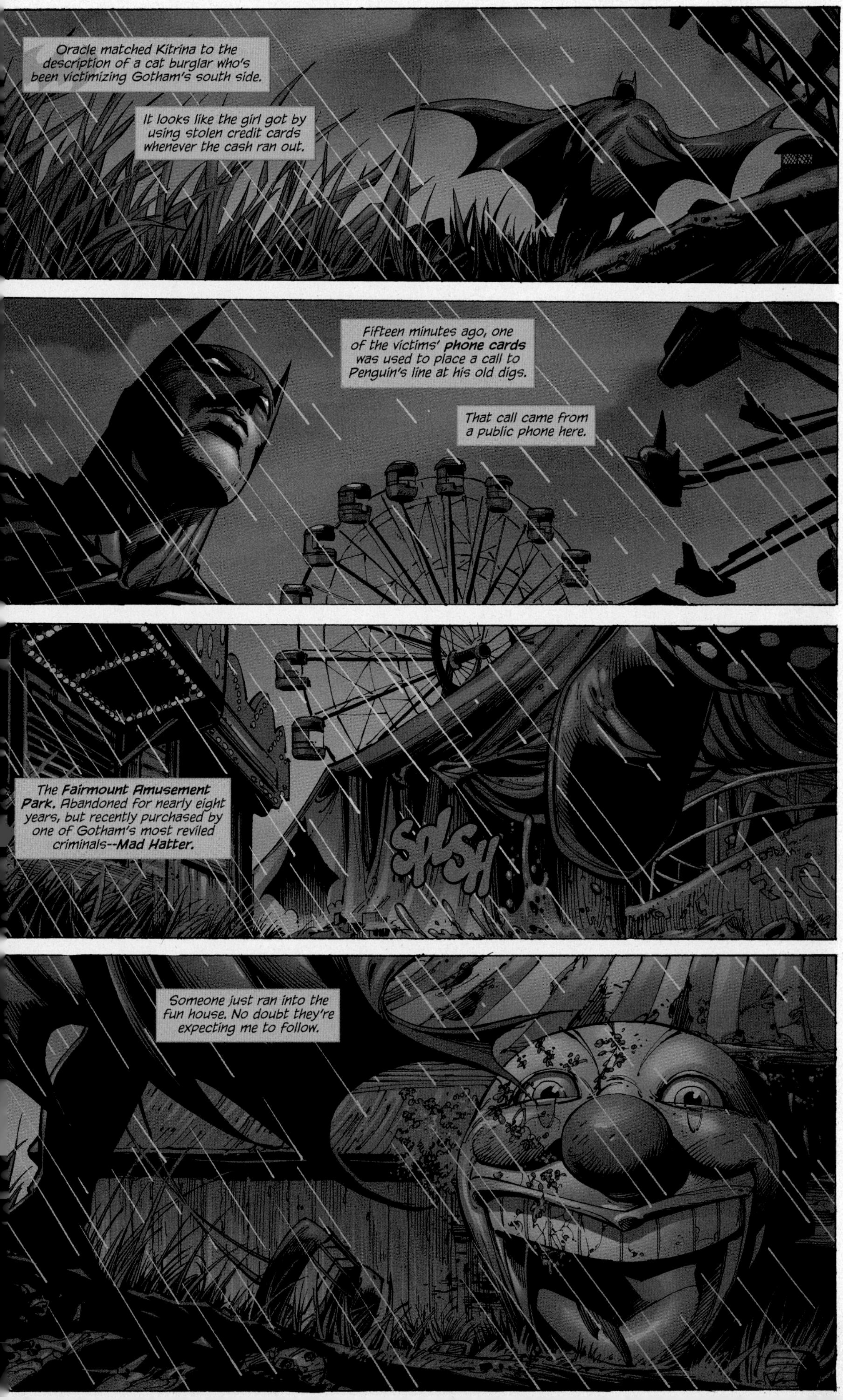

Oracle matched Kitrina to the description of a cat burglar who's been victimizing Gotham's south side.
It looks like the girl got by using stolen credit cards whenever the cash ran out.
Fifteen minutes ago, one of the victims' **phone cards** was used to place a call to Penguin's line at his old digs.
That call came from a public phone here.
The **Fairmount Amusement Park.** Abandoned for nearly eight years, but recently purchased by one of Gotham's most reviled criminals--**Mad Hatter.**
SPLSH
Someone just ran into the fun house. No doubt they're expecting me to follow.

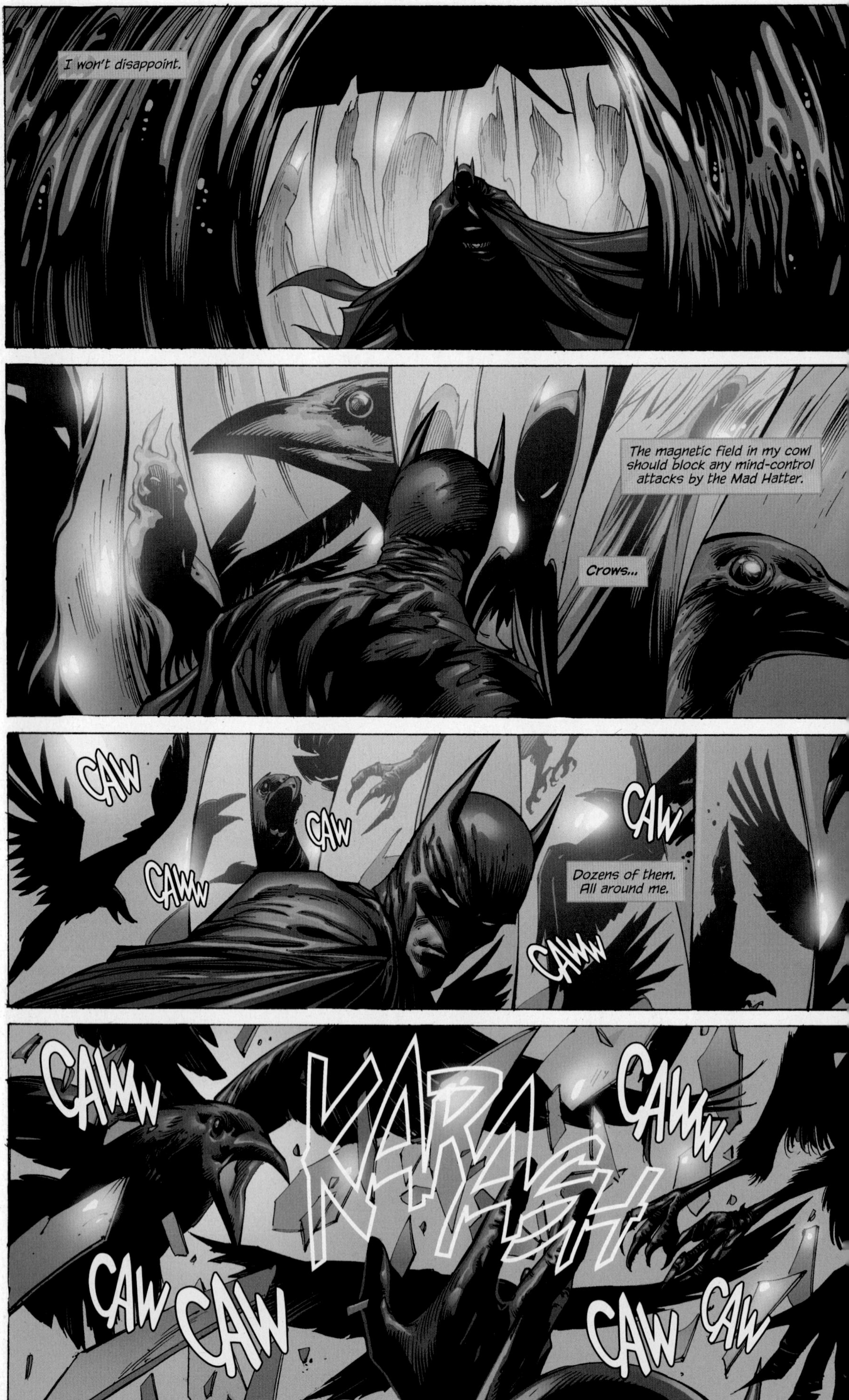

I won't disappoint.
The magnetic field in my cowl should block any mind-control attacks by the Mad Hatter.
Crows...
CAW
CAW
CAWW
CAW
Dozens of them. All around me.
CAWW
CAWW
KARASH
CAWW
CAW
CAW
CAW
CAW

Tearing into my flesh!

CAWW

CAW CAW

CAW CAWW CAWW

CAW CAWW CAW

Something on their beaks...

Poison...

CKKLIKKSHH KKKSHH

I've...got to...get out!

LOOK AT HIM. LOOKS LIKE A WOUNDED BIRD.

'CEPT HE'S A *BAT.*

WHO...?

HE DON'T LOOK SO TOUGH NOW, HUH?

THE BOSS LIKES HIM. HE'S HIS ONLY SHOT.

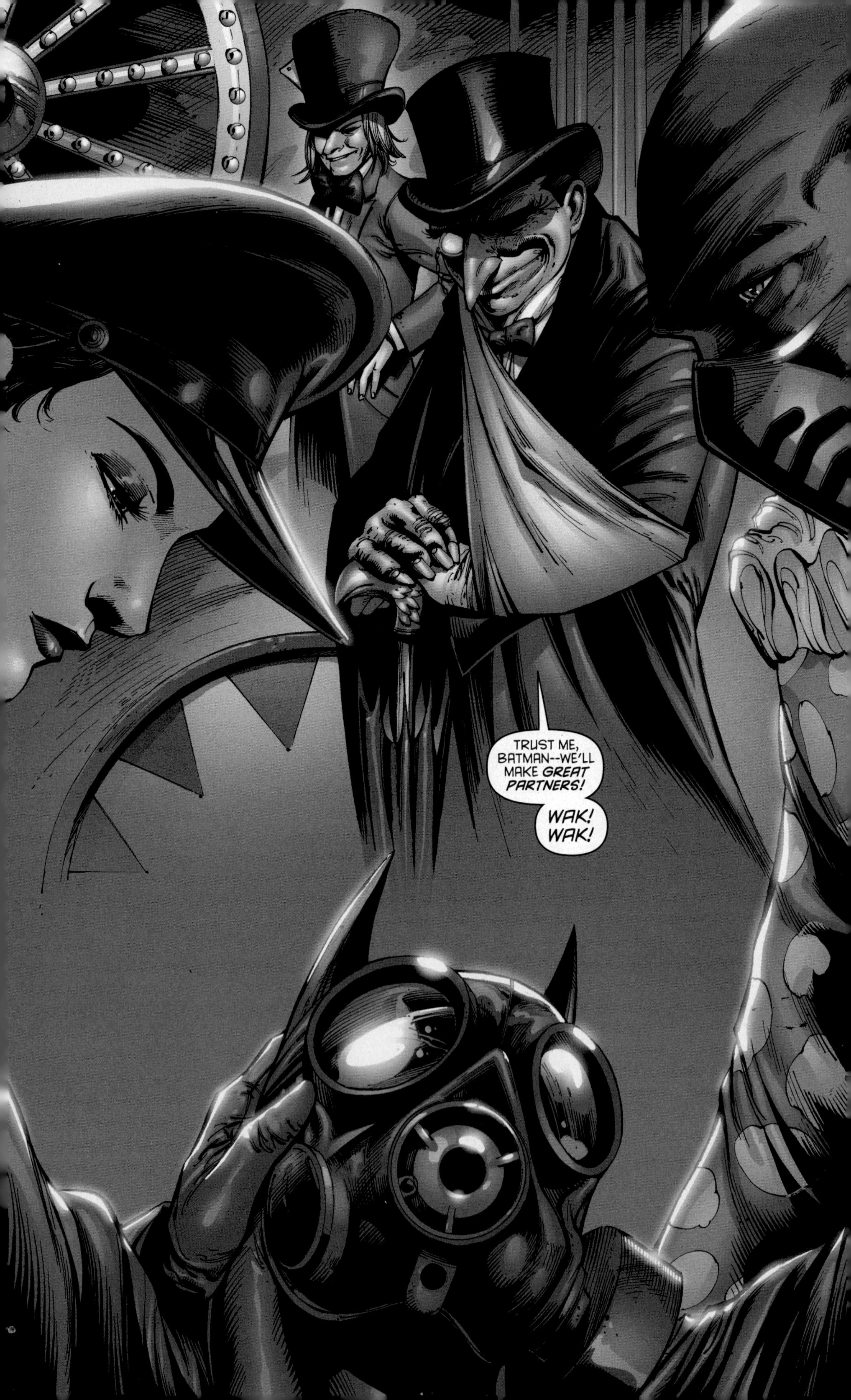
TRUST ME, BATMAN--WE'LL MAKE GREAT PARTNERS!
WAK! WAK!

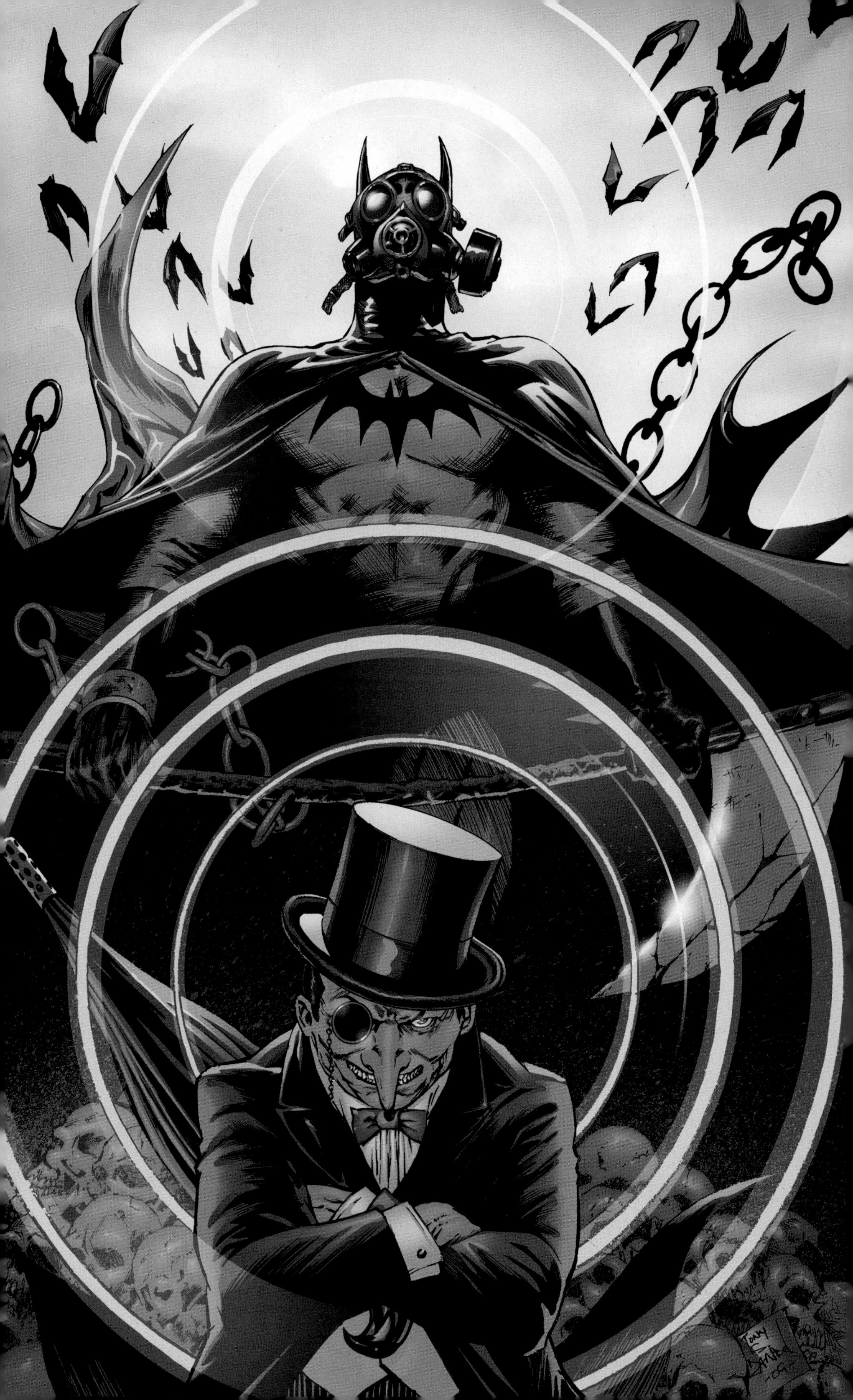

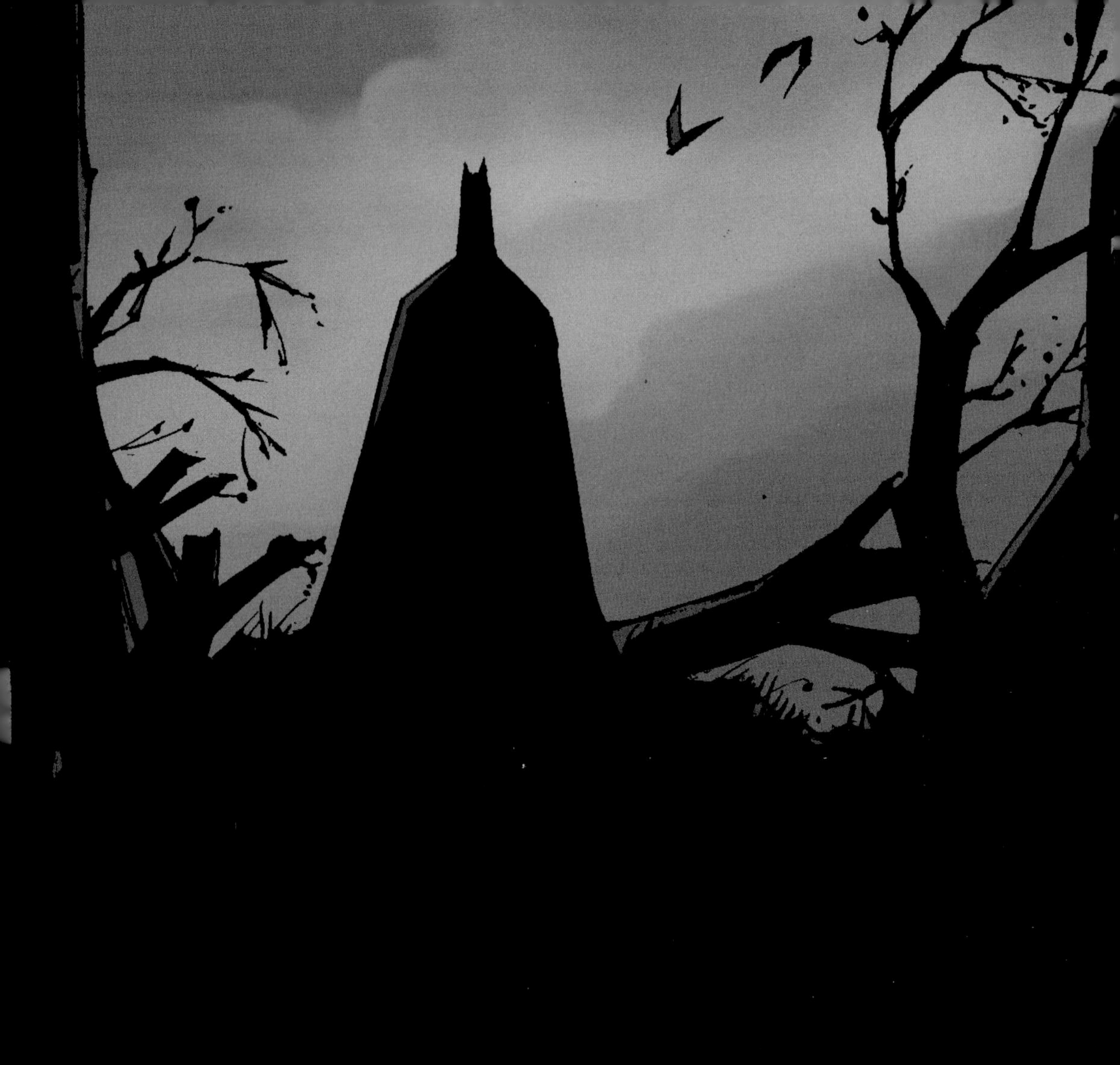

"You shouldn't feel any remorse for what you have to do to survive here."

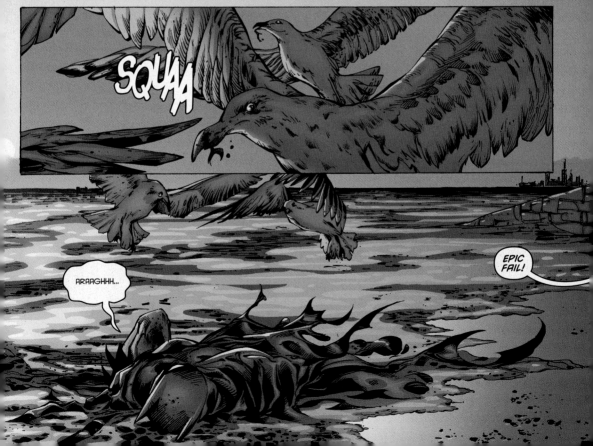

SQUAA

GOTHAM HARBOR. NOW.

SQUAA

SQUAA

SQUAA

ARAAGHHH...

EPIC FAIL!

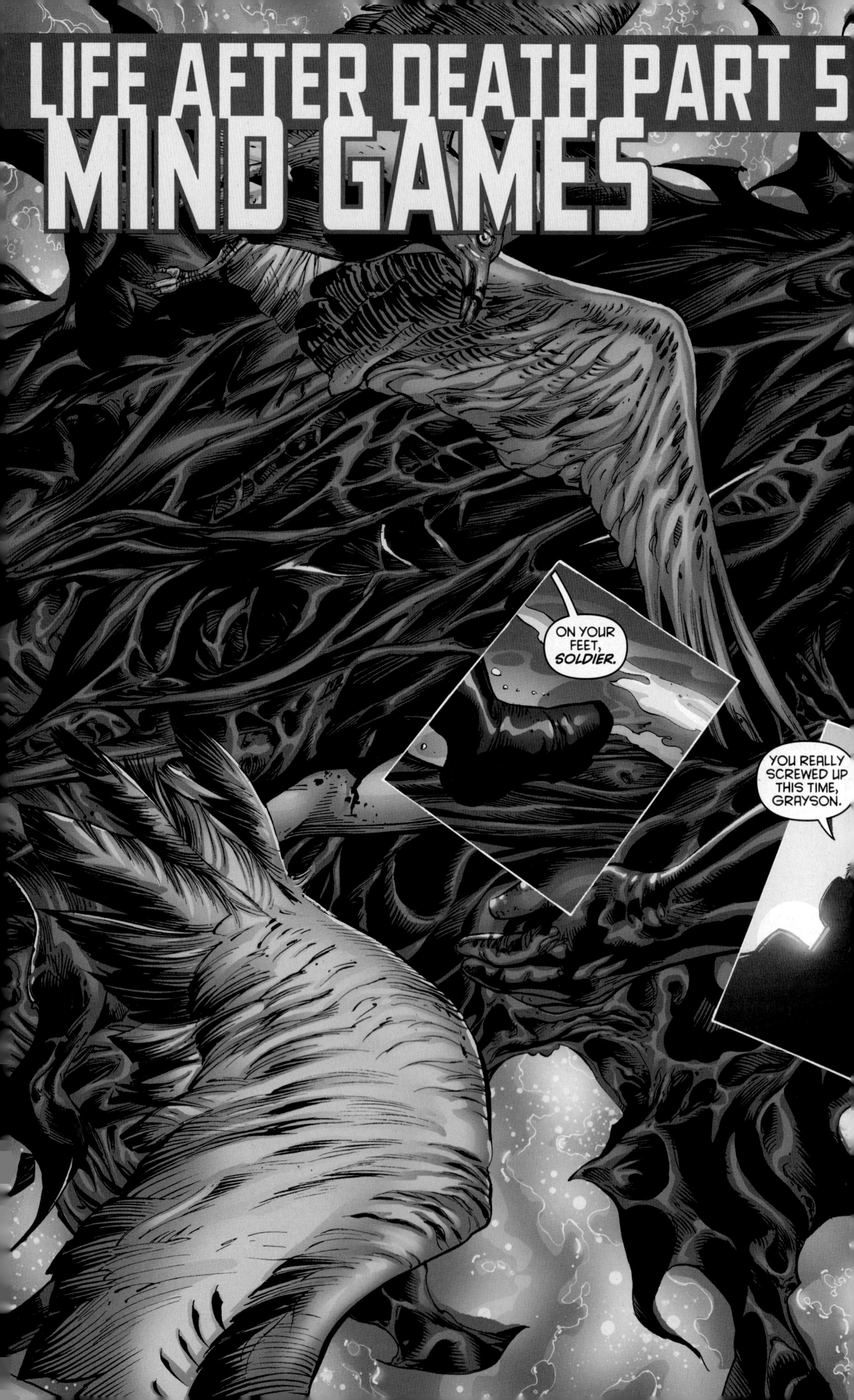
LIFE AFTER DEATH PART 5
MIND GAMES
ON YOUR FEET, SOLDIER.
YOU REALLY SCREWED UP THIS TIME, GRAYSON.

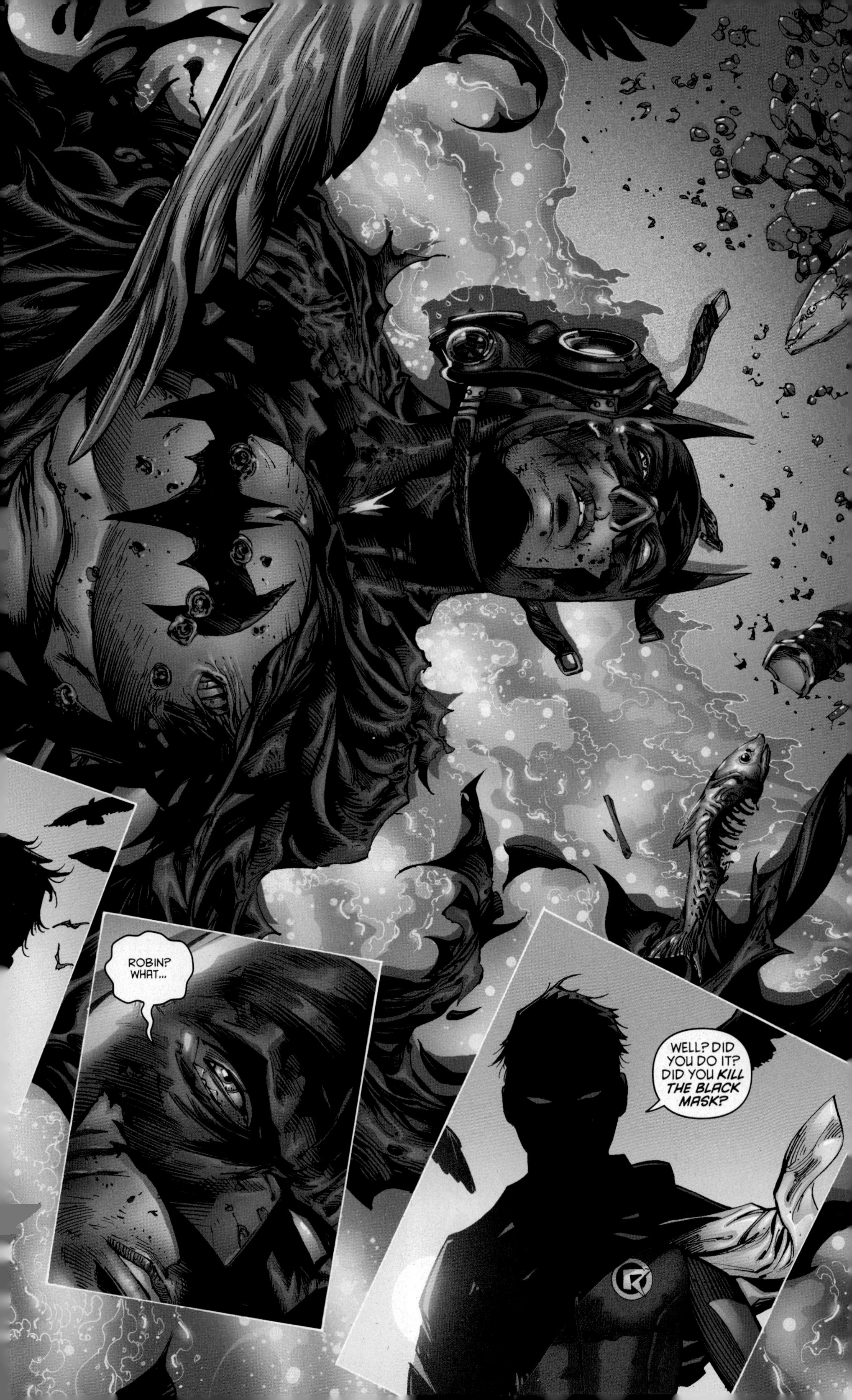
ROBIN? WHAT...
WELL? DID YOU DO IT? DID YOU KILL THE BLACK MASK?

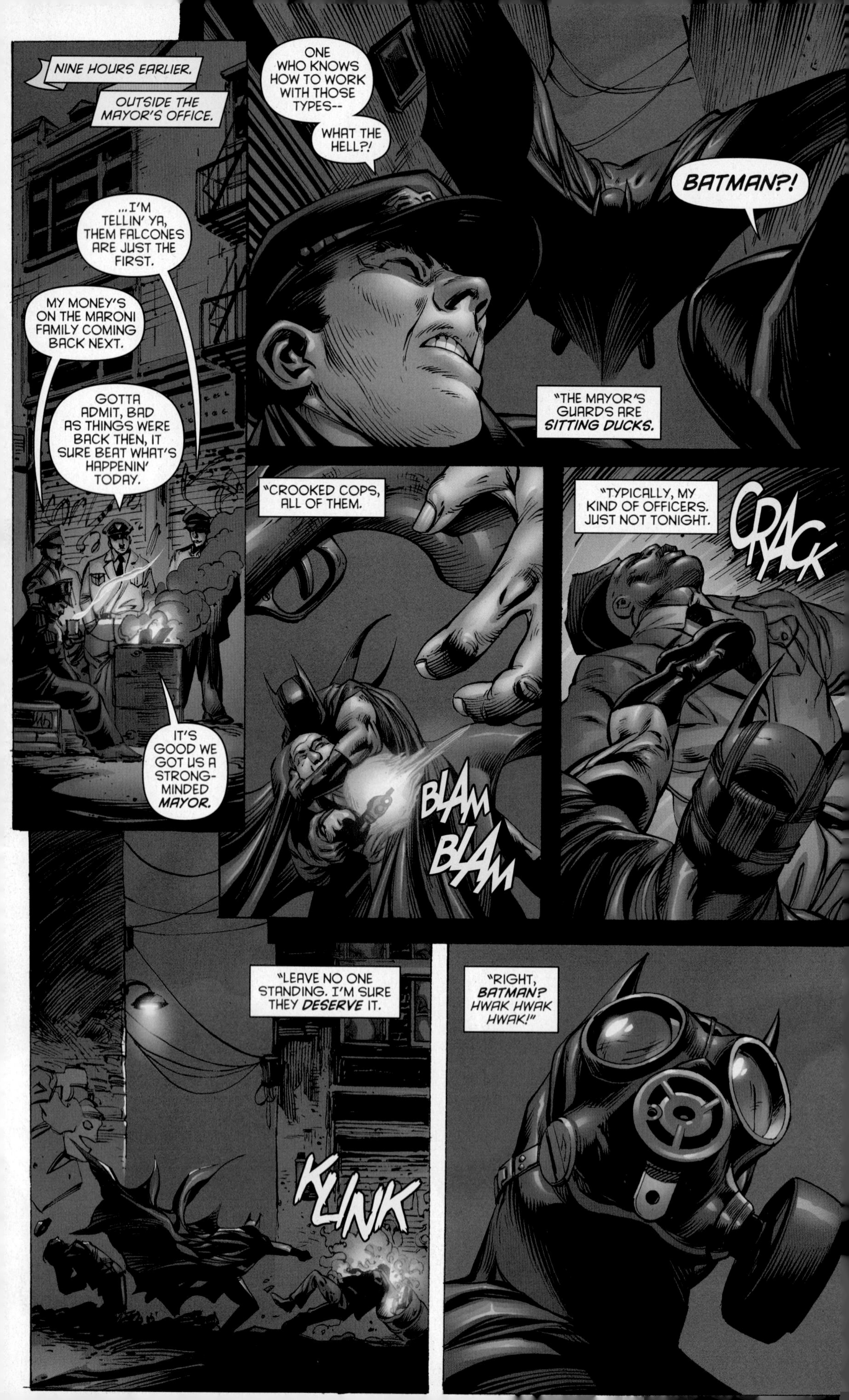
NINE HOURS EARLIER.
OUTSIDE THE MAYOR'S OFFICE.
...I'M TELLIN' YA, THEM FALCONES ARE JUST THE FIRST.
MY MONEY'S ON THE MARONI FAMILY COMING BACK NEXT.
GOTTA ADMIT, BAD AS THINGS WERE BACK THEN, IT SURE BEAT WHAT'S HAPPENIN' TODAY.
IT'S GOOD WE GOT US A STRONG-MINDED MAYOR.
ONE WHO KNOWS HOW TO WORK WITH THOSE TYPES--
WHAT THE HELL?!
BATMAN?!
"THE MAYOR'S GUARDS ARE SITTING DUCKS.
"CROOKED COPS, ALL OF THEM.
BLAM BLAM
"TYPICALLY, MY KIND OF OFFICERS. JUST NOT TONIGHT.
CRACK
"LEAVE NO ONE STANDING. I'M SURE THEY DESERVE IT.
KLINK
"RIGHT, BATMAN? HWAK HWAK HWAK!"

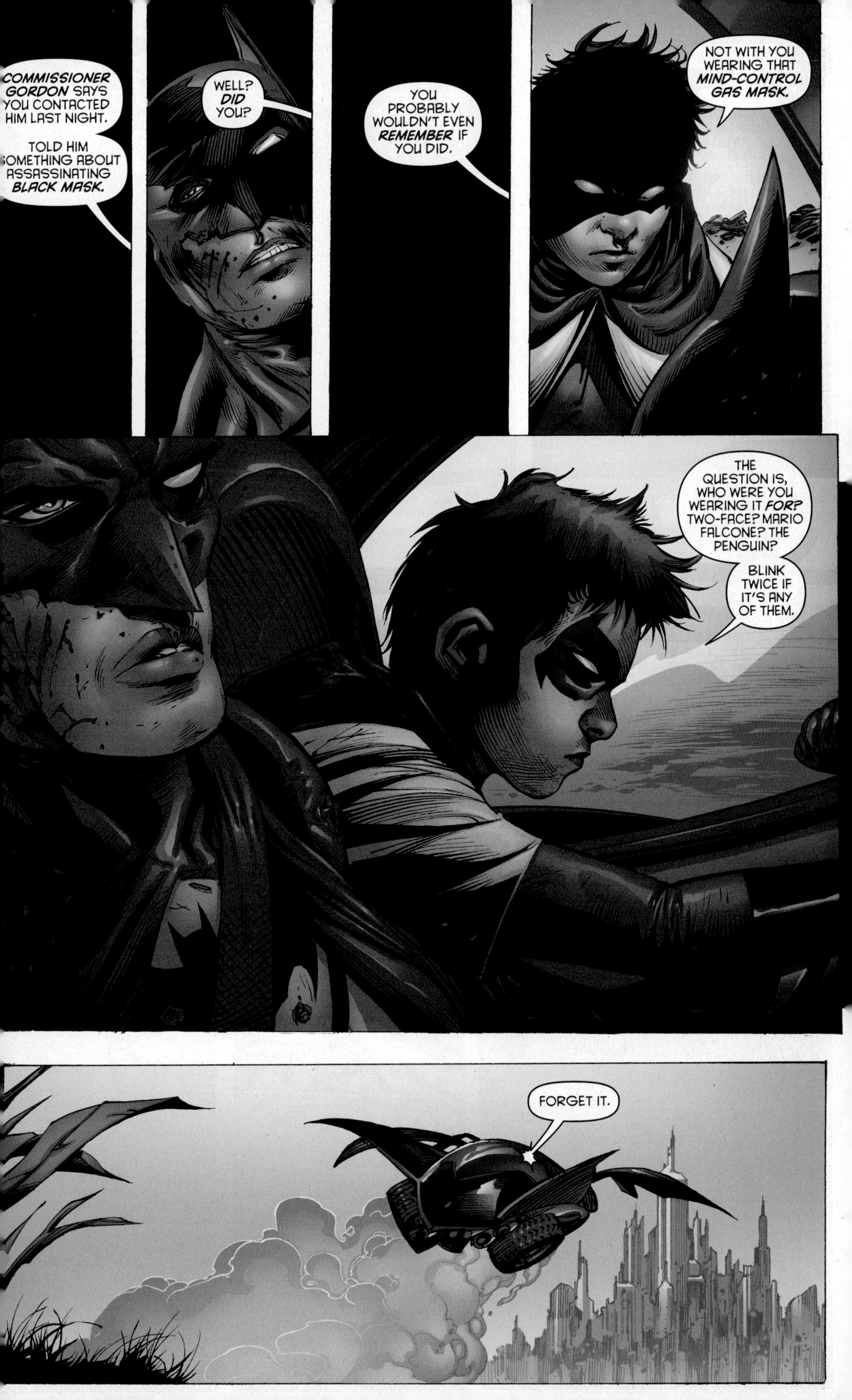
COMMISSIONER GORDON SAYS YOU CONTACTED HIM LAST NIGHT.
TOLD HIM SOMETHING ABOUT ASSASSINATING BLACK MASK.
WELL? DID YOU?
YOU PROBABLY WOULDN'T EVEN REMEMBER IF YOU DID.
NOT WITH YOU WEARING THAT MIND-CONTROL GAS MASK.
THE QUESTION IS, WHO WERE YOU WEARING IT FOR? TWO-FACE? MARIO FALCONE? THE PENGUIN?
BLINK TWICE IF IT'S ANY OF THEM.
FORGET IT.

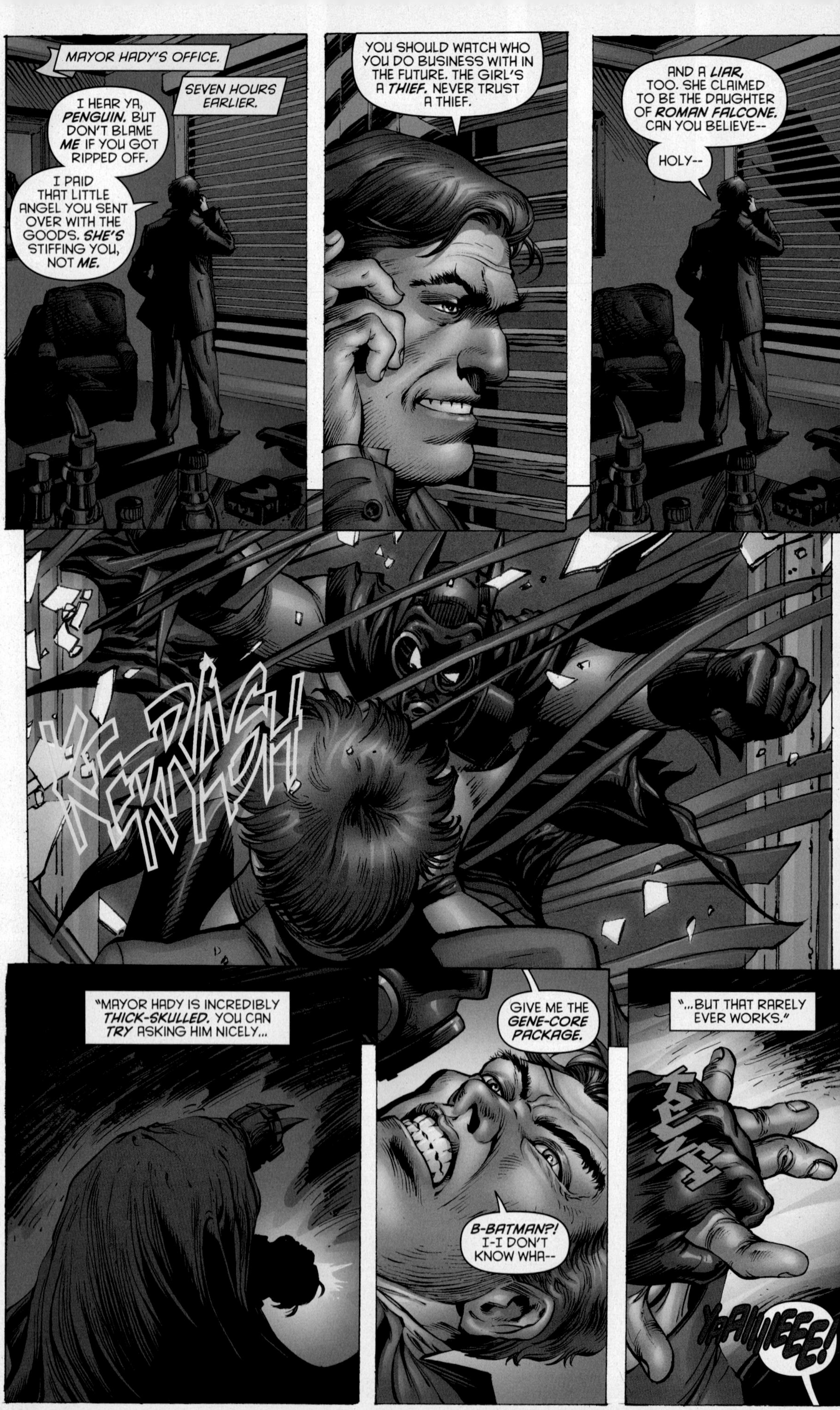
MAYOR HADY'S OFFICE.
SEVEN HOURS EARLIER.
I HEAR YA, PENGUIN. BUT DON'T BLAME ME IF YOU GOT RIPPED OFF.
I PAID THAT LITTLE ANGEL YOU SENT OVER WITH THE GOODS. SHE'S STIFFING YOU, NOT ME.
YOU SHOULD WATCH WHO YOU DO BUSINESS WITH IN THE FUTURE. THE GIRL'S A THIEF. NEVER TRUST A THIEF.
AND A LIAR, TOO. SHE CLAIMED TO BE THE DAUGHTER OF ROMAN FALCONE. CAN YOU BELIEVE--
HOLY--
KE-RASH
"MAYOR HADY IS INCREDIBLY THICK-SKULLED. YOU CAN TRY ASKING HIM NICELY...
GIVE ME THE GENE-CORE PACKAGE.
B-BATMAN?! I-I DON'T KNOW WHA--
"...BUT THAT RARELY EVER WORKS."
YAAIIIIEEE!

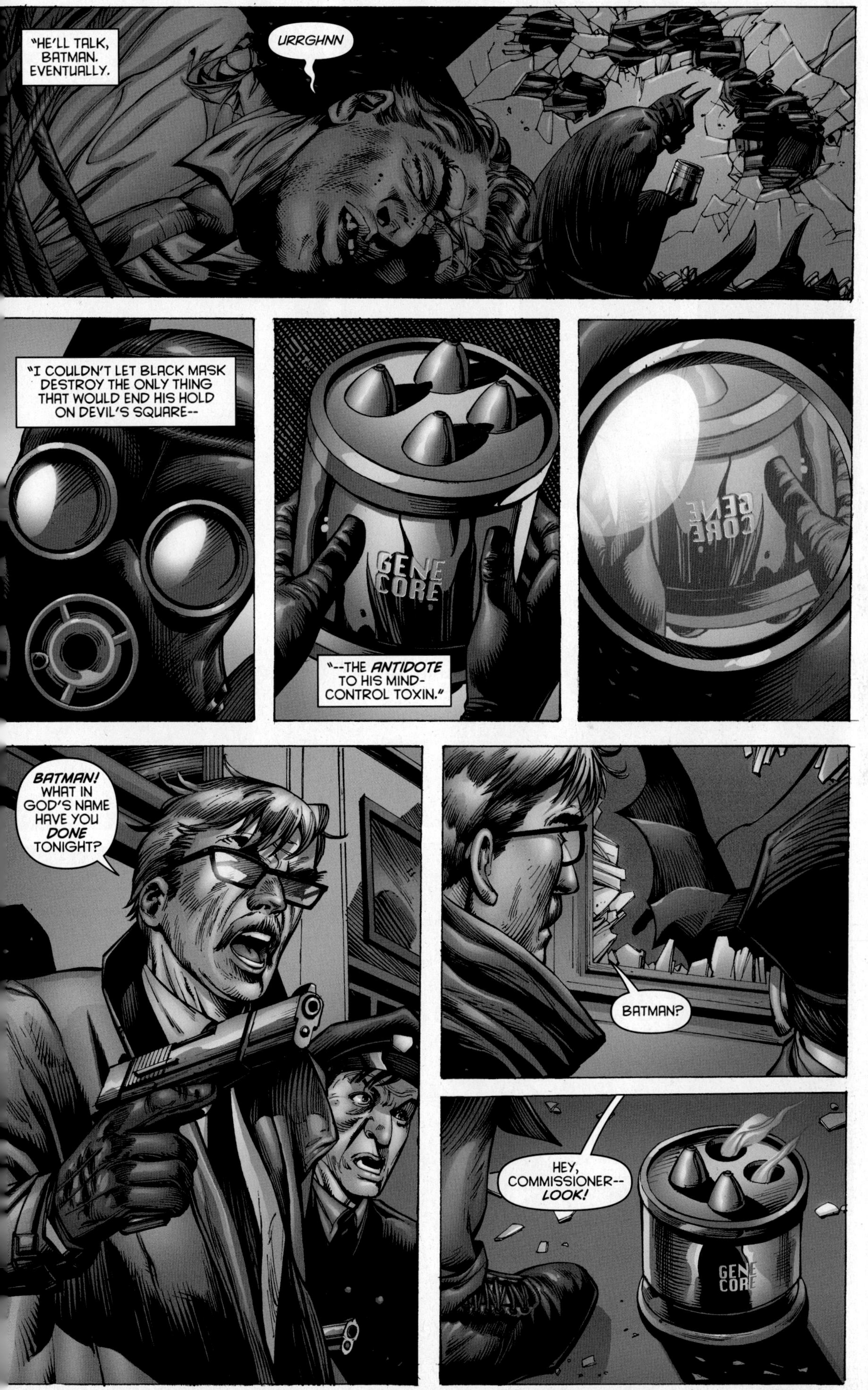
"HE'LL TALK, BATMAN. EVENTUALLY.
URRGHNN
"I COULDN'T LET BLACK MASK DESTROY THE ONLY THING THAT WOULD END HIS HOLD ON DEVIL'S SQUARE--
GENE CORE
"--THE ANTIDOTE TO HIS MIND-CONTROL TOXIN."
BATMAN! WHAT IN GOD'S NAME HAVE YOU DONE TONIGHT?
BATMAN?
HEY, COMMISSIONER-- LOOK!
GENE CORE

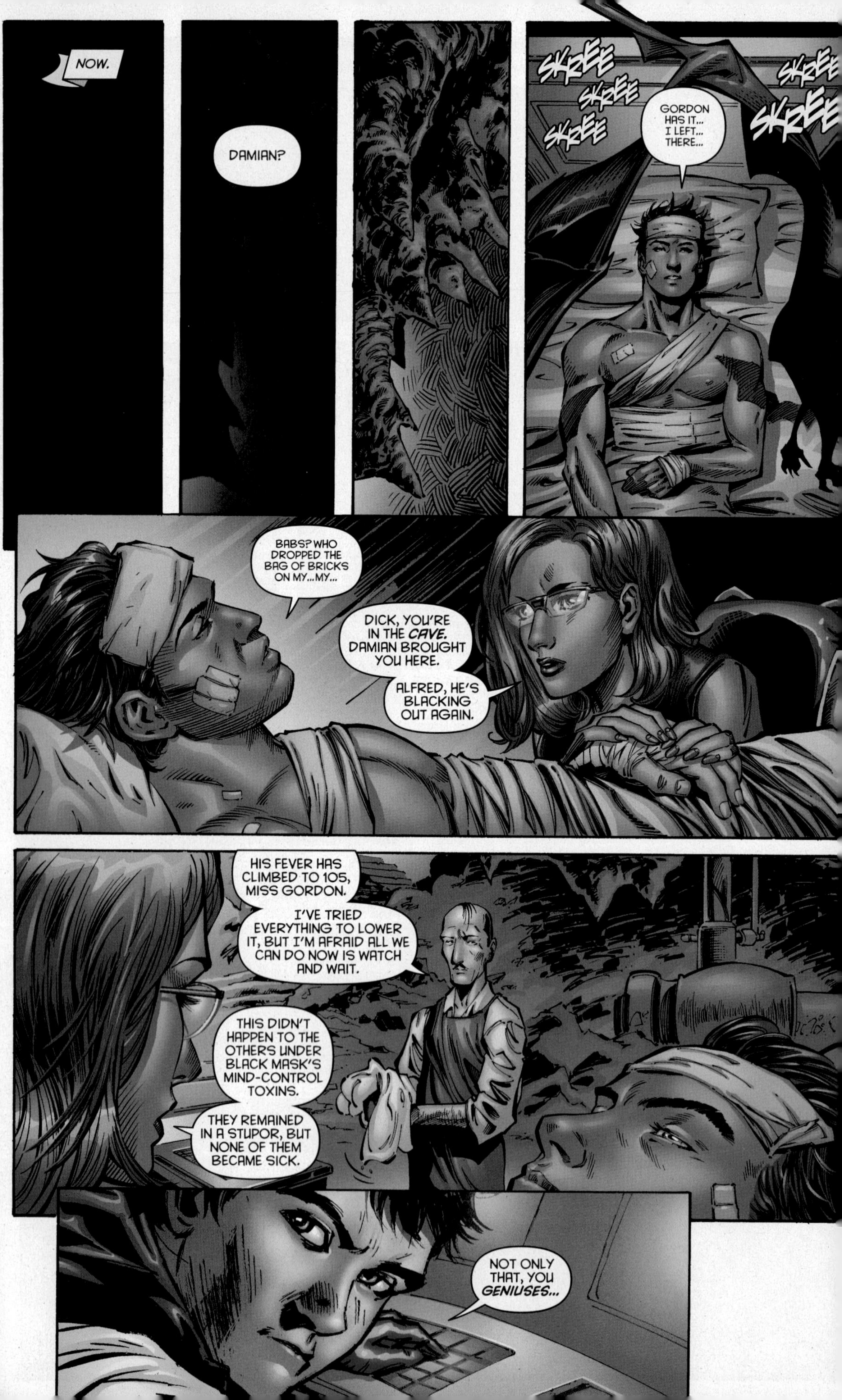
NOW.
DAMIAN?
SKREE SKREE SKREE
GORDON HAS IT... I LEFT... THERE...
SKREE SKREE
BABS? WHO DROPPED THE BAG OF BRICKS ON MY...MY...
DICK, YOU'RE IN THE *CAVE.* DAMIAN BROUGHT YOU HERE.
ALFRED, HE'S BLACKING OUT AGAIN.
HIS FEVER HAS CLIMBED TO 105, MISS GORDON.
I'VE TRIED EVERYTHING TO LOWER IT, BUT I'M AFRAID ALL WE CAN DO NOW IS WATCH AND WAIT.
THIS DIDN'T HAPPEN TO THE OTHERS UNDER BLACK MASK'S MIND-CONTROL TOXINS.
THEY REMAINED IN A STUPOR, BUT NONE OF THEM BECAME SICK.
NOT ONLY THAT, YOU *GENIUSES...*

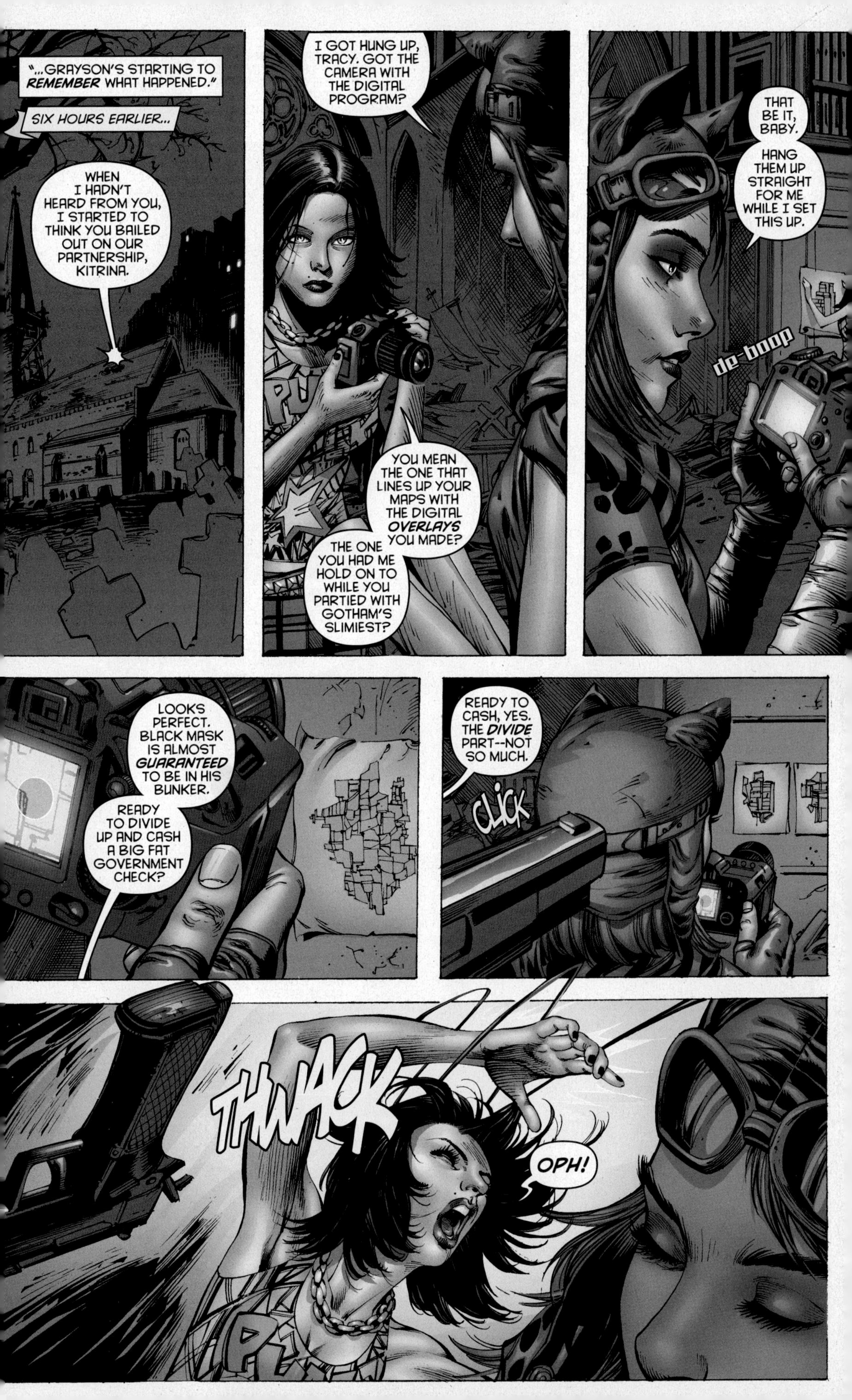
"...GRAYSON'S STARTING TO REMEMBER WHAT HAPPENED."
SIX HOURS EARLIER...
WHEN I HADN'T HEARD FROM YOU, I STARTED TO THINK YOU BAILED OUT ON OUR PARTNERSHIP, KITRINA.
I GOT HUNG UP, TRACY. GOT THE CAMERA WITH THE DIGITAL PROGRAM?
YOU MEAN THE ONE THAT LINES UP YOUR MAPS WITH THE DIGITAL OVERLAYS YOU MADE?
THE ONE YOU HAD ME HOLD ON TO WHILE YOU PARTIED WITH GOTHAM'S SLIMIEST?
THAT BE IT, BABY.
HANG THEM UP STRAIGHT FOR ME WHILE I SET THIS UP.
de-boop
LOOKS PERFECT. BLACK MASK IS ALMOST GUARANTEED TO BE IN HIS BUNKER.
READY TO DIVIDE UP AND CASH A BIG FAT GOVERNMENT CHECK?
READY TO CASH, YES. THE DIVIDE PART--NOT SO MUCH.
CLICK
THWACK
OPH!

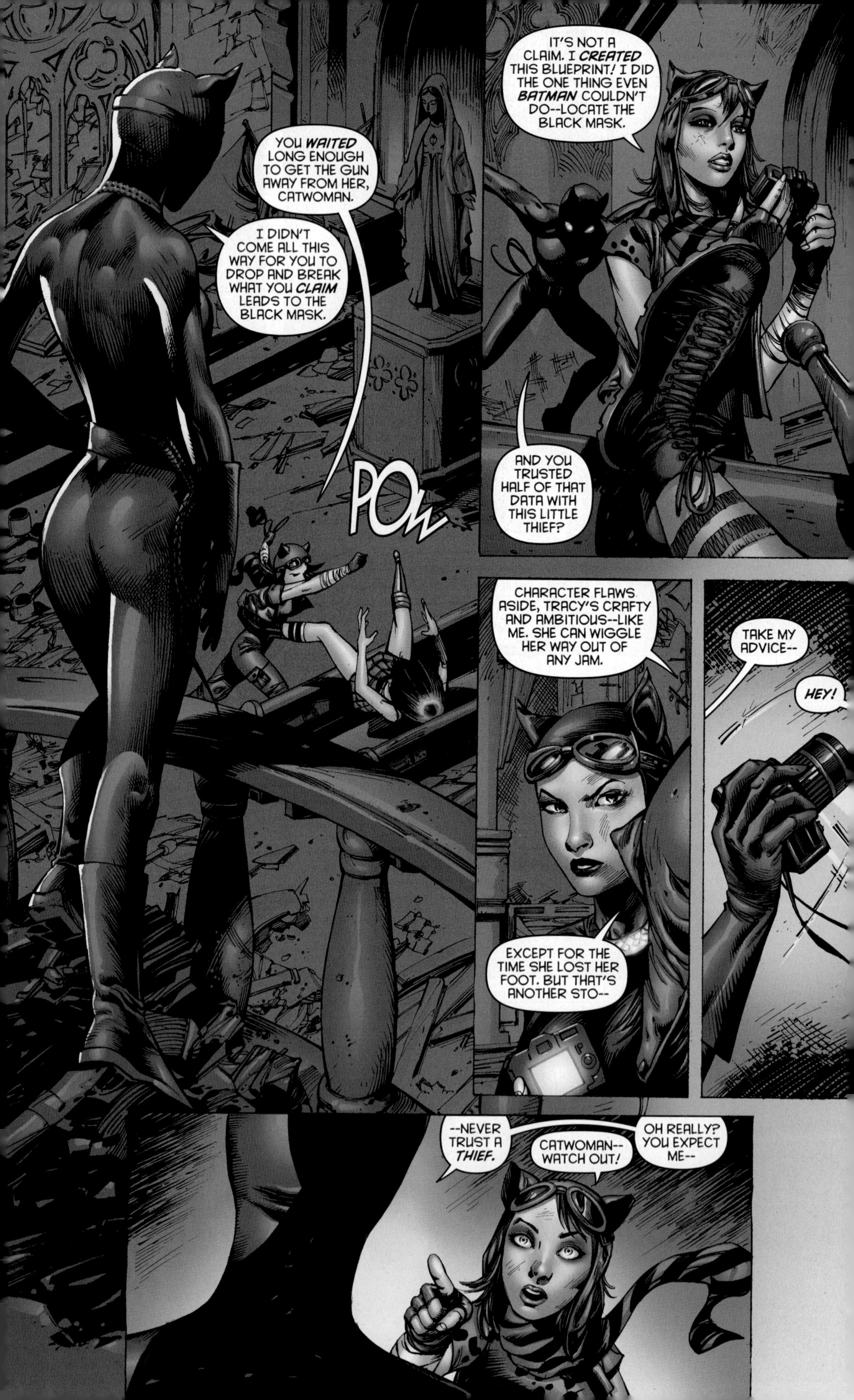
YOU *WAITED* LONG ENOUGH TO GET THE GUN AWAY FROM HER, CATWOMAN.
I DIDN'T COME ALL THIS WAY FOR YOU TO DROP AND BREAK WHAT YOU *CLAIM* LEADS TO THE BLACK MASK.
POW
IT'S NOT A CLAIM. I *CREATED* THIS BLUEPRINT! I DID THE ONE THING EVEN *BATMAN* COULDN'T DO--LOCATE THE BLACK MASK.
AND YOU TRUSTED HALF OF THAT DATA WITH THIS LITTLE THIEF?
CHARACTER FLAWS ASIDE, TRACY'S CRAFTY AND AMBITIOUS--LIKE ME. SHE CAN WIGGLE HER WAY OUT OF ANY JAM.
EXCEPT FOR THE TIME SHE LOST HER FOOT. BUT THAT'S ANOTHER STO--
TAKE MY ADVICE--
HEY!
--NEVER TRUST A *THIEF.*
OH REALLY? YOU EXPECT ME--
CATWOMAN-- WATCH OUT!

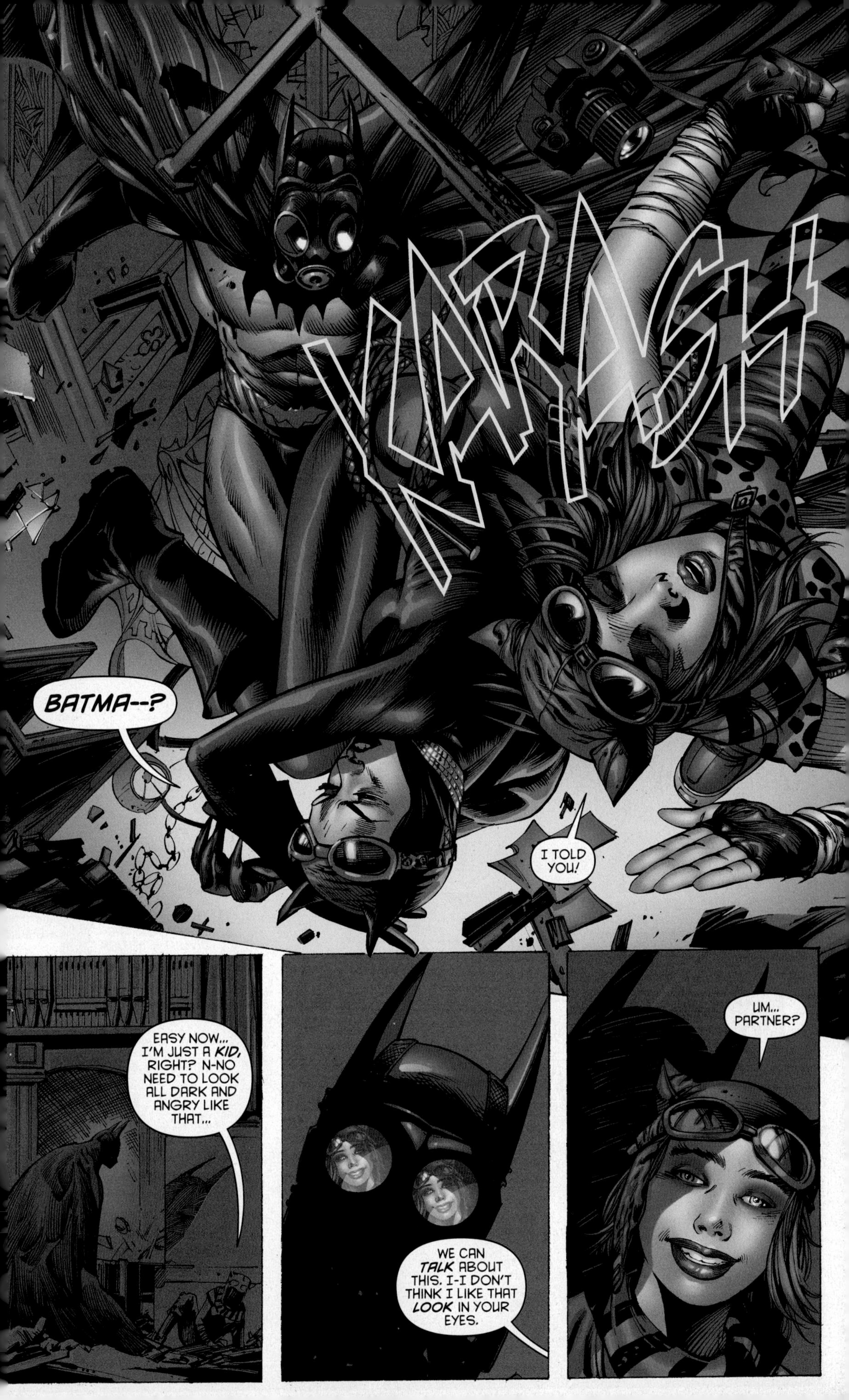
KRASH
BATMA--?
I TOLD YOU!
EASY NOW... I'M JUST A *KID,* RIGHT? N-NO NEED TO LOOK ALL DARK AND ANGRY LIKE THAT...
WE CAN *TALK* ABOUT THIS. I-I DON'T THINK I LIKE THAT *LOOK* IN YOUR EYES.
UM... PARTNER?

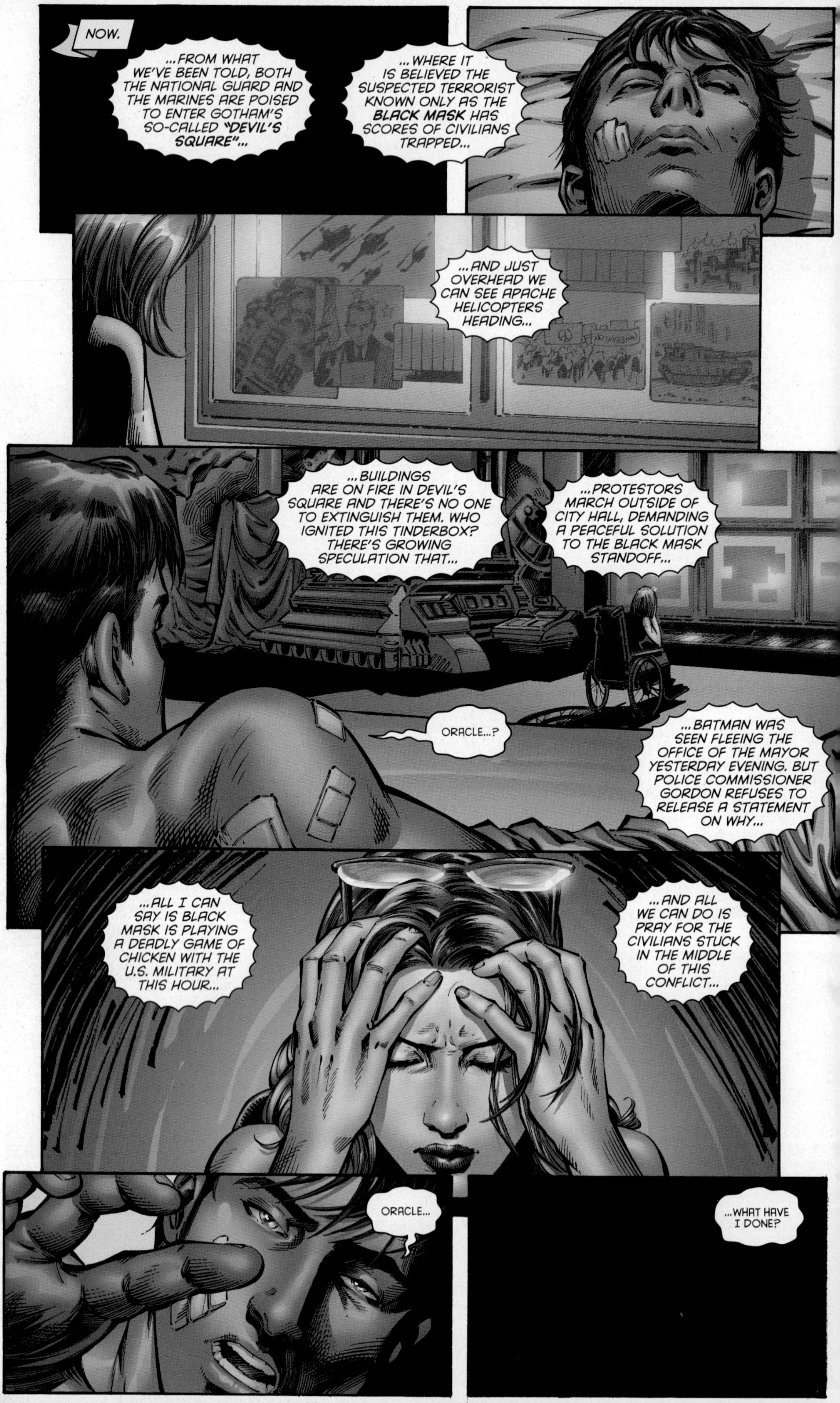
NOW.
...FROM WHAT WE'VE BEEN TOLD, BOTH THE NATIONAL GUARD AND THE MARINES ARE POISED TO ENTER GOTHAM'S SO-CALLED "DEVIL'S SQUARE"...
...WHERE IT IS BELIEVED THE SUSPECTED TERRORIST KNOWN ONLY AS THE BLACK MASK HAS SCORES OF CIVILIANS TRAPPED...
...AND JUST OVERHEAD WE CAN SEE APACHE HELICOPTERS HEADING...
...BUILDINGS ARE ON FIRE IN DEVIL'S SQUARE AND THERE'S NO ONE TO EXTINGUISH THEM. WHO IGNITED THIS TINDERBOX? THERE'S GROWING SPECULATION THAT...
...PROTESTORS MARCH OUTSIDE OF CITY HALL, DEMANDING A PEACEFUL SOLUTION TO THE BLACK MASK STANDOFF...
ORACLE...?
...BATMAN WAS SEEN FLEEING THE OFFICE OF THE MAYOR YESTERDAY EVENING. BUT POLICE COMMISSIONER GORDON REFUSES TO RELEASE A STATEMENT ON WHY...
...ALL I CAN SAY IS BLACK MASK IS PLAYING A DEADLY GAME OF CHICKEN WITH THE U.S. MILITARY AT THIS HOUR...
...AND ALL WE CAN DO IS PRAY FOR THE CIVILIANS STUCK IN THE MIDDLE OF THIS CONFLICT...
ORACLE...
...WHAT HAVE I DONE?

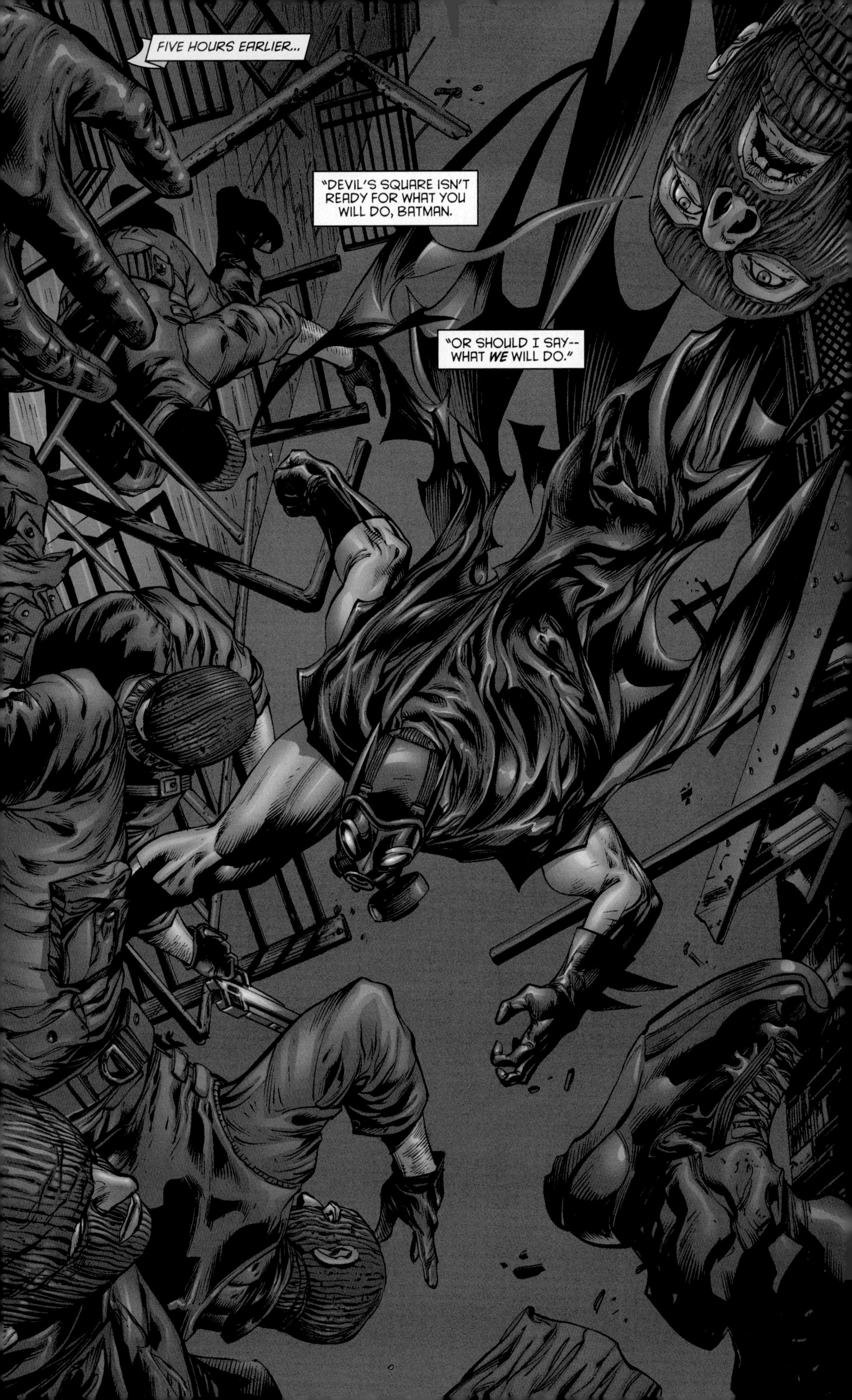
FIVE HOURS EARLIER...
"DEVIL'S SQUARE ISN'T READY FOR WHAT YOU WILL DO, BATMAN.
"OR SHOULD I SAY-- WHAT *WE* WILL DO."

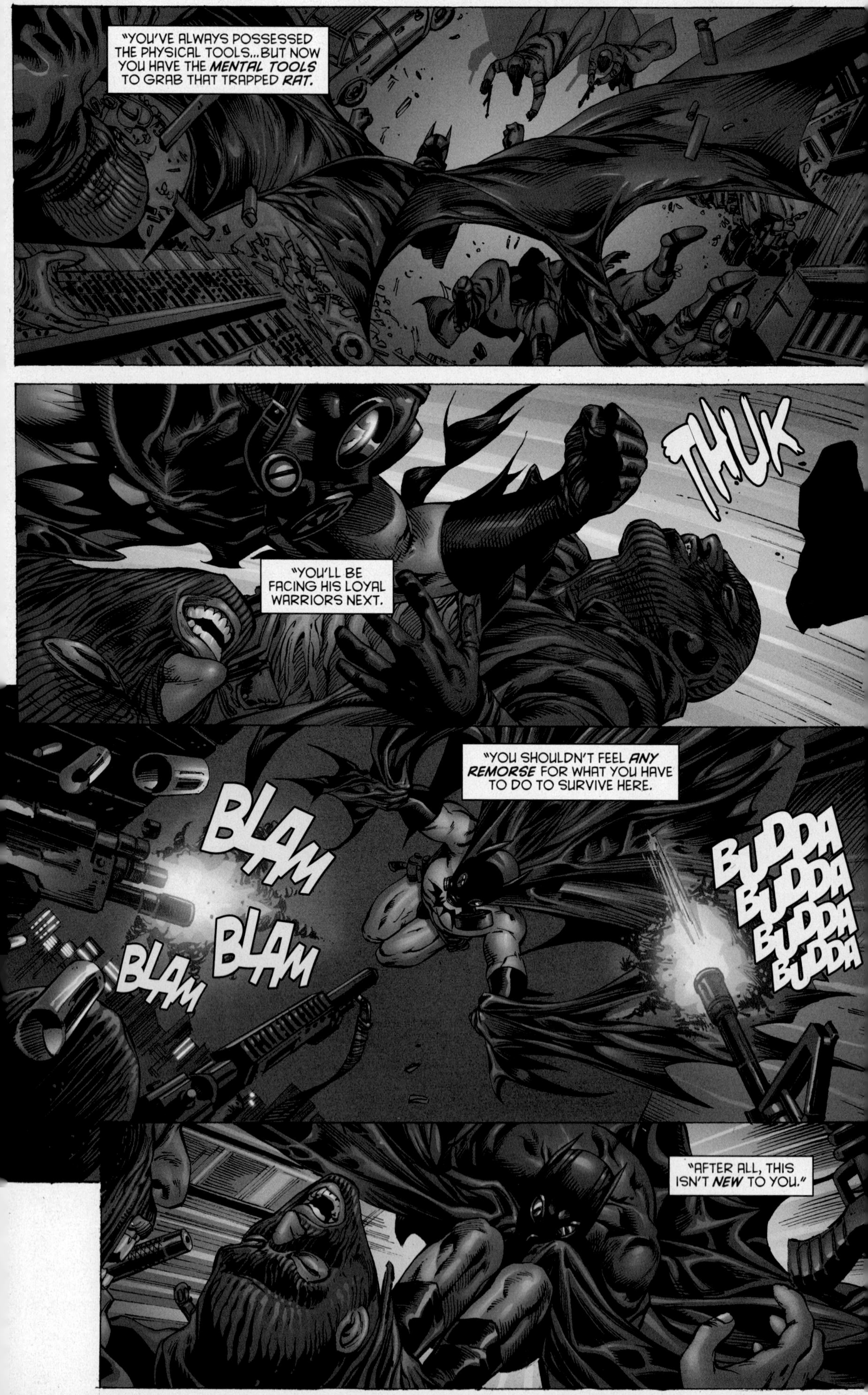
"YOU'VE ALWAYS POSSESSED THE PHYSICAL TOOLS...BUT NOW YOU HAVE THE *MENTAL TOOLS* TO GRAB THAT TRAPPED *RAT*.
THUK
"YOU'LL BE FACING HIS LOYAL WARRIORS NEXT.
"YOU SHOULDN'T FEEL *ANY REMORSE* FOR WHAT YOU HAVE TO DO TO SURVIVE HERE.
BLAM
BLAM
BLAM
BUDDA BUDDA BUDDA BUDDA
"AFTER ALL, THIS ISN'T *NEW* TO YOU."

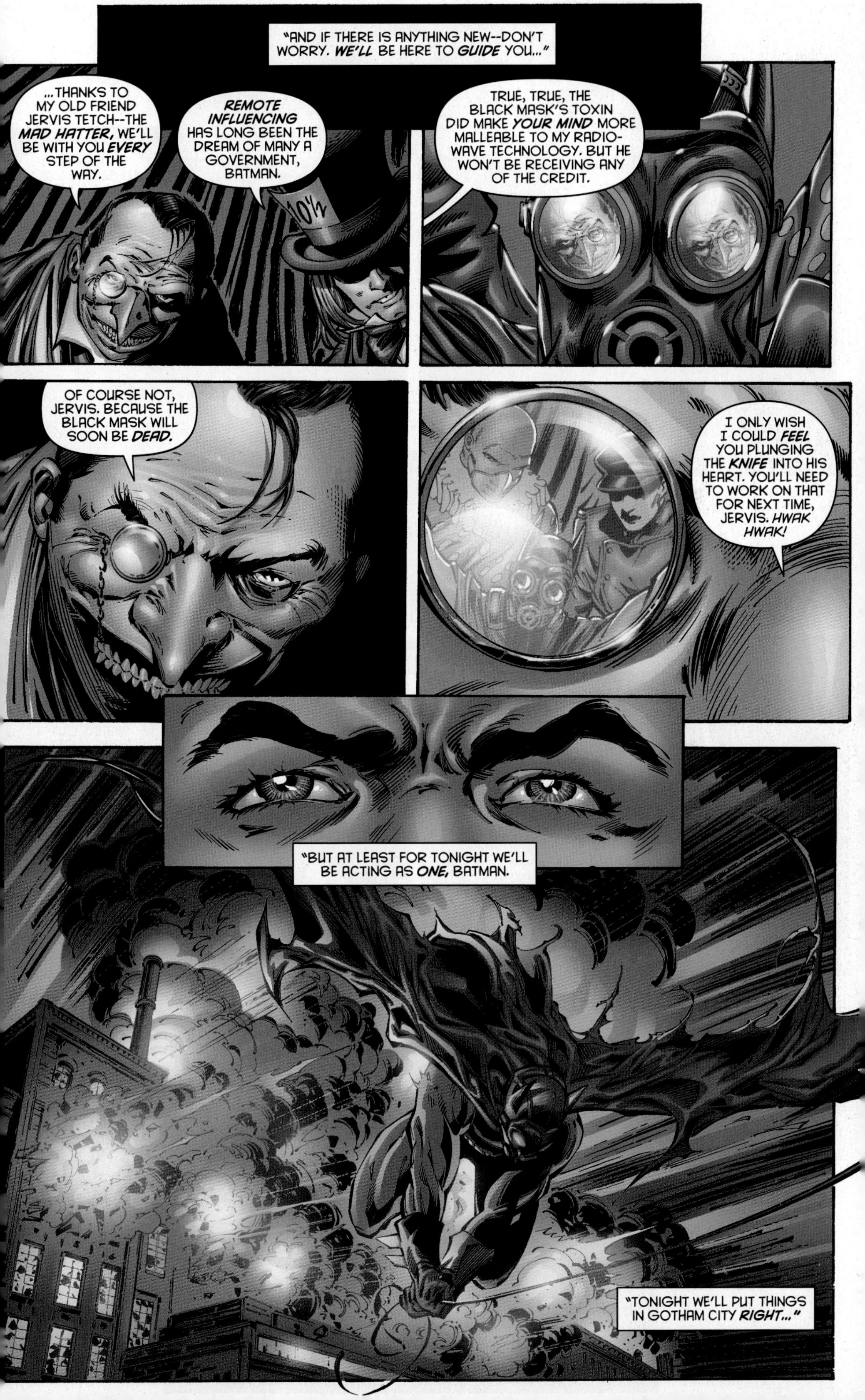
"AND IF THERE IS ANYTHING NEW--DON'T WORRY. WE'LL BE HERE TO GUIDE YOU..."
...THANKS TO MY OLD FRIEND JERVIS TETCH--THE MAD HATTER, WE'LL BE WITH YOU EVERY STEP OF THE WAY.
REMOTE INFLUENCING HAS LONG BEEN THE DREAM OF MANY A GOVERNMENT, BATMAN.
10½
TRUE, TRUE, THE BLACK MASK'S TOXIN DID MAKE YOUR MIND MORE MALLEABLE TO MY RADIO-WAVE TECHNOLOGY. BUT HE WON'T BE RECEIVING ANY OF THE CREDIT.
OF COURSE NOT, JERVIS. BECAUSE THE BLACK MASK WILL SOON BE DEAD.
I ONLY WISH I COULD FEEL YOU PLUNGING THE KNIFE INTO HIS HEART. YOU'LL NEED TO WORK ON THAT FOR NEXT TIME, JERVIS. HWAK HWAK!
"BUT AT LEAST FOR TONIGHT WE'LL BE ACTING AS ONE, BATMAN.
"TONIGHT WE'LL PUT THINGS IN GOTHAM CITY RIGHT..."

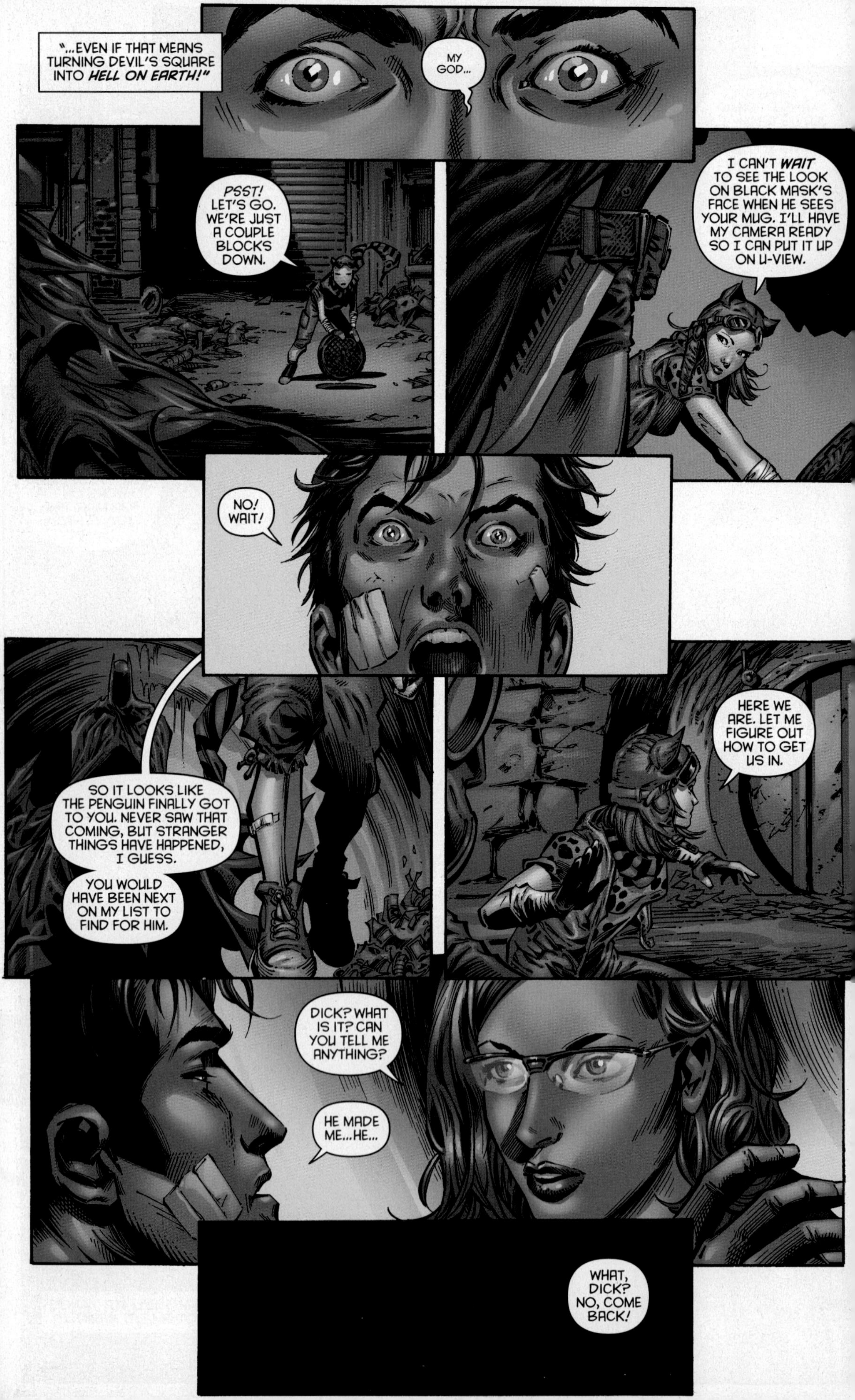
"...EVEN IF THAT MEANS TURNING DEVIL'S SQUARE INTO *HELL ON EARTH!*"
MY GOD...
PSST! LET'S GO. WE'RE JUST A COUPLE BLOCKS DOWN.
I CAN'T *WAIT* TO SEE THE LOOK ON BLACK MASK'S FACE WHEN HE SEES YOUR MUG. I'LL HAVE MY CAMERA READY SO I CAN PUT IT UP ON U-VIEW.
NO! WAIT!
SO IT LOOKS LIKE THE PENGUIN FINALLY GOT TO YOU. NEVER SAW THAT COMING, BUT STRANGER THINGS HAVE HAPPENED, I GUESS.
YOU WOULD HAVE BEEN NEXT ON MY LIST TO FIND FOR HIM.
HERE WE ARE. LET ME FIGURE OUT HOW TO GET US IN.
DICK? WHAT IS IT? CAN YOU TELL ME ANYTHING?
HE MADE ME...HE...
WHAT, DICK? NO, COME BACK!

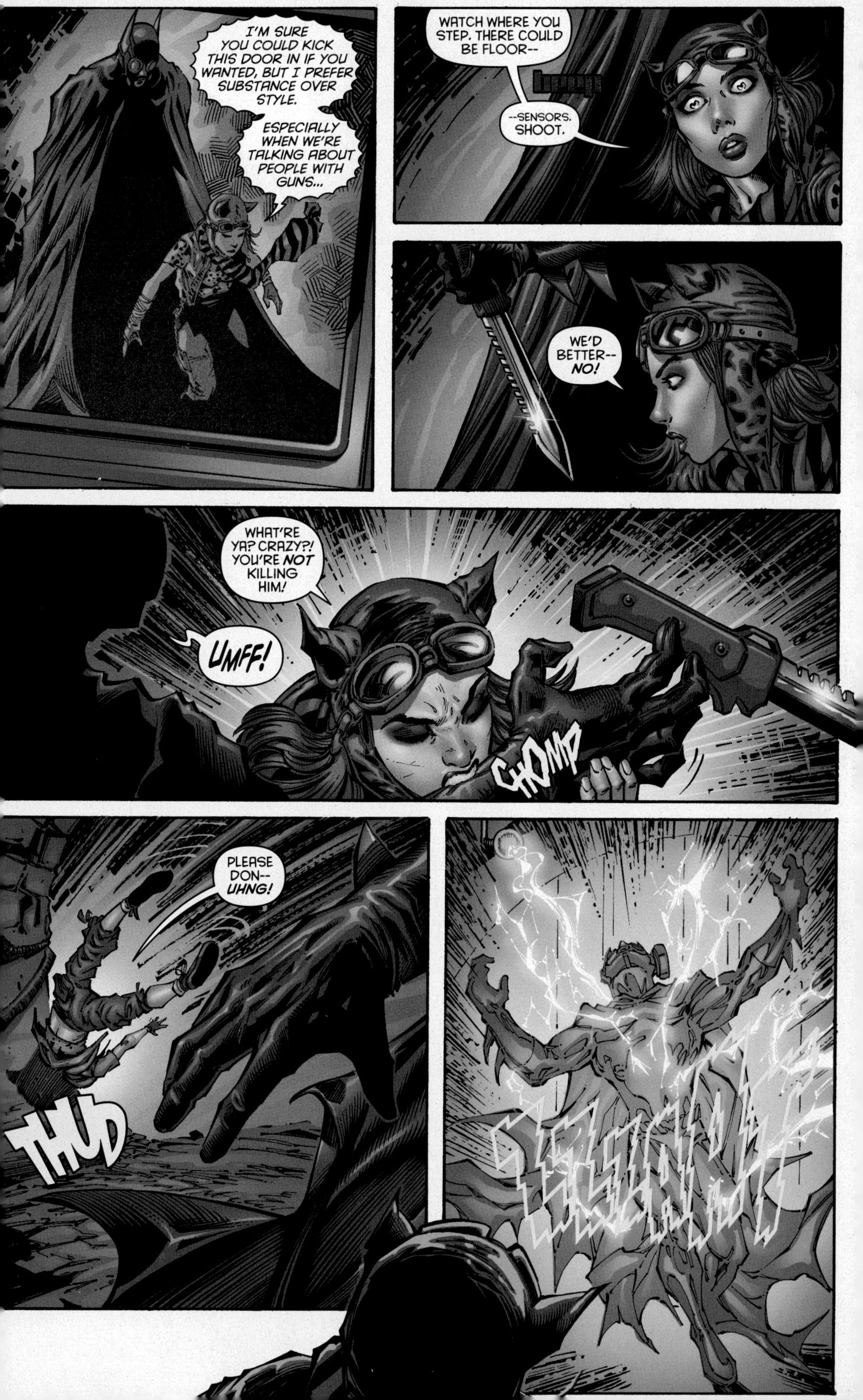
I'M SURE YOU COULD KICK THIS DOOR IN IF YOU WANTED, BUT I PREFER SUBSTANCE OVER STYLE.
ESPECIALLY WHEN WE'RE TALKING ABOUT PEOPLE WITH GUNS...
WATCH WHERE YOU STEP. THERE COULD BE FLOOR--
beep
--SENSORS. SHOOT.
WE'D BETTER-- NO!
WHAT'RE YA? CRAZY?! YOU'RE NOT KILLING HIM!
UMFF!
CHOMP
PLEASE DON-- UHNG!
THUD

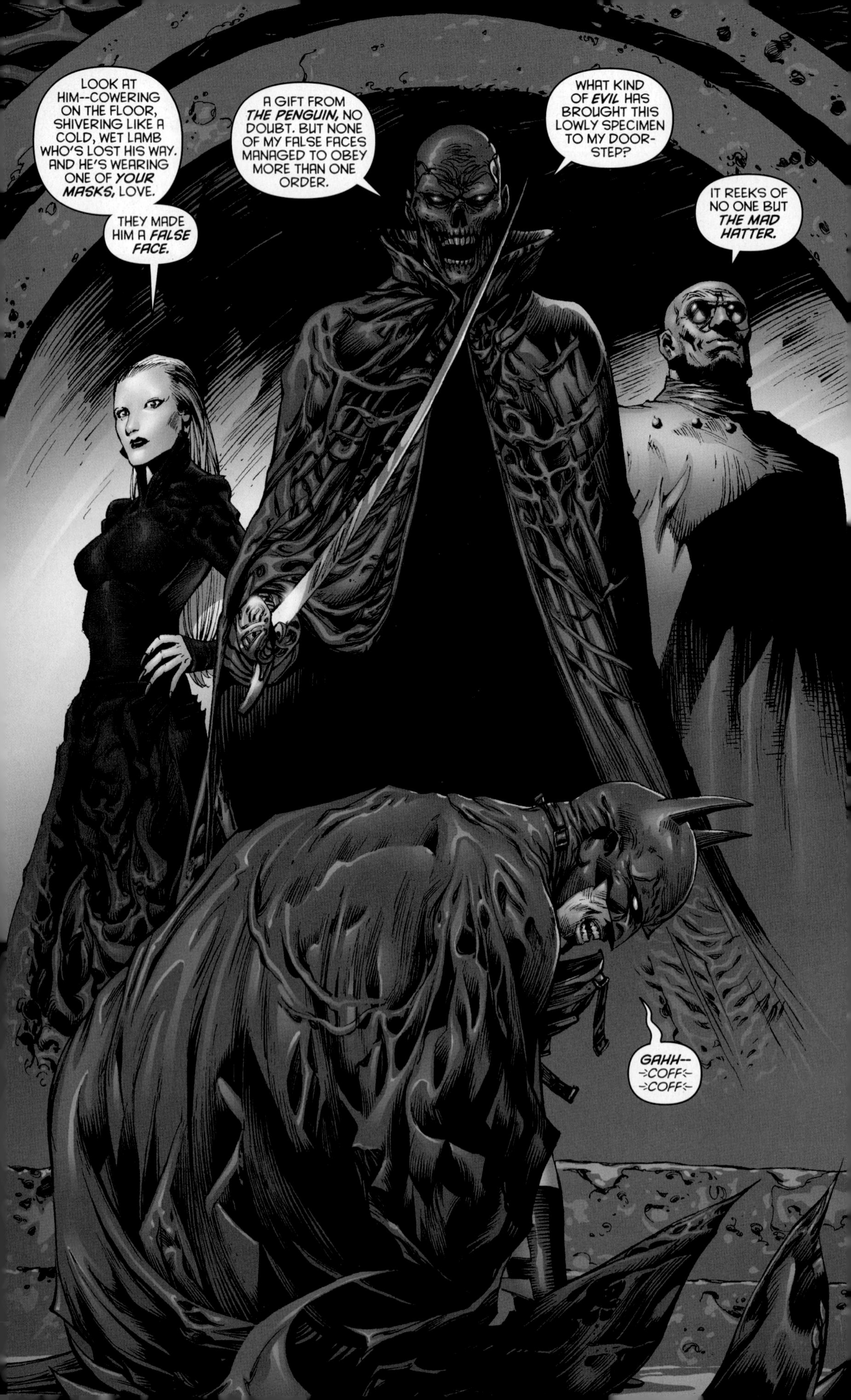
LOOK AT HIM--COWERING ON THE FLOOR, SHIVERING LIKE A COLD, WET LAMB WHO'S LOST HIS WAY. AND HE'S WEARING ONE OF *YOUR MASKS,* LOVE.
THEY MADE HIM A *FALSE FACE.*
A GIFT FROM *THE PENGUIN,* NO DOUBT. BUT NONE OF MY FALSE FACES MANAGED TO OBEY MORE THAN ONE ORDER.
WHAT KIND OF *EVIL* HAS BROUGHT THIS LOWLY SPECIMEN TO MY DOOR-STEP?
IT REEKS OF NO ONE BUT *THE MAD HATTER.*
GAHH-- -COFF- -COFF-

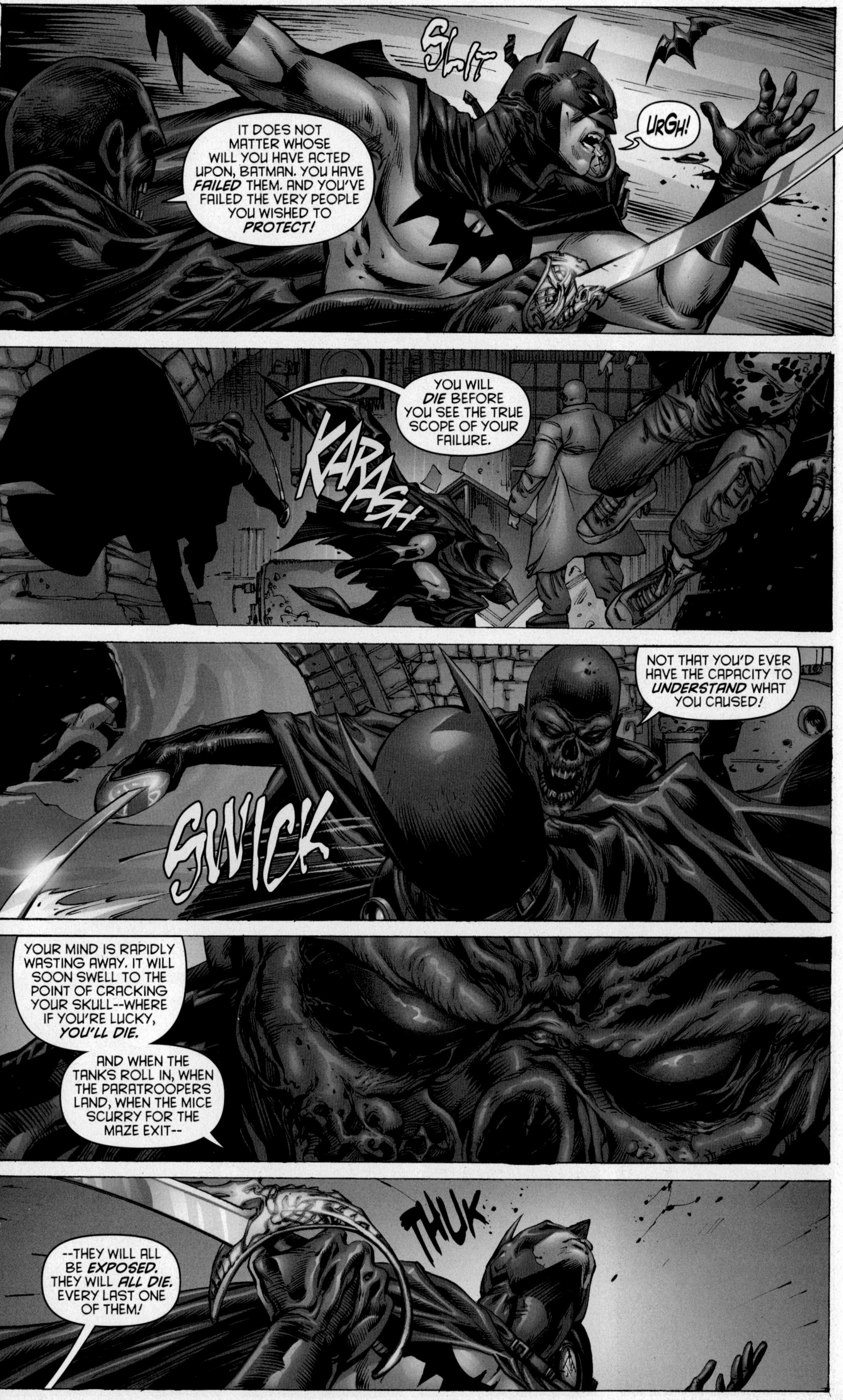
SLIT
IT DOES NOT MATTER WHOSE WILL YOU HAVE ACTED UPON, BATMAN. YOU HAVE FAILED THEM. AND YOU'VE FAILED THE VERY PEOPLE YOU WISHED TO PROTECT!
URGH!
YOU WILL DIE BEFORE YOU SEE THE TRUE SCOPE OF YOUR FAILURE.
KARASH
NOT THAT YOU'D EVER HAVE THE CAPACITY TO UNDERSTAND WHAT YOU CAUSED!
SWICK
YOUR MIND IS RAPIDLY WASTING AWAY. IT WILL SOON SWELL TO THE POINT OF CRACKING YOUR SKULL--WHERE IF YOU'RE LUCKY, YOU'LL DIE.
AND WHEN THE TANKS ROLL IN, WHEN THE PARATROOPERS LAND, WHEN THE MICE SCURRY FOR THE MAZE EXIT--
THUK
--THEY WILL ALL BE EXPOSED. THEY WILL ALL DIE. EVERY LAST ONE OF THEM!

AND BY THEN I'LL BE BACK IN MY OFFICE, WATCHING THE HORROR UNFOLD ON THE NEWS.

YOU'RE MAD. MAD AS HELL...

"NO GREAT GENIUS HAS EVER EXISTED WITHOUT SOME TOUCH OF MADNESS."

A QUOTE FROM *ARISTOTLE*. I--I GET IT...

HUSH UP. WHY IS HE TALKING? FALSE FACES DON'T TALK.

THAT'S RIGHT, MASK. WHY AM I TALKING?

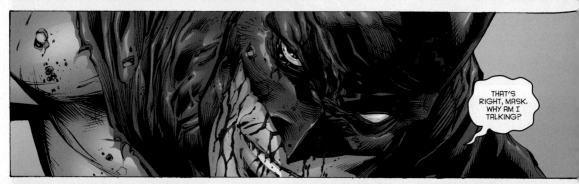

I'M NOT SUPPOSED TO...*AM* I?

I DISCOVERED HOW THE TOXINS IN YOUR MASKS WORK... ALL IT TOOK WAS A HEAVY DOSE OF BENZTROPINE...

...TO ENABLE ME *SOME* FREE WILL.

...ENOUGH FOR ME TO TAKE A COUPLE OF DOSES OF YOUR ANTIDOTE WITH ME...

JAB

IT'S *MUCH* TOO LATE FOR THAT. EVERYONE WILL BE *DEAD* SOON!

AND THERE'S *NOTHING* YOU CAN DO TO *STOP* ME!

THEN WHAT THE HELL DO YOU CALL--

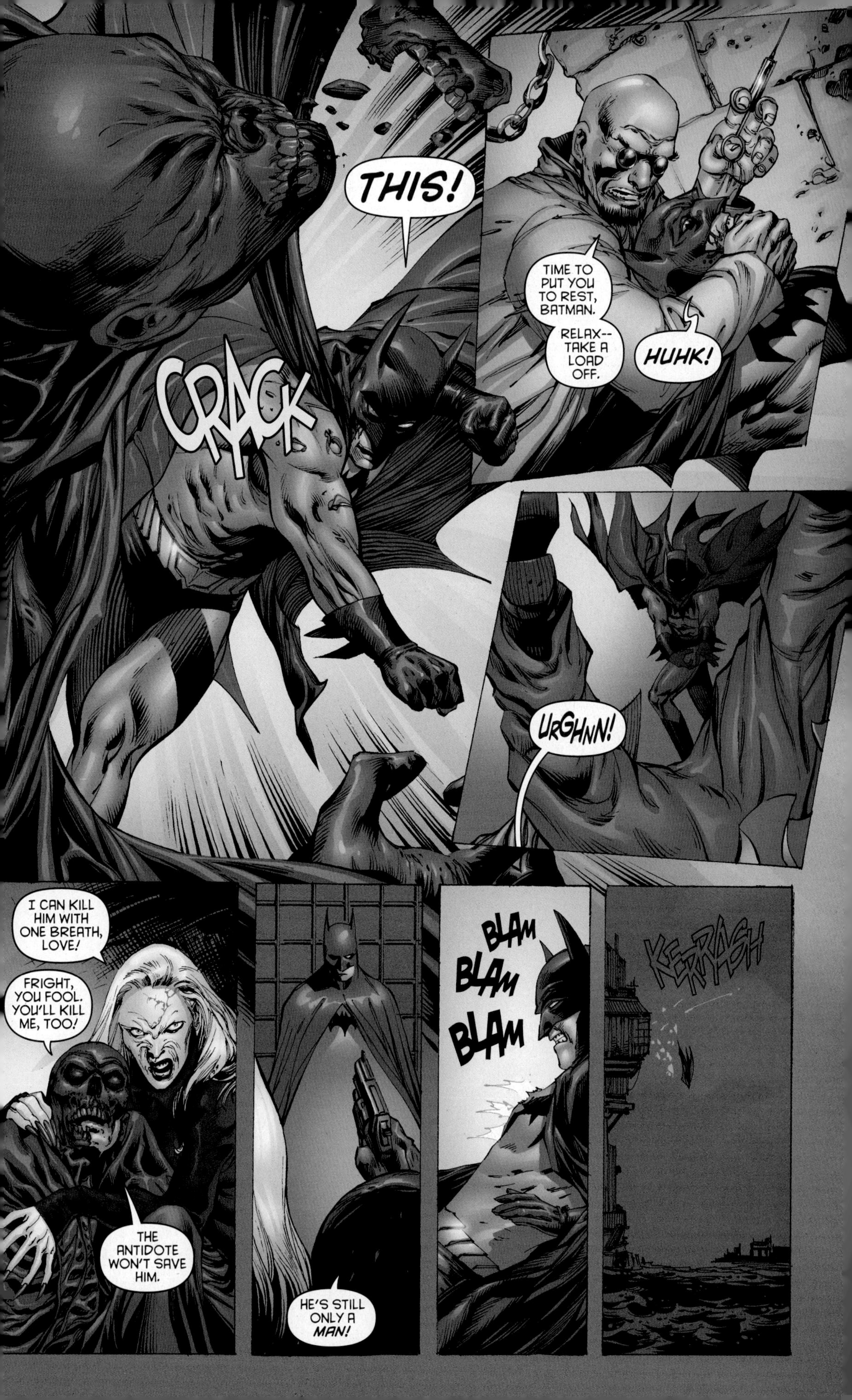
THIS!
CRACK
TIME TO PUT YOU TO REST, BATMAN.
RELAX-- TAKE A LOAD OFF.
HUHK!
URGHNN!
I CAN KILL HIM WITH ONE BREATH, LOVE!
FRIGHT, YOU FOOL. YOU'LL KILL ME, TOO!
THE ANTIDOTE WON'T SAVE HIM.
HE'S STILL ONLY A MAN!
BLAM
BLAM
BLAM
KERRASH

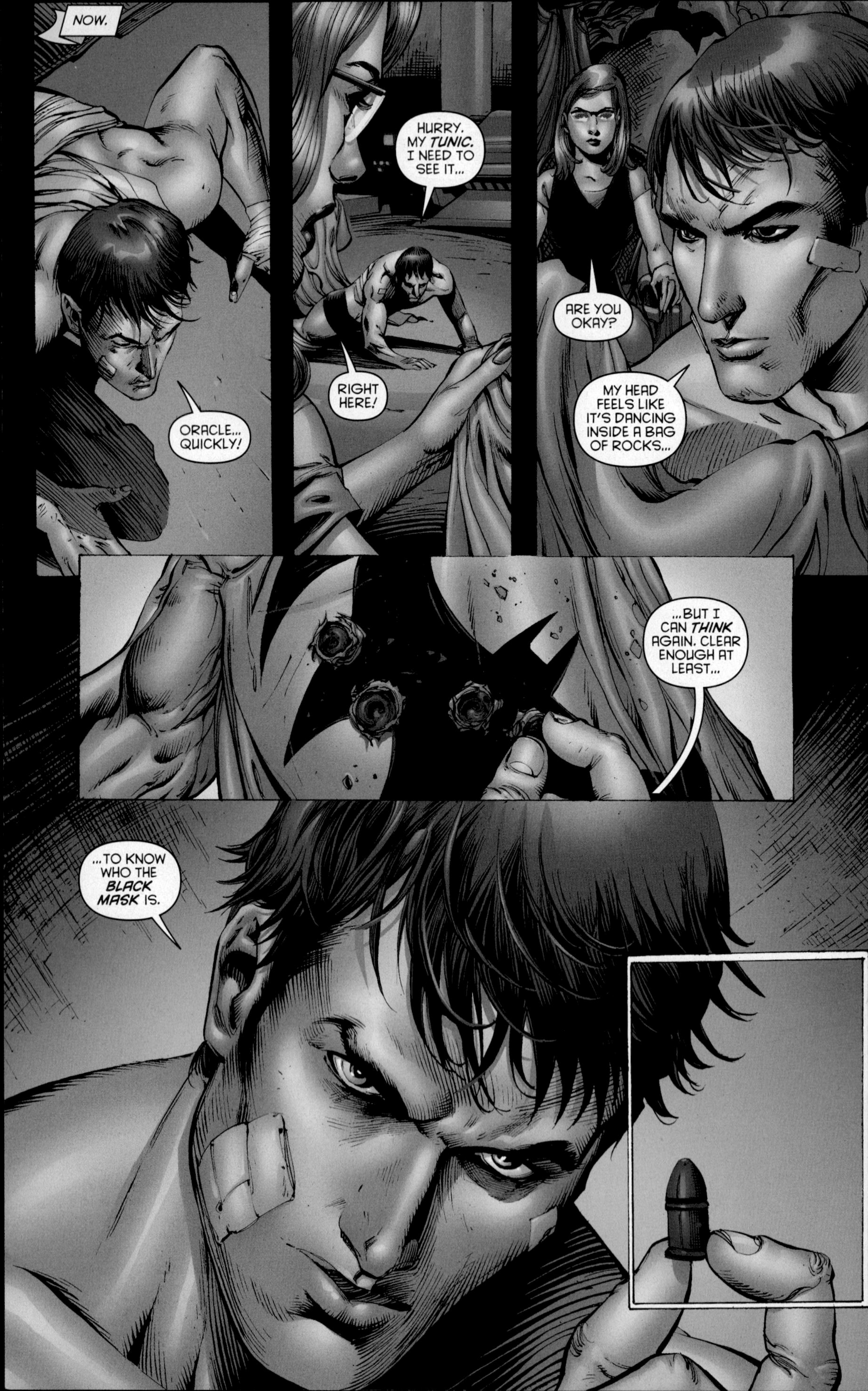
NOW.
ORACLE... QUICKLY!
HURRY. MY *TUNIC.* I NEED TO SEE IT...
RIGHT HERE!
ARE YOU OKAY?
MY HEAD FEELS LIKE IT'S DANCING INSIDE A BAG OF ROCKS...
...BUT I CAN *THINK* AGAIN. CLEAR ENOUGH AT LEAST...
...TO KNOW WHO THE *BLACK MASK* IS.

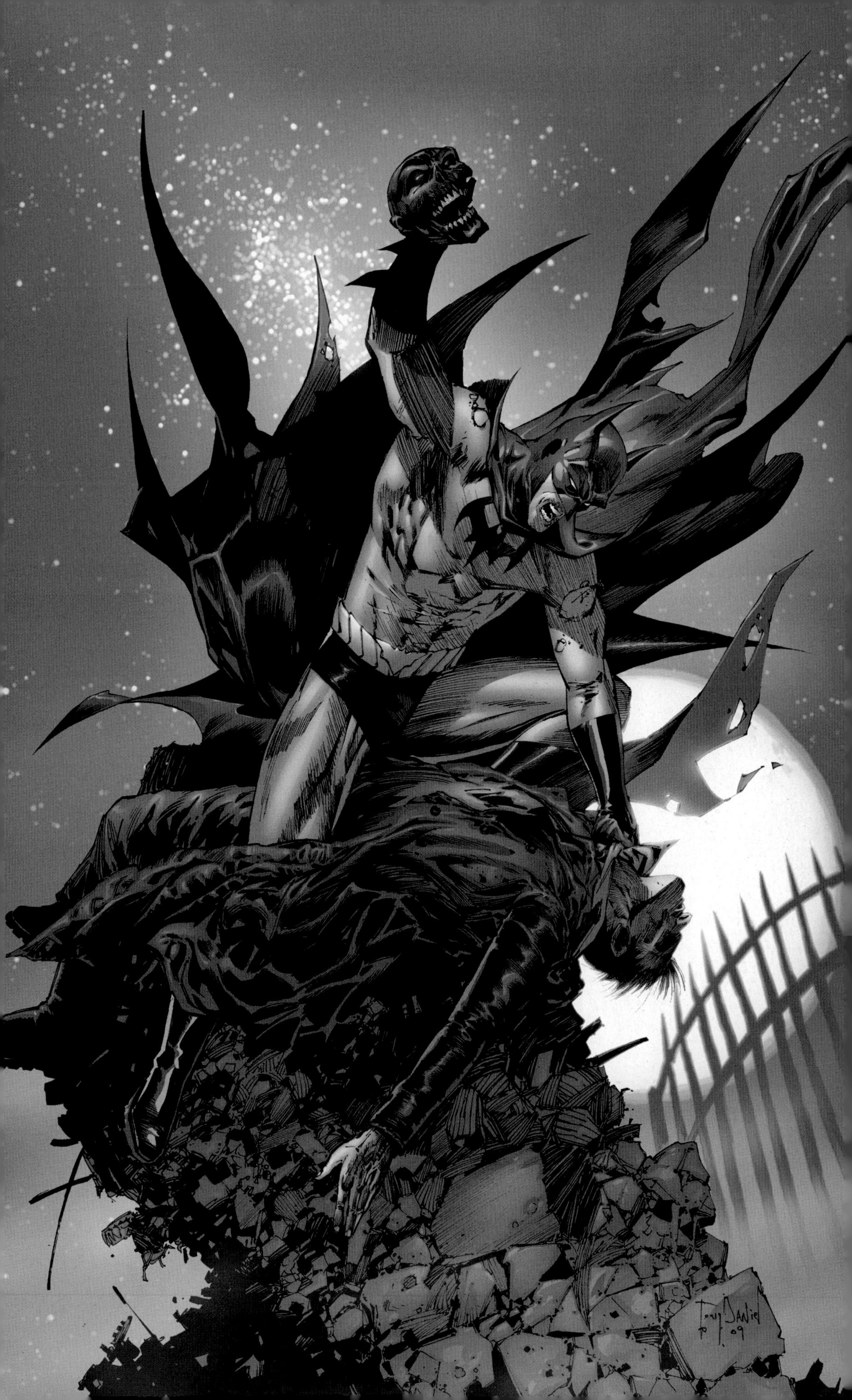

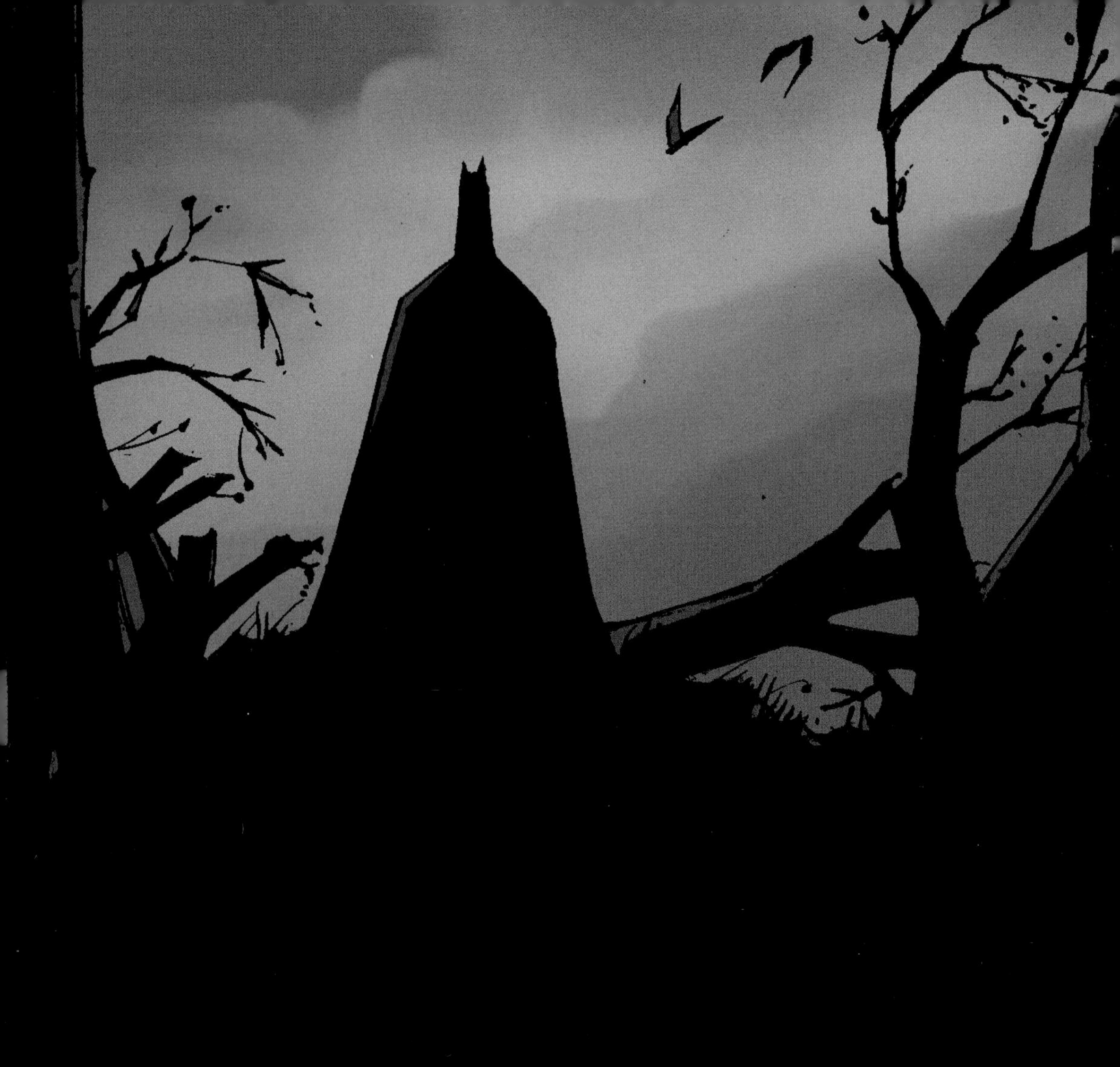

"I cannot be stopped. I always go on."

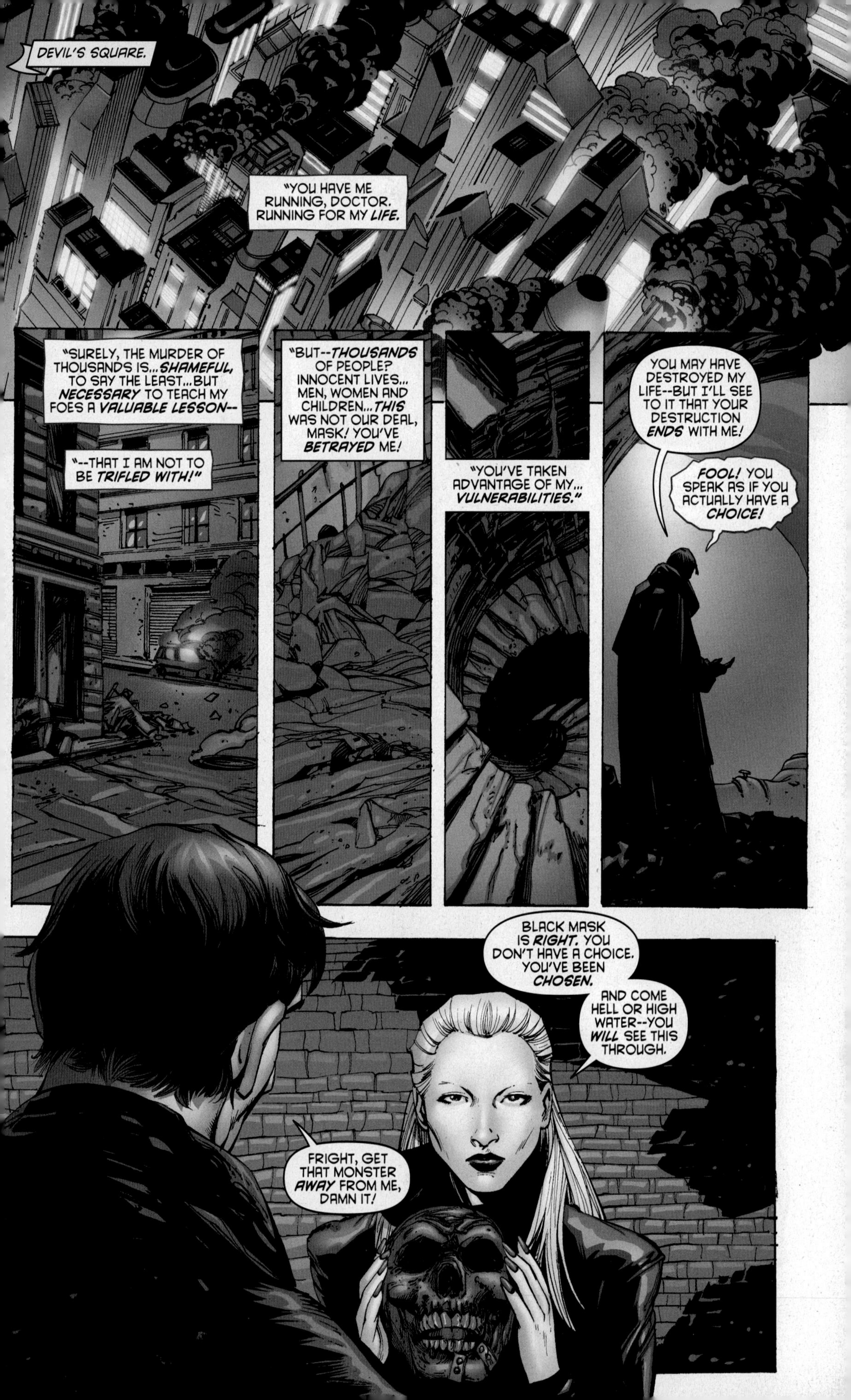
DEVIL'S SQUARE.
"YOU HAVE ME RUNNING, DOCTOR. RUNNING FOR MY LIFE.
"SURELY, THE MURDER OF THOUSANDS IS... SHAMEFUL, TO SAY THE LEAST... BUT NECESSARY TO TEACH MY FOES A VALUABLE LESSON--
"--THAT I AM NOT TO BE TRIFLED WITH!"
"BUT--THOUSANDS OF PEOPLE? INNOCENT LIVES... MEN, WOMEN AND CHILDREN... THIS WAS NOT OUR DEAL, MASK! YOU'VE BETRAYED ME!
"YOU'VE TAKEN ADVANTAGE OF MY... VULNERABILITIES."
YOU MAY HAVE DESTROYED MY LIFE--BUT I'LL SEE TO IT THAT YOUR DESTRUCTION ENDS WITH ME!
FOOL! YOU SPEAK AS IF YOU ACTUALLY HAVE A CHOICE!
BLACK MASK IS RIGHT. YOU DON'T HAVE A CHOICE. YOU'VE BEEN CHOSEN.
AND COME HELL OR HIGH WATER--YOU WILL SEE THIS THROUGH.
FRIGHT, GET THAT MONSTER AWAY FROM ME, DAMN IT!

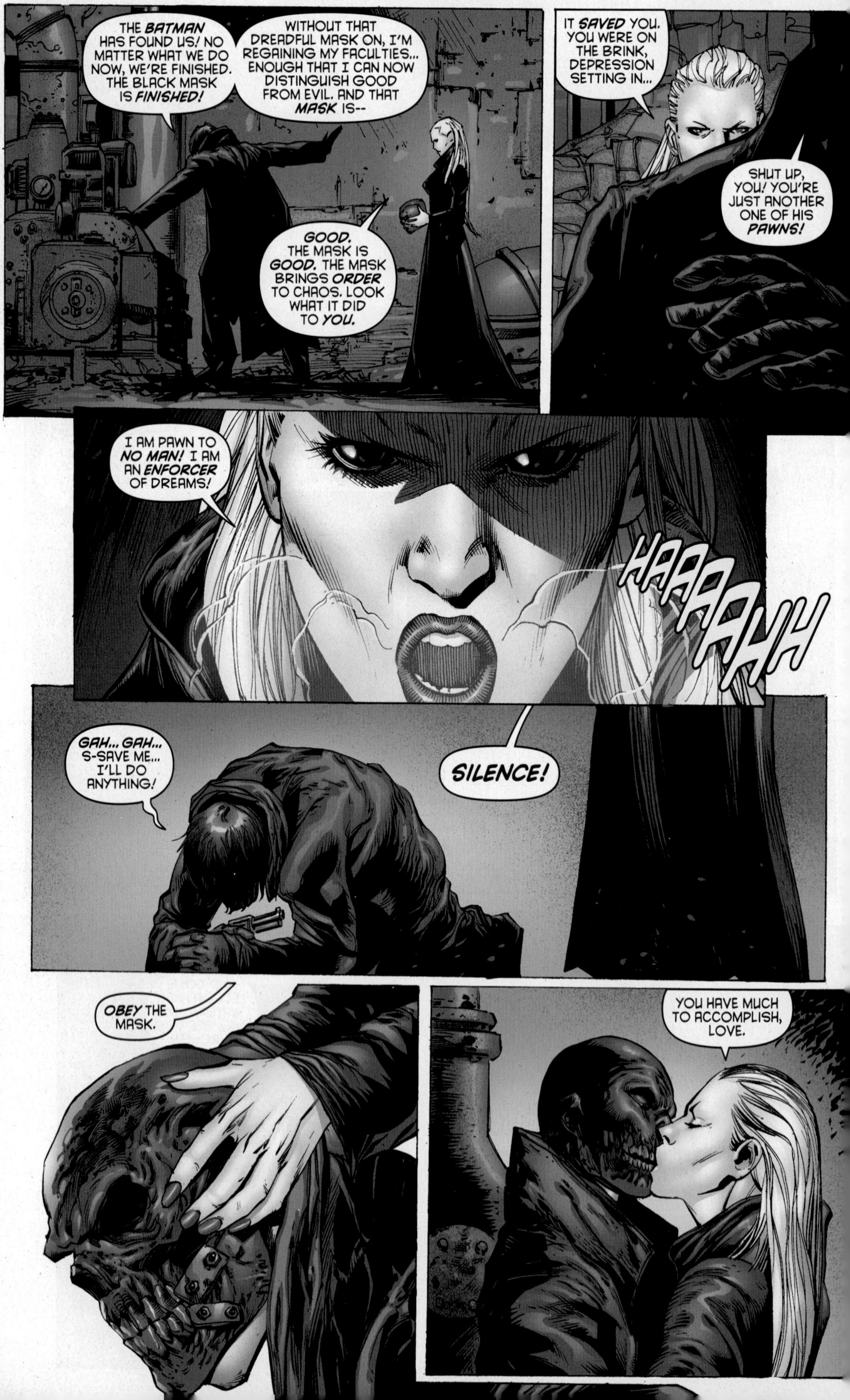
THE BATMAN HAS FOUND US! NO MATTER WHAT WE DO NOW, WE'RE FINISHED. THE BLACK MASK IS FINISHED!
WITHOUT THAT DREADFUL MASK ON, I'M REGAINING MY FACULTIES... ENOUGH THAT I CAN NOW DISTINGUISH GOOD FROM EVIL. AND THAT MASK IS--
GOOD. THE MASK IS GOOD. THE MASK BRINGS ORDER TO CHAOS. LOOK WHAT IT DID TO YOU.
IT SAVED YOU. YOU WERE ON THE BRINK, DEPRESSION SETTING IN...
SHUT UP, YOU! YOU'RE JUST ANOTHER ONE OF HIS PAWNS!
I AM PAWN TO NO MAN! I AM AN ENFORCER OF DREAMS!
HAAAAAHH
GAH... GAH... S-SAVE ME... I'LL DO ANYTHING!
SILENCE!
OBEY THE MASK.
YOU HAVE MUCH TO ACCOMPLISH, LOVE.

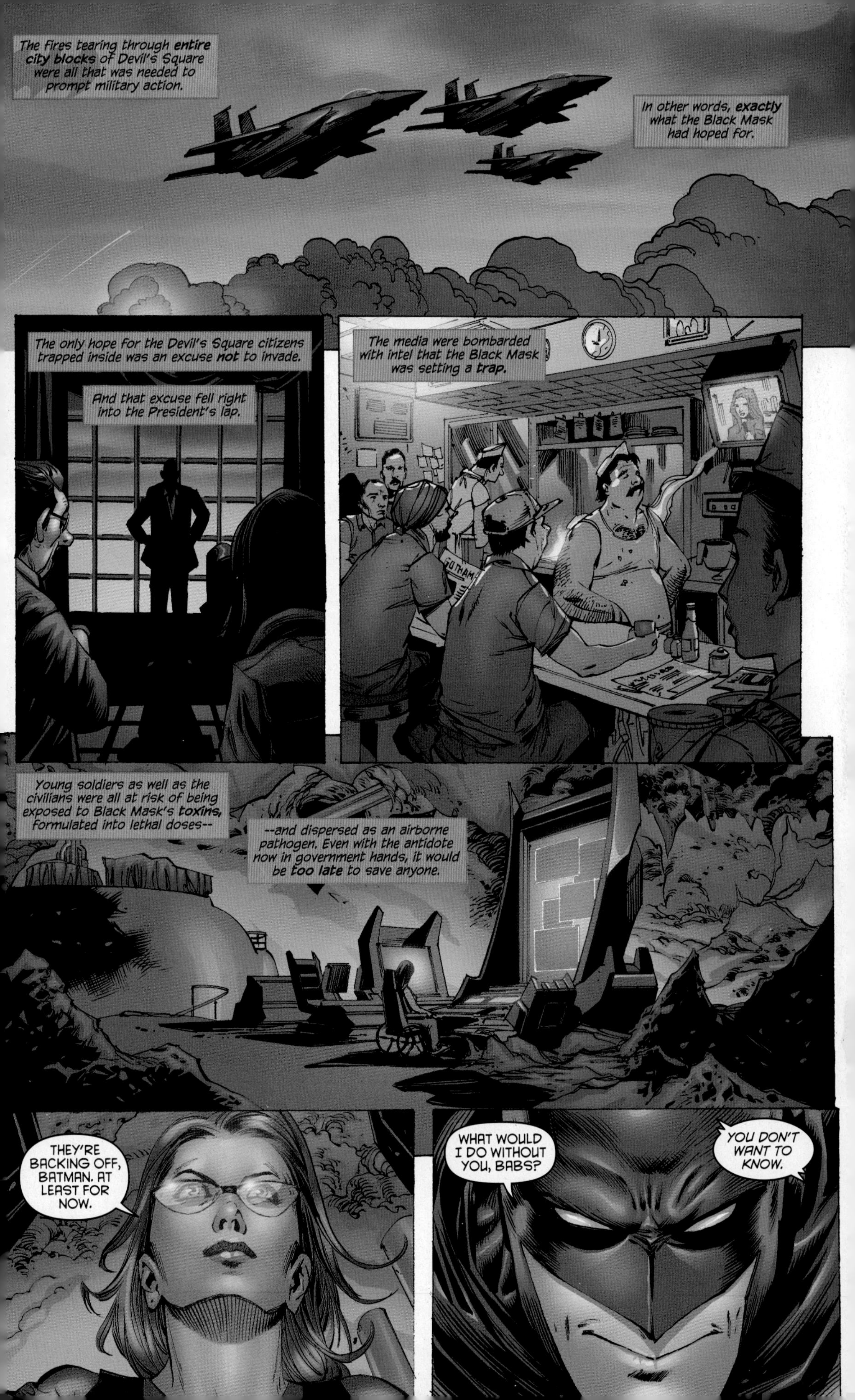
The fires tearing through entire city blocks of Devil's Square were all that was needed to prompt military action.
In other words, exactly what the Black Mask had hoped for.
The only hope for the Devil's Square citizens trapped inside was an excuse not to invade.
And that excuse fell right into the President's lap.
The media were bombarded with intel that the Black Mask was setting a trap.
GOTHAM
Young soldiers as well as the civilians were all at risk of being exposed to Black Mask's toxins, formulated into lethal doses--
--and dispersed as an airborne pathogen. Even with the antidote now in government hands, it would be too late to save anyone.
THEY'RE BACKING OFF, BATMAN. AT LEAST FOR NOW.
WHAT WOULD I DO WITHOUT YOU, BABS?
YOU DON'T WANT TO KNOW.

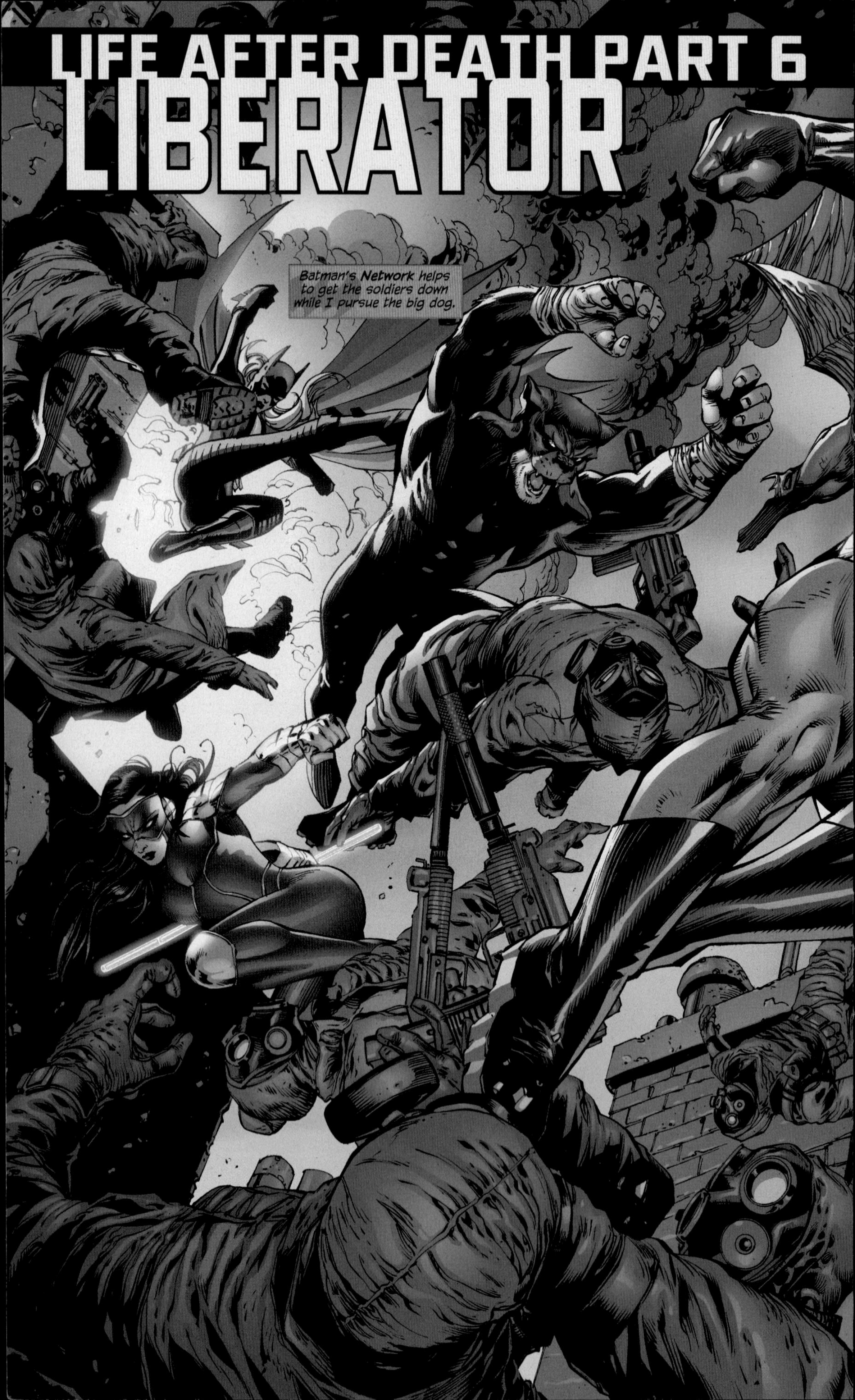
LIFE AFTER DEATH PART 6
LIBERATOR
Batman's **Network** helps to get the soldiers down while I pursue the big dog.

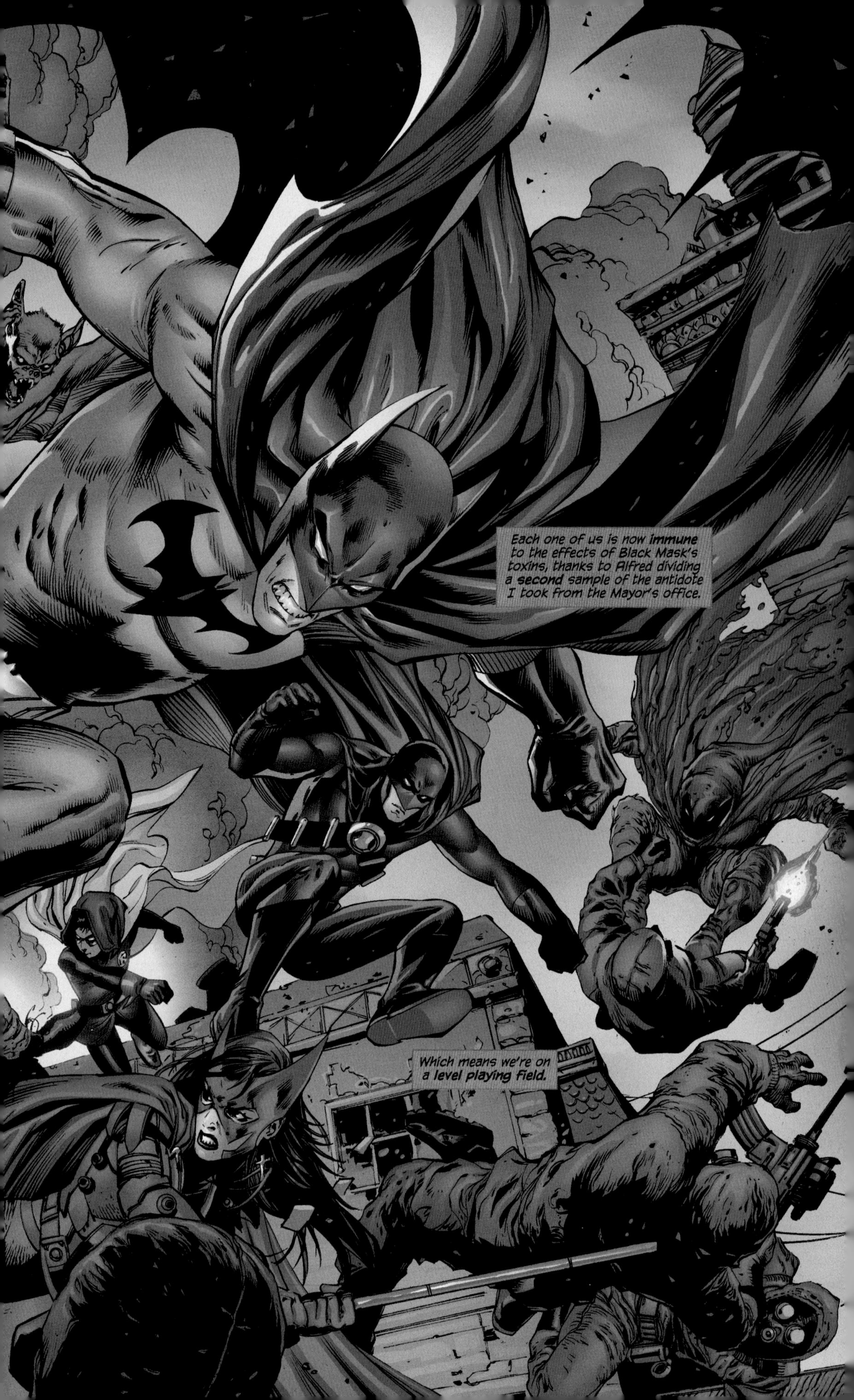
Each one of us is now immune to the effects of Black Mask's toxins, thanks to Alfred dividing a second sample of the antidote I took from the Mayor's office.
Which means we're on a level playing field.

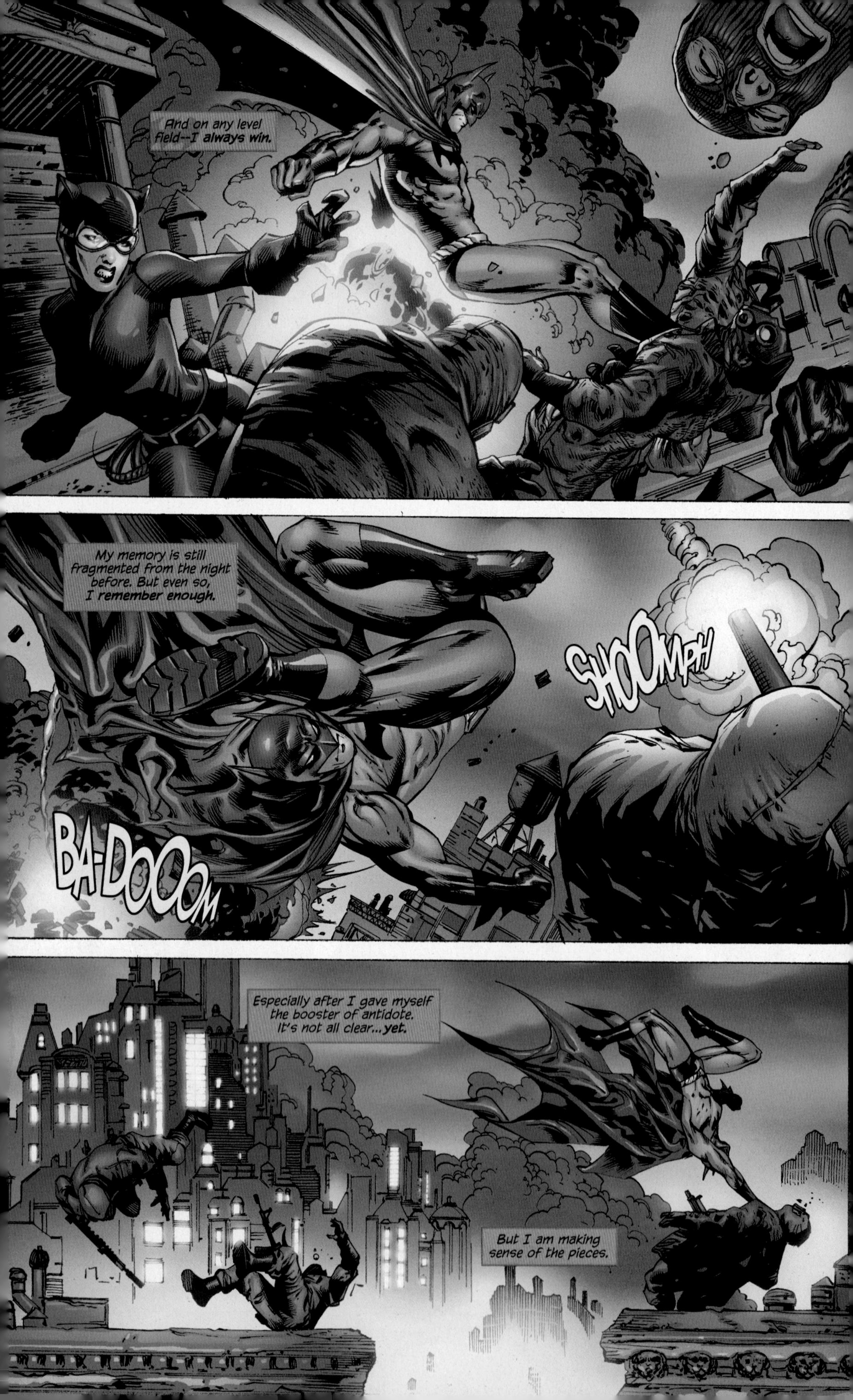
And on any level field--I always win.
My memory is still fragmented from the night before. But even so, I remember enough.
SHOOMPH
BA-DOOOM
Especially after I gave myself the booster of antidote. It's not all clear...yet.
But I am making sense of the pieces.

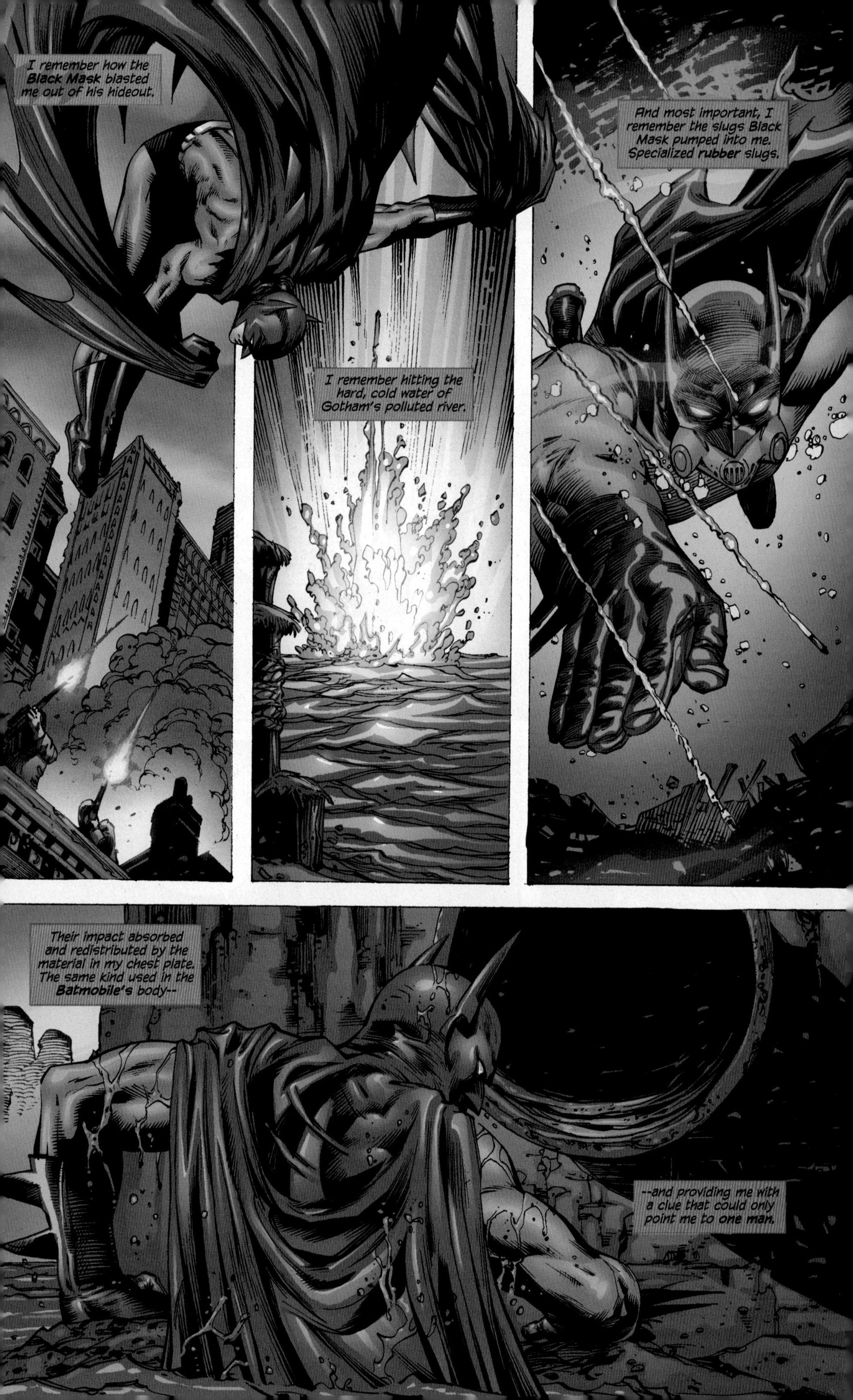
I remember how the Black Mask blasted me out of his hideout.
I remember hitting the hard, cold water of Gotham's polluted river.
And most important, I remember the slugs Black Mask pumped into me. Specialized rubber slugs.
Their impact absorbed and redistributed by the material in my chest plate. The same kind used in the Batmobile's body--
--and providing me with a clue that could only point me to one man.

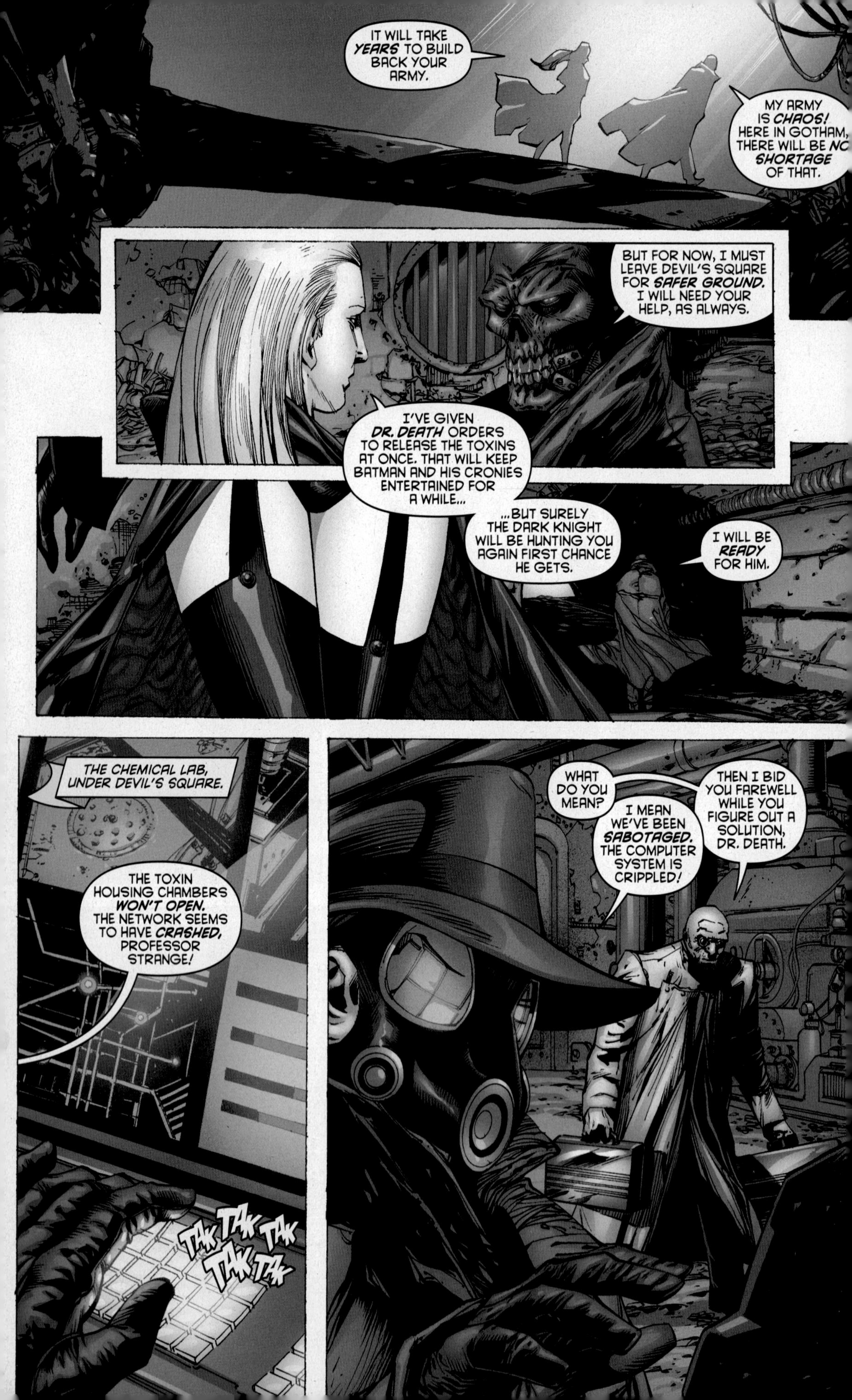
IT WILL TAKE YEARS TO BUILD BACK YOUR ARMY.
MY ARMY IS CHAOS! HERE IN GOTHAM, THERE WILL BE NO SHORTAGE OF THAT.
BUT FOR NOW, I MUST LEAVE DEVIL'S SQUARE FOR SAFER GROUND. I WILL NEED YOUR HELP, AS ALWAYS.
I'VE GIVEN DR. DEATH ORDERS TO RELEASE THE TOXINS AT ONCE. THAT WILL KEEP BATMAN AND HIS CRONIES ENTERTAINED FOR A WHILE...
...BUT SURELY THE DARK KNIGHT WILL BE HUNTING YOU AGAIN FIRST CHANCE HE GETS.
I WILL BE READY FOR HIM.
THE CHEMICAL LAB, UNDER DEVIL'S SQUARE.
THE TOXIN HOUSING CHAMBERS WON'T OPEN. THE NETWORK SEEMS TO HAVE CRASHED, PROFESSOR STRANGE!
TAK TAK TAK TAK TAK
WHAT DO YOU MEAN?
I MEAN WE'VE BEEN SABOTAGED. THE COMPUTER SYSTEM IS CRIPPLED!
THEN I BID YOU FAREWELL WHILE YOU FIGURE OUT A SOLUTION, DR. DEATH.

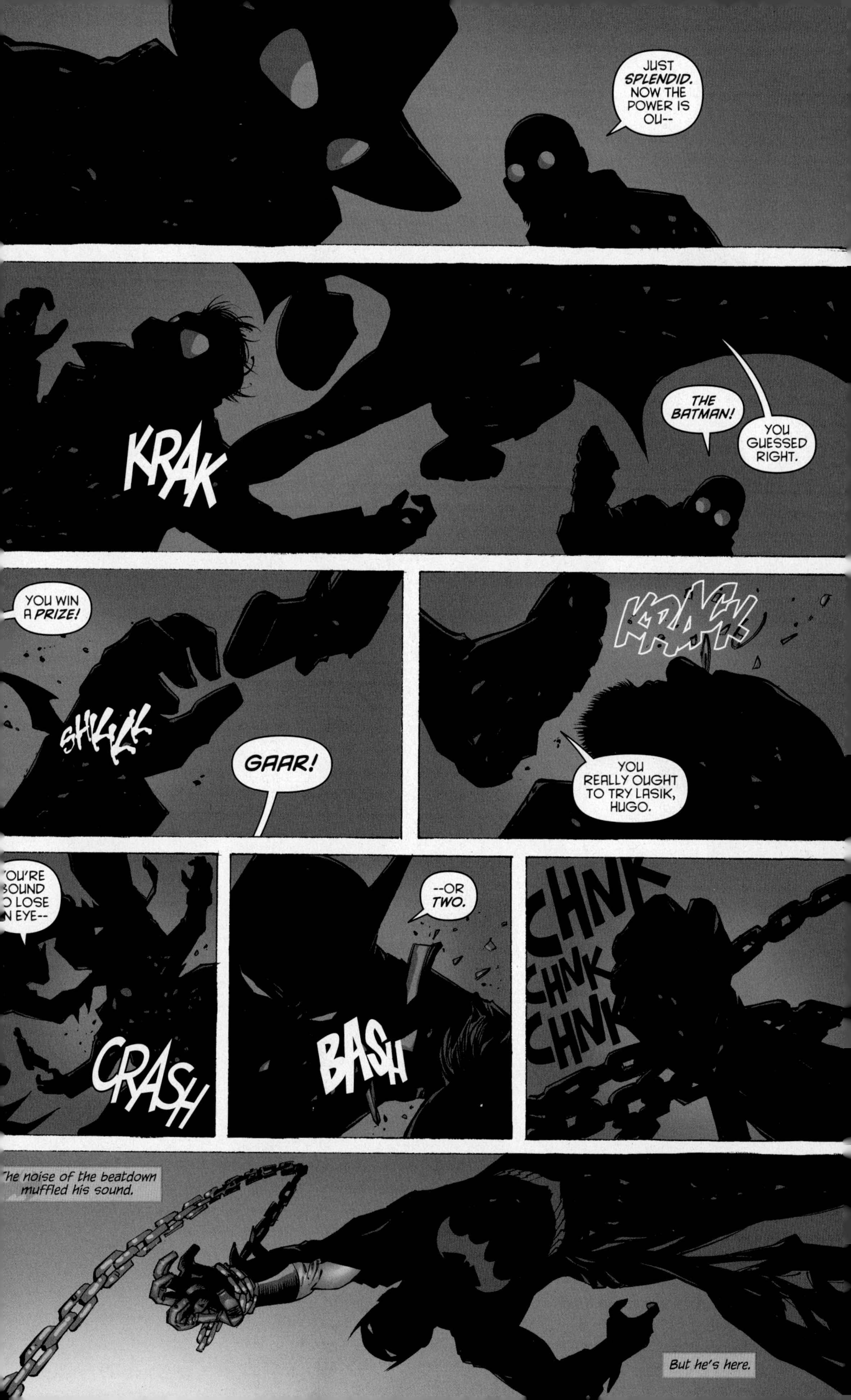
JUST SPLENDID. NOW THE POWER IS OU--
KRAK
THE BATMAN!
YOU GUESSED RIGHT.
YOU WIN A PRIZE!
SHKLK
GAAR!
KRACK
YOU REALLY OUGHT TO TRY LASIK, HUGO.
OU'RE BOUND O LOSE N EYE--
CRASH
--OR TWO.
BASH
CHNK
CHNK
CHNK
he noise of the beatdown muffled his sound.
But he's here.

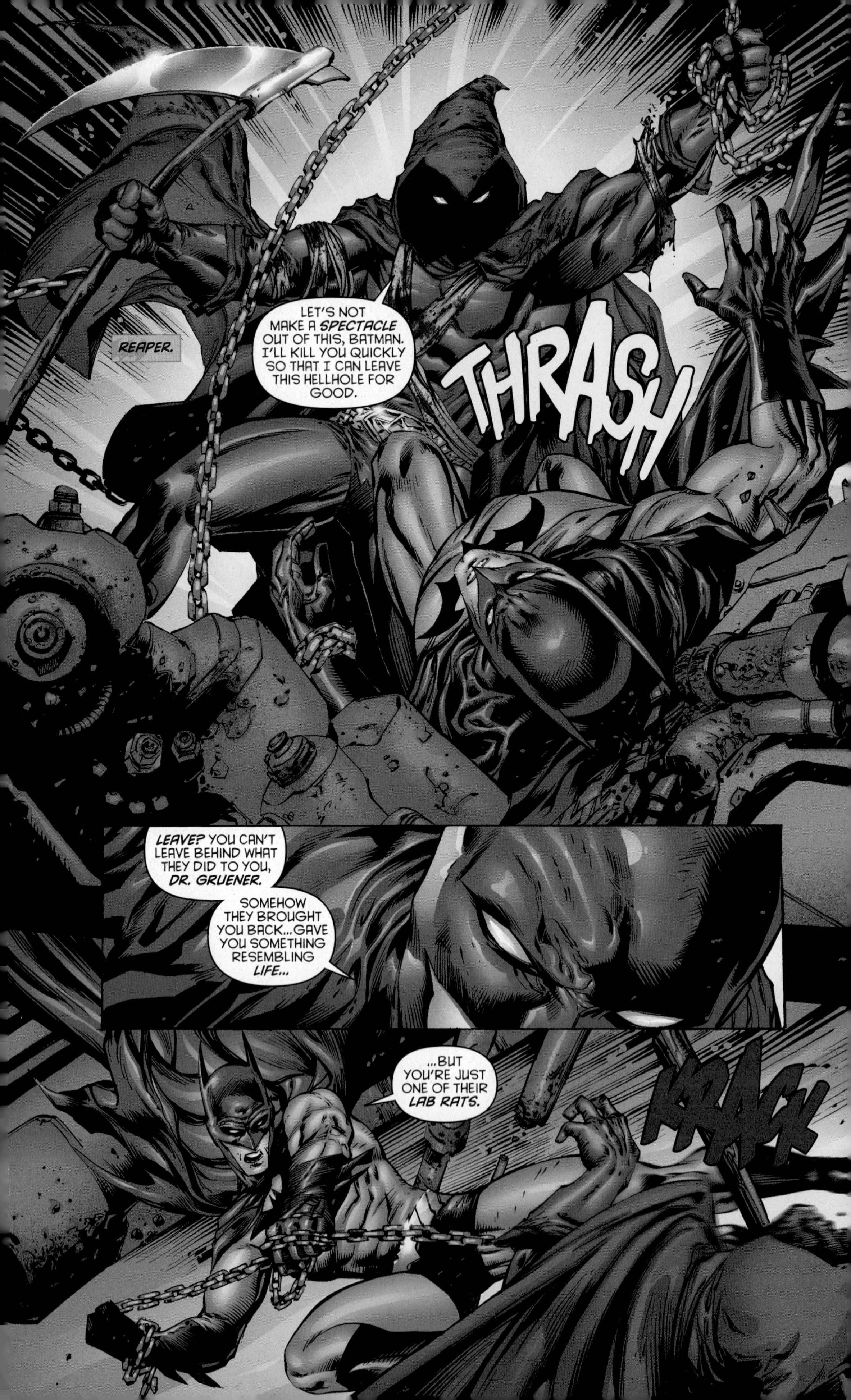
REAPER.
LET'S NOT MAKE A SPECTACLE OUT OF THIS, BATMAN. I'LL KILL YOU QUICKLY SO THAT I CAN LEAVE THIS HELLHOLE FOR GOOD.
THRASH
LEAVE? YOU CAN'T LEAVE BEHIND WHAT THEY DID TO YOU, DR. GRUENER.
SOMEHOW THEY BROUGHT YOU BACK...GAVE YOU SOMETHING RESEMBLING LIFE...
...BUT YOU'RE JUST ONE OF THEIR LAB RATS.
KRACK

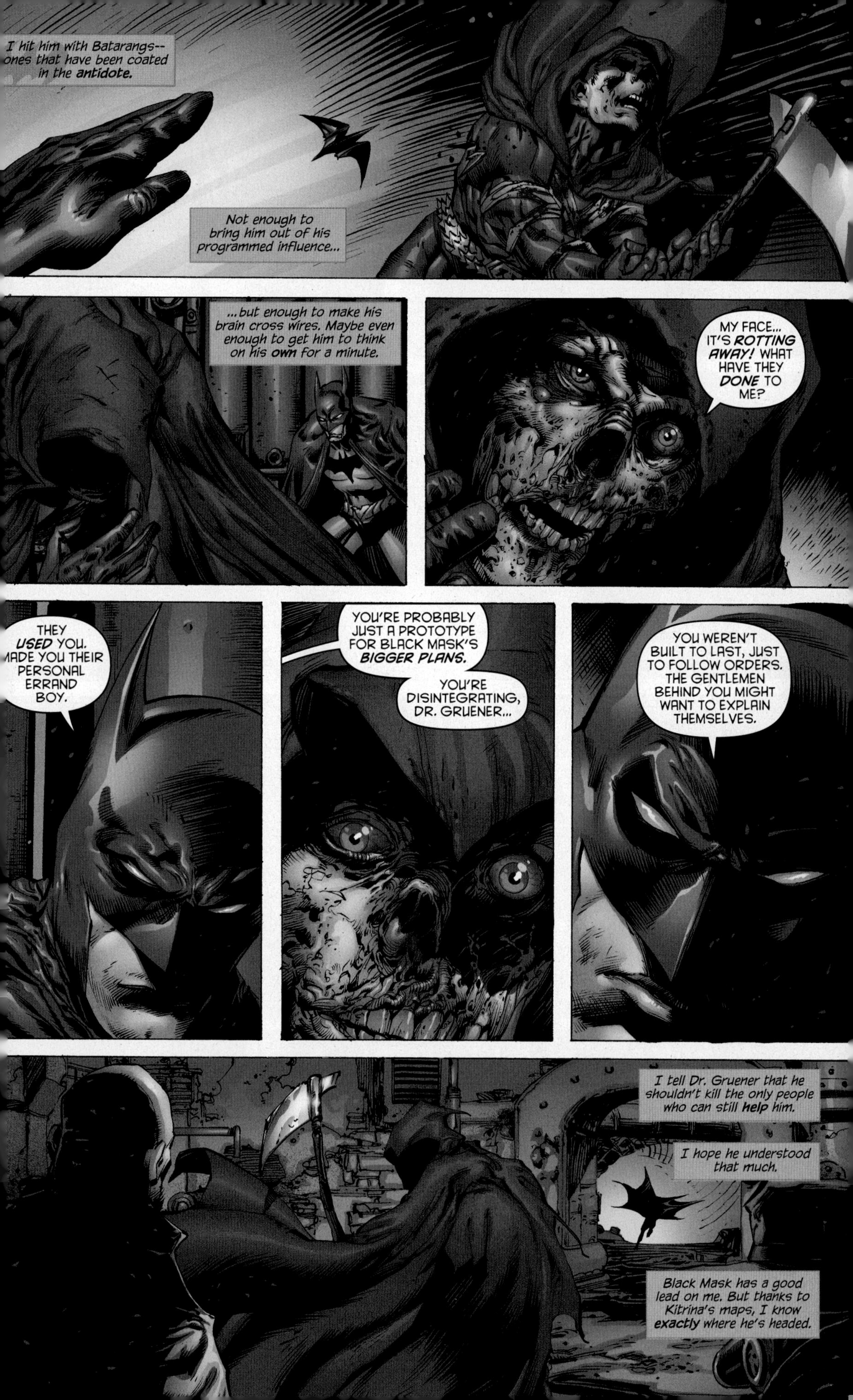

I hit him with Batarangs-- ones that have been coated in the **antidote.**
Not enough to bring him out of his programmed influence...
...but enough to make his brain cross wires. Maybe even enough to get him to think on his **own** for a minute.
MY FACE... IT'S ***ROTTING AWAY!*** WHAT HAVE THEY ***DONE*** TO ME?
THEY ***USED*** YOU. MADE YOU THEIR PERSONAL ERRAND BOY.
YOU'RE PROBABLY JUST A PROTOTYPE FOR BLACK MASK'S ***BIGGER PLANS.***
YOU'RE DISINTEGRATING, DR. GRUENER...
YOU WEREN'T BUILT TO LAST, JUST TO FOLLOW ORDERS. THE GENTLEMEN BEHIND YOU MIGHT WANT TO EXPLAIN THEMSELVES.
I tell Dr. Gruener that he shouldn't kill the only people who can still **help** him.
I hope he understood that much.
Black Mask has a good lead on me. But thanks to Kitrina's maps, I know **exactly** where he's headed.

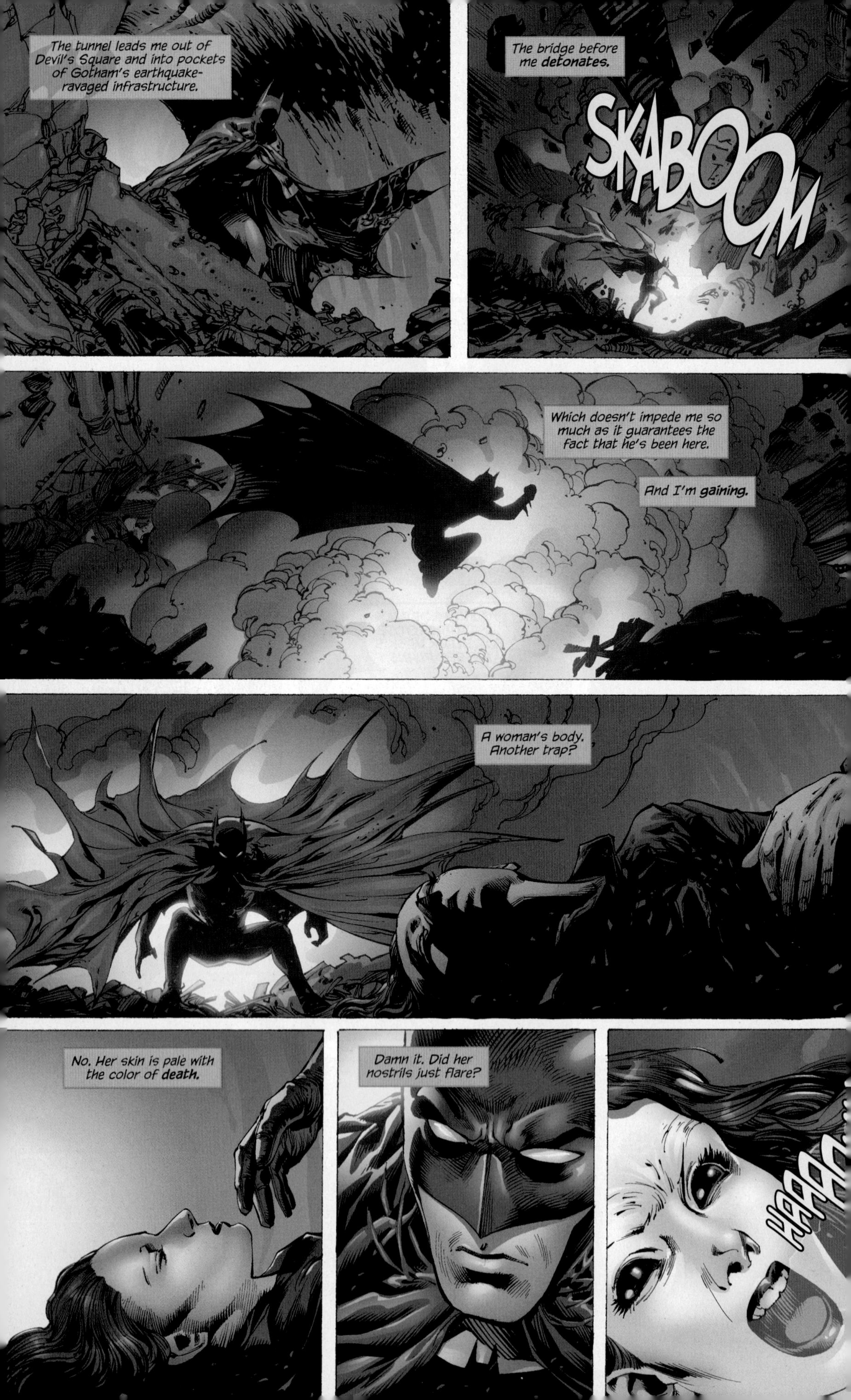
The tunnel leads me out of Devil's Square and into pockets of Gotham's earthquake-ravaged infrastructure.
The bridge before me **detonates.**
SKABOOM
Which doesn't impede me so much as it guarantees the fact that he's been here.
And I'm **gaining.**
A woman's body. Another trap?
No. Her skin is pale with the color of **death.**
Damn it. Did her nostrils just flare?

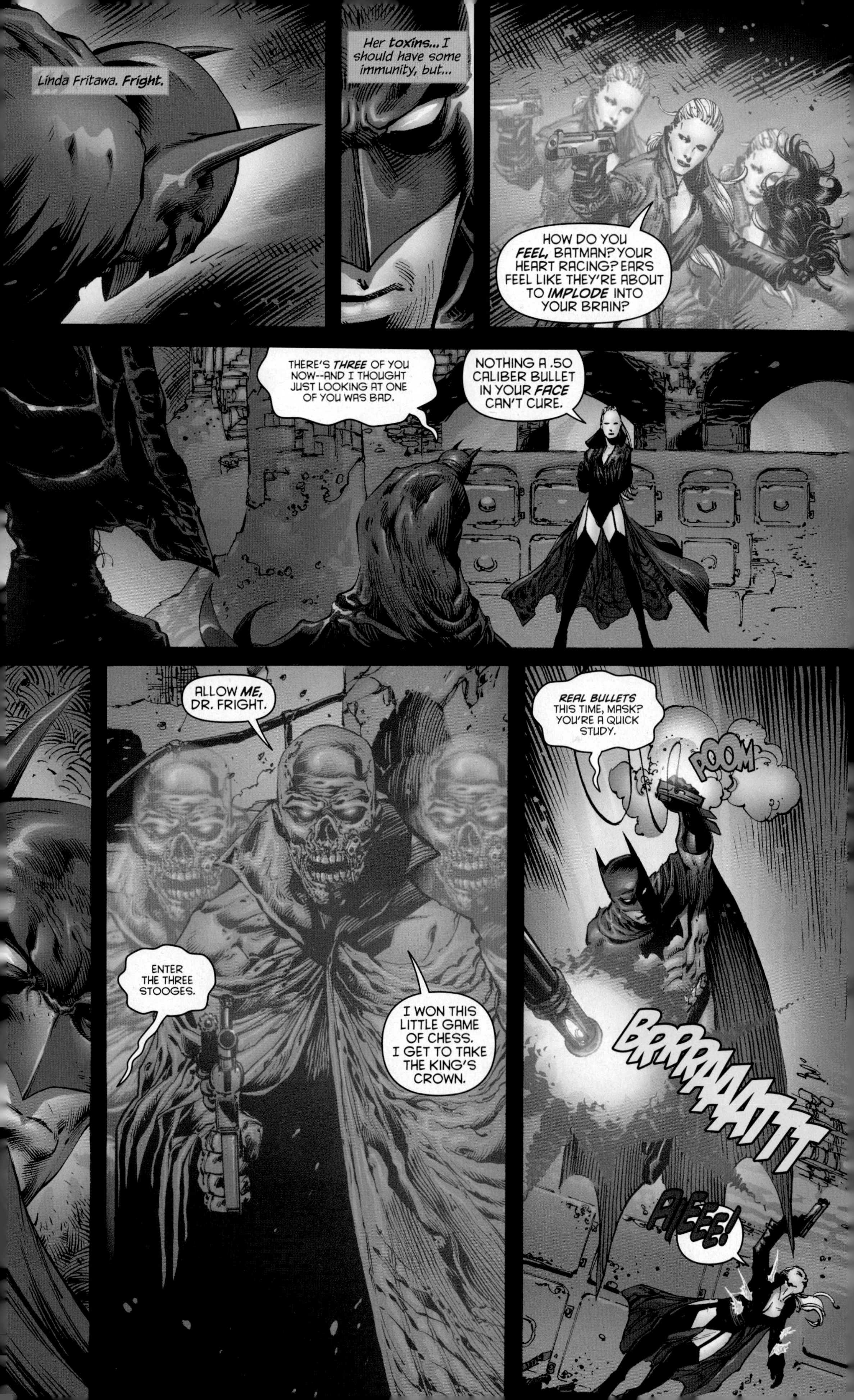
Linda Fritawa. Fright.
Her toxins... I should have some immunity, but...
HOW DO YOU FEEL, BATMAN? YOUR HEART RACING? EARS FEEL LIKE THEY'RE ABOUT TO IMPLODE INTO YOUR BRAIN?
THERE'S THREE OF YOU NOW--AND I THOUGHT JUST LOOKING AT ONE OF YOU WAS BAD.
NOTHING A .50 CALIBER BULLET IN YOUR FACE CAN'T CURE.
ALLOW ME, DR. FRIGHT.
ENTER THE THREE STOOGES.
I WON THIS LITTLE GAME OF CHESS. I GET TO TAKE THE KING'S CROWN.
REAL BULLETS THIS TIME, MASK? YOU'RE A QUICK STUDY.
POOM
BRRRAAATTT
AIEEE!

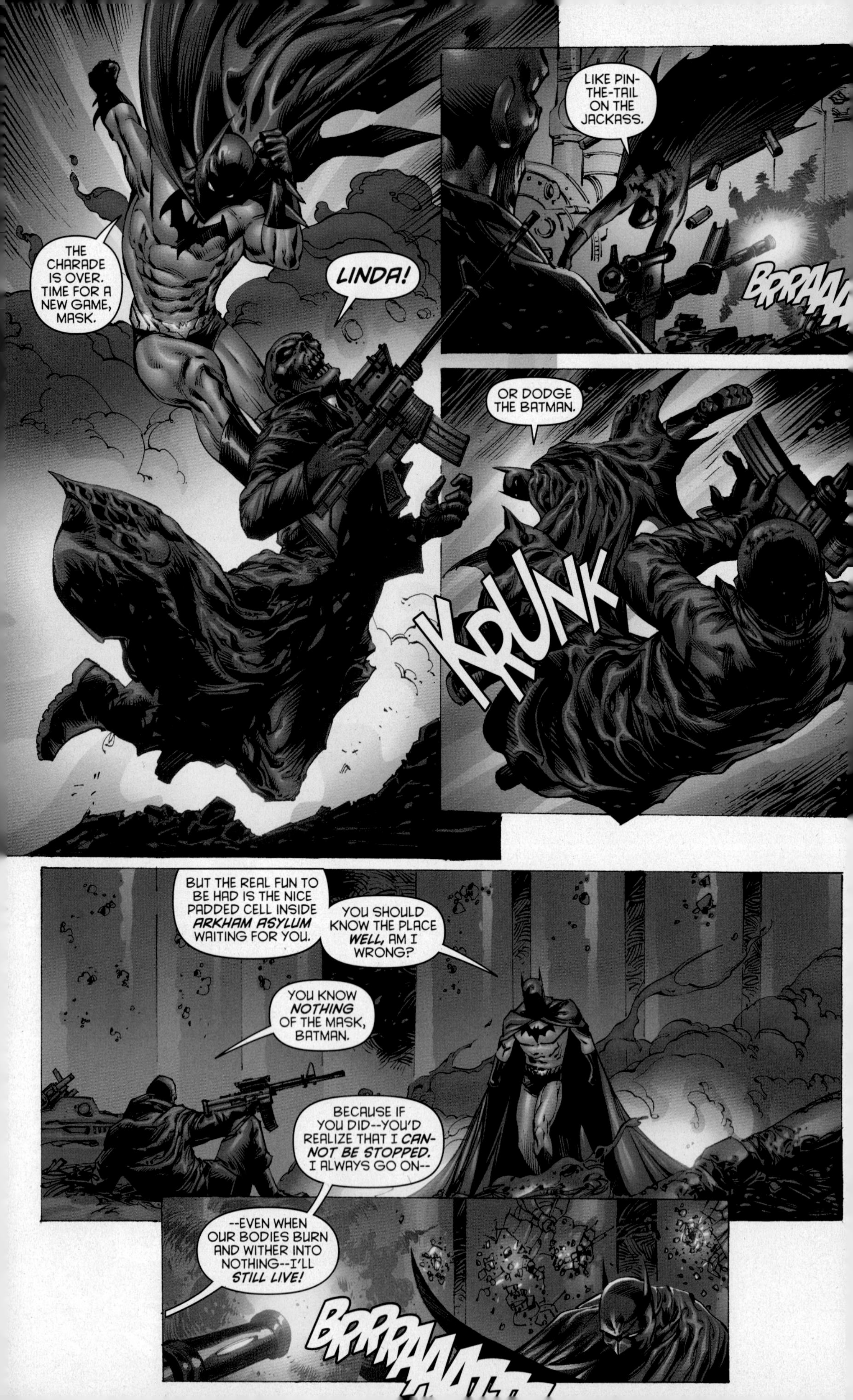
THE CHARADE IS OVER. TIME FOR A NEW GAME, MASK.
LINDA!
LIKE PIN-THE-TAIL ON THE JACKASS.
BRRRAAA
OR DODGE THE BATMAN.
KRUNK
BUT THE REAL FUN TO BE HAD IS THE NICE PADDED CELL INSIDE ARKHAM ASYLUM WAITING FOR YOU.
YOU SHOULD KNOW THE PLACE WELL, AM I WRONG?
YOU KNOW NOTHING OF THE MASK, BATMAN.
BECAUSE IF YOU DID--YOU'D REALIZE THAT I CAN-NOT BE STOPPED. I ALWAYS GO ON--
--EVEN WHEN OUR BODIES BURN AND WITHER INTO NOTHING--I'LL STILL LIVE!
BRRRAAAT

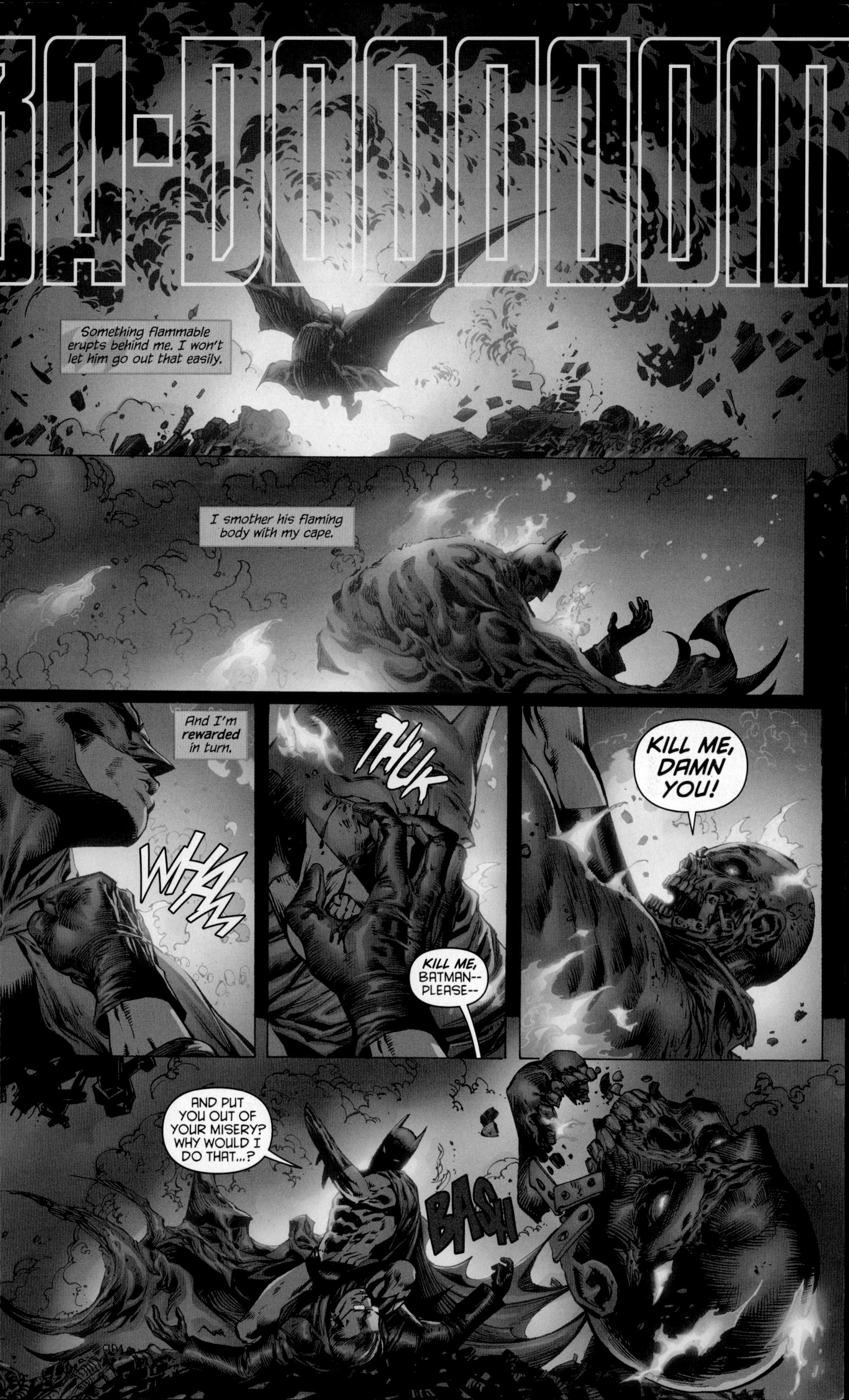
A-DOOOOOM
Something flammable erupts behind me. I won't let him go out that easily.
I smother his flaming body with my cape.
And I'm rewarded in turn.
WHAM
THUK
KILL ME, BATMAN-- PLEASE--
KILL ME, DAMN YOU!
AND PUT YOU OUT OF YOUR MISERY? WHY WOULD I DO THAT...?
BASH

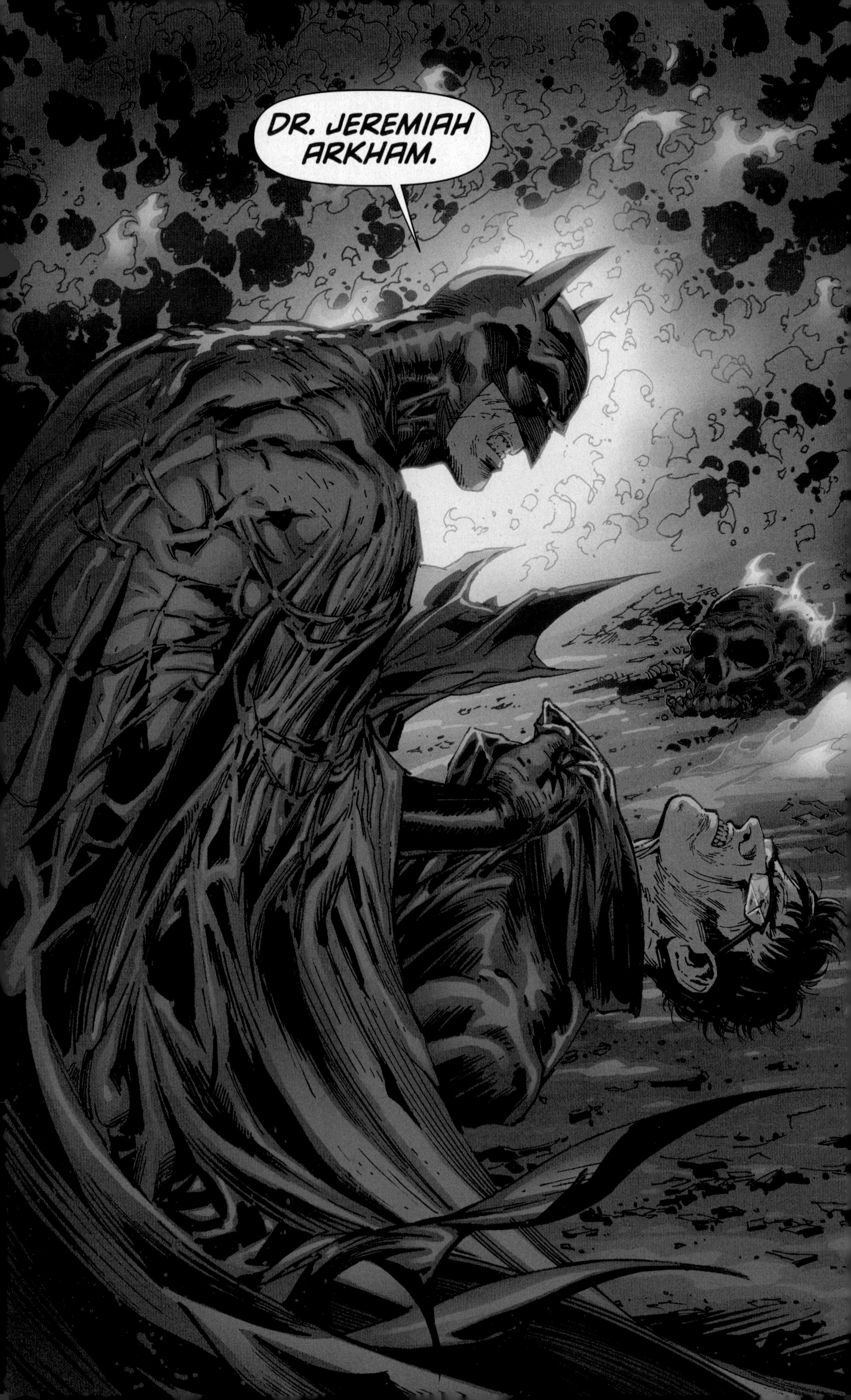
DR. JEREMIAH ARKHAM.

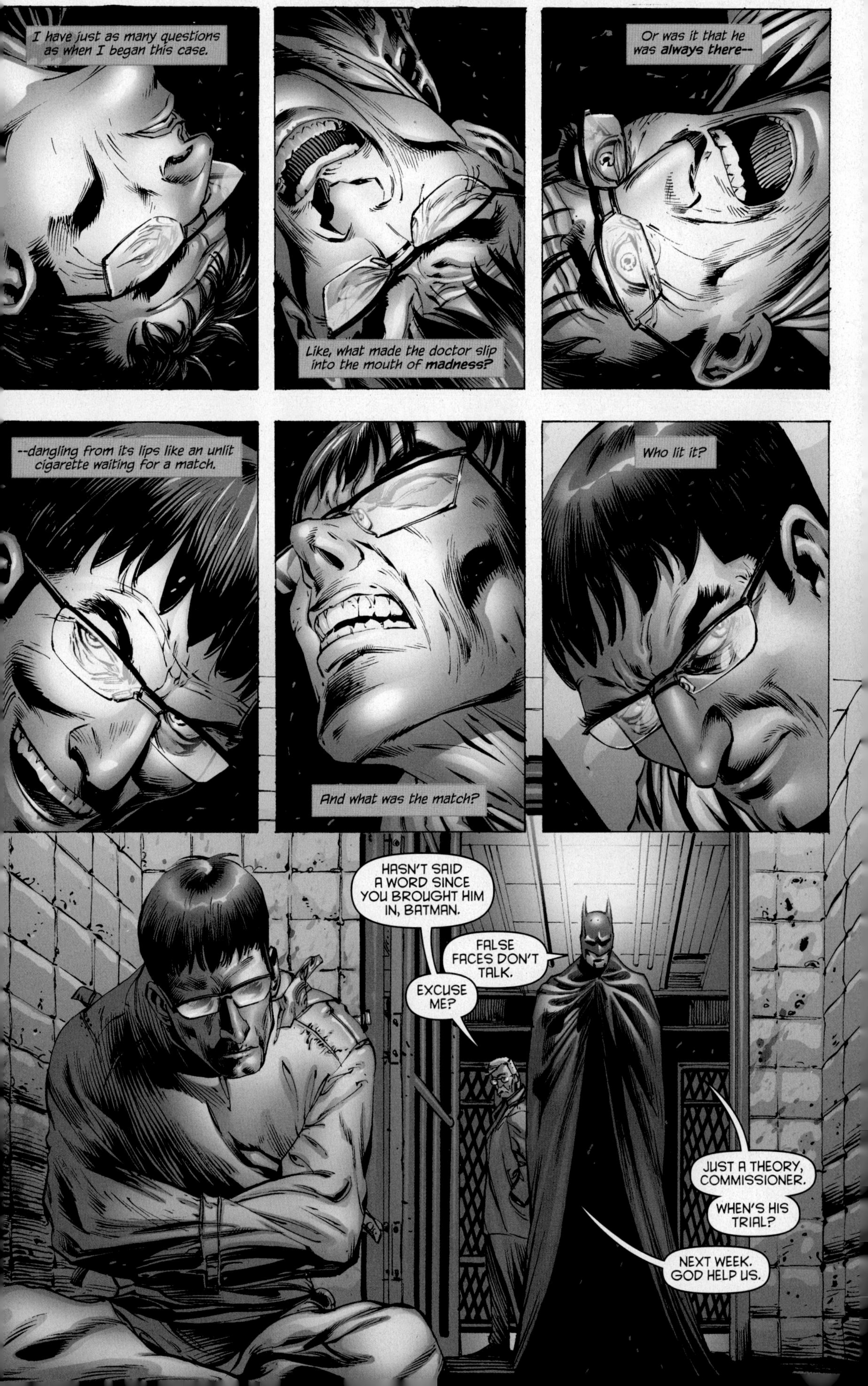
I have just as many questions as when I began this case.
Like, what made the doctor slip into the mouth of madness?
Or was it that he was always there--
--dangling from its lips like an unlit cigarette waiting for a match.
And what was the match?
Who lit it?
HASN'T SAID A WORD SINCE YOU BROUGHT HIM IN, BATMAN.
FALSE FACES DON'T TALK.
EXCUSE ME?
JUST A THEORY, COMMISSIONER.
WHEN'S HIS TRIAL?
NEXT WEEK. GOD HELP US.

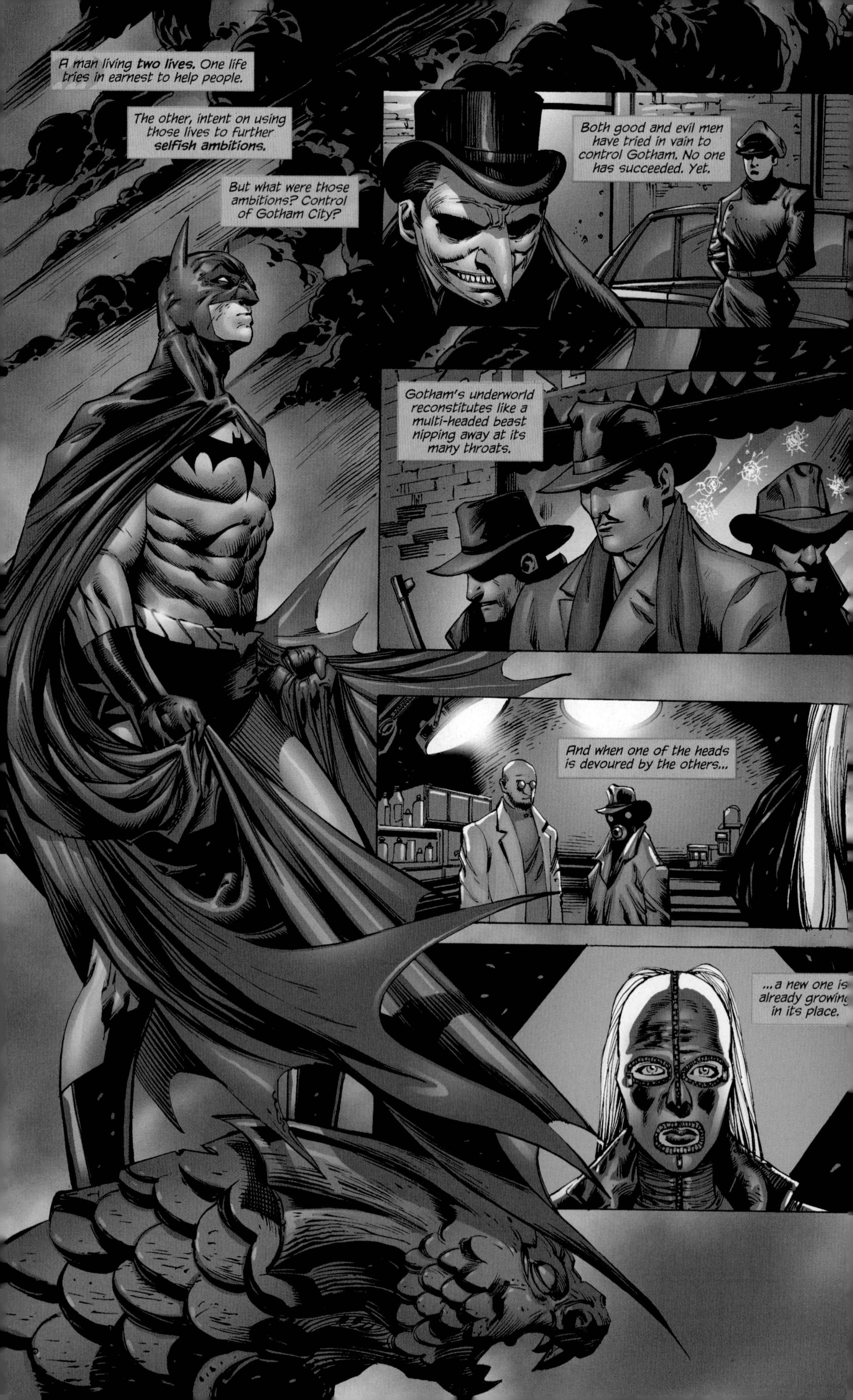
A man living **two lives.** One life tries in earnest to help people.
The other, intent on using those lives to further **selfish ambitions.**
But what were those ambitions? Control of Gotham City?
Both good and evil men have tried in vain to control Gotham. No one has succeeded. Yet.
Gotham's underworld reconstitutes like a multi-headed beast nipping away at its many throats.
And when one of the heads is devoured by the others...
...a new one is already growing in its place.

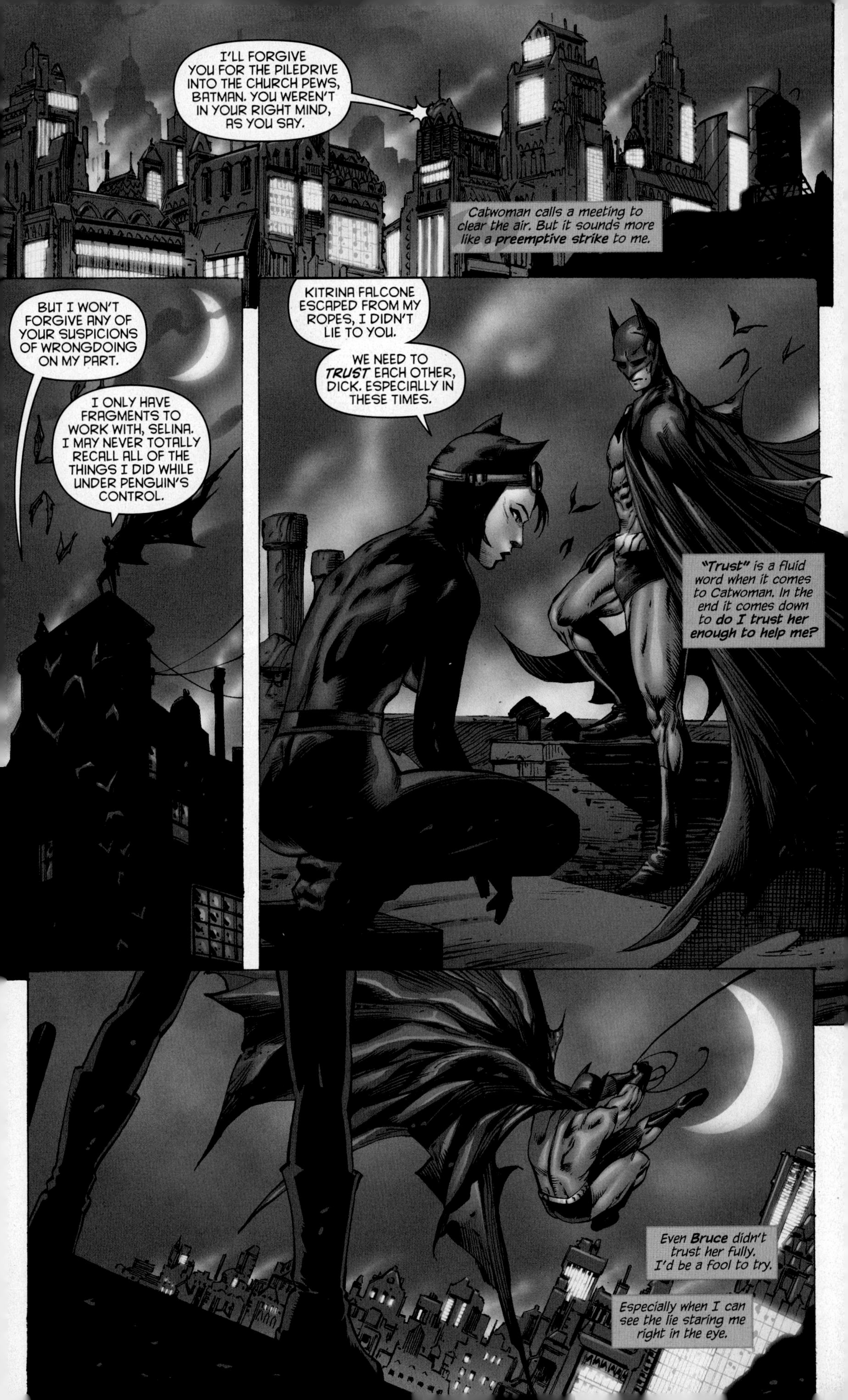

I'LL FORGIVE YOU FOR THE PILEDRIVE INTO THE CHURCH PEWS, BATMAN. YOU WEREN'T IN YOUR RIGHT MIND, AS YOU SAY.
Catwoman calls a meeting to clear the air. But it sounds more like a **preemptive strike** to me.
BUT I WON'T FORGIVE ANY OF YOUR SUSPICIONS OF WRONGDOING ON MY PART.
I ONLY HAVE FRAGMENTS TO WORK WITH, SELINA. I MAY NEVER TOTALLY RECALL ALL OF THE THINGS I DID WHILE UNDER PENGUIN'S CONTROL.
KITRINA FALCONE ESCAPED FROM MY ROPES, I DIDN'T LIE TO YOU.
WE NEED TO ***TRUST*** EACH OTHER, DICK. ESPECIALLY IN THESE TIMES.
"Trust" is a fluid word when it comes to Catwoman. In the end it comes down to **do I trust her enough to help me?**
Even **Bruce** didn't trust her fully. I'd be a fool to try.
Especially when I can see the lie staring me right in the eye.

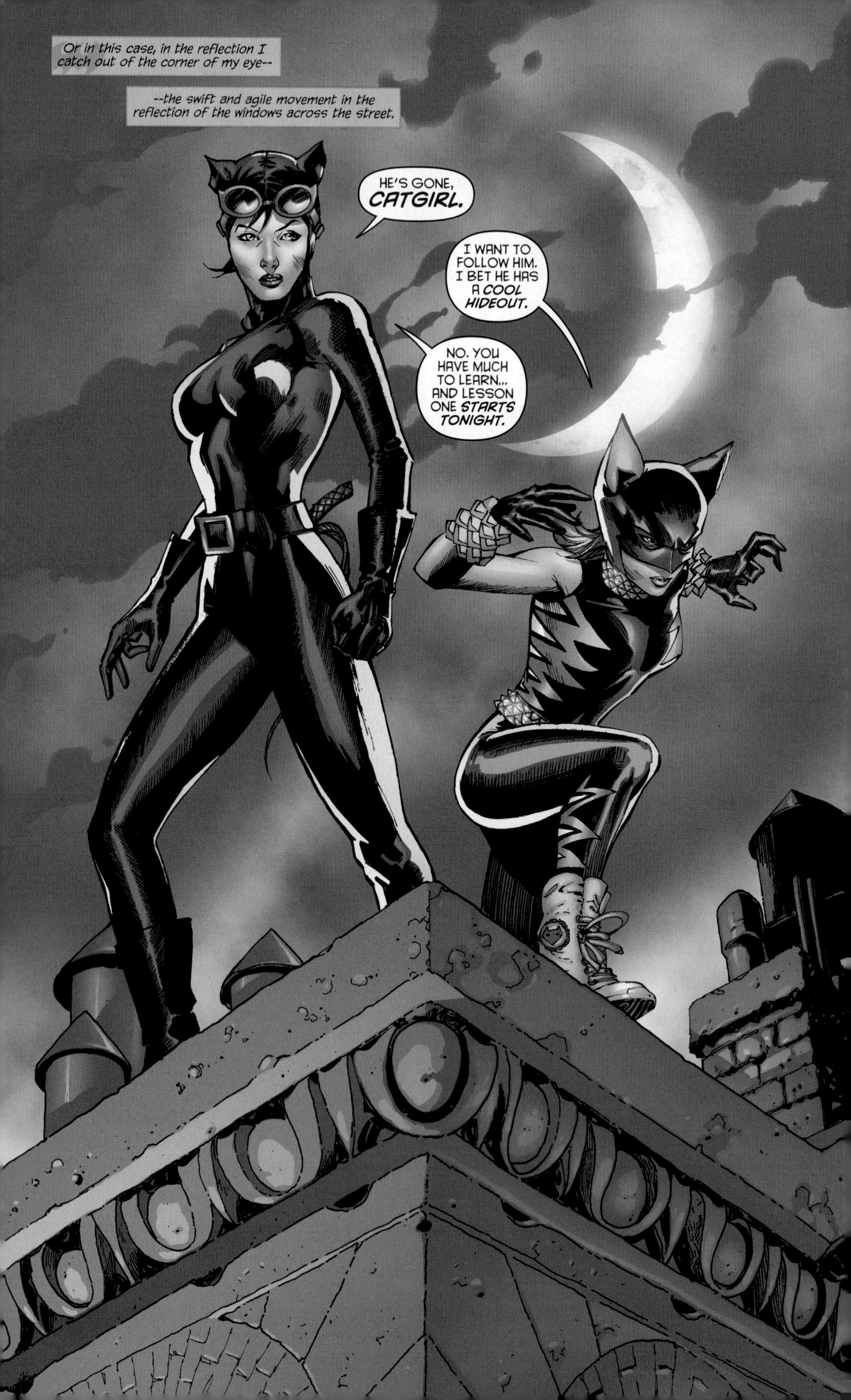
Or in this case, in the reflection I catch out of the corner of my eye--
--the swift and agile movement in the reflection of the windows across the street.
HE'S GONE, CATGIRL.
I WANT TO FOLLOW HIM. I BET HE HAS A COOL HIDEOUT.
NO. YOU HAVE MUCH TO LEARN... AND LESSON ONE STARTS TONIGHT.

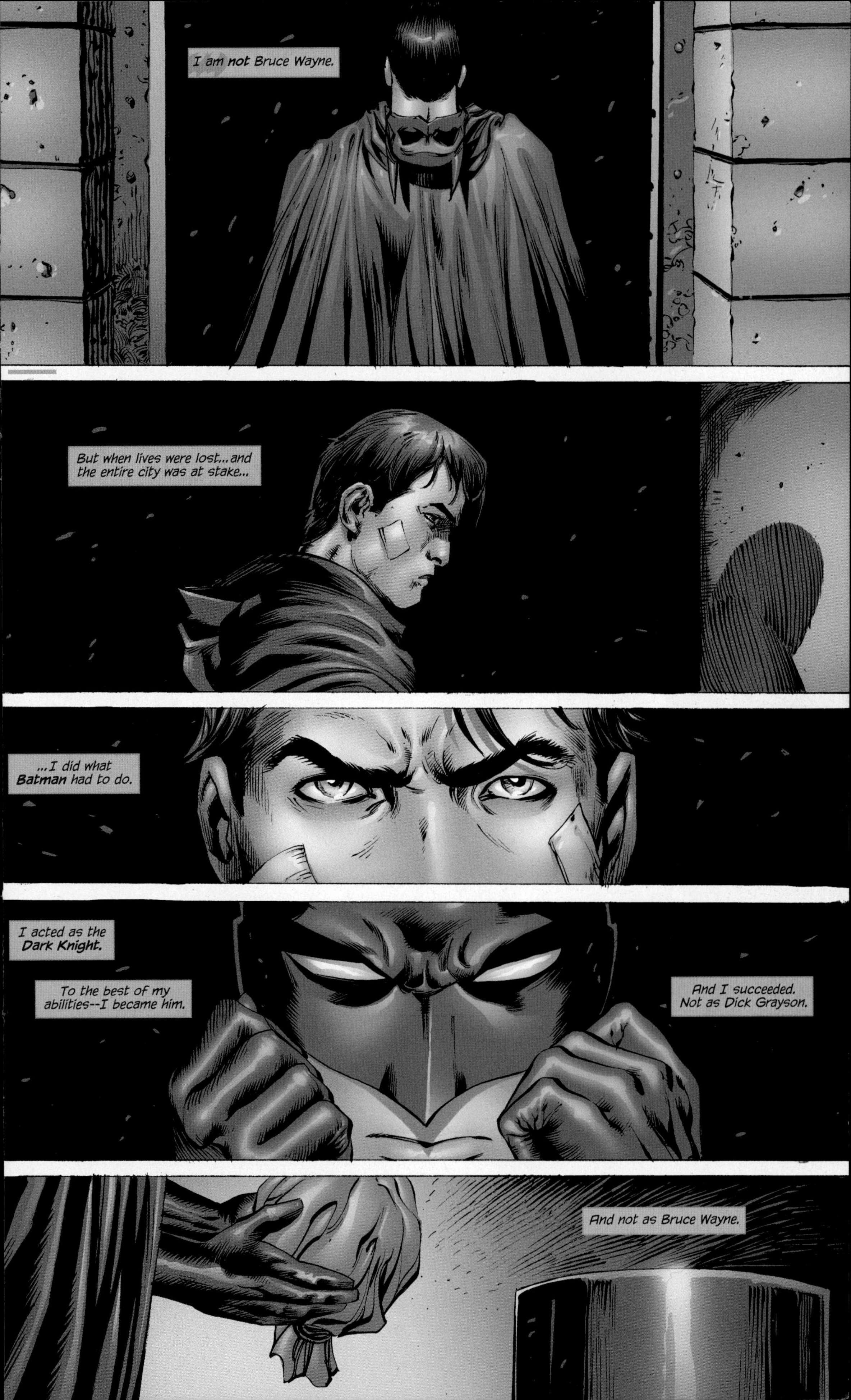
I am **not** Bruce Wayne.
But when lives were lost...and the entire city was at stake...
...I did what **Batman** had to do.
I acted as the **Dark Knight.**
To the best of my abilities--I became him.
And I succeeded. Not as Dick Grayson.
And not as Bruce Wayne.

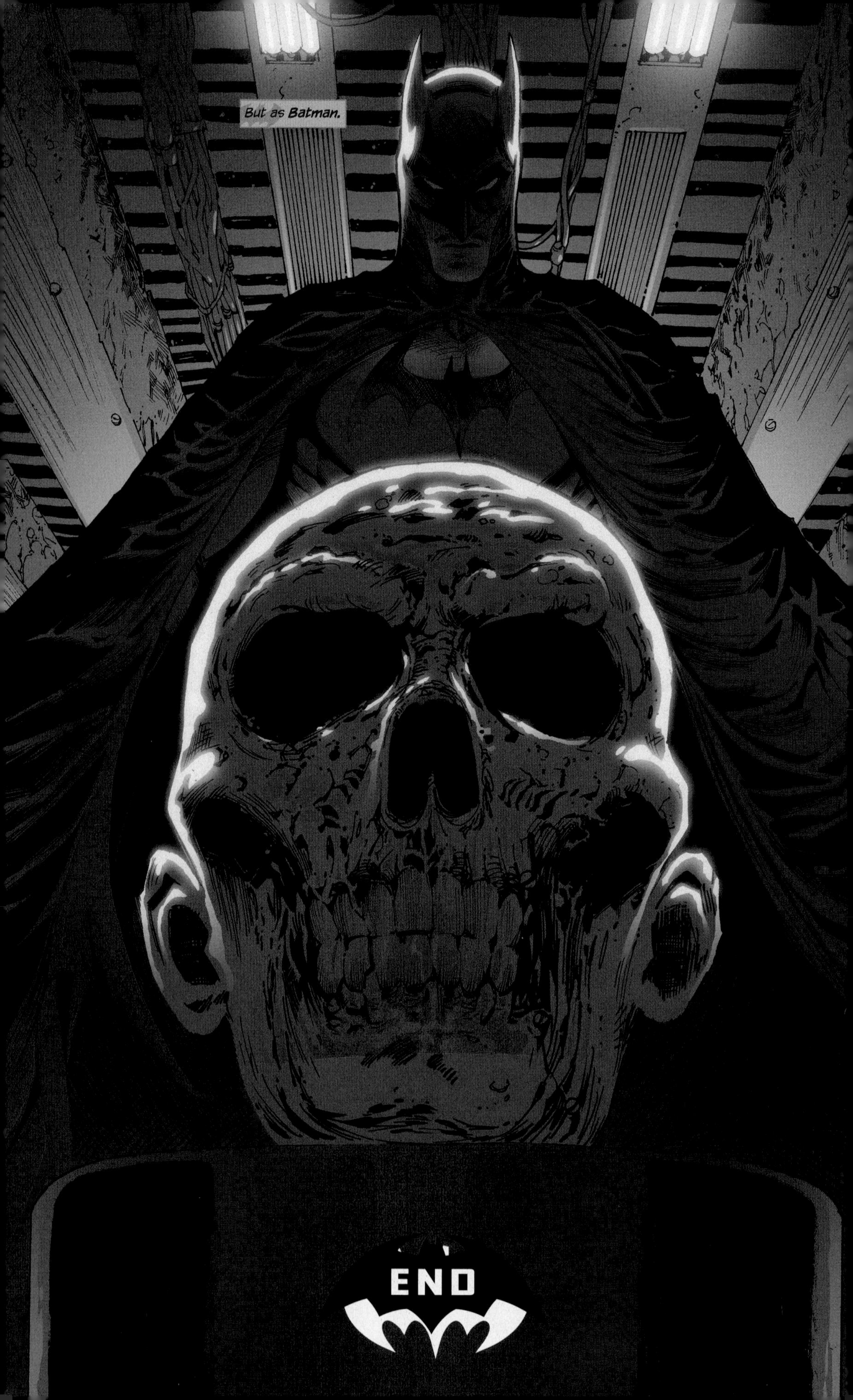
But as Batman.
END

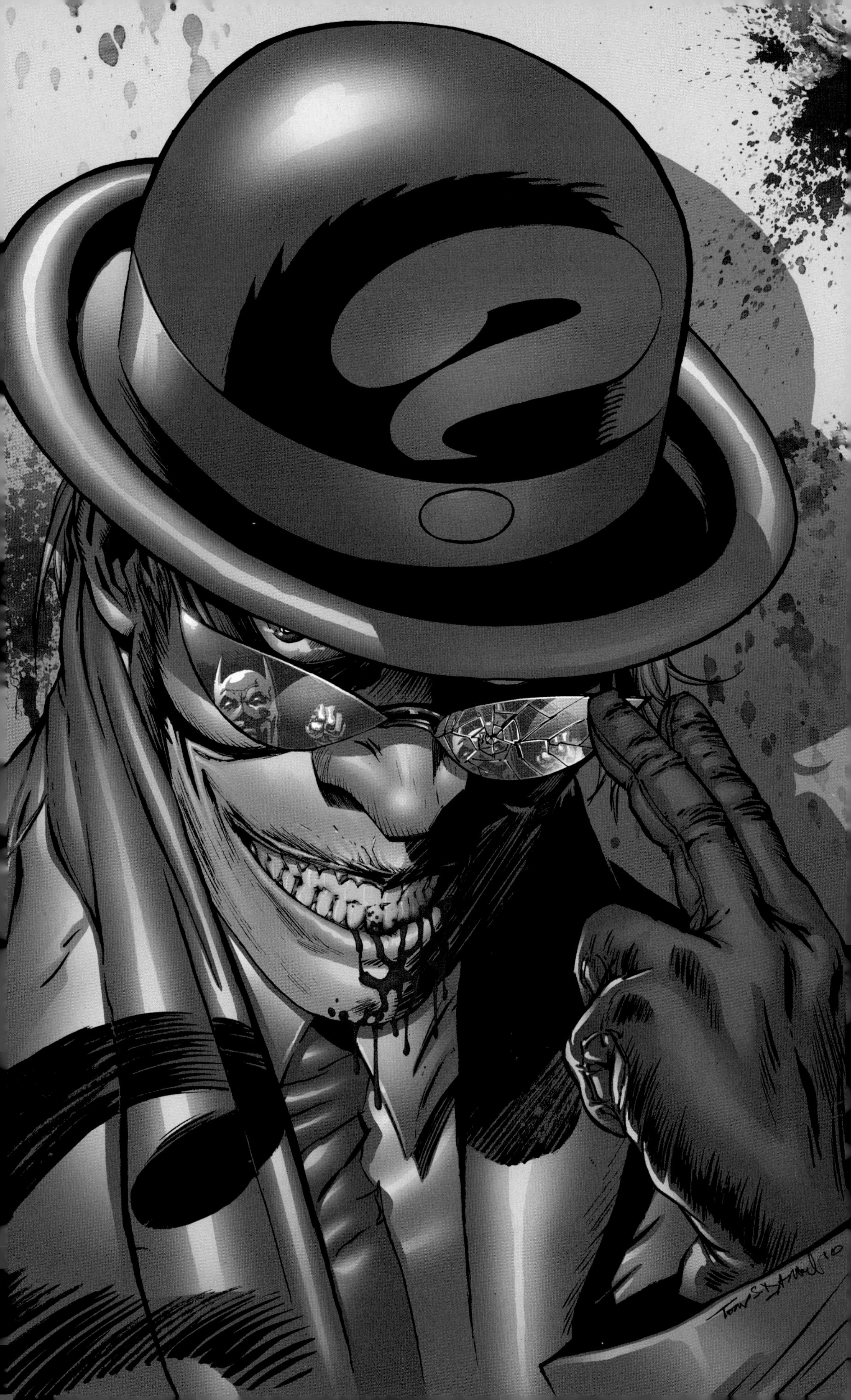

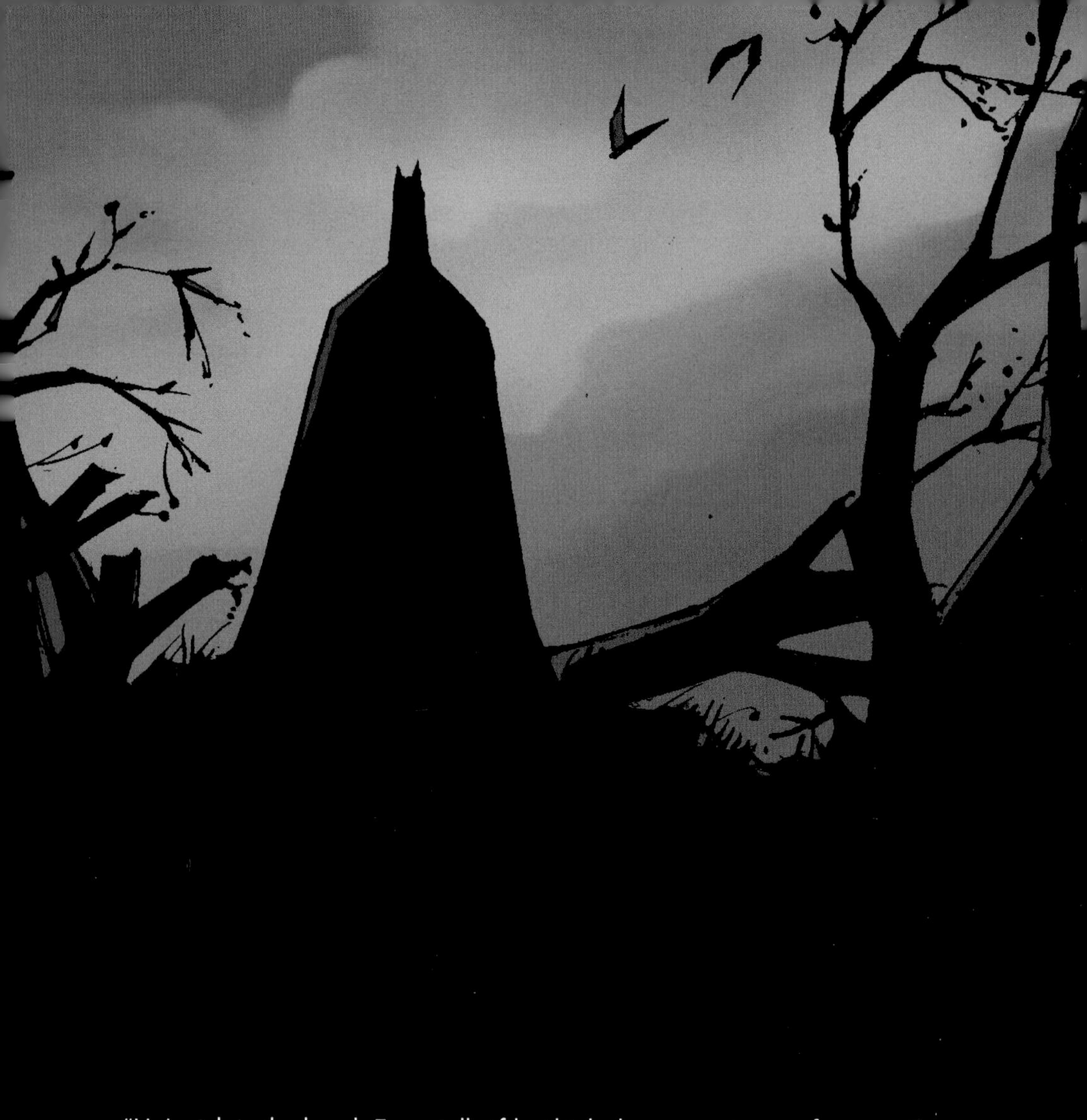

"He's sick in the head. Especially if he thinks he can get away from me."

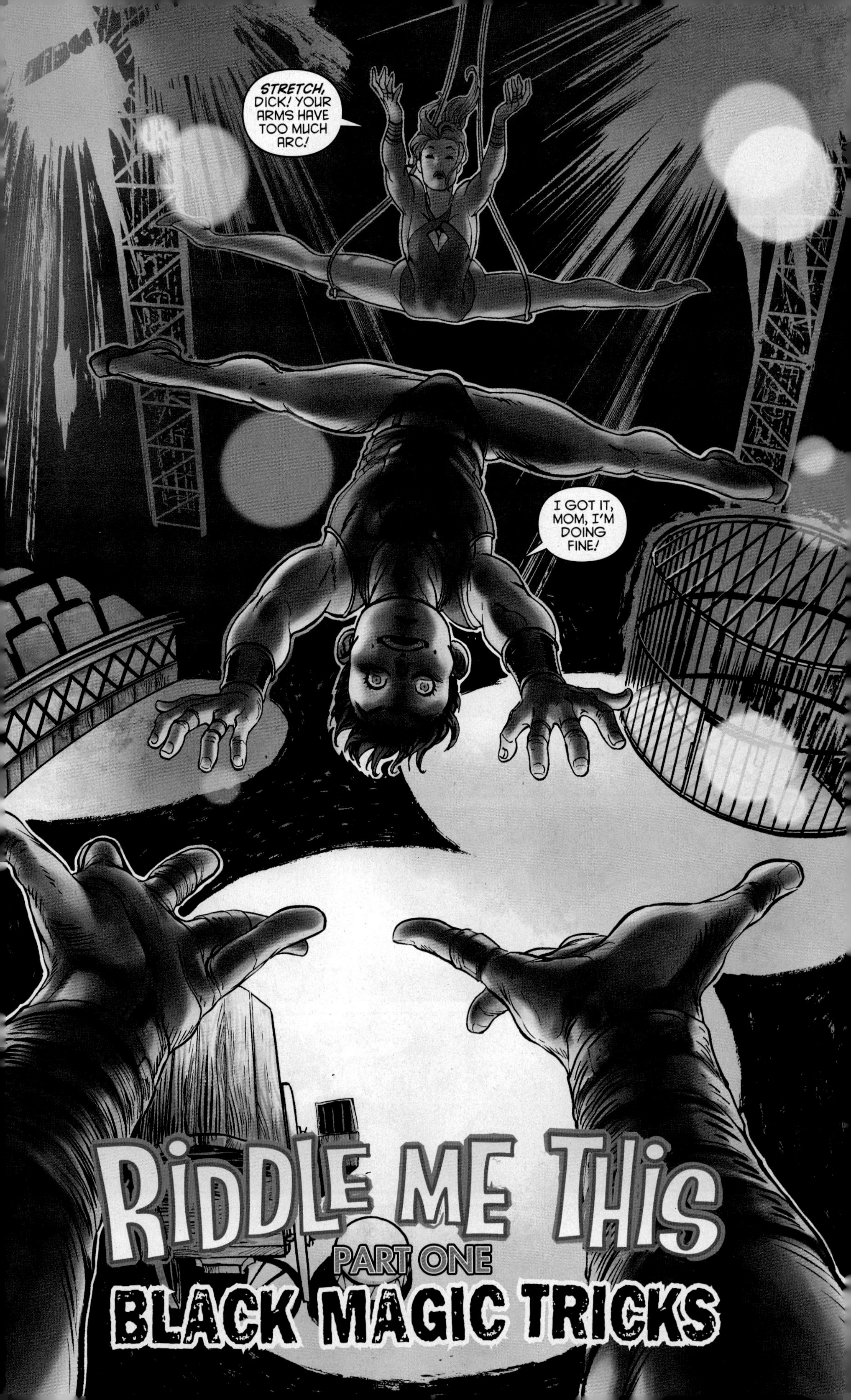
STRETCH, DICK! YOUR ARMS HAVE TOO MUCH ARC!
I GOT IT, MOM, I'M DOING FINE!
RIDDLE ME THIS
PART ONE
BLACK MAGIC TRICKS

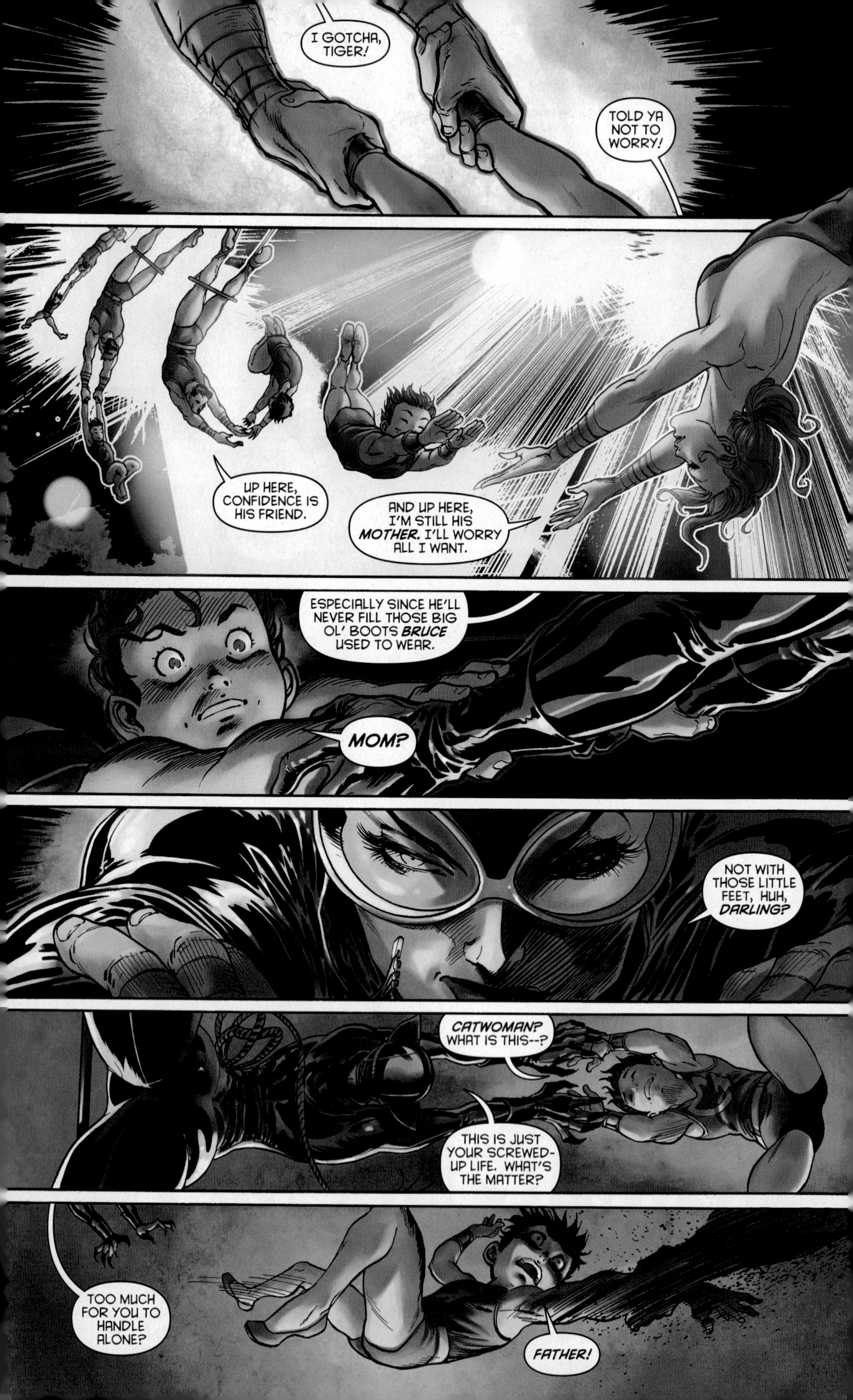

I GOTCHA, TIGER!
TOLD YA NOT TO WORRY!
UP HERE, CONFIDENCE IS HIS FRIEND.
AND UP HERE, I'M STILL HIS *MOTHER.* I'LL WORRY ALL I WANT.
ESPECIALLY SINCE HE'LL NEVER FILL THOSE BIG OL' BOOTS *BRUCE* USED TO WEAR.
MOM?
NOT WITH THOSE LITTLE FEET, HUH, *DARLING?*
CATWOMAN? WHAT IS THIS--?
THIS IS JUST YOUR SCREWED-UP LIFE. WHAT'S THE MATTER?
TOO MUCH FOR YOU TO HANDLE ALONE?
FATHER!

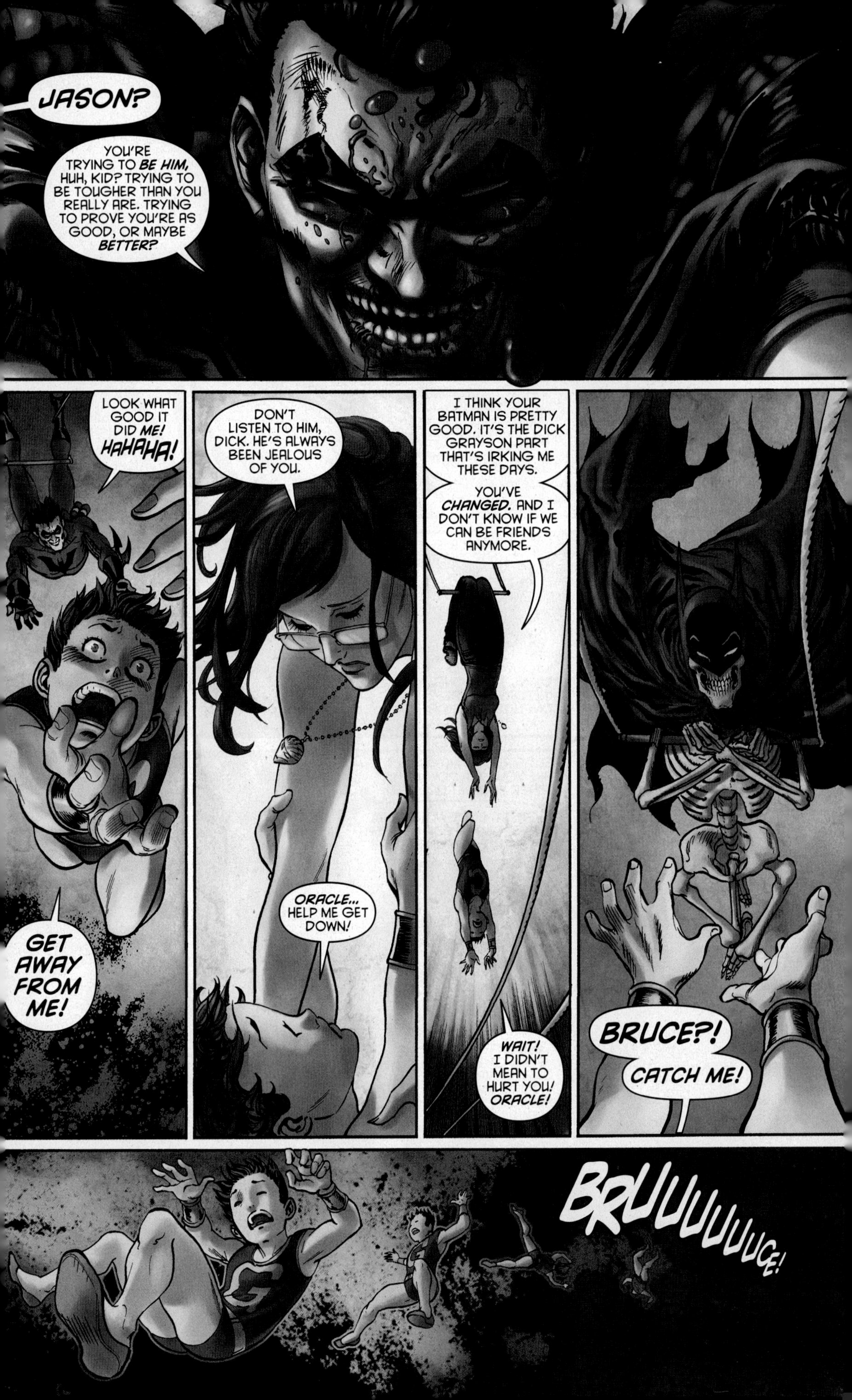

JASON?
YOU'RE TRYING TO BE HIM, HUH, KID? TRYING TO BE TOUGHER THAN YOU REALLY ARE. TRYING TO PROVE YOU'RE AS GOOD, OR MAYBE BETTER?
LOOK WHAT GOOD IT DID ME! HAHAHA!
GET AWAY FROM ME!
DON'T LISTEN TO HIM, DICK. HE'S ALWAYS BEEN JEALOUS OF YOU.
ORACLE... HELP ME GET DOWN!
I THINK YOUR BATMAN IS PRETTY GOOD. IT'S THE DICK GRAYSON PART THAT'S IRKING ME THESE DAYS.
YOU'VE CHANGED. AND I DON'T KNOW IF WE CAN BE FRIENDS ANYMORE.
WAIT! I DIDN'T MEAN TO HURT YOU! ORACLE!
BRUCE?!
CATCH ME!
BRUUUUUUUCE!

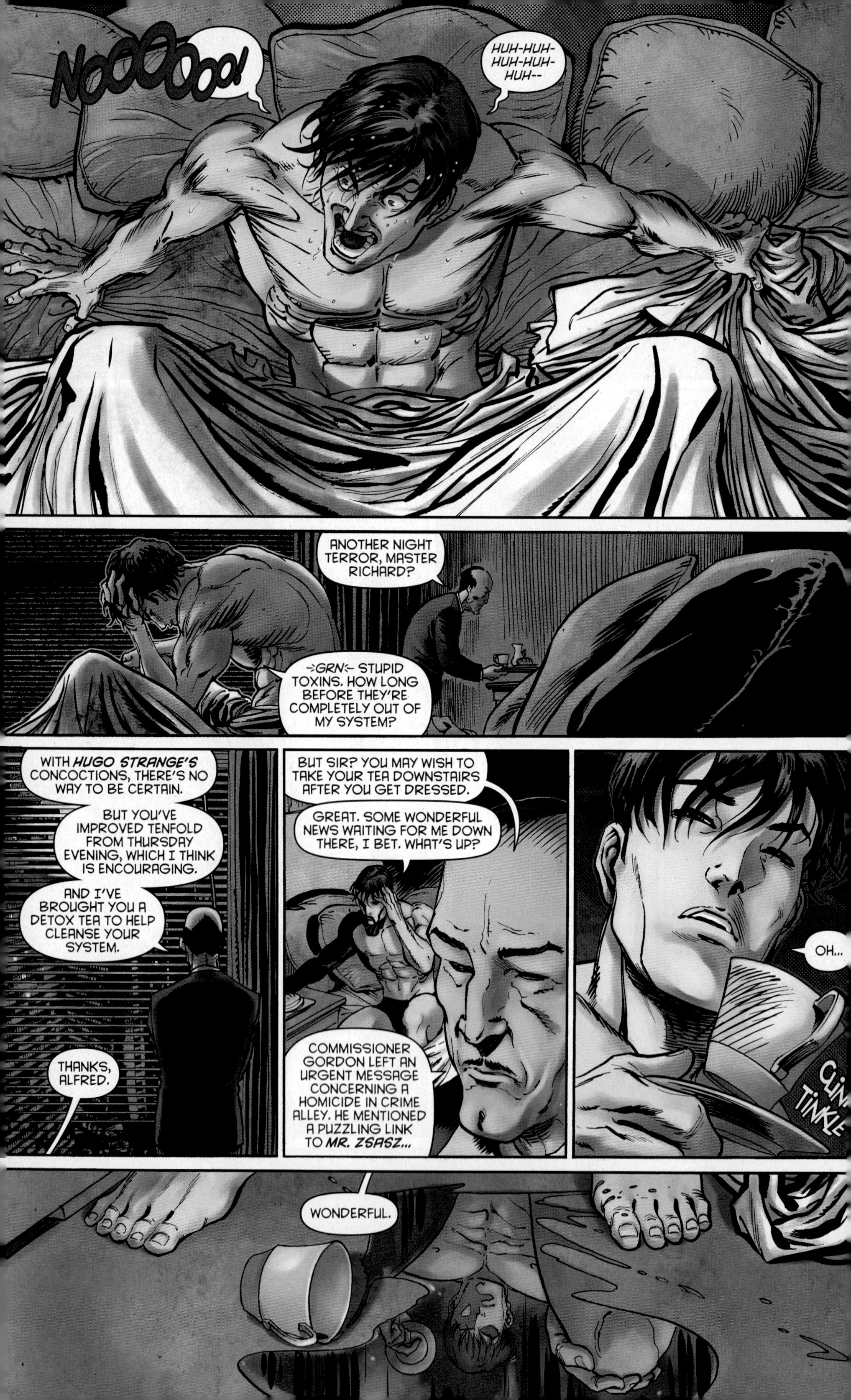
NOOOOOOO!
HUH-HUH-HUH-HUH-HUH--
ANOTHER NIGHT TERROR, MASTER RICHARD?
GRN STUPID TOXINS. HOW LONG BEFORE THEY'RE COMPLETELY OUT OF MY SYSTEM?
WITH HUGO STRANGE'S CONCOCTIONS, THERE'S NO WAY TO BE CERTAIN.
BUT YOU'VE IMPROVED TENFOLD FROM THURSDAY EVENING, WHICH I THINK IS ENCOURAGING.
AND I'VE BROUGHT YOU A DETOX TEA TO HELP CLEANSE YOUR SYSTEM.
THANKS, ALFRED.
BUT SIR? YOU MAY WISH TO TAKE YOUR TEA DOWNSTAIRS AFTER YOU GET DRESSED.
GREAT. SOME WONDERFUL NEWS WAITING FOR ME DOWN THERE, I BET. WHAT'S UP?
COMMISSIONER GORDON LEFT AN URGENT MESSAGE CONCERNING A HOMICIDE IN CRIME ALLEY. HE MENTIONED A PUZZLING LINK TO MR. ZSASZ...
OH...
TINKLE
WONDERFUL.

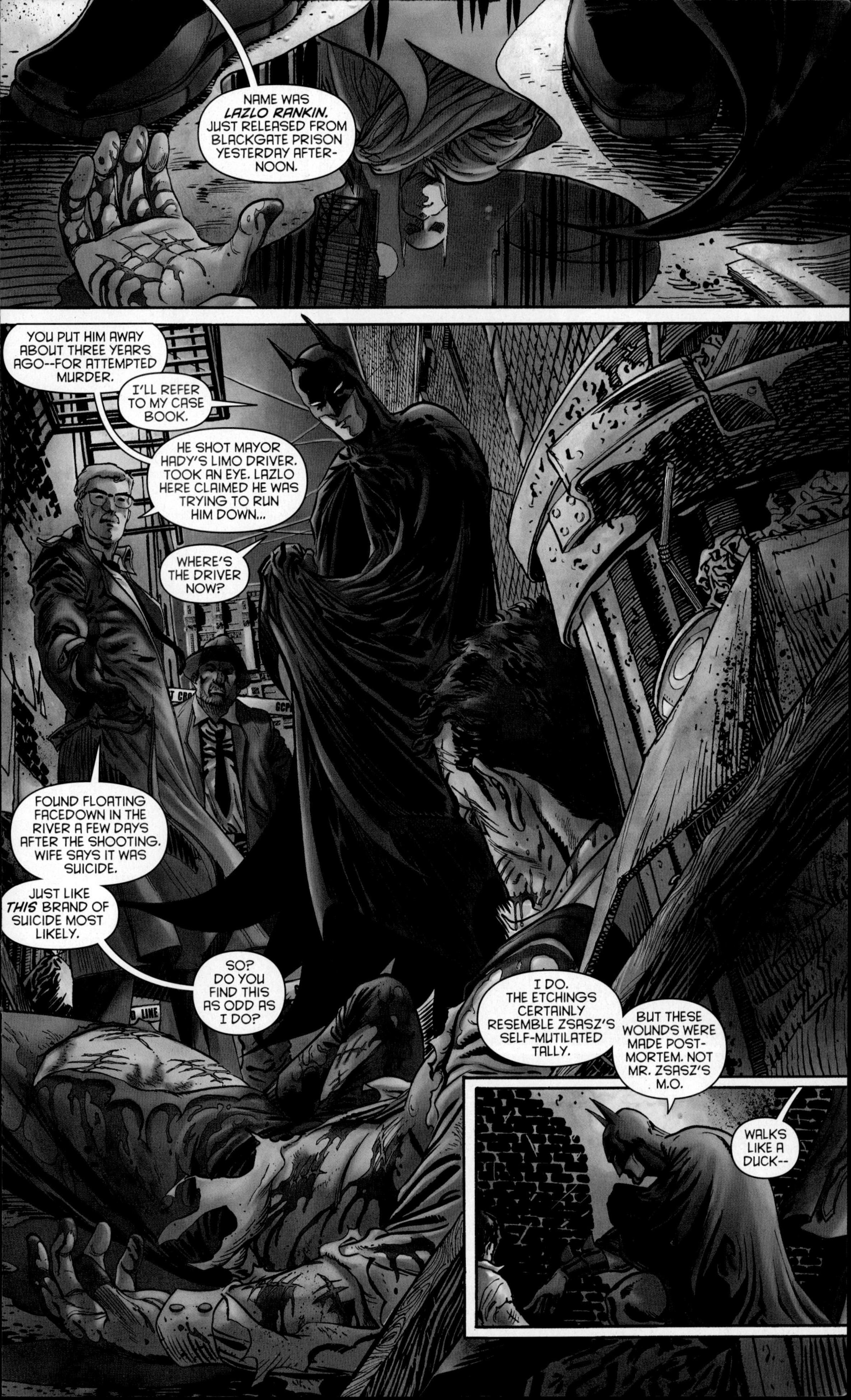
NAME WAS *LAZLO RANKIN.* JUST RELEASED FROM BLACKGATE PRISON YESTERDAY AFTER-NOON.
YOU PUT HIM AWAY ABOUT THREE YEARS AGO--FOR ATTEMPTED MURDER.
I'LL REFER TO MY CASE BOOK.
HE SHOT MAYOR HADY'S LIMO DRIVER. TOOK AN EYE. LAZLO HERE CLAIMED HE WAS TRYING TO RUN HIM DOWN...
WHERE'S THE DRIVER NOW?
FOUND FLOATING FACEDOWN IN THE RIVER A FEW DAYS AFTER THE SHOOTING. WIFE SAYS IT WAS SUICIDE.
JUST LIKE *THIS* BRAND OF SUICIDE MOST LIKELY.
SO? DO YOU FIND THIS AS ODD AS I DO?
I DO. THE ETCHINGS CERTAINLY RESEMBLE ZSASZ'S SELF-MUTILATED TALLY.
BUT THESE WOUNDS WERE MADE POST-MORTEM. NOT MR. ZSASZ'S M.O.
WALKS LIKE A DUCK--

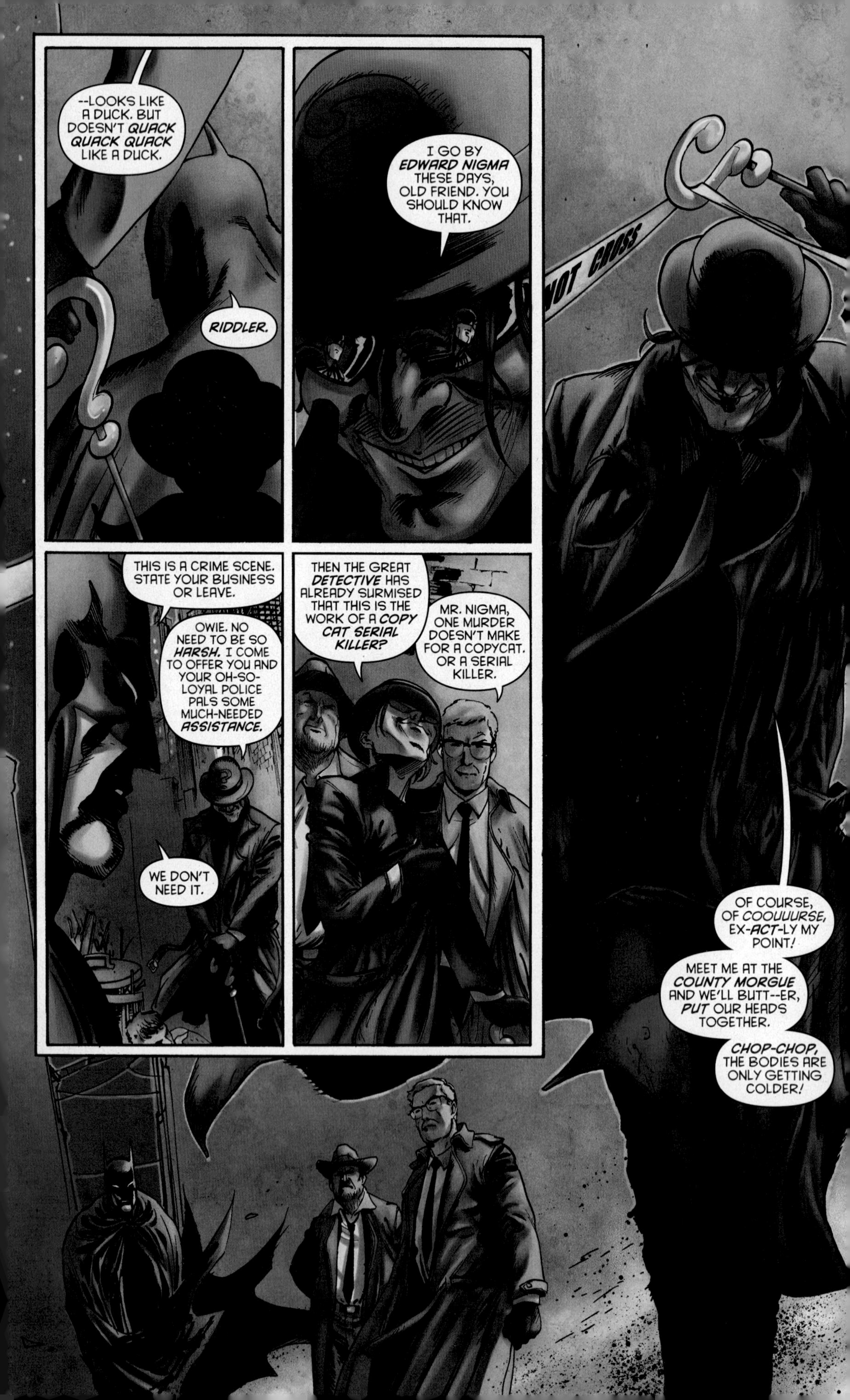

--LOOKS LIKE A DUCK. BUT DOESN'T QUACK QUACK QUACK LIKE A DUCK.
I GO BY EDWARD NIGMA THESE DAYS, OLD FRIEND. YOU SHOULD KNOW THAT.
RIDDLER.
DO NOT CROSS
THIS IS A CRIME SCENE. STATE YOUR BUSINESS OR LEAVE.
OWIE. NO NEED TO BE SO HARSH. I COME TO OFFER YOU AND YOUR OH-SO-LOYAL POLICE PALS SOME MUCH-NEEDED ASSISTANCE.
WE DON'T NEED IT.
THEN THE GREAT DETECTIVE HAS ALREADY SURMISED THAT THIS IS THE WORK OF A COPY CAT SERIAL KILLER?
MR. NIGMA, ONE MURDER DOESN'T MAKE FOR A COPYCAT. OR A SERIAL KILLER.
OF COURSE, OF COOUUURSE, EX-ACT-LY MY POINT!
MEET ME AT THE COUNTY MORGUE AND WE'LL BUTT--ER, PUT OUR HEADS TOGETHER.
CHOP-CHOP, THE BODIES ARE ONLY GETTING COLDER!

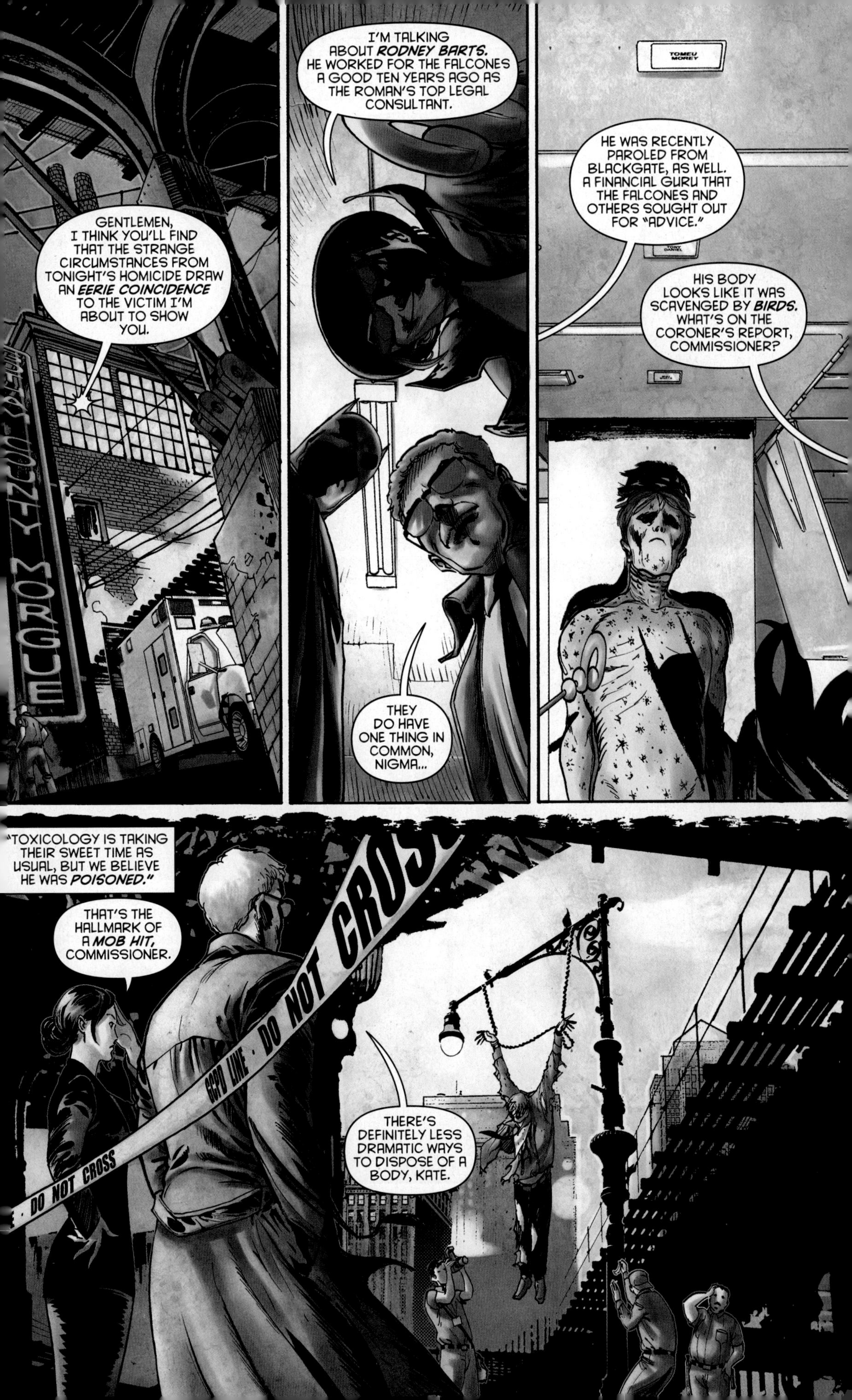

GENTLEMEN, I THINK YOU'LL FIND THAT THE STRANGE CIRCUMSTANCES FROM TONIGHT'S HOMICIDE DRAW AN *EERIE COINCIDENCE* TO THE VICTIM I'M ABOUT TO SHOW YOU.
MORGUE
I'M TALKING ABOUT *RODNEY BARTS.* HE WORKED FOR THE FALCONES A GOOD TEN YEARS AGO AS THE ROMAN'S TOP LEGAL CONSULTANT.
THEY DO HAVE ONE THING IN COMMON, NIGMA...
TOMEU MOREY
HE WAS RECENTLY PAROLED FROM BLACKGATE, AS WELL. A FINANCIAL GURU THAT THE FALCONES AND OTHERS SOUGHT OUT FOR "ADVICE."
HIS BODY LOOKS LIKE IT WAS SCAVENGED BY *BIRDS.* WHAT'S ON THE CORONER'S REPORT, COMMISSIONER?
"TOXICOLOGY IS TAKING THEIR SWEET TIME AS USUAL, BUT WE BELIEVE HE WAS *POISONED.*"
THAT'S THE HALLMARK OF A *MOB HIT,* COMMISSIONER.
GCPD LINE · DO NOT CROSS
DO NOT CROSS
THERE'S DEFINITELY LESS DRAMATIC WAYS TO DISPOSE OF A BODY, KATE.

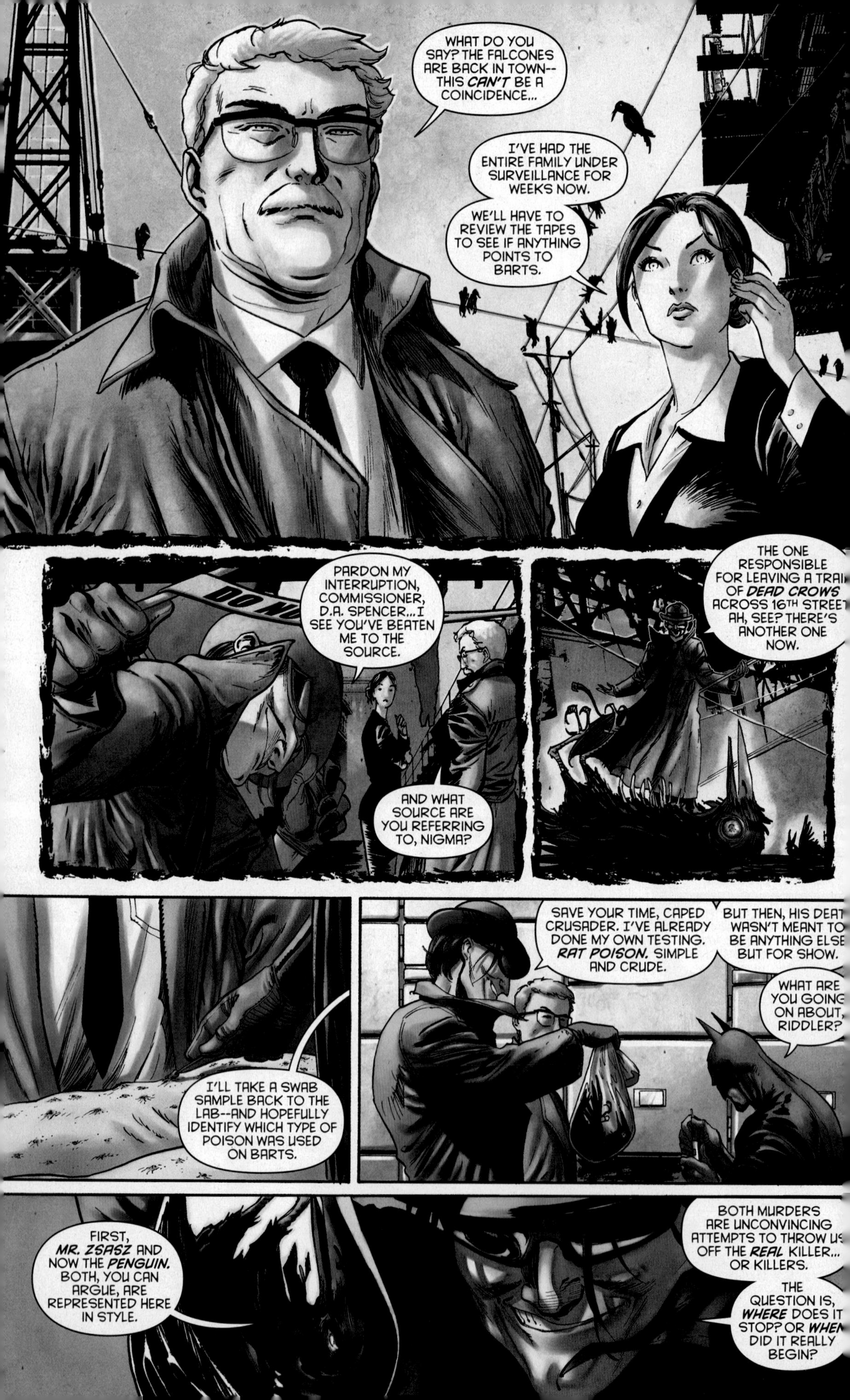
WHAT DO YOU SAY? THE FALCONES ARE BACK IN TOWN-- THIS CAN'T BE A COINCIDENCE...
I'VE HAD THE ENTIRE FAMILY UNDER SURVEILLANCE FOR WEEKS NOW.
WE'LL HAVE TO REVIEW THE TAPES TO SEE IF ANYTHING POINTS TO BARTS.
DO NO
PARDON MY INTERRUPTION, COMMISSIONER, D.A. SPENCER...I SEE YOU'VE BEATEN ME TO THE SOURCE.
AND WHAT SOURCE ARE YOU REFERRING TO, NIGMA?
THE ONE RESPONSIBLE FOR LEAVING A TRAI OF DEAD CROWS ACROSS 16TH STREET AH, SEE? THERE'S ANOTHER ONE NOW.
I'LL TAKE A SWAB SAMPLE BACK TO THE LAB--AND HOPEFULLY IDENTIFY WHICH TYPE OF POISON WAS USED ON BARTS.
SAVE YOUR TIME, CAPED CRUSADER. I'VE ALREADY DONE MY OWN TESTING. RAT POISON. SIMPLE AND CRUDE.
BUT THEN, HIS DEAT WASN'T MEANT TO BE ANYTHING ELSE BUT FOR SHOW.
WHAT ARE YOU GOING ON ABOUT, RIDDLER?
FIRST, MR. ZSASZ AND NOW THE PENGUIN. BOTH, YOU CAN ARGUE, ARE REPRESENTED HERE IN STYLE.
BOTH MURDERS ARE UNCONVINCING ATTEMPTS TO THROW US OFF THE REAL KILLER... OR KILLERS.
THE QUESTION IS, WHERE DOES IT STOP? OR WHEN DID IT REALLY BEGIN?

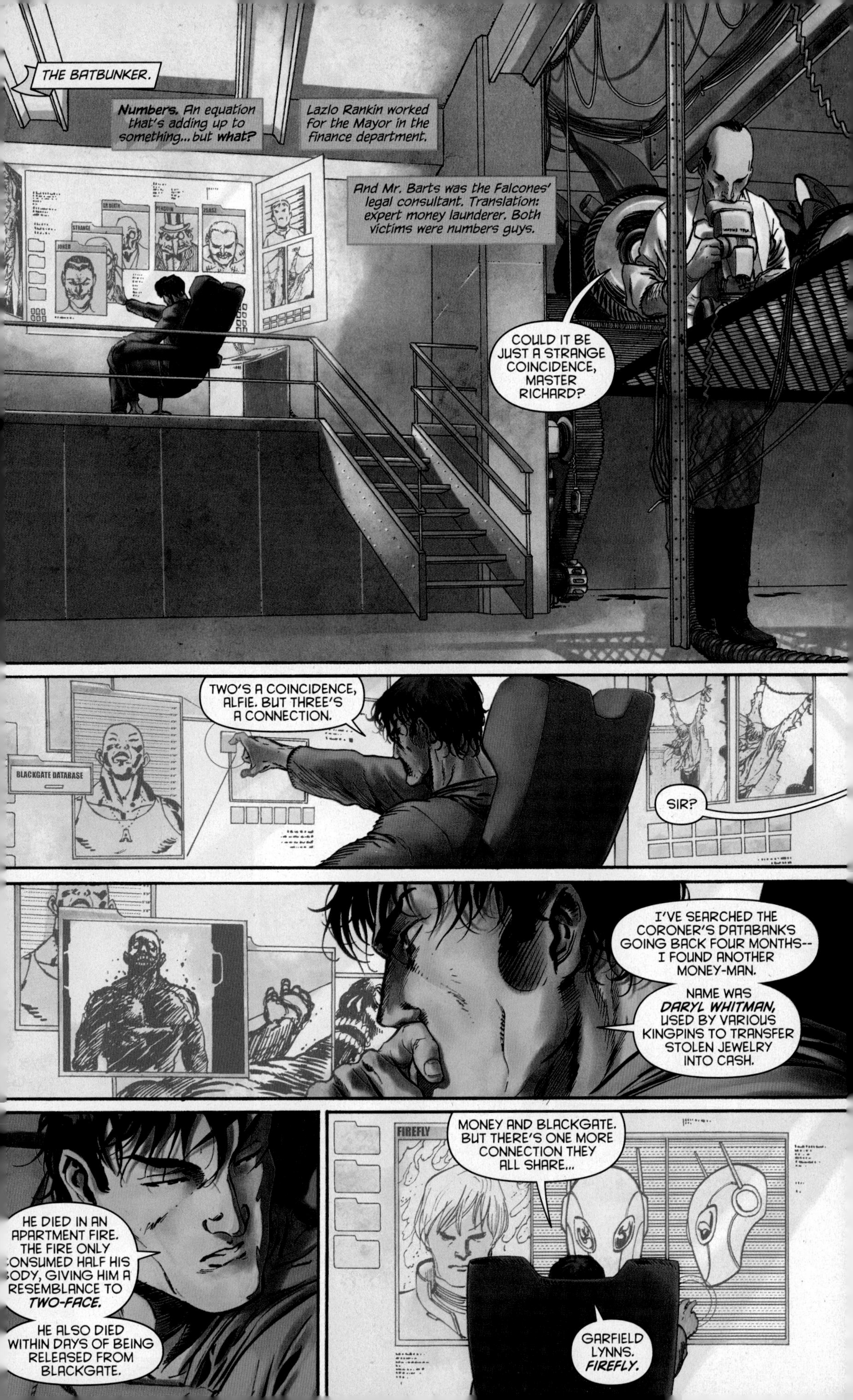
THE BATBUNKER.
Numbers. An equation that's adding up to something... but what?
Lazlo Rankin worked for the Mayor in the finance department.
And Mr. Barts was the Falcones' legal consultant. Translation: expert money launderer. Both victims were numbers guys.
COULD IT BE JUST A STRANGE COINCIDENCE, MASTER RICHARD?
TWO'S A COINCIDENCE, ALFIE. BUT THREE'S A CONNECTION.
BLACKGATE DATABASE
SIR?
I'VE SEARCHED THE CORONER'S DATABANKS GOING BACK FOUR MONTHS-- I FOUND ANOTHER MONEY-MAN.
NAME WAS DARYL WHITMAN, USED BY VARIOUS KINGPINS TO TRANSFER STOLEN JEWELRY INTO CASH.
HE DIED IN AN APARTMENT FIRE. THE FIRE ONLY CONSUMED HALF HIS BODY, GIVING HIM A RESEMBLANCE TO TWO-FACE.
HE ALSO DIED WITHIN DAYS OF BEING RELEASED FROM BLACKGATE.
MONEY AND BLACKGATE. BUT THERE'S ONE MORE CONNECTION THEY ALL SHARE...
FIREFLY
GARFIELD LYNNS. FIREFLY.

ARKHAM ASYLUM.

Finding Firefly is easy. Getting him to talk is always the challenge.

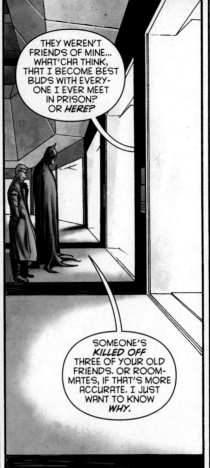

THEY WEREN'T FRIENDS OF MINE... WHAT'CHA THINK, THAT I BECOME BEST BUDS WITH EVERY-ONE I EVER MEET IN PRISON? OR *HERE*?

SOMEONE'S *KILLED OFF* THREE OF YOUR OLD FRIENDS. OR ROOM-MATES, IF THAT'S MORE ACCURATE. I JUST WANT TO KNOW *WHY*.

HELL IF I KNOW. PEOPLE MAKE ENEMIES IN THIS TOWN. ANYWAY, IT'S NONE OF MY BUSINESS.

ESPECIALLY SINCE I DON'T SEE HOW IT HELPS *ME* OUT ANY. SMELL WHAT I'M SNIFFIN', BATMAN?

I WON'T CUT YOU ANY DEALS, LYNN. BUT TELLING ME WHO ELSE WAS INVOLVED IN WHATEVER BROUGHT THIS ON MIGHT SAVE A LIFE.

WHO KNOWS? MAYBE EVEN *YOUR OWN*.

B-DEEPEEP B-DEEPEEP

GORDON HERE.

ER, BATMAN? IT'S FOR YOU.

WHO IS THIS?

YOU HAVE *FIVE MINUTES* TO SAVE A LIFE. WILL YOU COME OUT IN A BLAZE OF GLORY OR WILL YOU LOSE YOUR COOL?

CLICK

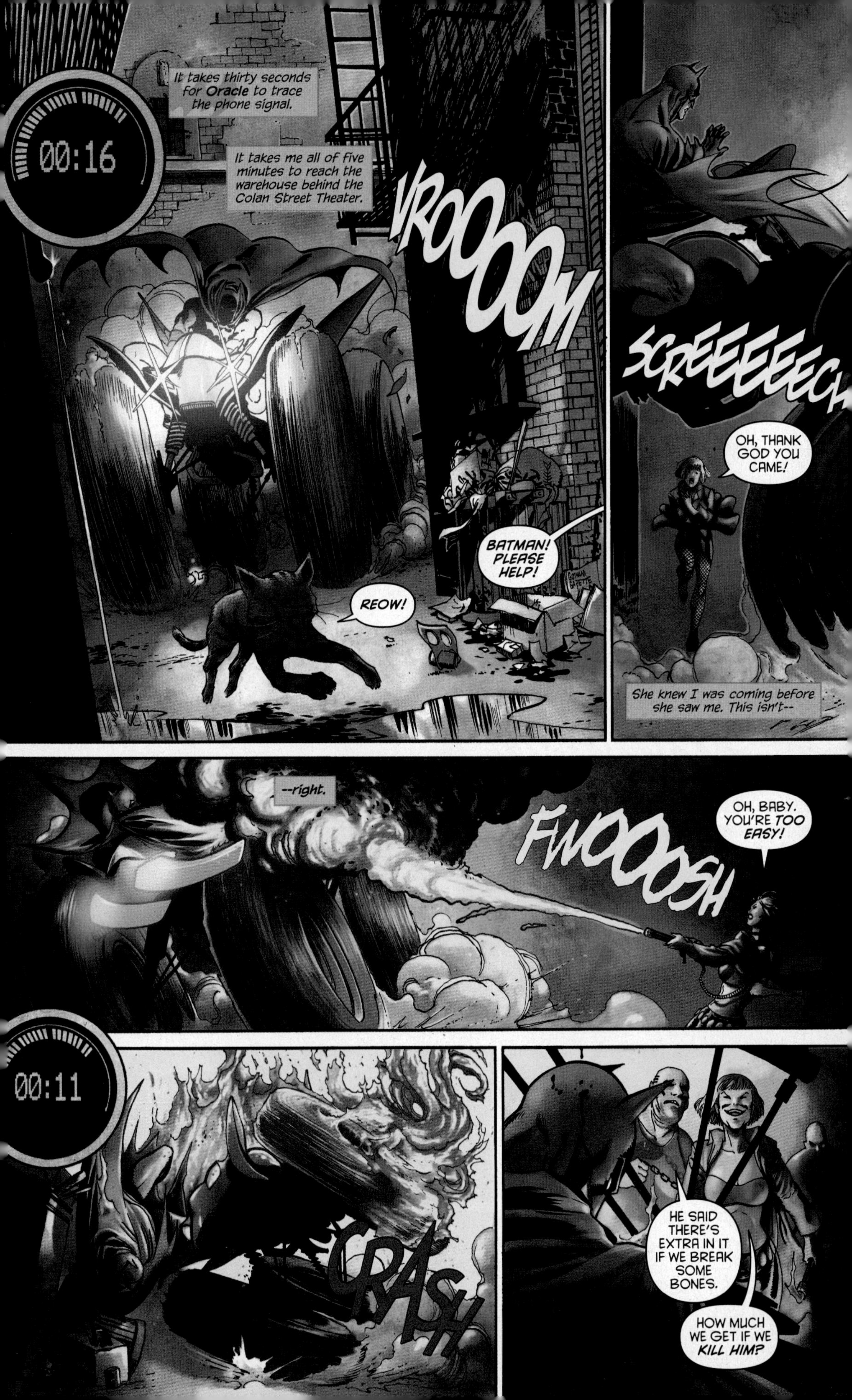

It takes thirty seconds for Oracle to trace the phone signal.
00:16
It takes me all of five minutes to reach the warehouse behind the Colan Street Theater.
VROOOOOM
BATMAN! PLEASE HELP!
REOW!
GOTHAM GAZETTE
SCREEEEECH
OH, THANK GOD YOU CAME!
She knew I was coming before she saw me. This isn't--
--right.
FWOOOOSH
OH, BABY. YOU'RE TOO EASY!
00:11
CRASH
HE SAID THERE'S EXTRA IN IT IF WE BREAK SOME BONES.
HOW MUCH WE GET IF WE KILL HIM?

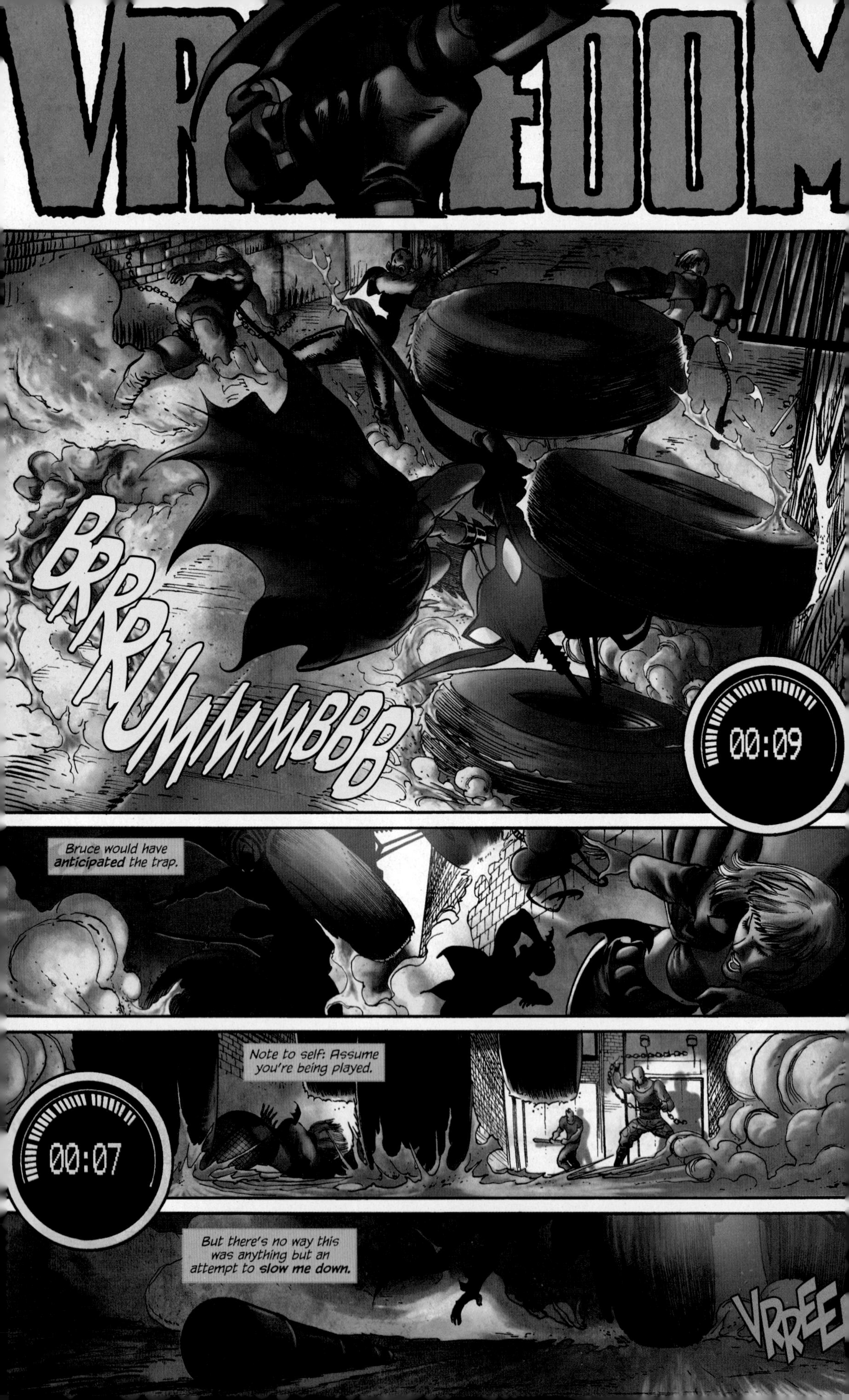

BRRRUMMMBBB
00:09
Bruce would have anticipated the trap.
Note to self: Assume you're being played.
00:07
But there's no way this was anything but an attempt to slow me down.
VRREE

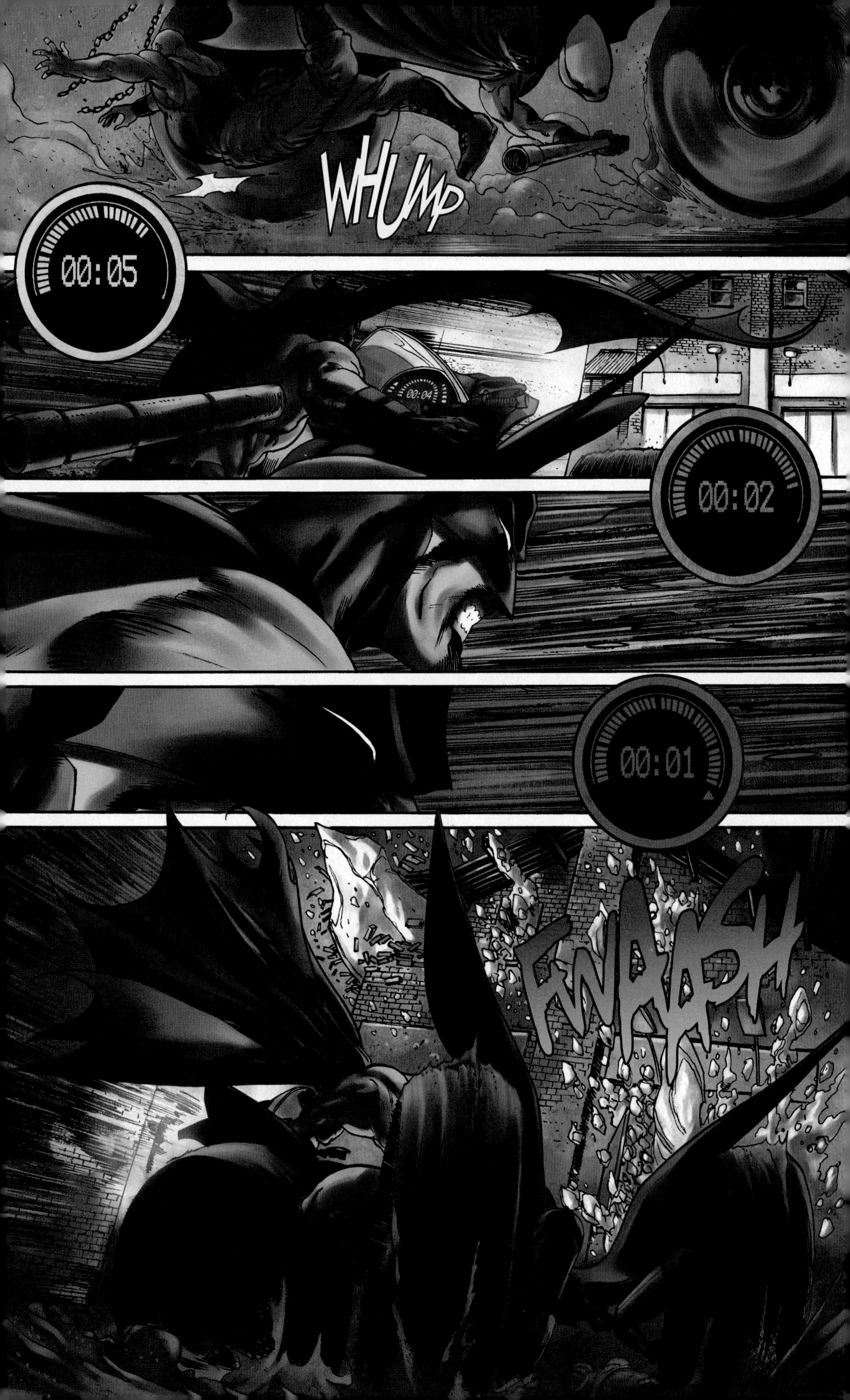
WHUMP
00:05
00:04
00:02
00:01
FWASH

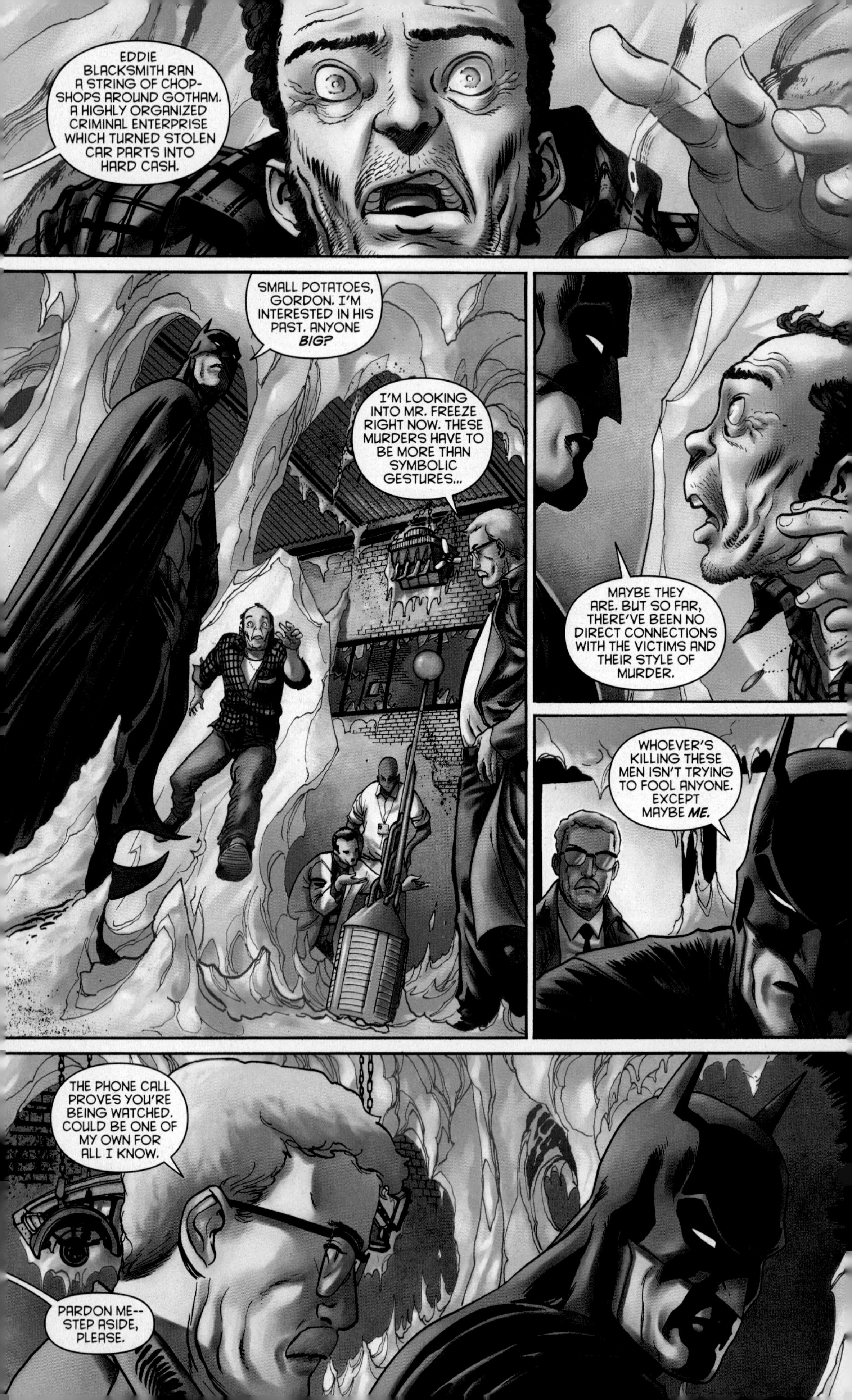
EDDIE BLACKSMITH RAN A STRING OF CHOP-SHOPS AROUND GOTHAM. A HIGHLY ORGANIZED CRIMINAL ENTERPRISE WHICH TURNED STOLEN CAR PARTS INTO HARD CASH.
SMALL POTATOES, GORDON. I'M INTERESTED IN HIS PAST. ANYONE *BIG?*
I'M LOOKING INTO MR. FREEZE RIGHT NOW. THESE MURDERS HAVE TO BE MORE THAN SYMBOLIC GESTURES...
MAYBE THEY ARE. BUT SO FAR, THERE'VE BEEN NO DIRECT CONNECTIONS WITH THE VICTIMS AND THEIR STYLE OF MURDER.
WHOEVER'S KILLING THESE MEN ISN'T TRYING TO FOOL ANYONE. EXCEPT MAYBE *ME.*
THE PHONE CALL PROVES YOU'RE BEING WATCHED. COULD BE ONE OF MY OWN FOR ALL I KNOW.
PARDON ME-- STEP ASIDE, PLEASE.

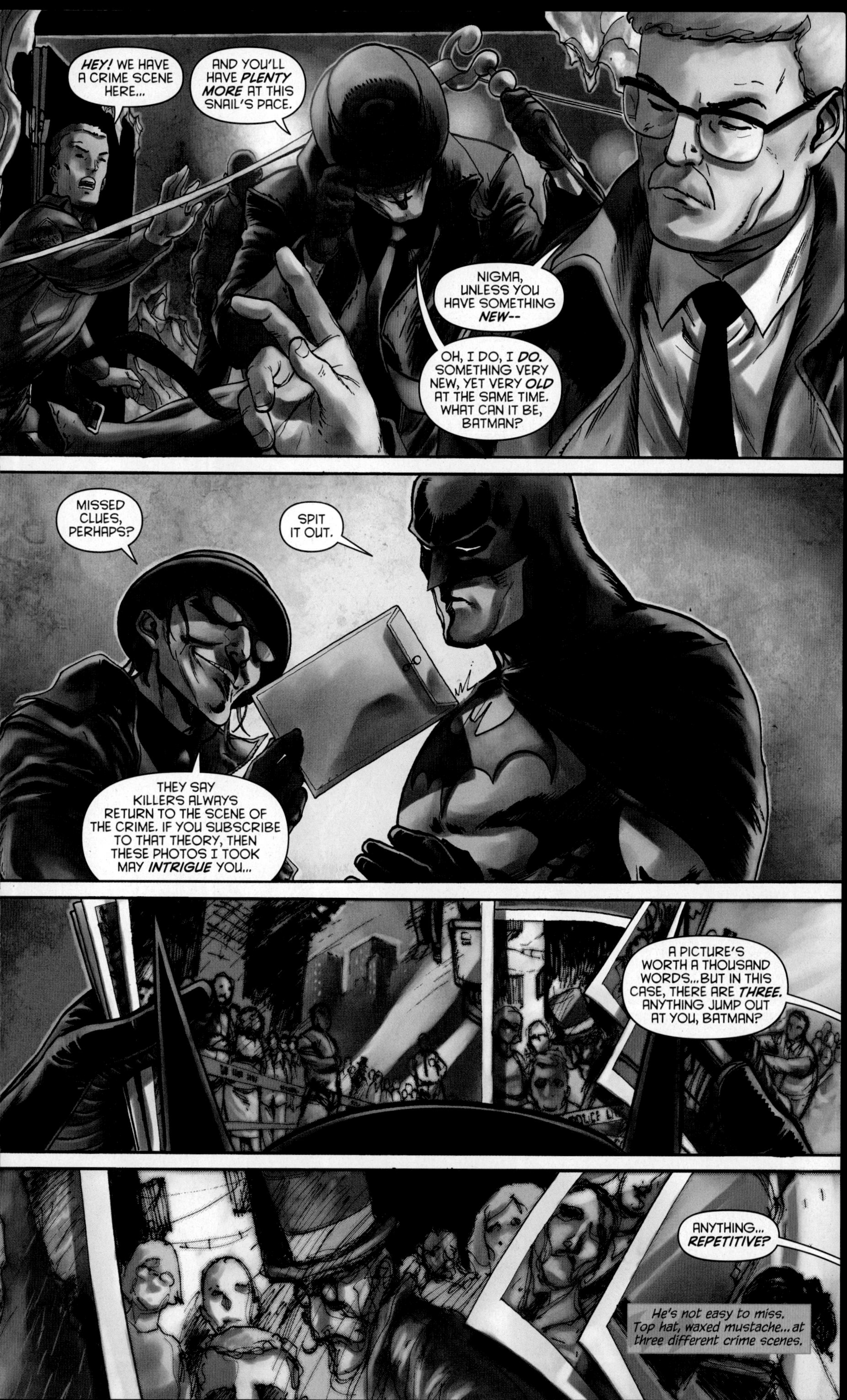
HEY! WE HAVE A CRIME SCENE HERE...
AND YOU'LL HAVE PLENTY MORE AT THIS SNAIL'S PACE.
NIGMA, UNLESS YOU HAVE SOMETHING NEW--
OH, I DO, I DO. SOMETHING VERY NEW, YET VERY OLD AT THE SAME TIME. WHAT CAN IT BE, BATMAN?
MISSED CLUES, PERHAPS?
SPIT IT OUT.
THEY SAY KILLERS ALWAYS RETURN TO THE SCENE OF THE CRIME. IF YOU SUBSCRIBE TO THAT THEORY, THEN THESE PHOTOS I TOOK MAY INTRIGUE YOU...
A PICTURE'S WORTH A THOUSAND WORDS...BUT IN THIS CASE, THERE ARE THREE. ANYTHING JUMP OUT AT YOU, BATMAN?
ANYTHING... REPETITIVE?
He's not easy to miss. Top hat, waxed mustache...at three different crime scenes.

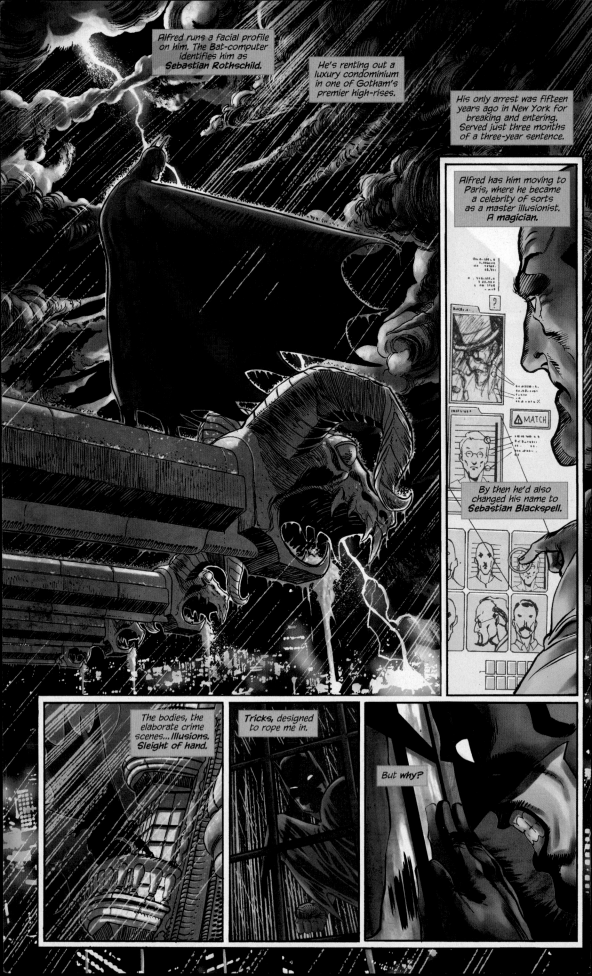

Alfred runs a facial profile on him. The Bat-computer identifies him as **Sebastian Rothschild.**

He's renting out a luxury condominium in one of Gotham's premier high-rises.

His only arrest was fifteen years ago in New York for breaking and entering. Served just three months of a three-year sentence.

Alfred has him moving to Paris, where he became a celebrity of sorts as a master illusionist. **A magician.**

By then he'd also changed his name to **Sebastian Blackspell.**

The bodies, the elaborate crime scenes...Illusions. **Sleight of hand.**

Tricks, designed to rope me in.

But why?

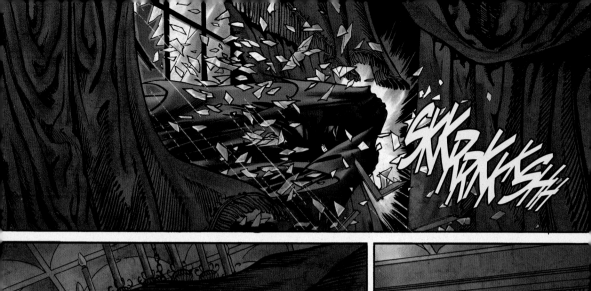

SKK RIK KSH

Blood. And only a few hours old.

A struggle... someone seriously wounded and dragged...

...to the smoking gun.

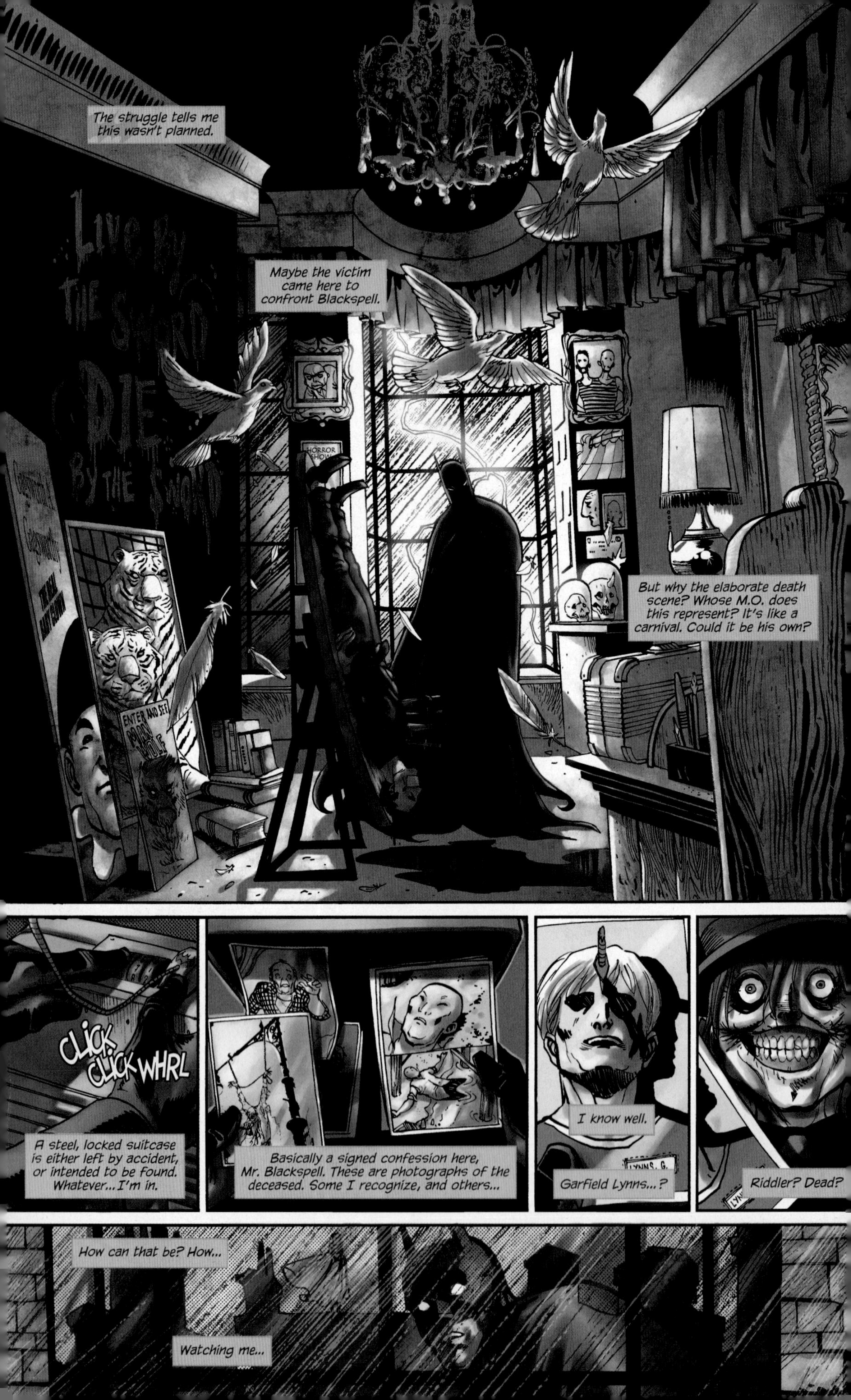

The struggle tells me this wasn't planned.
LIVE BY THE SWORD DIE BY THE SWORD
Maybe the victim came here to confront Blackspell.
HORROR SHOW
But why the elaborate death scene? Whose M.O. does this represent? It's like a carnival. Could it be his own?
ENTER AND SEE
CLICK CLICK WHRL
A steel, locked suitcase is either left by accident, or intended to be found. Whatever...I'm in.
Basically a signed confession here, Mr. Blackspell. These are photographs of the deceased. Some I recognize, and others...
I know well.
LYNNS, G.
Garfield Lynns...?
Riddler? Dead?
How can that be? How...
Watching me...

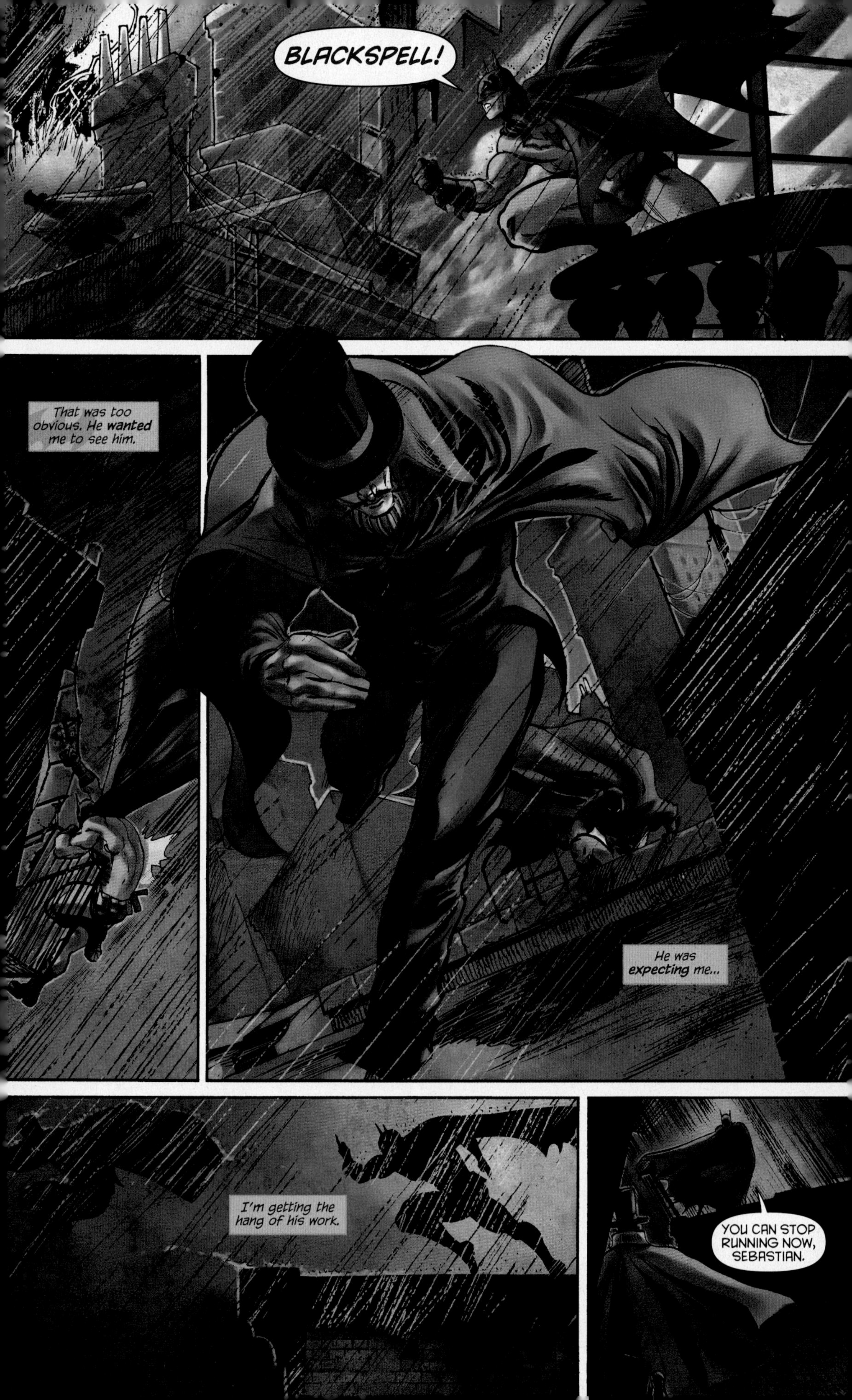

BLACKSPELL!
That was too obvious. He wanted me to see him.
He was expecting me...
I'm getting the hang of his work.
YOU CAN STOP RUNNING NOW, SEBASTIAN.

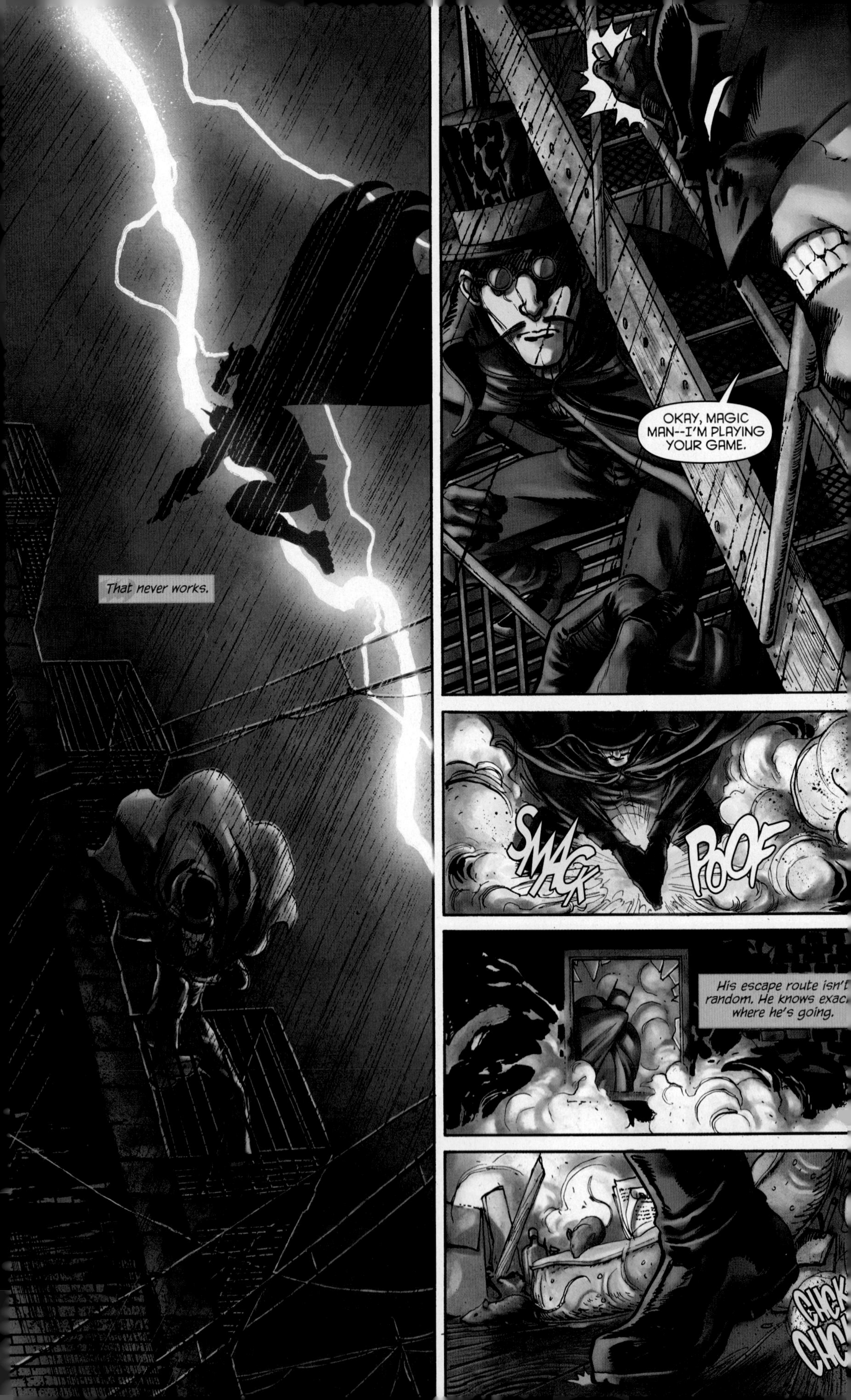
That never works.
OKAY, MAGIC MAN--I'M PLAYING YOUR GAME.
SMACK
POOF
His escape route isn't random. He knows exac where he's going.
CHCK CHC

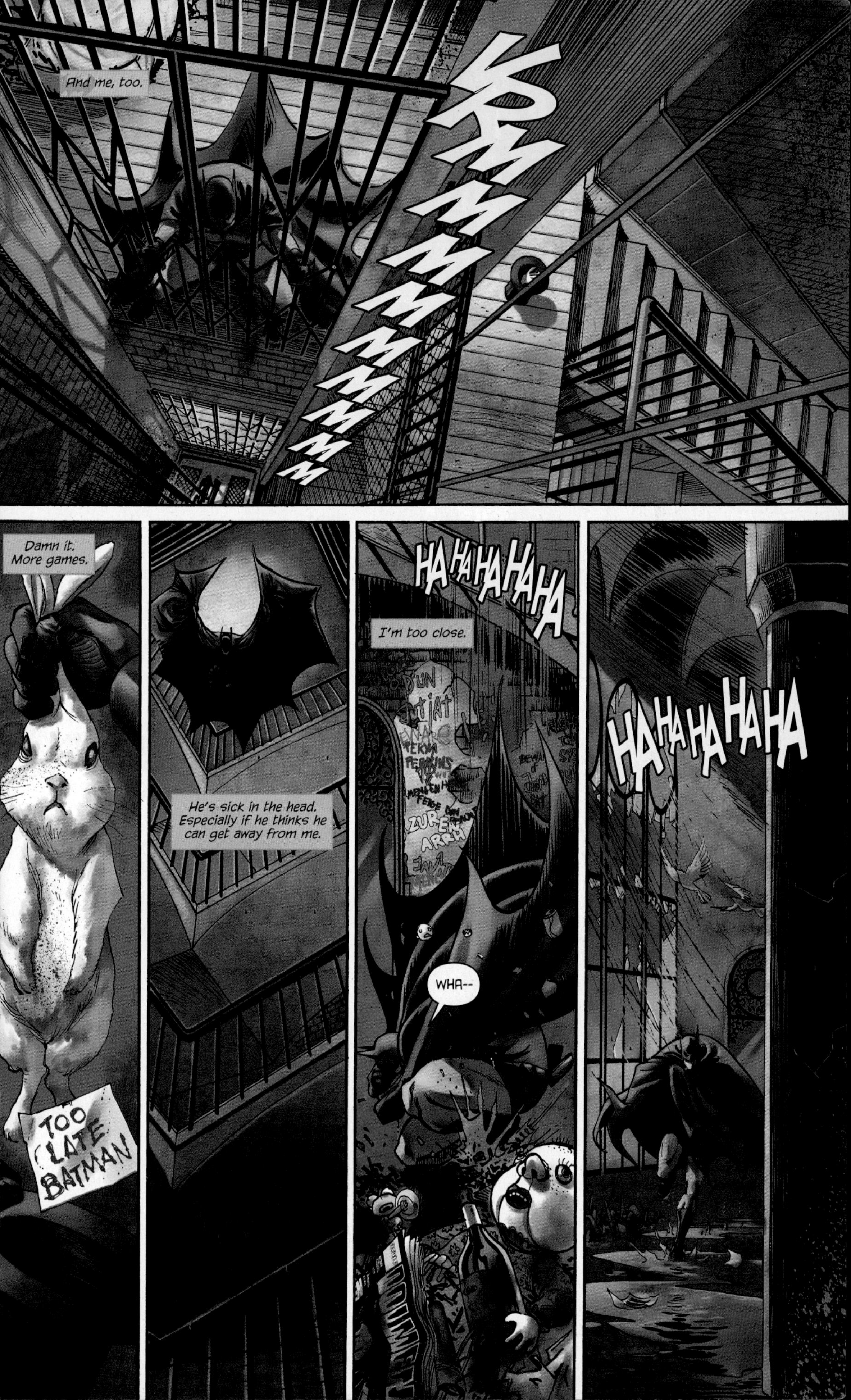
And me, too.
KRMMMMMMMMM
Damn it. More games.
TOO LATE BATMAN
He's sick in the head. Especially if he thinks he can get away from me.
HAHAHAHAHAHA
I'm too close.
WHA--
HAHAHAHAHAHA

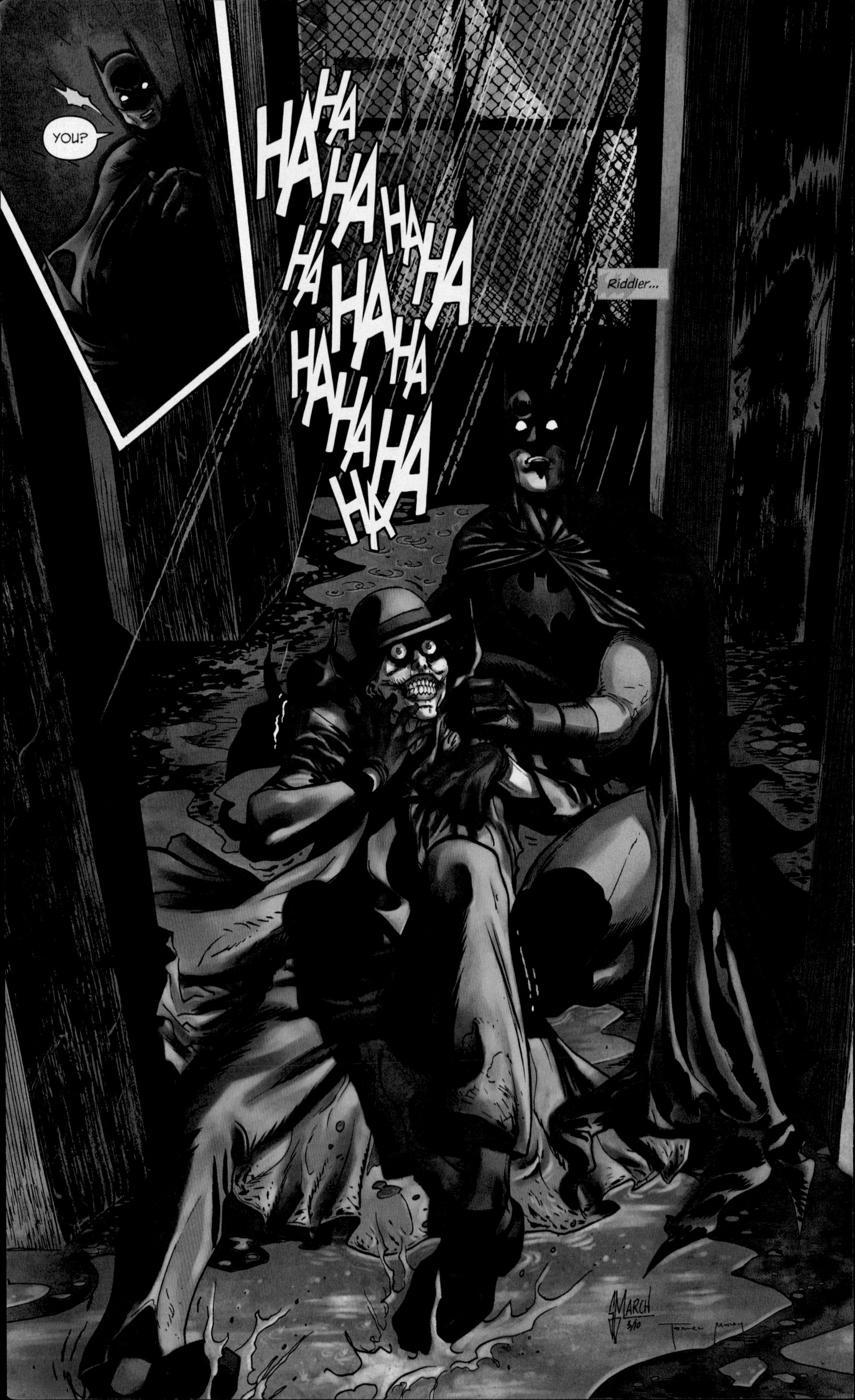
YOU?
HAHA HAHA HAHA HA HAHA HAHA HAHA HAHAHAHA HA
Riddler...

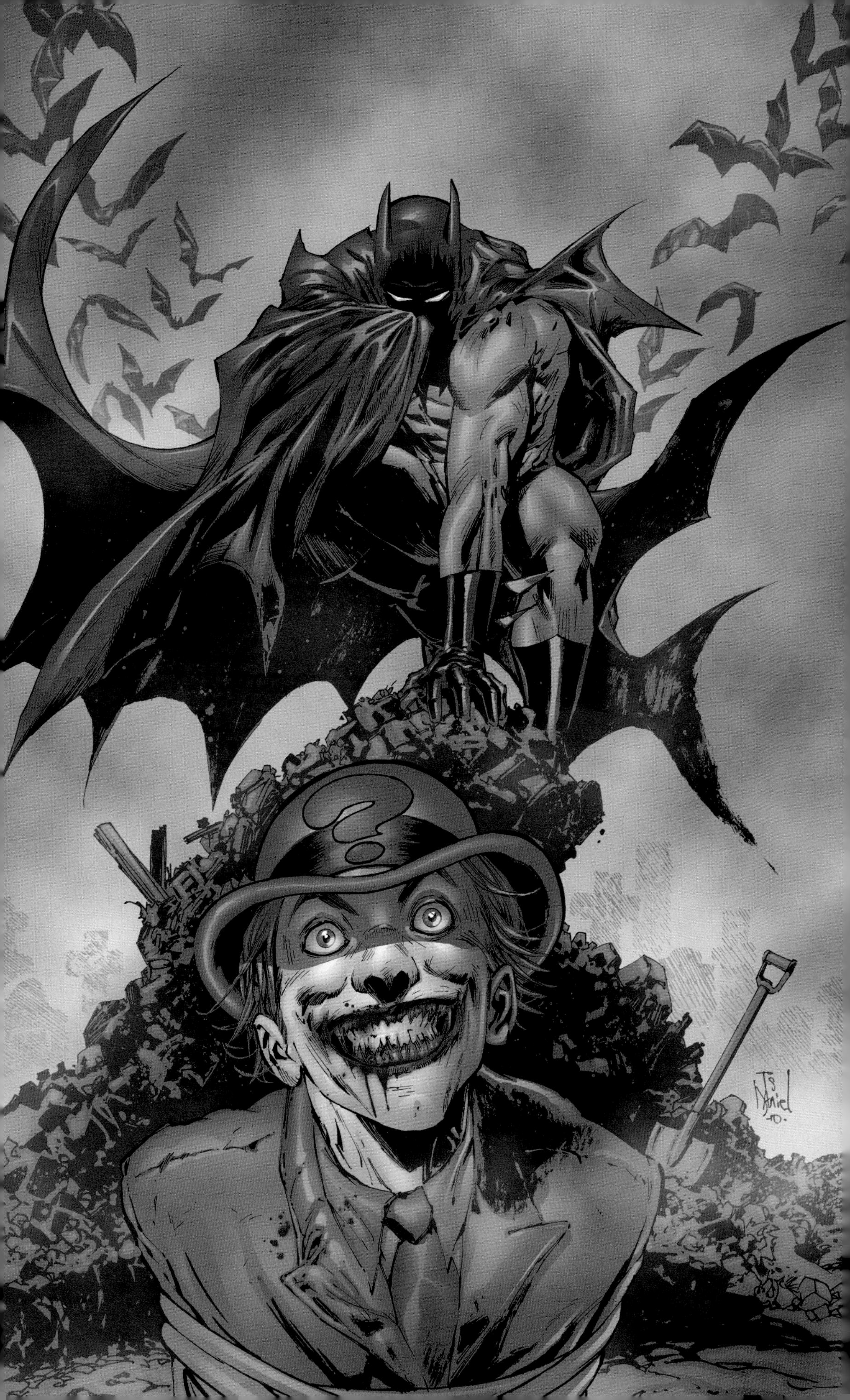

"Be thankful I will need you one day."

GOTHAM HOSPITAL.

It wasn't the real Joker toxin. Just a cheap imitation.

The doctors say Riddler's lucky to be alive.

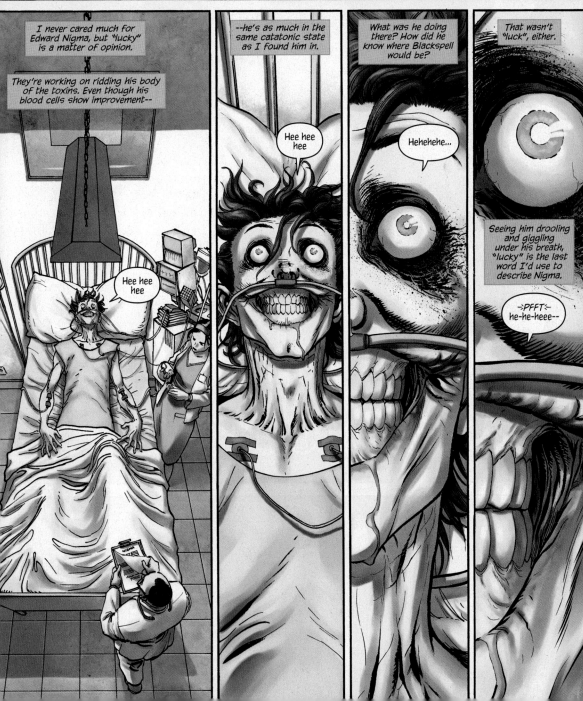

I never cared much for Edward Nigma, but "lucky" is a matter of opinion.

They're working on ridding his body of the toxins. Even though his blood cells show improvement--

Hee hee hee

--he's as much in the same catatonic state as I found him in.

Hee hee hee

What was he doing there? How did he know where Blackspell would be?

Hehehehe...

That wasn't "luck", either.

Seeing him drooling and giggling under his breath, "lucky" is the last word I'd use to describe Nigma.

->PFFT<- he-he-heee--

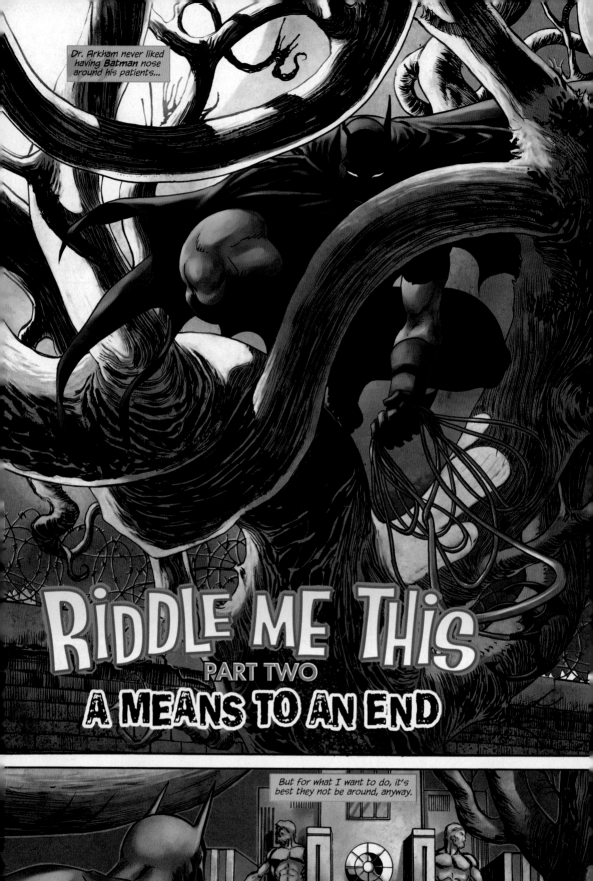

Dr. Arkham never liked having *Batman* nose around his patients...

RiDDLe ME THiS

PART TWO

A MEANS TO AN END

But for what I want to do, it's best they not be around, anyway.

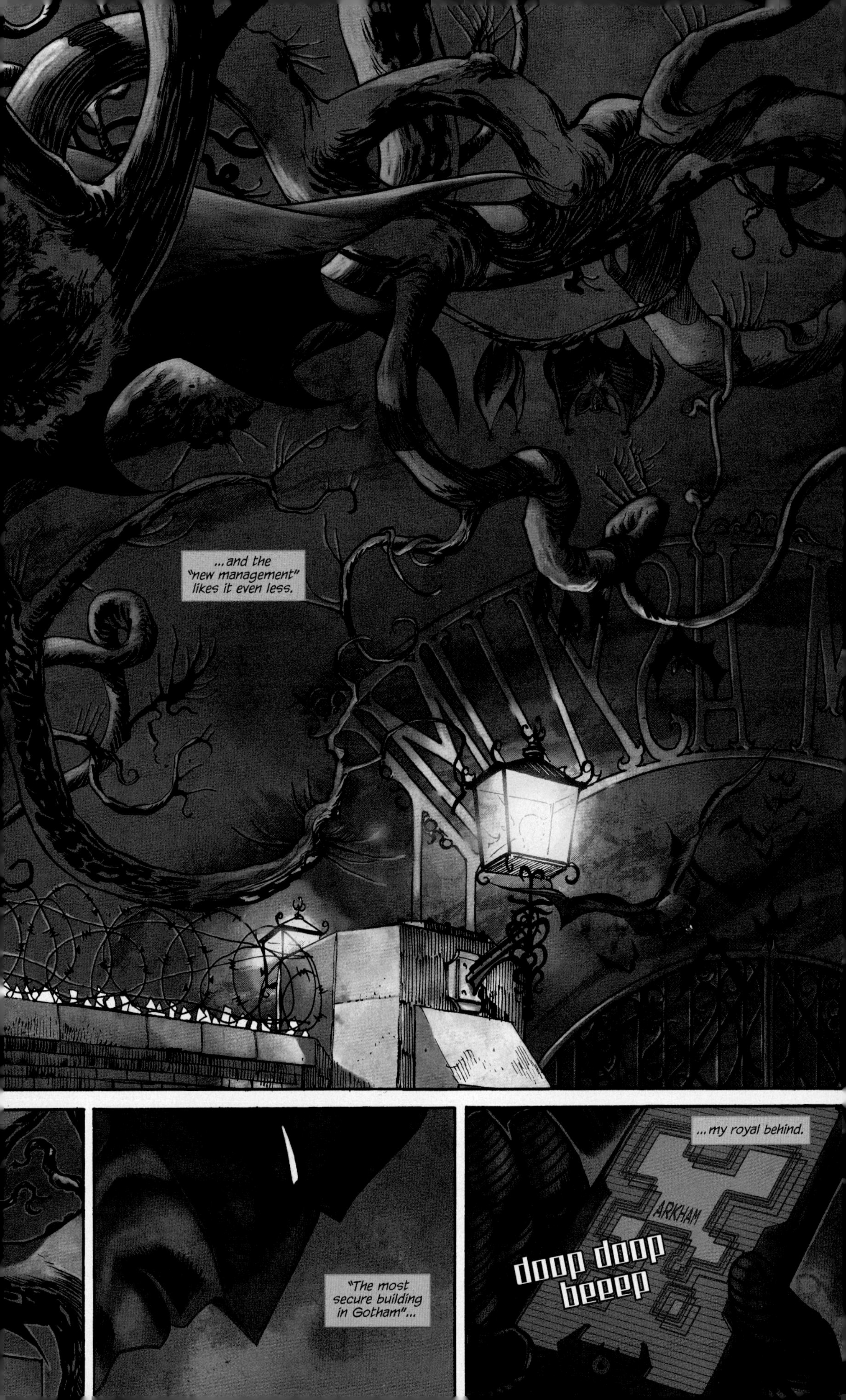
...and the "new management" likes it even less.
"The most secure building in Gotham"...
...my royal behind.
ARKHAM
doop doop beeep

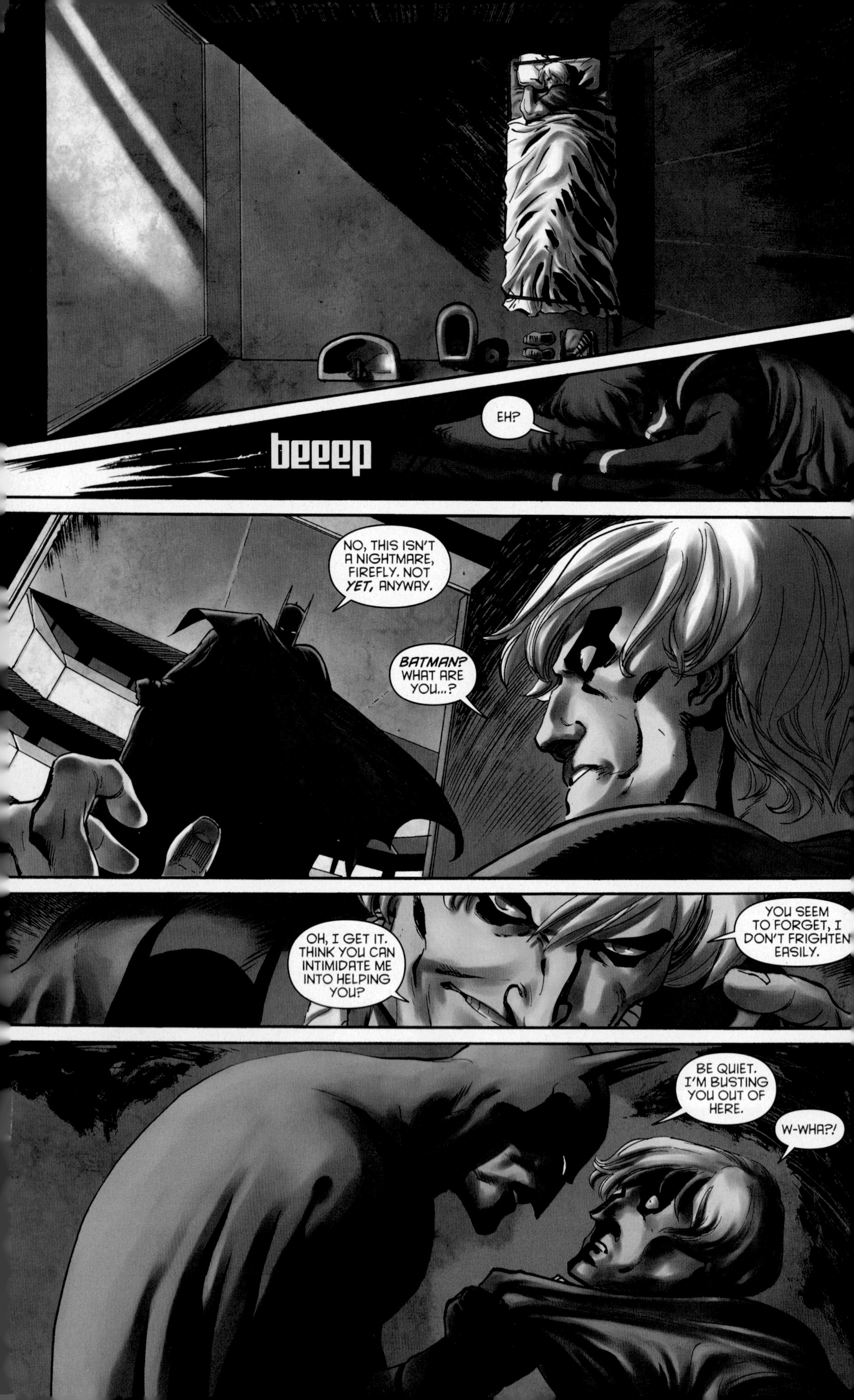
EH?
beeep
NO, THIS ISN'T A NIGHTMARE, FIREFLY. NOT *YET,* ANYWAY.
BATMAN? WHAT ARE YOU...?
OH, I GET IT. THINK YOU CAN INTIMIDATE ME INTO HELPING YOU?
YOU SEEM TO FORGET, I DON'T FRIGHTEN EASILY.
BE QUIET. I'M BUSTING YOU OUT OF HERE.
W-WHA?!

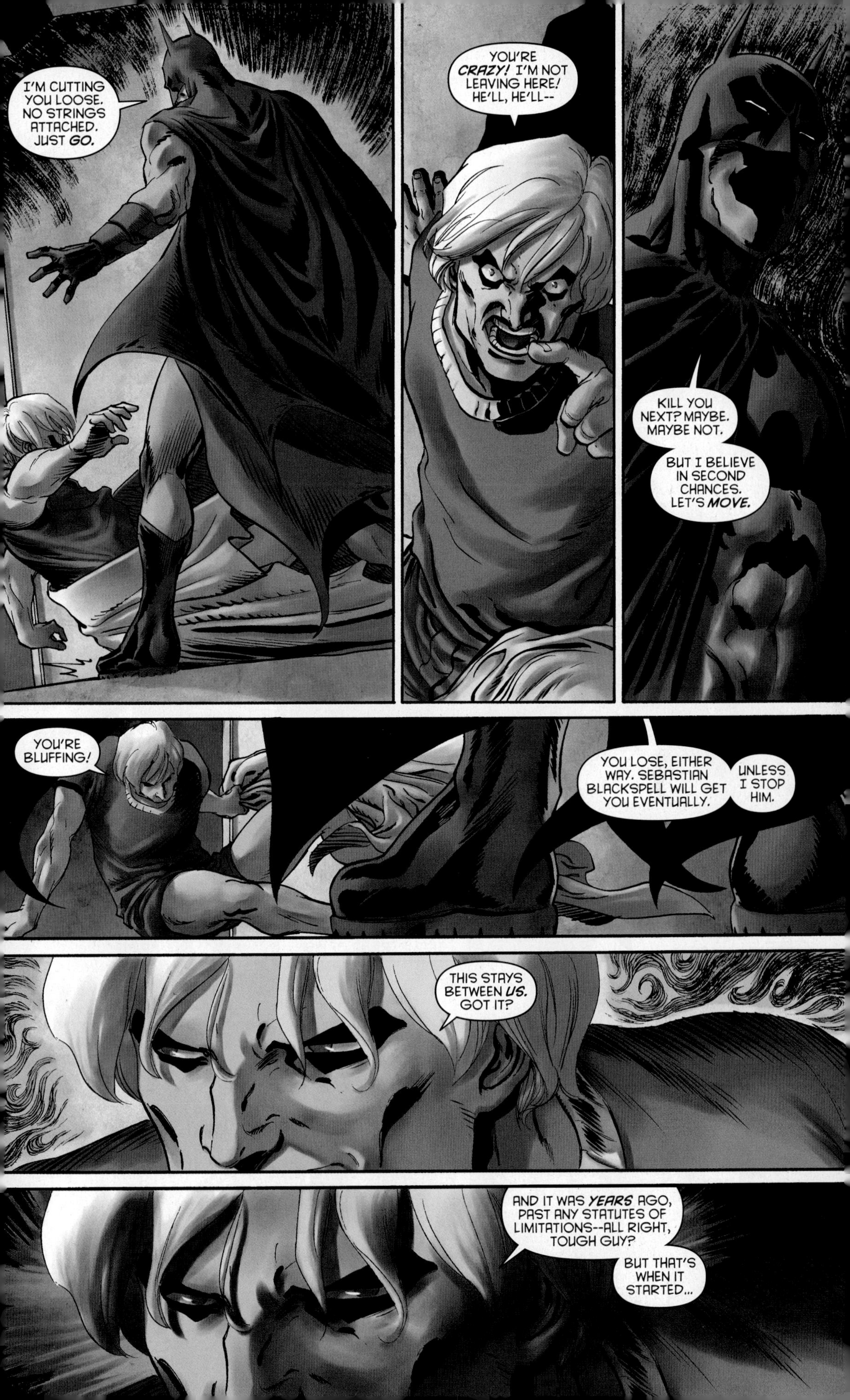
I'M CUTTING YOU LOOSE. NO STRINGS ATTACHED. JUST GO.
YOU'RE CRAZY! I'M NOT LEAVING HERE! HE'LL, HE'LL--
KILL YOU NEXT? MAYBE. MAYBE NOT.
BUT I BELIEVE IN SECOND CHANCES. LET'S MOVE.
YOU'RE BLUFFING!
YOU LOSE, EITHER WAY. SEBASTIAN BLACKSPELL WILL GET YOU EVENTUALLY.
UNLESS I STOP HIM.
THIS STAYS BETWEEN US. GOT IT?
AND IT WAS YEARS AGO, PAST ANY STATUTES OF LIMITATIONS--ALL RIGHT, TOUGH GUY?
BUT THAT'S WHEN IT STARTED...

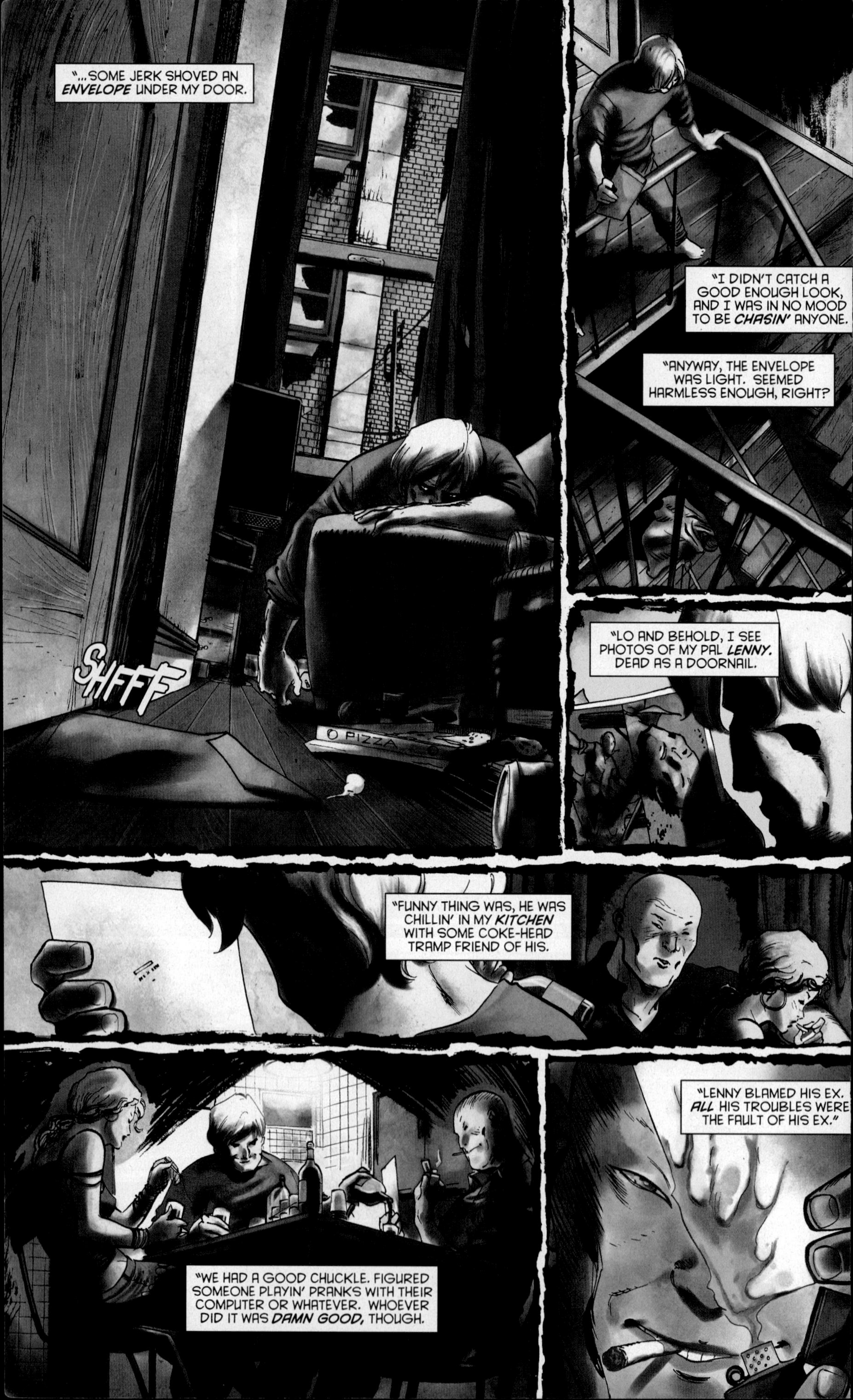
"...SOME JERK SHOVED AN ENVELOPE UNDER MY DOOR.
SHFFF
"I DIDN'T CATCH A GOOD ENOUGH LOOK, AND I WAS IN NO MOOD TO BE CHASIN' ANYONE.
"ANYWAY, THE ENVELOPE WAS LIGHT. SEEMED HARMLESS ENOUGH, RIGHT?
PIZZA
"LO AND BEHOLD, I SEE PHOTOS OF MY PAL LENNY. DEAD AS A DOORNAIL.
"FUNNY THING WAS, HE WAS CHILLIN' IN MY KITCHEN WITH SOME COKE-HEAD TRAMP FRIEND OF HIS.
"WE HAD A GOOD CHUCKLE. FIGURED SOMEONE PLAYIN' PRANKS WITH THEIR COMPUTER OR WHATEVER. WHOEVER DID IT WAS DAMN GOOD, THOUGH.
"LENNY BLAMED HIS EX. ALL HIS TROUBLES WERE THE FAULT OF HIS EX."

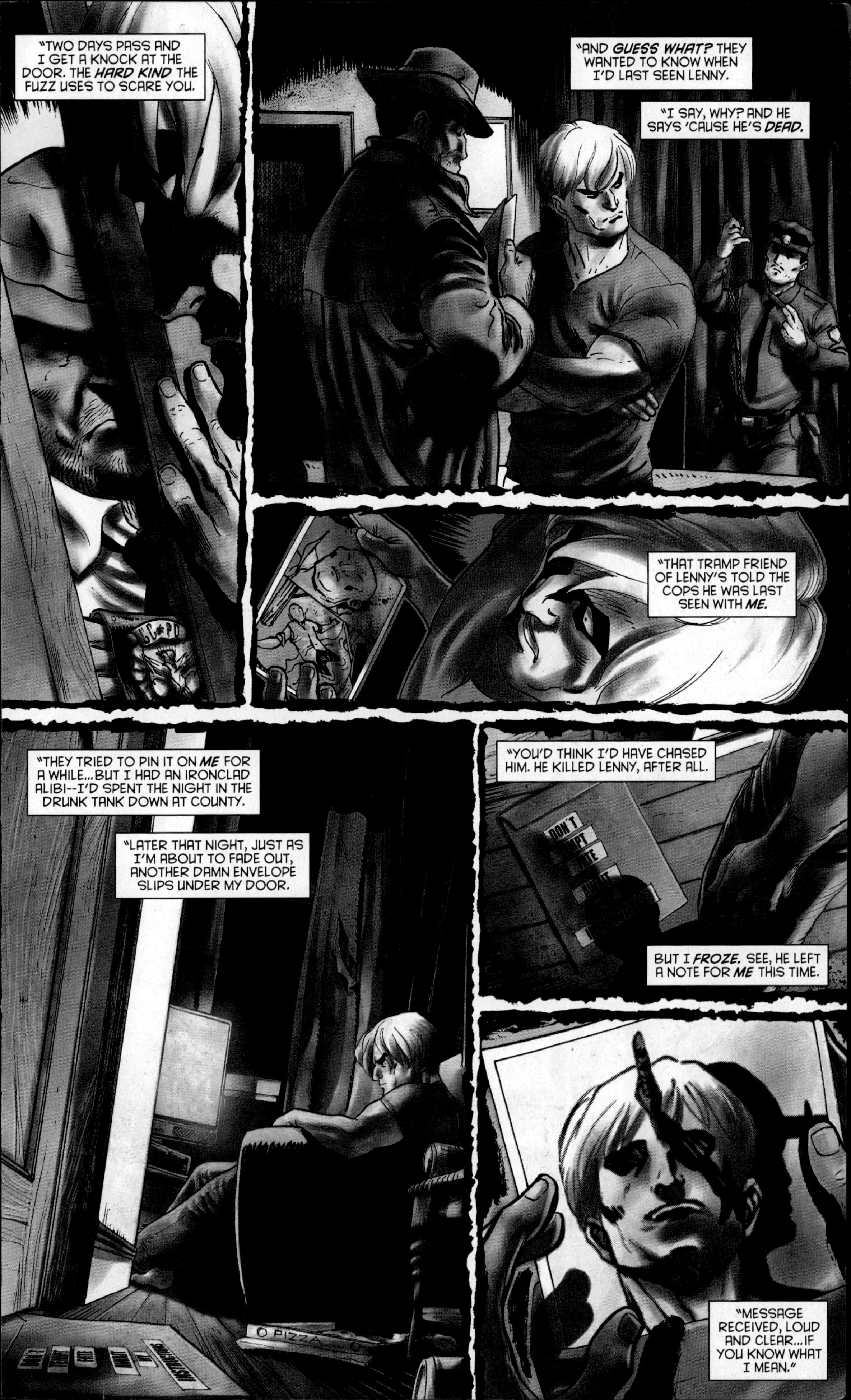
"TWO DAYS PASS AND I GET A KNOCK AT THE DOOR. THE HARD KIND THE FUZZ USES TO SCARE YOU.
"AND GUESS WHAT? THEY WANTED TO KNOW WHEN I'D LAST SEEN LENNY.
"I SAY, WHY? AND HE SAYS 'CAUSE HE'S DEAD.
"THAT TRAMP FRIEND OF LENNY'S TOLD THE COPS HE WAS LAST SEEN WITH ME.
"THEY TRIED TO PIN IT ON ME FOR A WHILE...BUT I HAD AN IRONCLAD ALIBI--I'D SPENT THE NIGHT IN THE DRUNK TANK DOWN AT COUNTY.
"LATER THAT NIGHT, JUST AS I'M ABOUT TO FADE OUT, ANOTHER DAMN ENVELOPE SLIPS UNDER MY DOOR.
PIZZA
"YOU'D THINK I'D HAVE CHASED HIM. HE KILLED LENNY, AFTER ALL.
BUT I FROZE. SEE, HE LEFT A NOTE FOR ME THIS TIME.
"MESSAGE RECEIVED, LOUD AND CLEAR...IF YOU KNOW WHAT I MEAN."

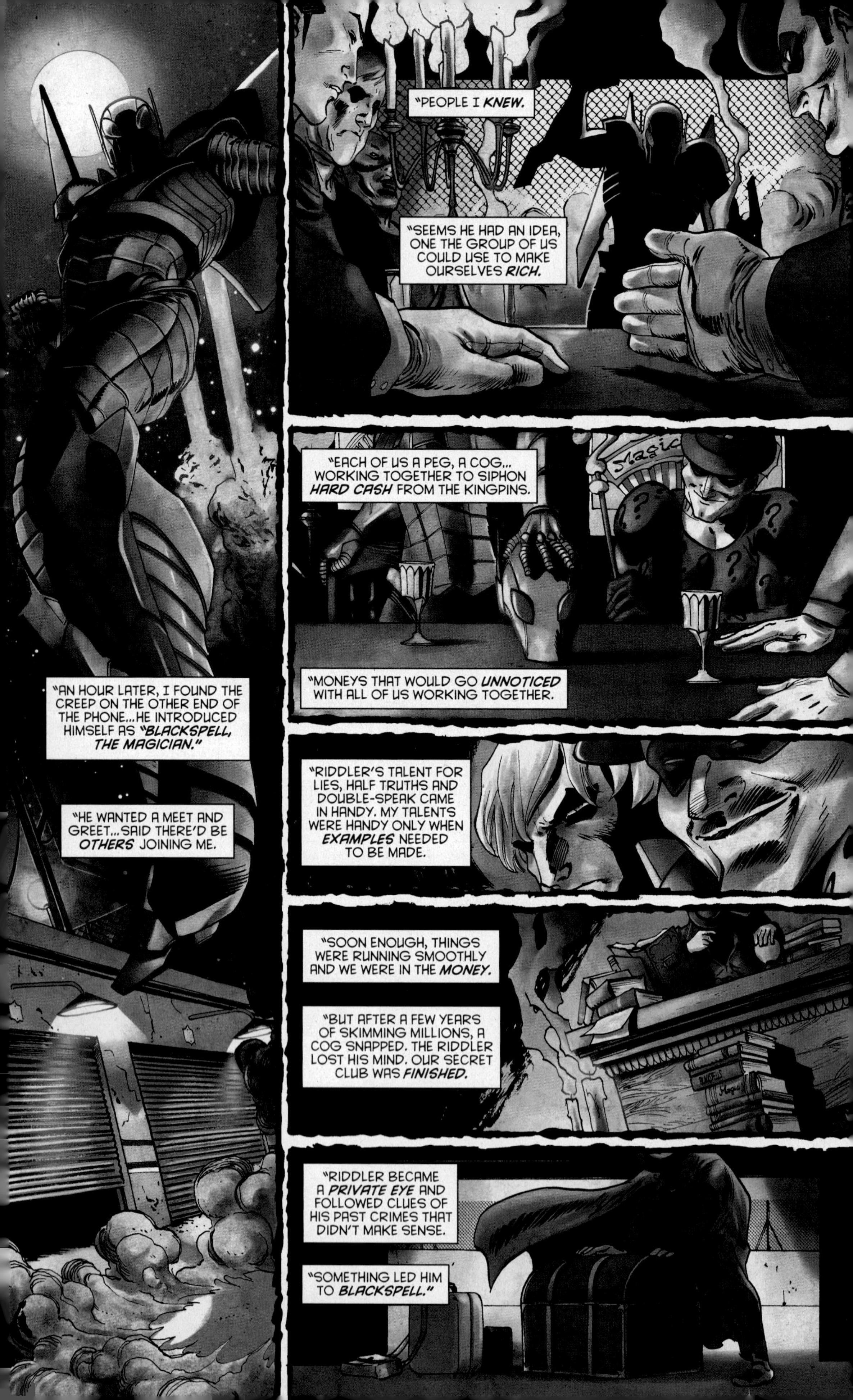
"AN HOUR LATER, I FOUND THE CREEP ON THE OTHER END OF THE PHONE...HE INTRODUCED HIMSELF AS "BLACKSPELL, THE MAGICIAN."
"HE WANTED A MEET AND GREET...SAID THERE'D BE OTHERS JOINING ME.
"PEOPLE I KNEW.
"SEEMS HE HAD AN IDEA, ONE THE GROUP OF US COULD USE TO MAKE OURSELVES RICH.
"EACH OF US A PEG, A COG... WORKING TOGETHER TO SIPHON HARD CASH FROM THE KINGPINS.
"MONEYS THAT WOULD GO UNNOTICED WITH ALL OF US WORKING TOGETHER.
"RIDDLER'S TALENT FOR LIES, HALF TRUTHS AND DOUBLE-SPEAK CAME IN HANDY. MY TALENTS WERE HANDY ONLY WHEN EXAMPLES NEEDED TO BE MADE.
"SOON ENOUGH, THINGS WERE RUNNING SMOOTHLY AND WE WERE IN THE MONEY.
"BUT AFTER A FEW YEARS OF SKIMMING MILLIONS, A COG SNAPPED. THE RIDDLER LOST HIS MIND. OUR SECRET CLUB WAS FINISHED.
"RIDDLER BECAME A PRIVATE EYE AND FOLLOWED CLUES OF HIS PAST CRIMES THAT DIDN'T MAKE SENSE.
"SOMETHING LED HIM TO BLACKSPELL."

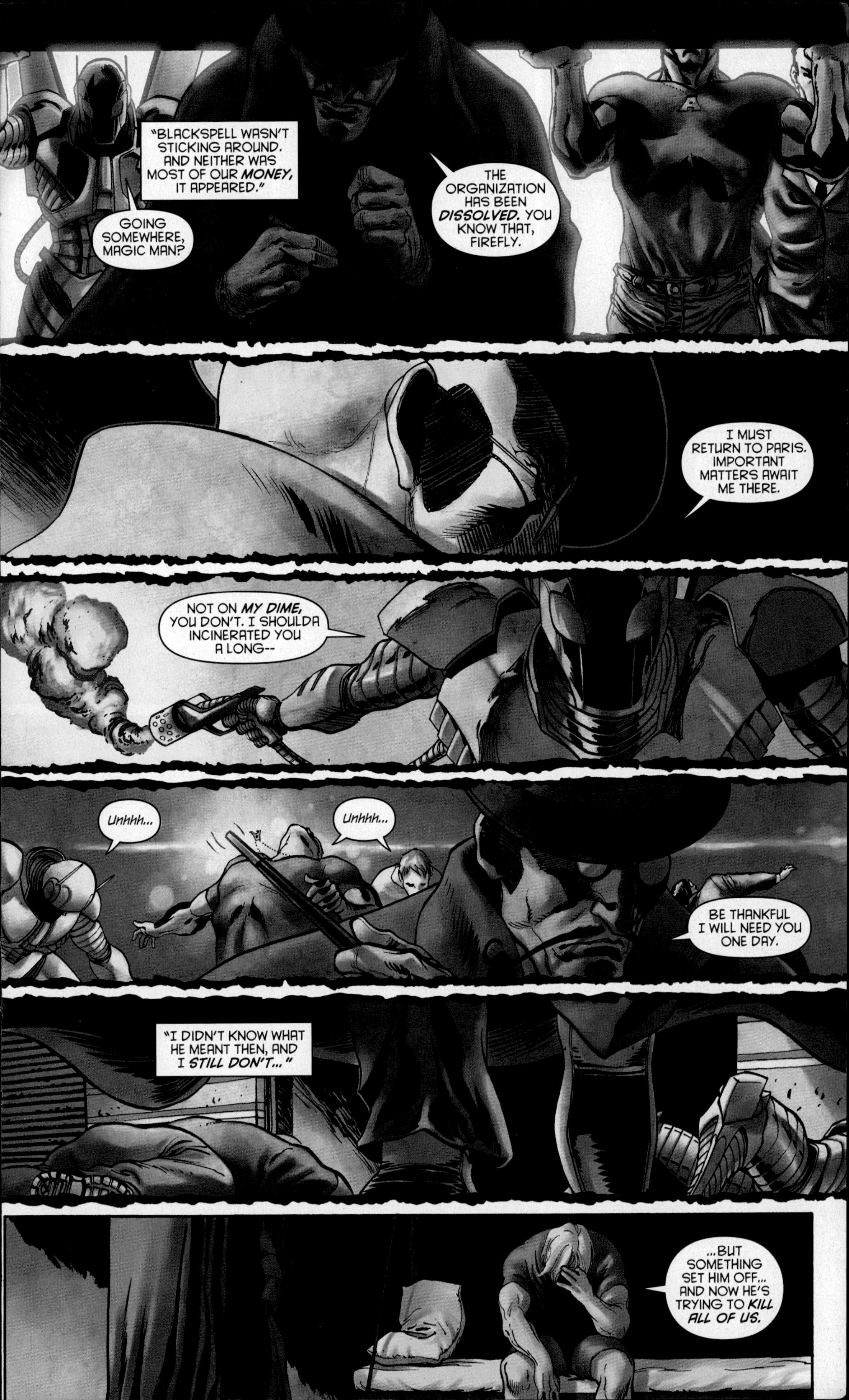
"BLACKSPELL WASN'T STICKING AROUND. AND NEITHER WAS MOST OF OUR *MONEY,* IT APPEARED."
GOING SOMEWHERE, MAGIC MAN?
THE ORGANIZATION HAS BEEN *DISSOLVED.* YOU KNOW THAT, FIREFLY.
I MUST RETURN TO PARIS. IMPORTANT MATTERS AWAIT ME THERE.
NOT ON *MY DIME,* YOU DON'T. I SHOULDA INCINERATED YOU A LONG--
Unhhh...
Unhhh...
BE THANKFUL I WILL NEED YOU ONE DAY.
"I DIDN'T KNOW WHAT HE MEANT THEN, AND I *STILL DON'T...*"
...BUT SOMETHING SET HIM OFF... AND NOW HE'S TRYING TO *KILL ALL OF US.*

OUTSIDE SEBASTIAN BLACKSPELL'S PENTHOUSE...

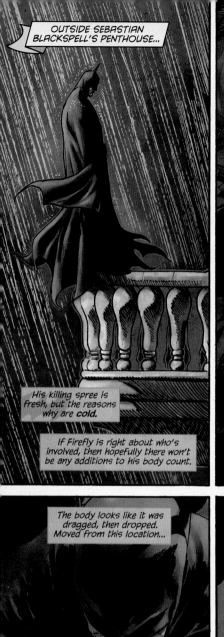

His killing spree is fresh, but the reasons why are **cold**.

If Firefly is right about who's involved, then hopefully there won't be any additions to his body count.

Something's been bothering me about this crime scene.

In my haste to pursue Blackspell, perhaps there's something I overlooked.

Or didn't examine close enough...

The body looks like it was dragged, then dropped. Moved from this location...

...but to **where?** The wheel where the victim's body was found?

Forensics searched for fingerprints and signs of blood here--but they didn't catch the **bleach** on the doorknob. Someone **cleaned** it.

A gloved handprint from the same chemical on that wall. The blood spatters on the tile, the abrupt movement of the fallen body...

...there were **two** victims in this room.

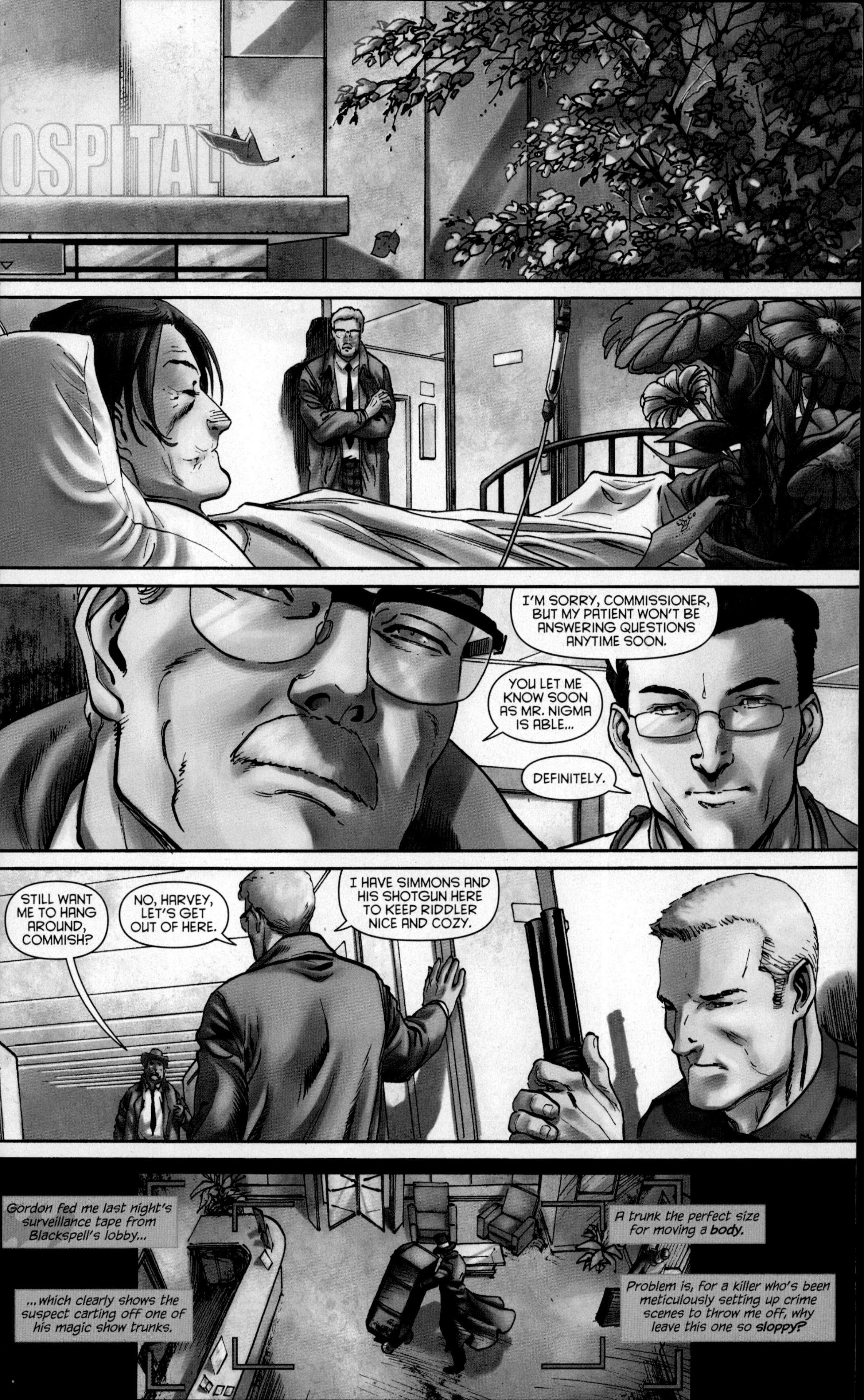
OSPITAL
I'M SORRY, COMMISSIONER, BUT MY PATIENT WON'T BE ANSWERING QUESTIONS ANYTIME SOON.
YOU LET ME KNOW SOON AS MR. NIGMA IS ABLE...
DEFINITELY.
STILL WANT ME TO HANG AROUND, COMMISH?
NO, HARVEY, LET'S GET OUT OF HERE.
I HAVE SIMMONS AND HIS SHOTGUN HERE TO KEEP RIDDLER NICE AND COZY.
Gordon fed me last night's surveillance tape from Blackspell's lobby...
...which clearly shows the suspect carting off one of his magic show trunks.
A trunk the perfect size for moving a **body.**
Problem is, for a killer who's been meticulously setting up crime scenes to throw me off, why leave this one so ***sloppy?***

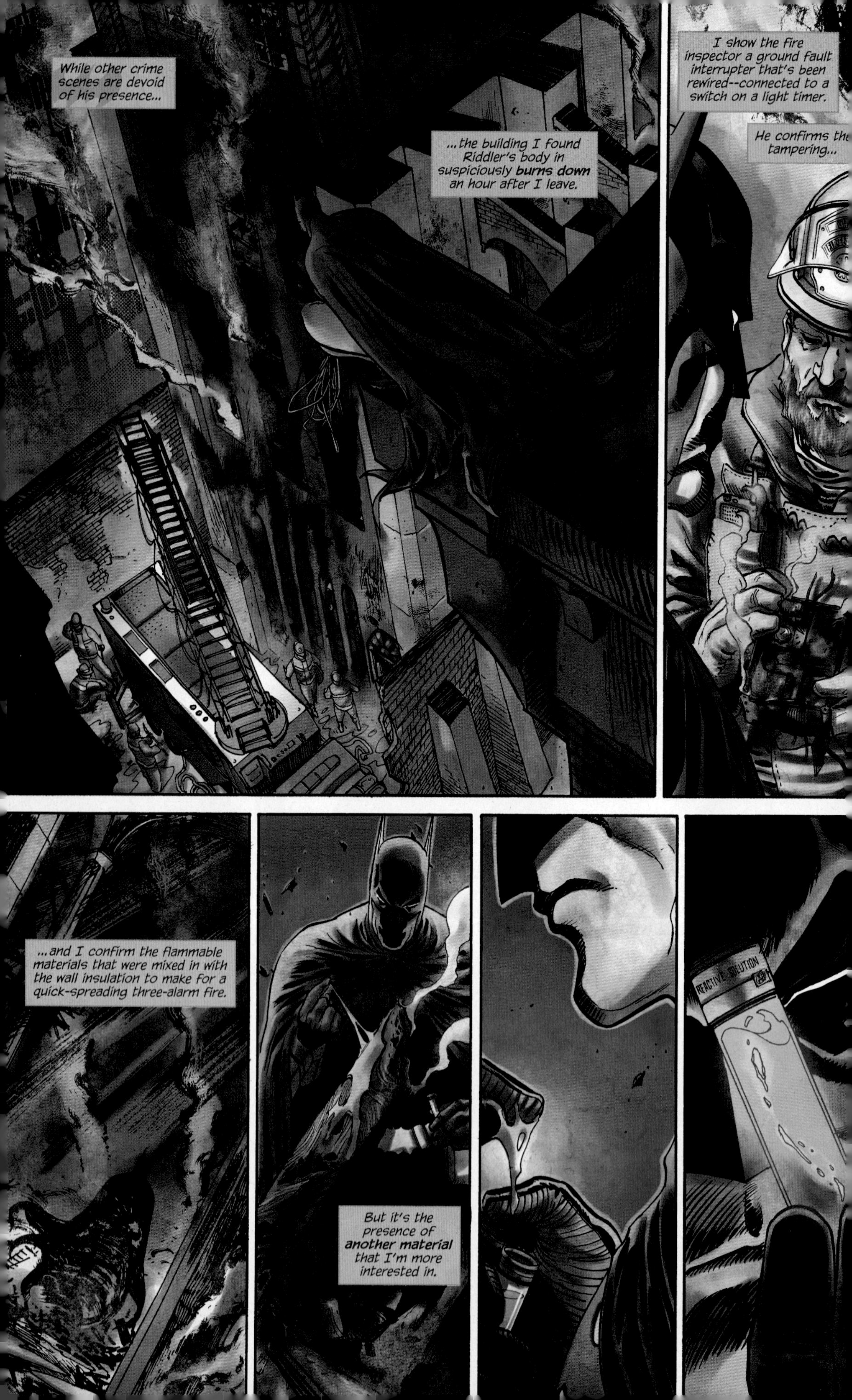

While other crime scenes are devoid of his presence...
...the building I found Riddler's body in suspiciously **burns down** an hour after I leave.
I show the fire inspector a ground fault interrupter that's been rewired--connected to a switch on a light timer.
He confirms the tampering...
...and I confirm the flammable materials that were mixed in with the wall insulation to make for a quick-spreading three-alarm fire.
But it's the presence of **another material** that I'm more interested in.
REACTIVE SOLUTION

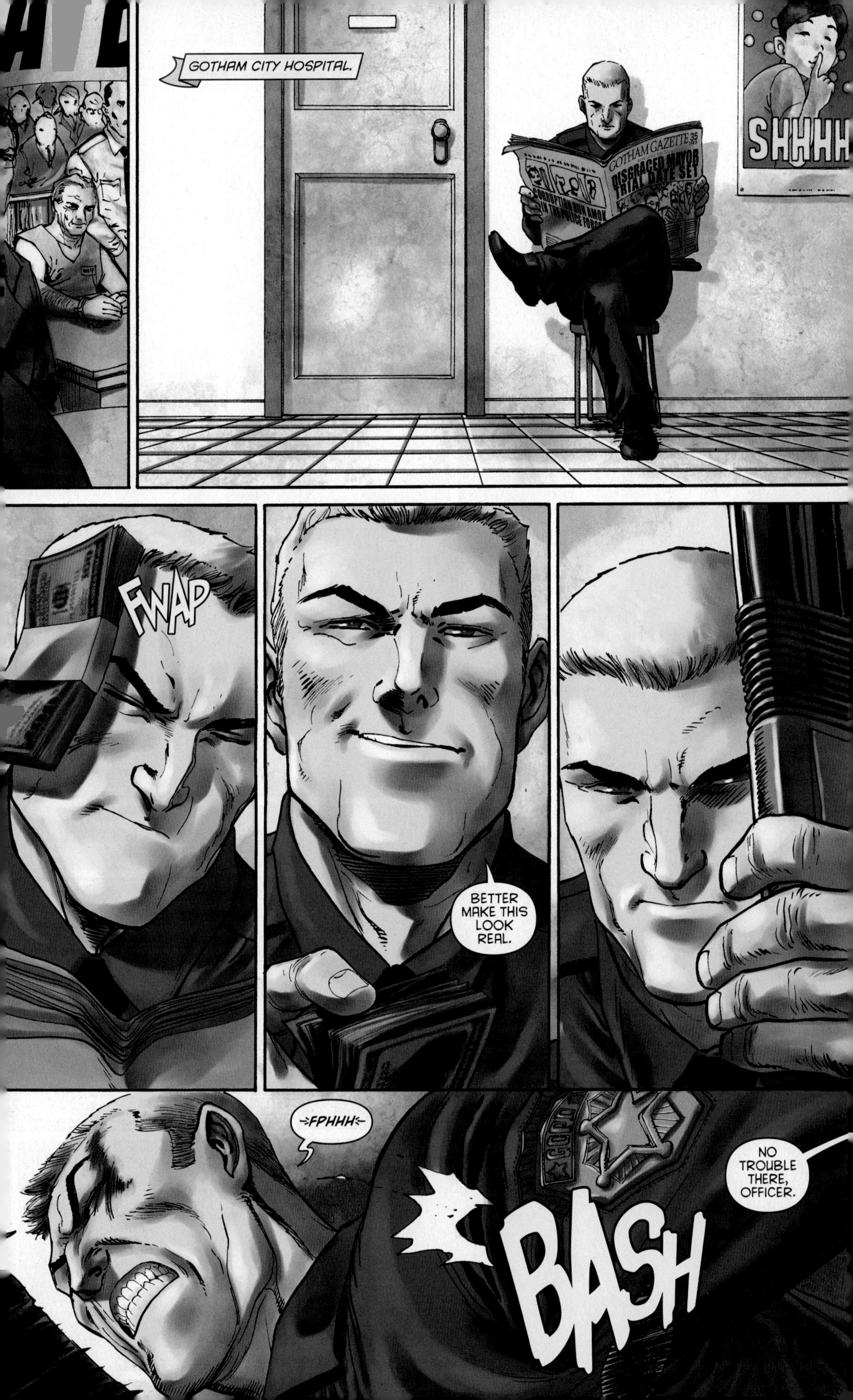
GOTHAM CITY HOSPITAL.
GOTHAM GAZETTE
DISGRACED MAYOR TRIAL DATE SET
SHHHH
FWAP
BETTER MAKE THIS LOOK REAL.
FPHHH
NO TROUBLE THERE, OFFICER.
BASH

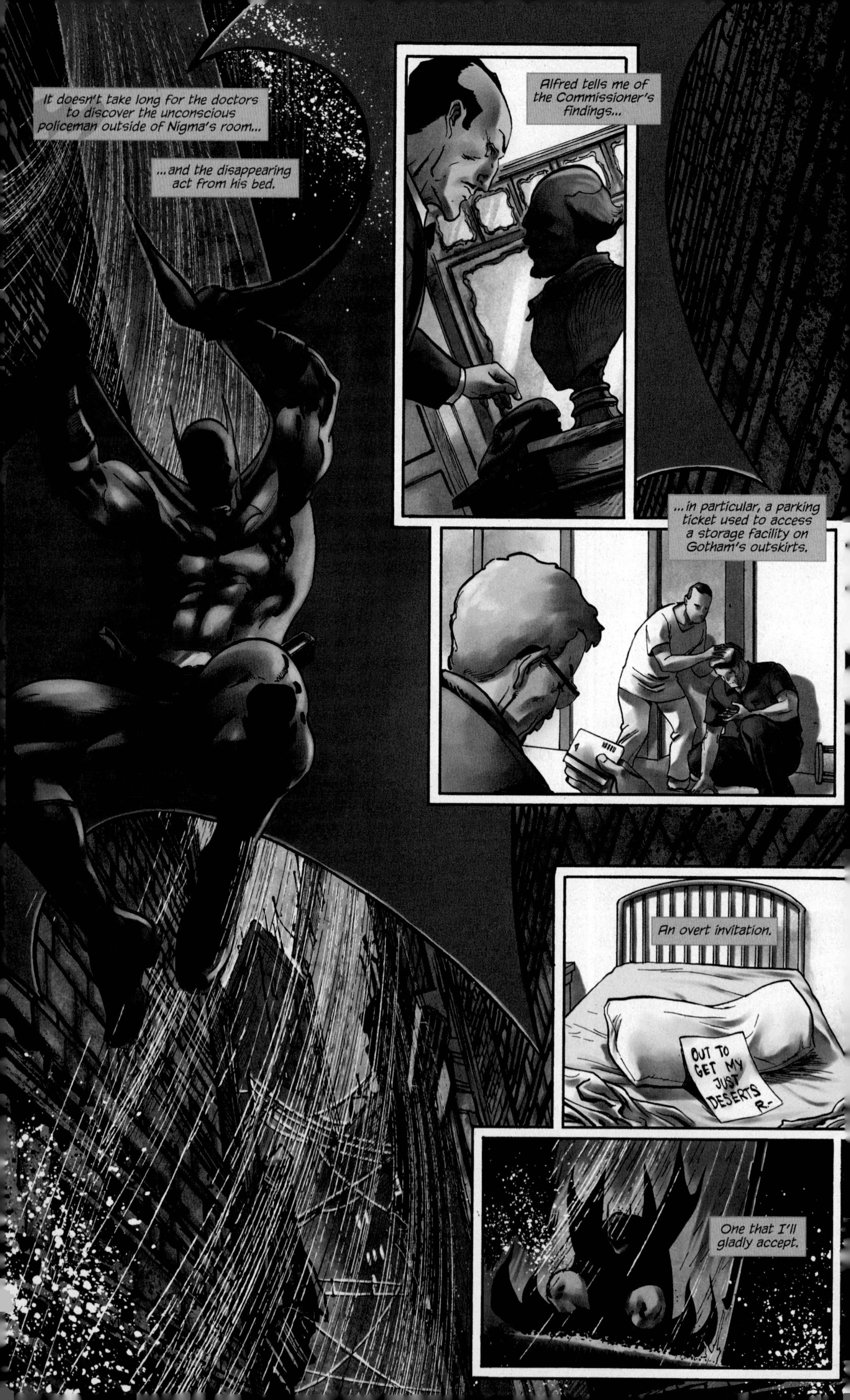
It doesn't take long for the doctors to discover the unconscious policeman outside of Nigma's room...
...and the disappearing act from his bed.
Alfred tells me of the Commissioner's findings...
...in particular, a parking ticket used to access a storage facility on Gotham's outskirts.
An overt invitation.
OUT TO GET MY JUST DESERTS R.-
One that I'll gladly accept.

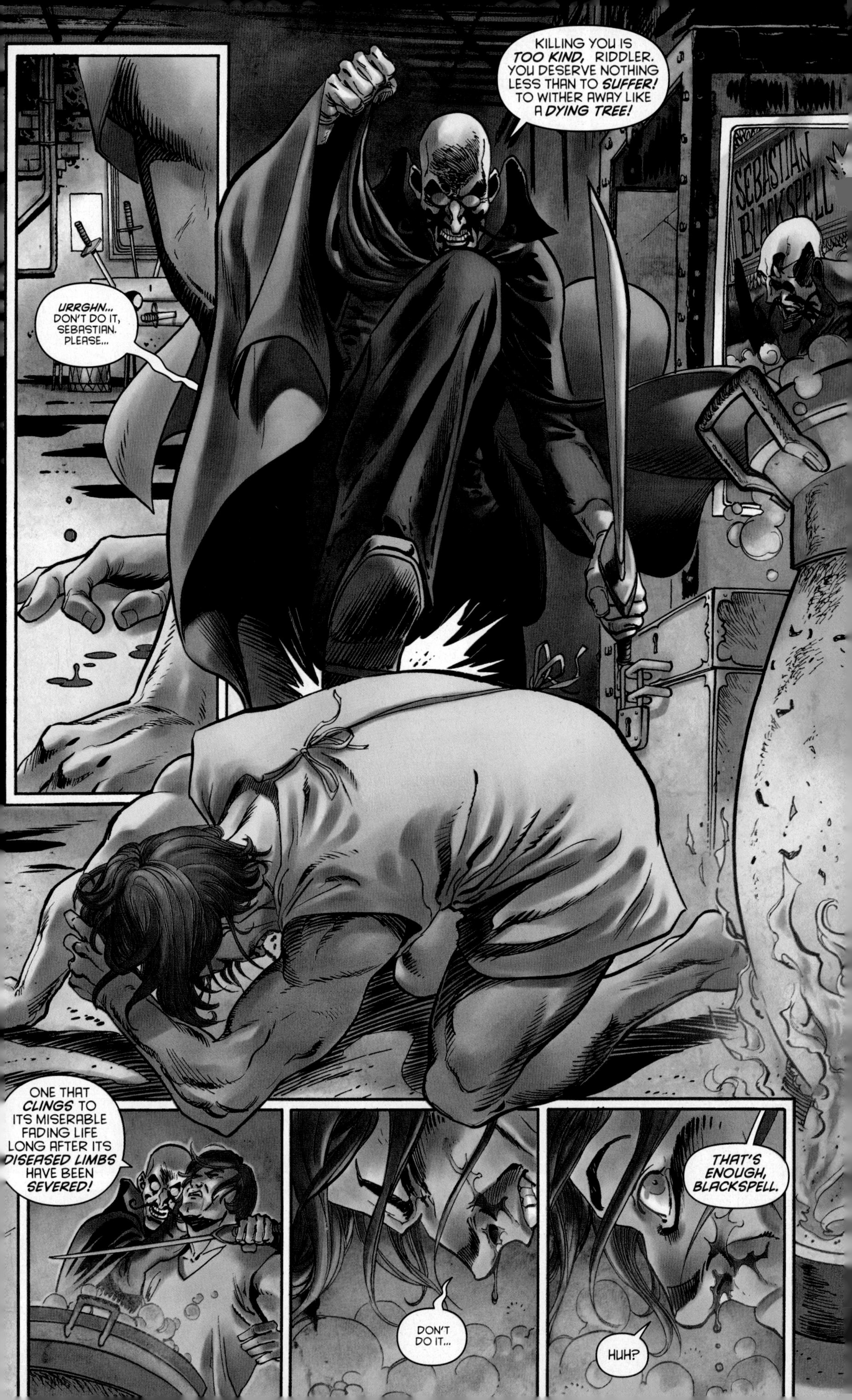
KILLING YOU IS TOO KIND, RIDDLER. YOU DESERVE NOTHING LESS THAN TO SUFFER! TO WITHER AWAY LIKE A DYING TREE!
URRGHN... DON'T DO IT, SEBASTIAN. PLEASE...
SEBASTIAN BLACKSPELL
ONE THAT CLINGS TO ITS MISERABLE FADING LIFE LONG AFTER ITS DISEASED LIMBS HAVE BEEN SEVERED!
DON'T DO IT...
THAT'S ENOUGH, BLACKSPELL.
HUH?

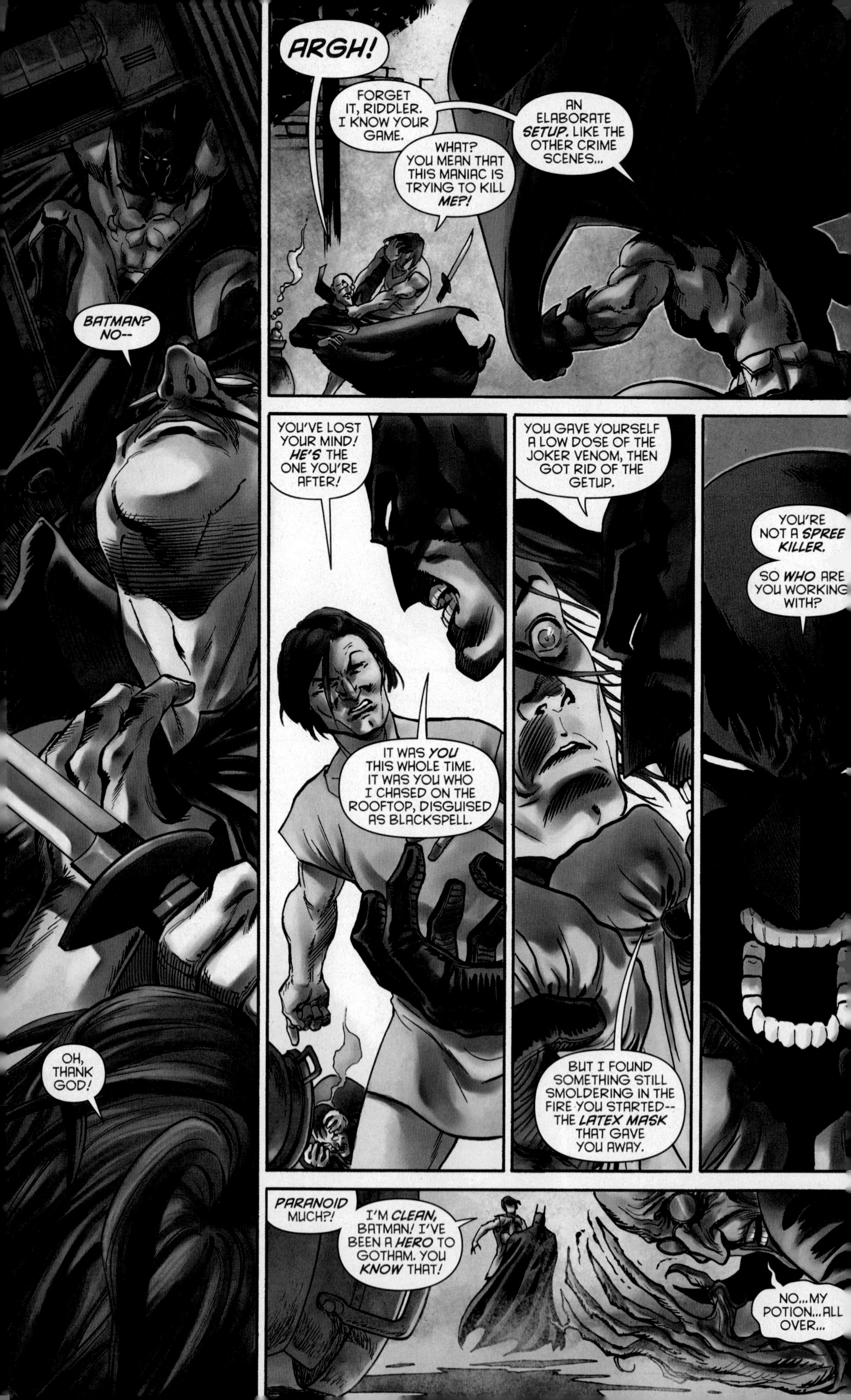
BATMAN? NO--
OH, THANK GOD!
ARGH!
FORGET IT, RIDDLER. I KNOW YOUR GAME.
WHAT? YOU MEAN THAT THIS MANIAC IS TRYING TO KILL ME?!
AN ELABORATE SETUP. LIKE THE OTHER CRIME SCENES...
YOU'VE LOST YOUR MIND! HE'S THE ONE YOU'RE AFTER!
IT WAS YOU THIS WHOLE TIME. IT WAS YOU WHO I CHASED ON THE ROOFTOP, DISGUISED AS BLACKSPELL.
YOU GAVE YOURSELF A LOW DOSE OF THE JOKER VENOM, THEN GOT RID OF THE GETUP.
BUT I FOUND SOMETHING STILL SMOLDERING IN THE FIRE YOU STARTED-- THE LATEX MASK THAT GAVE YOU AWAY.
YOU'RE NOT A SPREE KILLER.
SO WHO ARE YOU WORKING WITH?
PARANOID MUCH?!
I'M CLEAN, BATMAN! I'VE BEEN A HERO TO GOTHAM. YOU KNOW THAT!
NO...MY POTION...ALL OVER...

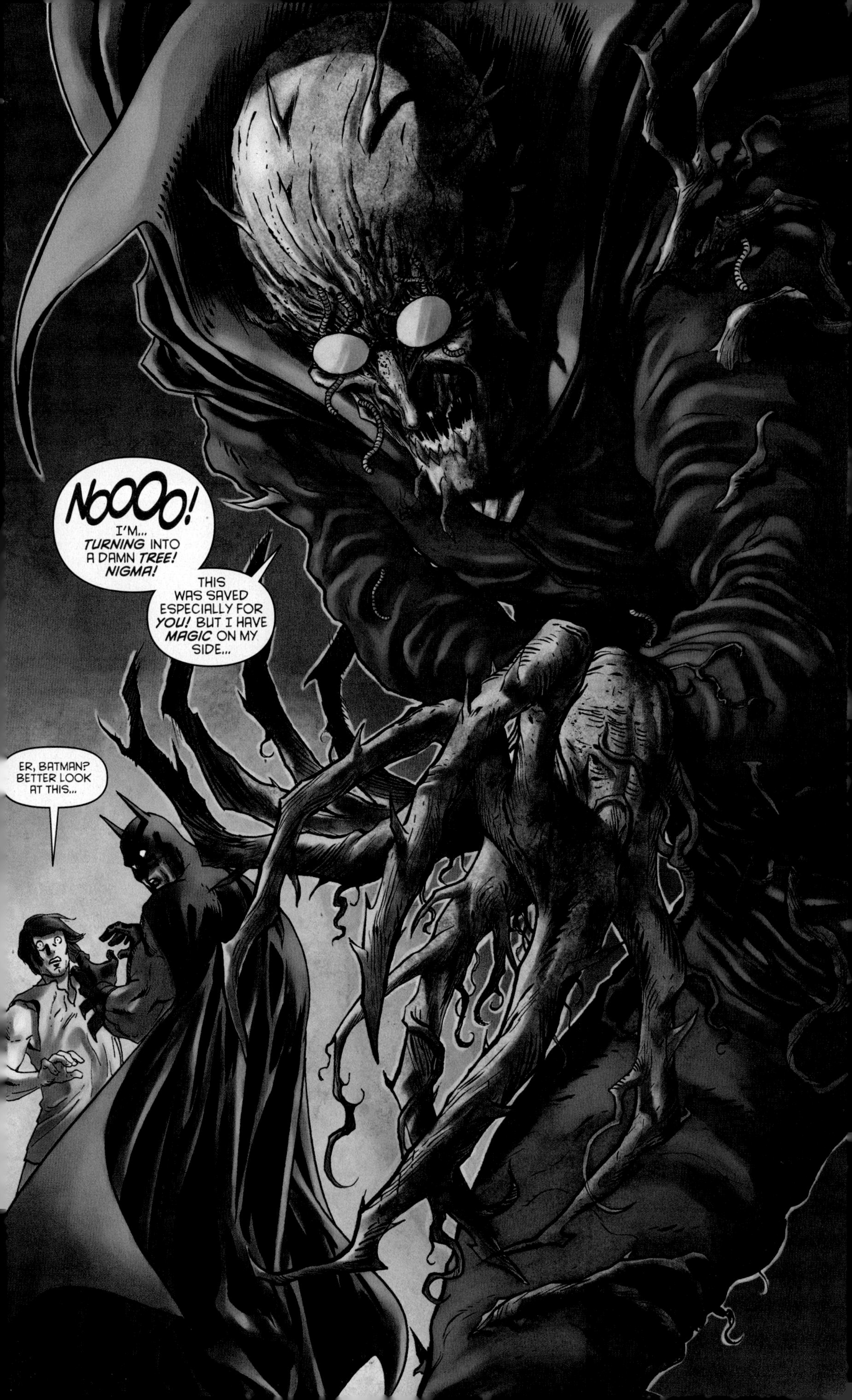
NOOOO! I'M... TURNING INTO A DAMN TREE! NIGMA!
THIS WAS SAVED ESPECIALLY FOR YOU! BUT I HAVE MAGIC ON MY SIDE...
ER, BATMAN? BETTER LOOK AT THIS...

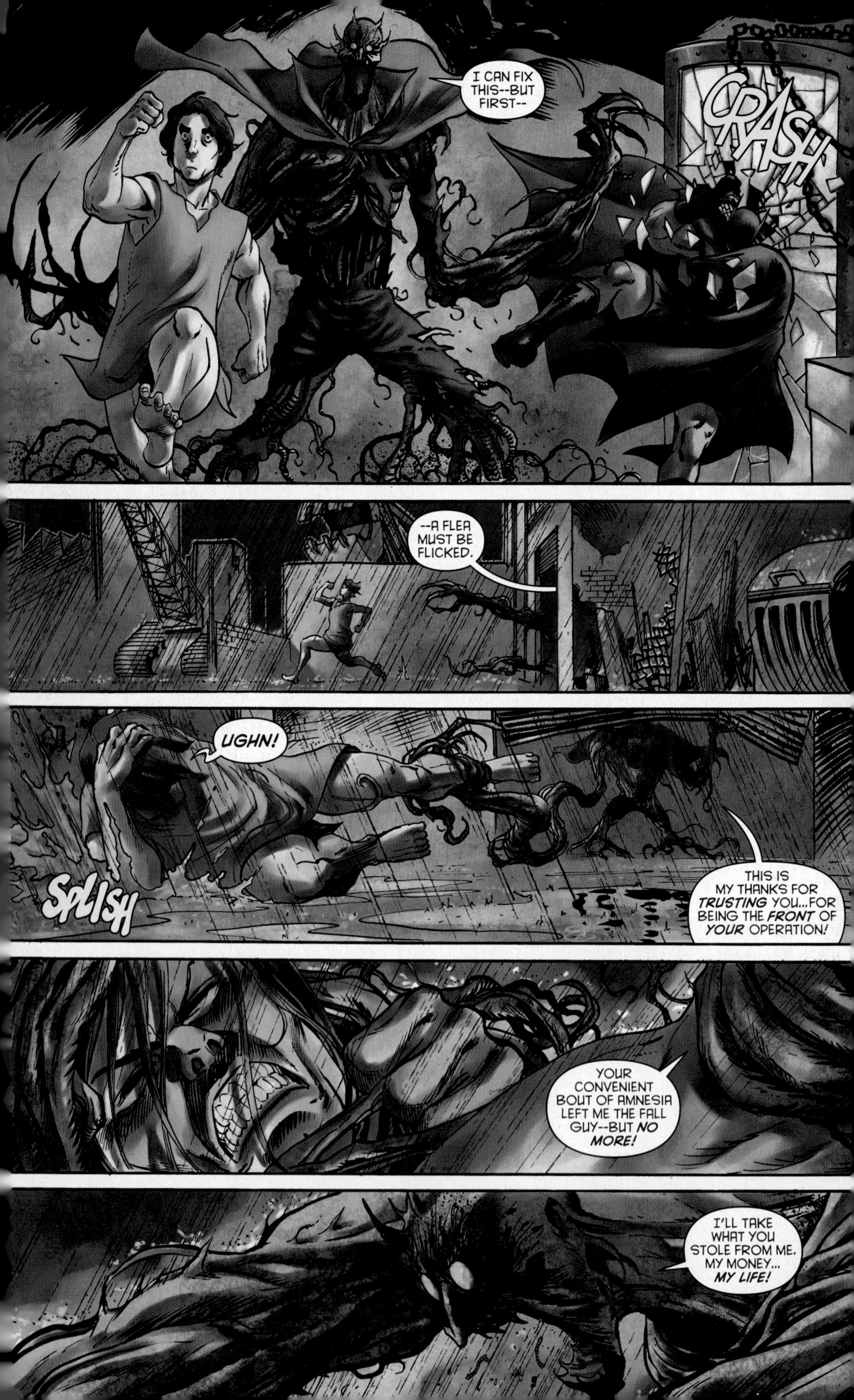
I CAN FIX THIS--BUT FIRST--
CRASH
--A FLEA MUST BE FLICKED.
UGHN!
SPLISH
THIS IS MY THANKS FOR TRUSTING YOU...FOR BEING THE FRONT OF YOUR OPERATION!
YOUR CONVENIENT BOUT OF AMNESIA LEFT ME THE FALL GUY--BUT NO MORE!
I'LL TAKE WHAT YOU STOLE FROM ME. MY MONEY... MY LIFE!

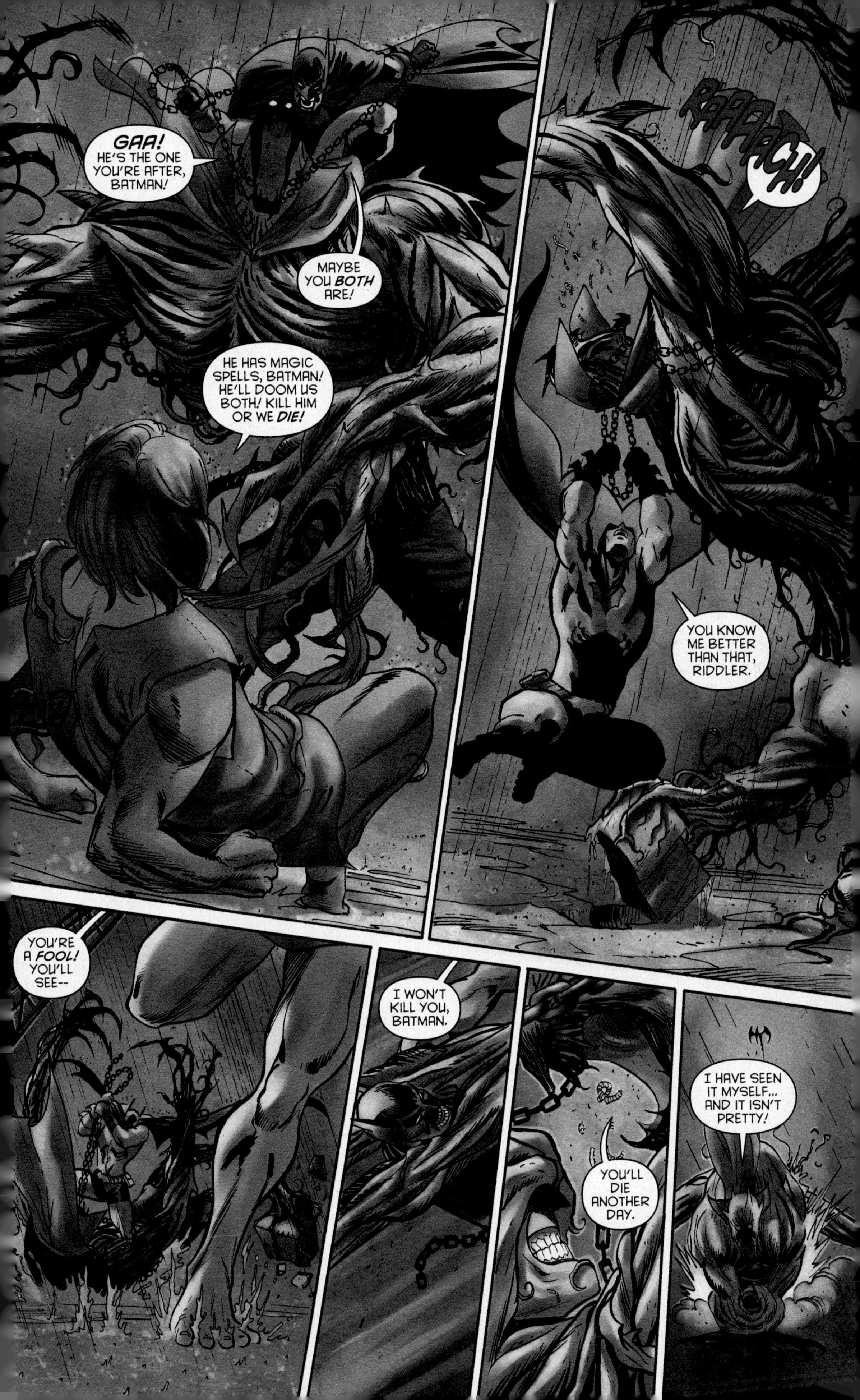
GAA! HE'S THE ONE YOU'RE AFTER, BATMAN!
MAYBE YOU BOTH ARE!
HE HAS MAGIC SPELLS, BATMAN! HE'LL DOOM US BOTH! KILL HIM OR WE DIE!
RAAAACH!!
YOU KNOW ME BETTER THAN THAT, RIDDLER.
YOU'RE A FOOL! YOU'LL SEE--
I WON'T KILL YOU, BATMAN.
YOU'LL DIE ANOTHER DAY.
I HAVE SEEN IT MYSELF... AND IT ISN'T PRETTY!

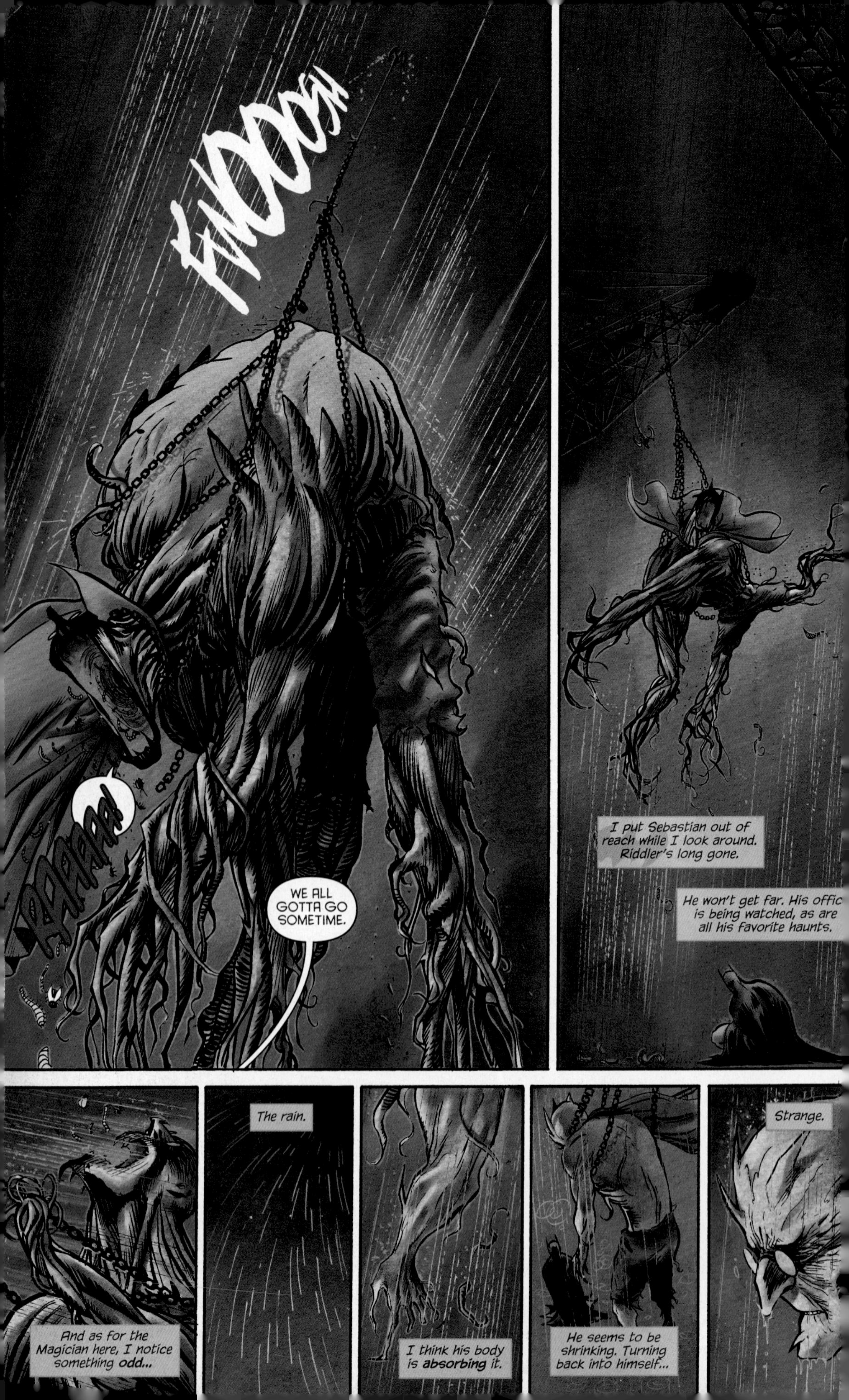
FWOOOSH
RAAAAA!
WE ALL GOTTA GO SOMETIME.
I put Sebastian out of reach while I look around. Riddler's long gone.
He won't get far. His offic is being watched, as are all his favorite haunts.
And as for the Magician here, I notice something **odd...**
The rain.
I think his body is **absorbing** it.
He seems to be shrinking. Turning back into himself...
Strange.

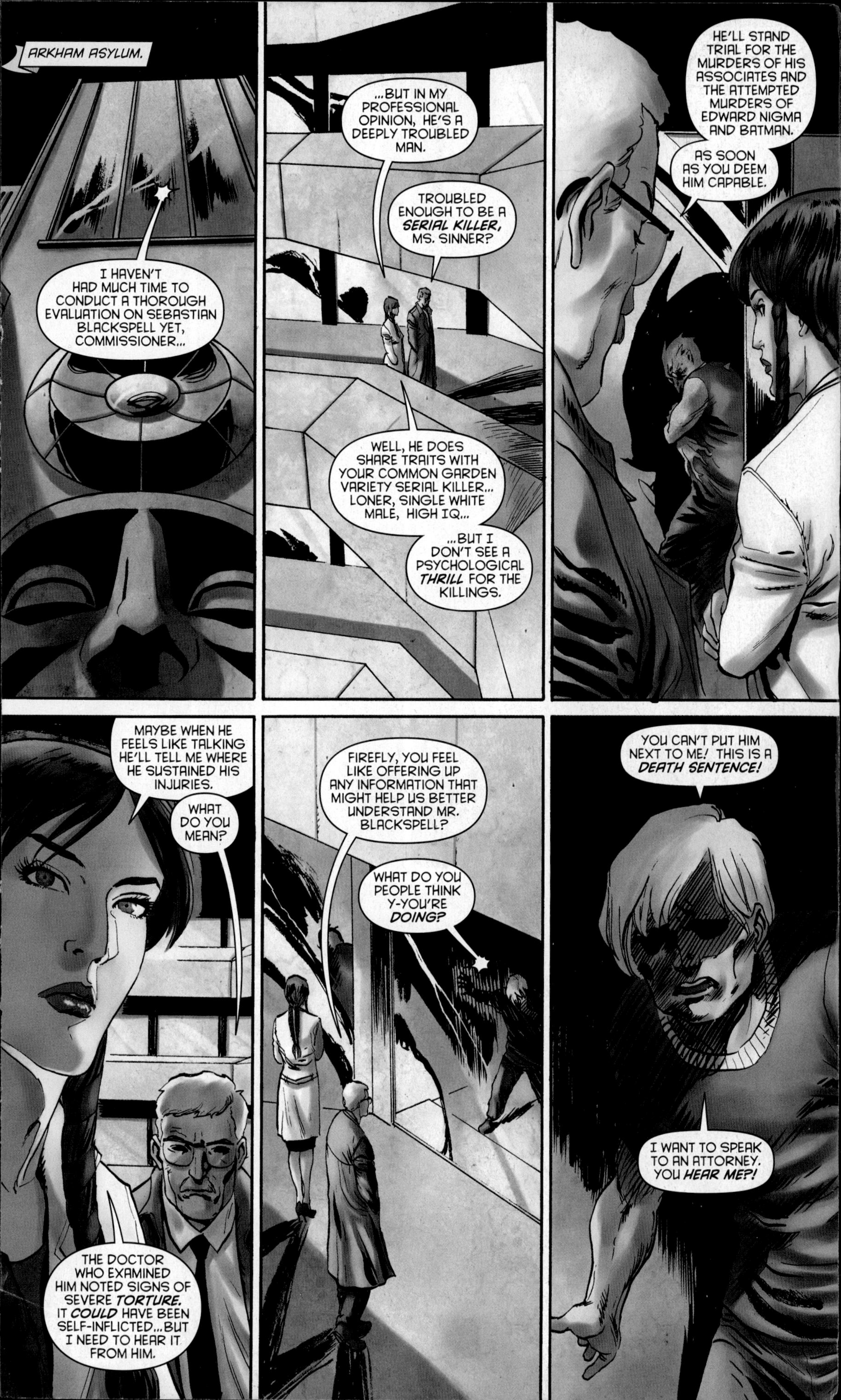

ARKHAM ASYLUM.
I HAVEN'T HAD MUCH TIME TO CONDUCT A THOROUGH EVALUATION ON SEBASTIAN BLACKSPELL YET, COMMISSIONER...
...BUT IN MY PROFESSIONAL OPINION, HE'S A DEEPLY TROUBLED MAN.
TROUBLED ENOUGH TO BE A SERIAL KILLER, MS. SINNER?
WELL, HE DOES SHARE TRAITS WITH YOUR COMMON GARDEN VARIETY SERIAL KILLER... LONER, SINGLE WHITE MALE, HIGH IQ...
...BUT I DON'T SEE A PSYCHOLOGICAL THRILL FOR THE KILLINGS.
HE'LL STAND TRIAL FOR THE MURDERS OF HIS ASSOCIATES AND THE ATTEMPTED MURDERS OF EDWARD NIGMA AND BATMAN.
AS SOON AS YOU DEEM HIM CAPABLE.
MAYBE WHEN HE FEELS LIKE TALKING HE'LL TELL ME WHERE HE SUSTAINED HIS INJURIES.
WHAT DO YOU MEAN?
THE DOCTOR WHO EXAMINED HIM NOTED SIGNS OF SEVERE TORTURE. IT COULD HAVE BEEN SELF-INFLICTED...BUT I NEED TO HEAR IT FROM HIM.
FIREFLY, YOU FEEL LIKE OFFERING UP ANY INFORMATION THAT MIGHT HELP US BETTER UNDERSTAND MR. BLACKSPELL?
WHAT DO YOU PEOPLE THINK Y-YOU'RE DOING?
YOU CAN'T PUT HIM NEXT TO ME! THIS IS A DEATH SENTENCE!
I WANT TO SPEAK TO AN ATTORNEY. YOU HEAR ME?!

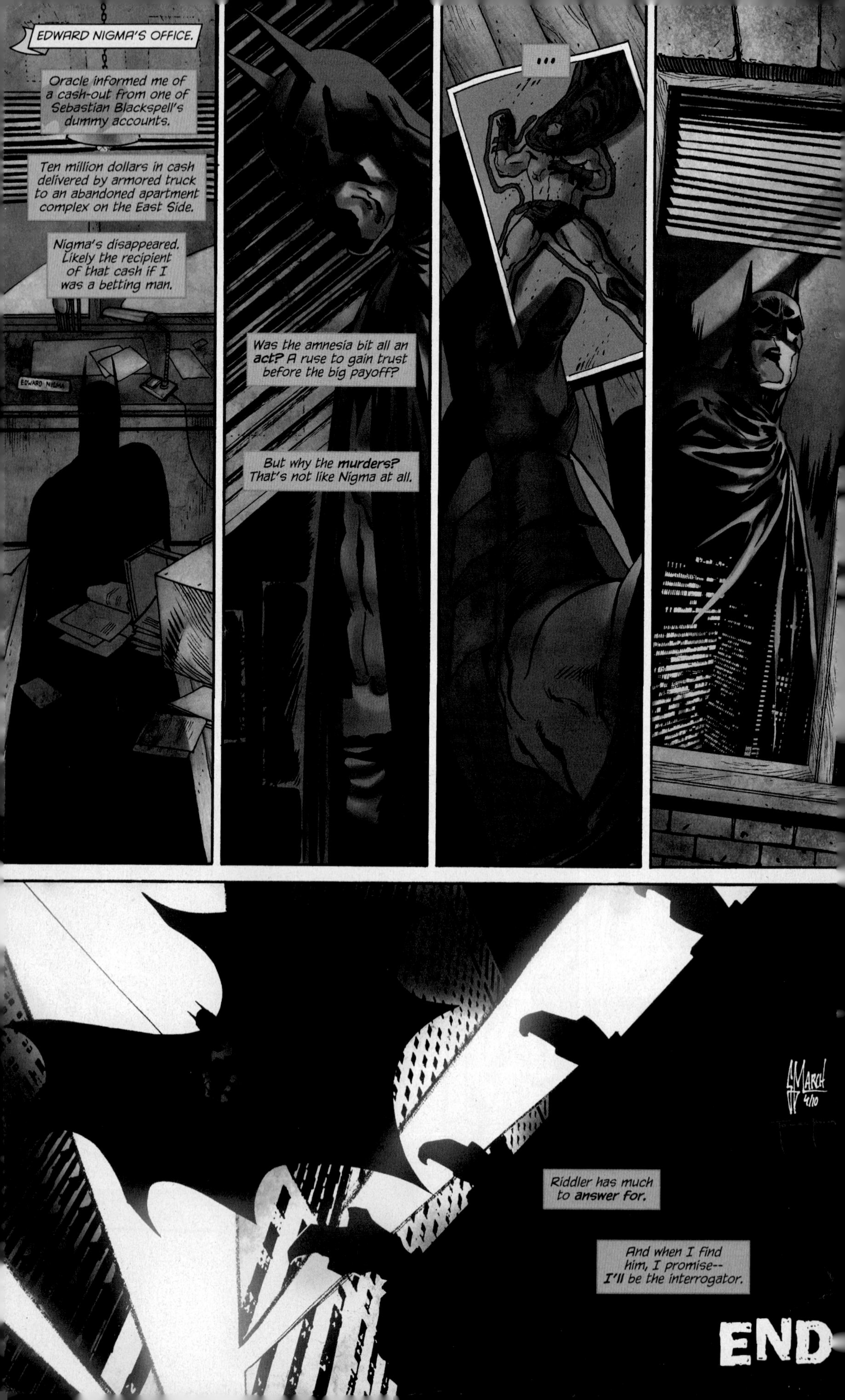
EDWARD NIGMA'S OFFICE.
Oracle informed me of a cash-out from one of Sebastian Blackspell's dummy accounts.
Ten million dollars in cash delivered by armored truck to an abandoned apartment complex on the East Side.
Nigma's disappeared. Likely the recipient of that cash if I was a betting man.
EDWARD NIGMA
Was the amnesia bit all an act? A ruse to gain trust before the big payoff?
But why the murders? That's not like Nigma at all.
...
Riddler has much to answer for.
And when I find him, I promise-- I'll be the interrogator.
END

MORE CLASSIC TALES OF THE DARK KNIGHT

BATMAN: HUSH

JEPH LOEB
JIM LEE

BATMAN: UNDER THE HOOD
VOLS. 1 & 2

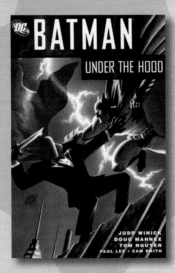

JUDD WINICK
DOUG MAHNKE

BATMAN:
THE LONG HALLOWEEN

JEPH LOEB
TIM SALE

BATMAN:
DARK VICTORY

JEPH LOEB
TIM SALE

BATMAN:
HAUNTED KNIGHT

JEPH LOEB
TIM SALE

BATMAN:
YEAR 100

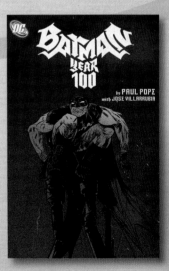

PAUL POPE

SEARCH THE GRAPHIC NOVELS SECTION OF
DCCOMICS.COM
FOR ART AND INFORMATION ON ALL OF OUR BOOKS!

FROM THE WRITER OF
300 & SIN CITY

FRANK MILLER

Frank Miller's classic graphic novel features a Gotham City that has sunk into decadence and lawlessness ten years after an aging Batman retired. The Dark Knight returns in a blaze of glory when his city needs him most to end the threat of a brutal new generation of criminals while encountering the Joker, Two-Face and the Man of Steel for the final time.

"Groundbreaking."
– USA TODAY

"It's film noir in cartoon panels."
–VANITY FAIR

BATMAN: THE DARK KNIGHT RETURNS
FRANK MILLER
WITH KLAUS JANSON and LYNN VARLEY

BATMAN:
THE DARK KNIGHT
STRIKES AGAIN

BATMAN: YEAR ONE

ALL STAR BATMAN & ROBIN,
THE BOY WONDER VOL. I

with
DAVID MAZZUCCHELLI

with
JIM LEE

SEARCH THE GRAPHIC NOVELS SECTION OF
DCCOMICS.COM
FOR ART AND INFORMATION ON ALL OF OUR BOOKS!